To E. William Horr— This volume tell the story of thirty years of effort by the Friends Committee on National Legislation to influence our government toward peace, justice and freedom. We still have a long ways to go! With the best wishes of the Author

E. Raymond Wilson
Sandy Spring, Maryland
August 15, 1978

UPHILL FOR PEACE

UPHILL FOR PEACE

Quaker Impact on Congress

by

E. Raymond Wilson

RICHMOND
INDIANA

Published by
Friends United Press
Richmond, Indiana

Library of Congress Cataloging in Publication Data

Wilson, Edward Raymond, 1896-
  Uphill for peace.

  Bibliography: p.
  Includes index.
  1. Friends, Society of — Political activity. 2. Lobbying. 3. Friends
Committee on National Legislation, Washington, D.C. I. Title.
BX7748.C5W54   328.73'07'8   74-29428
ISBN 0-913408-16-6

Printed in the United States of America
by
R.R. Donnelley & Sons Company

To Miriam

Who shared the journey
for thirty-three years
uphill for peace

Preface

Why try to work *uphill for peace*, justice and freedom on *Capitol Hill* at a time when cynicism about the character and operation of government and government officials is widespread, and when disillusionment about the church and organized religion is so common and so vocal? Because religion should be vital and relevant and because the health and the future of democracy rest upon responsible participation by informed and concerned citizens.

A world without war, without conscription and militarism has still to be achieved. Even in the United States the price of liberty is still eternal vigilance. The battle for justice is never-ending. A world dominated by military, economic and political power easily forgets fairness and compassion for the disadvantaged and dispossessed at home and abroad.

To strive for these and similar goals has been the role of the Friends Committee on National Legislation.

Even a volume of this size can give only a fragmentary account of the variety and intensity of the thirty years' effort by those who have joined together in the FCNL to share the process of decision-making in Congress on the crucial issues of this period. It has not been possible to give full credit to the many staff and committee members and thousands in our constituency who have labored valiantly for their vision of a better future for humanity.

Following are some of the questions dealt with only slightly or not at all. I listened on the Capitol lawn when President Harry S. Truman announced his Point IV proposal for technical assistance. For many years the FCNL was an active participant in the Point IV Information Committee which strove for an enlarged program of economic aid and technical assistance to help underdeveloped countries help themselves, aided by American and UN personnel and money. In recent years, for many supporters, including the FCNL, much of the U.S. aid and Food for Peace program soured, because of increasing diversion to military purposes.

The FCNL Policy Committee struggled through nine revisions in nine months in evolving a statement on Jobs and Assured Income in order to define a position on guaranteed minimum income as one essential step in abolishing dire and involuntary poverty in the United States. This is still one of our many unachieved goals.

This history does not fully reflect FCNL actions, which were not as vigorous as they should have been, against the blight of McCarthyism on individuals and organizations that aroused the unfounded accusations of sympathy for Communism by the Senator from Wisconsin in the early nineteen fifties. We cannot defend freedom abroad by deserting it at home.

Little emphasis has been placed on the organization and decision-making process within the FCNL. No account has been included of the series of Tenth, Twentieth and Thirtieth Anniversary Celebrations held in various parts of the country which brought together loyal supporters of the FCNL and which raised reserve funds that helped provide financial stability when receipts were low and gave opportunities for staff and program expansion at critical times. In 1953, for example, following a Tenth Anniversary Conference in June, twenty-two dinner meetings and two other evening meetings were held in different places. The goal that year of $25,000 for special reserve funds was reached. Norman R. Morrison wrote in the *Baltimore Monthly Meeting Newsletter*, April 1, 1963, "It took John Woolman nearly forty years to persuade Quakers to give up slaves. We should not be discouraged that the FCNL has not succeeded in its first twenty years in getting governments to give up wars."

The task of building bridges of reconciliation between various elements in a sharply divided world and efforts to melt the Cold War deserve fuller treatment than they have received in this volume. A more detailed history of the three years' work against conscription by the forerunner of the FCNL, the Friends War Problems Committee, was sacrificed for lack of space. Much more has been done on legislation for American Indians than has been recounted. Many more memorable interviews might have been recorded. Little emphasis has been given to the many expressions of appreciation from members of Congress for the initiatives and activities of the FCNL.

There are many difficult and cruel dilemmas which an organization like the FCNL faces much of the time. The answer is not so much all of one to the exclusion of the other but which one should have the major priority. One of the most frequent has been whether our efforts should be concentrated on short-range crisis efforts, of which there are always plenty, or on more fundamental long-range solutions. My reflective judgment is that on balance we have spent too large a proportion of time on rushing to put out legislative or other brush fires and less time than we should have on the long-range and imperative things which have to be done if peace is to be finally achieved.

However much more might and should have been done, of which we are very conscious, may it be said that within the limitations of time, energy and resources, the Friends Committee on National Legislation has sought, in company with many other unofficial and nongovernmental organizations, to serve its time and generation.

E. RAYMOND WILSON

MAY 7, 1974

Acknowledgments

This history of three decades of Quaker lobbying was launched by the award of a T. Wistar Brown Fellowship from Haverford College, and furthered by a later grant from the Anna H. and Elizabeth M. Chace Fund of the Philadelphia Yearly Meeting of Friends. The Friends Committee on National Legislation graciously gave me leave from the turmoil of Washington in order to concentrate on this study in the Haverford and Swarthmore College libraries.

Aid for the publishing of this book at a nominal price was given by the Monthly Meeting of Friends of Philadelphia (Arch Street), the Book Association of Friends, the Book and Publications Committee, the Central Monthly Meeting of Philadelphia, the Shoemaker Fund and by a number of Friends.

My deep appreciation goes to those who have helped in editing, including Tom Abrams and Earl Conn. Heartfelt thanks are due the persons who have aided in research and/or in typing various stages of the manuscript. These include Margot Bronner, Betty Endo, Virginia Davis, Donna Hoffman, Ann Klein, Patricia Kutzner, Clemence A. Ravacon, Lynne Shivers and Nancy Zimmer. Marion Glaeser not only contributed throughout in many ways to this enterprise, but prepared the index. I benefited very much from the keen suggestions of Carroll Streeter, former editor of the *Farm Journal*, regarding title and chapter headings.

The staff of the Friends Historical Library at Haverford College were very cooperative, including Edwin Bronner, Elizabeth Tritle and Barbara Curtis. J. William Frost and Jane Rittenhouse and their colleagues in the Swarthmore Friends Historical Library extended me many courtesies in tracking down historical reference material.

Most of the research and writing during the past two years has been done in the Swarthmore College Peace Collection where the archives of the Friends Committee on National Legislation are on deposit as well as my own personal papers. Jeanette Hadley years ago took the initiative in organizing the records of the FCNL for the first twenty years and having the minutes and publications bound. These volumes at present are on file in the FCNL office in Washington. Marjorie Risley worked with me for some time organizing the reference material in the FCNL library for deposit in the Swarthmore College Peace Collection.

The Swarthmore College Peace Collection has developed into what is probably the most unique library in the world of the records of peace organizations, peace activities and peace leaders. The curator, Bernice Nichols, and her associates have been untiring in providing advice and assistance.

E. RAYMOND WILSON

Contents

Introduction

On August 7, 1964, the United States Congress effectively abdicated its responsibility in determining the foreign policy stance of this nation toward Vietnam. Ten years and 50,000 American lives later we are able to see the results of this particular act of corporate irresponsibility. The Gulf of Tonkin resolution which gave to the President tremendous discretionary powers to wage war in Southeast Asia was so all encompassing that even after its repeal in 1970, United States involvement in the Vietnamese war continued unhindered by the lack of statutory authority.

Our tragic role in that remote part of the world was initiated by the refusal of Congress to play a significant part in the shaping of our foreign policy. Yet our continuing commitment in lives and resources was kept alive, at least initially, by the noninvolvement by many concerned citizens.

W.H. Auden writes in a poem about a young soldier:
> "Boy , the quarrel was before your time, the aggressor
> No one you know."

Those haunting words continue to reverberate in my mind as I ponder the question of political responsibility.

A country was allowed to shatter its national soul because too few people would say, "This is enough." The major reason given for such inaction was the lack of sufficient knowledge of foreign policy and the void of moral commitment. Thus, the government was given a free rein to wage destruction. It was only after the inhumanity of the war was brought home to millions via the television medium that significant opposition was raised.

In a Faulkner novel, a character says, "Thank God men have done learned how to forget quick what they aren't brave enough to try to cure." The tragic truth of this statement was pointed out in the general citizenry's understanding indifference, even now, to the continuing suffering in Indochina and it is reinforced by our apparent indifference to the plight of the poor in our nation and in our world.

Some recent statistics bear consideration: The upper fifth of our population receives 40% of our national income, owns 77% of the wealth, and 97% of the corporate stock. Only 6% of the national income goes to the bottom fifth of our people. These income distribution patterns have not changed in a generation.

The discrepancies between the rich and the poor on the international level are even greater. After conducting an extensive survey of poverty in Asia, the *New York Times* reported:

> "There are more poor people than ever. . .and more of them than ever before are born into malnutrition and disease. Physically and mentally stunted, they live wretchedly foreclosed lives in which the future means little more than tomorrow's struggle to survive. They die young and hopeless."

Two-thirds of the deaths in the world each year can be traced to hunger or disease due to hunger. In the face of these facts, it is terribly sobering to hear that the earth could only support one-half billion people at the level of the American standard of living.

Because of our rate of consumption of nonrenewable resources and the resulting pollution factor, our planet could only accommodate 500,000,000 Americans, and no one else.

But the problems of one part of humanity affect us all. The child that lies awake at night hungry cannot be forgotten for he, too, is a part of the whole, a creature of infinite value in the sight of God. To refuse to respond both individually and collectively to the cries of the world is to deny our ultimate unity with all of creation. It is to accept the destructive premise that we, as individuals, share no common bond with the rest of humanity, except as we care to consciously create. Surely the economic interdependence alone of the modern world has given the lie to that presumption.

We are creatures who find our identity in groups. It is through the interaction of individuals that the human personality is formed. In man's most profound moments he has sensed his own individual incompleteness. In the community — be it family, nation, or humanity itself — the individual involves himself in something beyond his own person in order to answer his quest for a final meaning to his existence. Although the ultimate answer does not reside in human groups, but rather in the Creator himself, still much of what is essentially human can be known through participation in a community.

However, groups and communities do not evolve naturally into a just order. Inevitably, owing to man's nature, domination of one individual by another or one group by another will occur. Thus, rules must be established to prevent oppression. In a society of laws, these rules become the legal system by which the state operates. They are processes by which the society orders itself into a functioning whole.

A democracy affirms the right of all individuals to establish the laws by which they are governed. Our Constitution begins, "We, the People. . . ." The Declaration of Independence affirms "certain unalienable Rights" for which governments are established to protect.

As participants in a system from which all power is derived from the people, we, as citizens, have a moral responsibility to involve ourselves within the political process or risk its dissolution. The truth of the statement that tyranny triumphs only when enough good men do nothing can hardly be debated.

The tragedy of noninvolvement is epitomized by the general reluctance of Church members to become involved with social and political concerns. The traditional view of the Church as a sanctuary from the world has so reinforced our dichotomy of church and state that it is easy to forget our prophetic mission to the culture.

There is a great tendency, particularly amid the frantic pace of today's world, to see the Church as an insulator from the pressures of twentieth-century life. However, inherent in this view is a temptation to see the Church cut off from the rest of the world, alone in a realm of its own, casting influence only over what we ambiguously label "spiritual things." If the mission of the Church is reduced to ministering exclusively to the restricted world within its four walls, then it has misunderstood its commission to feed the hungry, clothe the poor, and minister to all of mankind.

In a society where decisions are made on the basis of expediency, there is a crying need for someone to hold out the moral imperatives that must illuminate the decision-making process.

To a world that acknowledges violence as the final arbiter of disputes, the standard of peace must be raised. In the midst of a creation that appears chaotic and disjointed, the community of mankind must be proclaimed.

In its own small way this has been the mission of the Friends Committee on National Legislation. Born in the violent world of 1943, the FCNL has joined the ongoing struggle for peace and a better world. Attempting to influence national policy through its role as the first registered church lobby, the FCNL has fought a wide variety of battles since its inception.

The road to peace has not been easy, and the tangible results of the FCNL may at first glance seem minimal. But the Society of Friends has been extremely sensitive to its call as an agent of reconciliation, and through the FCNL, has responded in faith. The influence of this powerful witness to a vision of peace and justice should not be measured merely in successful votes in Congress, but its impact cannot be denied.

There is an old Jewish proverb which says:

> "God gives you the task. He does not ask that you succeed, but He does ask that you not lay the task aside."

The Friends Committee on National Legislation has understood its task and remains today faithful to that call. It is my prayer that its vision may one day become a reality.

Whenever I am with Raymond Wilson and others who share this mission, I am prompted to think and say that the world has been run by "realists" for these past decades, and look where it's gotten us. Isn't it about time that we give the idealists a chance?

SENATOR MARK O. HATFIELD

MARCH, 1974

UPHILL FOR PEACE

CHAPTER 1

The Quakers Started Something

*Quakers have been engaged in lobbying — that is to say in seeking
to influence legislators by personal visits — ever since 1659. . . . The
weightiest Friends in England including George Fox and William
Penn, busied themselves buttonholing members of Parliament and
appearing at committee hearings. The Yearly Meeting even rented a
room in a coffee house hard by the Houses of Parliament for a
headquarters — a kind of Friends Committee on National
Legislation office. . . .*

*The legislative struggle for religious liberty was substantially won in
1659 with the passage of the great Toleration Act, but the lobbying
efforts went on, until Friends were finally granted the right to
substitute a simple affirmation for a formal oath in 1722. From time
to time in the course of this campaign the Meeting for Sufferings
urged Friends to write their Parliament-men on the subject. If
anyone thinks the techniques of the FCNL are a modern innovation,
he knows little of Quaker History.*

> — Frederick B. Tolles
> *Quakerism and Politics*, pp. 10-11
>
> The Ward Lecture, 1956
> Guilford College, N.C.

The Friends Committee on National Legislation was a natural
outgrowth of three centuries of Quaker efforts to influence
governmental decisions. Since the seventeenth century, Friends in
England and America have encouraged or opposed the decisions of

their governments on such issues as war, slavery and the treatment of American Indians.

Francis Bugg, in 1699, issued a two-page broadside in London addressed to Parliament, complaining that what the Parliament did one day was made null and void by the Quakers* the next day. His reason why "the Quaker Principles and Practices should be Examined, and Censured or Suppressed" dealt in part with their political activities in opposition to laws passed by Parliament. By virtue of their adherence to a "Superior Power to that of King, Lords and Commons," he complained:

> . . .what is made Lawful to Day at Westminster. . .they Null and make Void to Morrow at *Grace-Church-Street*, as not only Unlawful, but Antichristian; and how far this affects the Government, I humbly submit to our Legislators. [1]

Among the many causes championed by English Friends over the years were abolition of compulsory church tithes, repeal of the oppressive Corn Laws, extension of the franchise to vote, abolition of capital punishment and slavery, emancipation of the Jews from civil disabilities based on prejudice, and drastic reduction of armaments.

WILLIAM PENN CHAMPIONS RIGHT OF FAIR JURY TRIAL

One of the landmarks of influencing the judicial branch of government was the trial of William Penn at Old Bailey in London in September 1670.

Parliament had passed the Conventicle Act which declared seditious and unlawful the assemblage of more than five persons for any religious worship according to any other rite than the national rite. The act prescribed penalties for the first offense of a fine of five pounds or imprisonment for three months; for the second offense a fine of ten pounds or six months' imprisonment. The penalty for the third offense was a fine of one hundred pounds and transportation beyond the seas for seven years.

When Penn and a few of his fellow Quakers, on August 14, 1690, went to their meetinghouse on Gracechurch Street in London, they found the doors closed and guarded by soldiers. William Penn defied their ban, took off his hat and began to preach in the street. He and William Mead were arrested. They pled not guilty and conducted their own defense demanding the right of freedom of worship. William Penn pleaded to the jury "Give not away your right"; after the jury stood eight to four with no hope of a verdict, the judge told

---

* The terms Friends and Quakers are used interchangeably in this volume.

the jury that they could not be released until they had reached a verdict. Later the judge told the jury that they would not be dismissed until they reached a verdict that the court could accept. After being detained all night they returned a verdict that William Penn was "not guilty." Whereupon the court fined each juror forty marks for contempt of court and ordered each committed to Newgate Prison until his fine was paid. Penn and Mead were also sent to Newgate Prison until they had paid the forty marks' fine. Four of the jurors refused to pay their fine and went to prison; it was more than a year before their cases were heard. The justices in a unanimous decision ruled that the jury had been illegally fined and imprisoned and that a jury could not be punished for its verdict.[2]

From that day forward no longer could a judge threaten or harass a jury into doing his bidding.

In Penn's words:

It is established for Law, That the Judges, how great soever they be, have no Right to Fine, imprison, or punish a Jury, for not finding a Verdict according to the Direction of the Court. And this I hope is sufficient to prove that Jurymen are to see with their own Eyes, to hear with their own Ears, and to make use of their own Consciences and the Understandings in judging of the Lives, Liberties or Estates of their fellow Subjects. [3]

In the United States Quakers oscillated between active participation in government, as in William Penn's "Holy Experiment" in Pennsylvania, and quietist withdrawal from the compromises and corruptions of political life. On two issues, in particular, the Quakers carried on a long and persistent campaign — the abolition of slavery and better treatment for the American Indians.

SEEKING AN END TO SLAVERY

In 1676, William Edmondson challenged his fellow Quakers in a general letter of advice in which he declared that Negro slavery was a sin. One hundred years elapsed, however, before the last Quaker slaveholders freed their slaves. More than eighty-five years dragged on after that long-delayed achievement before the slaves were freed by the Civil War and President Lincoln's Emancipation Proclamation in 1863. In Great Britain, by contrast, the slaves had been freed without war and by legislative enactment, when the country outlawed the slave trade in 1807 and abolished slavery in 1833.

In his book *Quakers and Slavery in America*, Thomas Drake cites more than sixty attempts by American or English Friends to ameliorate or abolish Negro slavery. For example, slavery in Pennsylvania became illegal after 1780 when Anthony Benezet personally and successfully solicited "every member of the government" of the state, on behalf of an act for gradual emancipation, the first of its kind in America.[4] William Dillwyn of Burlington carried a petition, signed by three thousand people, to the Assembly in Trenton, New Jersey, in 1774, advocating emancipation for all the slaves in the province.[5]

Over the years either personal lobbying efforts or petitions were directed to the legislatures of Connecticut, Delaware, Indiana, Maryland, Massachusetts, Pennsylvania, North Carolina, Ohio and Rhode Island, and to the American Confederation, the Constitutional Convention, the Congress and the British House of Commons. William Rotch, the Nantucket-New Bedford whaling merchant, voiced his concern, and probably that of many others, in a letter to Moses Brown, saying that, while he approved of many parts in the proposed American Constitution, "it is evident to me that it is founded on *Slavery* and that is on *Blood*."[6]

In Indiana Friends petitioned Congress against the proposed admission of Texas into the Union.[7] Philadelphia and Baltimore Quakers asked Congress to assist the British in policing the sea against slave runners. Their memorials contributed to the passage of legislation in 1819 and 1820 declaring foreign slave trade to be punishable as piracy.[8]

Many protested the Fugitive Slave Law of 1793 which required the return of fleeing slaves.[9] The Green Plain, Ohio, Meeting condemned the Fugitive Slave Law of 1850, declaring they would aid fugitive Negroes as they had in the past. "If it be really a constitutional obligation," they wrote, "that all who live under the government shall be kidnappers and slave catchers for Southern tyrants, WE GO FOR REVOLUTION, by such instrumentalities as are in accordance with the laws of God," possibly referring to the Underground Railroad as an instrumentality.[10]

The Quakers were defended and denounced time and again for their attempts to influence Congress. A Philadelphia Representative in Congress vigorously opposed the extension into the territories of the slavery compromises of the Constitution, praised the Quaker policy on slavery and said to his fellow members, "Would to God we were all Quakers, in order that there might be less oppression, evil, and bloodshed in the land!"[11]

When Representative Hartley of Pennsylvania introduced the

Philadelphia Quakers' petition on February 11, 1790, asking Congress to apply a "remedy against the gross national inequity of trafficking in the persons of fellow men," it stirred up a torrent of discussions. Jackson of Georgia declared that the abolition of the slave trade would point toward complete emancipation. The Bible sanctioned slavery, and why should the Quakers set themselves up above the Bible? "Did they," he asked, "by their arms or contributions, establish our independence?" Burke of South Carolina accused them of having acted as British spies during the Revolution. Smith, also from South Carolina, in referring to the compromises that were involved in establishing the Federal Government, complained, "We took each other with our mutual bad habits and respective evils, for better, for worse. The Northern states adopted us with our slaves, and we adopted them with their Quakers."[12]

Since Quakers had led in the freeing of their own slaves and had played a large part in launching the movement for abolishing slavery, why were they not more successful during the eighteen-thirties, -forties and -fifties in helping to eliminate slavery by legislation as England had done in 1833? Slavery was rapidly being undermined by moral and religious protests against it and by economic developments in the South which were making it less profitable.

One reason was that the Society of Friends was torn apart by the separation between the Orthodox and Hicksite branches in 1827-28. Another factor was the swing to quietism and political nonparticipation in the Philadelphia and North Carolina Yearly Meetings. Quakers were never a dominant majority in the population of the United States.

And third — and this has lessons for us today — the Society of Friends was unable to unite on a consistent and prolonged strategy regarding abolition itself. Some manned the Underground Railroad, helping thousands of slaves to escape to the North or to Canada. Some joined the militant wing of the abolitionists.[13] Some worked for steps toward restricting or eliminating slavery by state or national legislation. Thus during the twenty years before the outbreak of the Civil War, Friends were divided between the activists and the conservatives, and between the cautious and complacent city dwellers and the more radical rural people. There was no overall united strategy developed for the political emancipation of the slaves without violence. The dilemma was never resolved and the nation floundered into war over the Union and slavery.

There were some proposals made before the Civil War to

compensate slaveholders who would free their slaves. At the request
of Abraham Lincoln in 1862, members of Congress from the border
states placed an estimated value of 300 dollars on each slave.
Assuming the number of four million, which is probably high, the
value of all the slaves in the United States was $1,200,000,000. The
Secretary of the Treasury in 1880 declared that the cost of the war to
the Northern Army alone from 1861 to 1879, not counting the lives
lost, was $6,796,798,508, or sufficient to have purchased every slave
at five times his market value.[14]

Quakers Strive for Indian Justice

When Gandhi died in 1948, J.N. Darling (Ding), the great
cartoonist for the *Des Moines Register*, drew a remarkable cartoon of
Father Time with his scythe over his shoulder standing before the
open pages of history. There was a bookmark between the open
pages with the words, "Love and Non-Violence." The inscription
below the cartoon read, "Put a Bookmark in the Pages of History
Here."

In the blood-spattered record of the white man in America the
treatment of the Indians by the Quakers might merit a "bookmark in
the pages of history here." The contrast is vividly illustrated by the
words in the charter which King Charles II granted to William Penn
in 1681 as proprietor of Pennsylvania and the message of Penn to the
Indians a year before he came over to America.

As Rayner W. Kelsey relates in his *Friends and the Indians,
1655-1917*, the royal charter gave to the proprietor the privilege of
making war on the savages and of pursuing them "even without the
limits of the said province, and by God's assistance, to vanquish and
take them; and being taken, to put them to death, by the law of war,
or to save them," at his pleasure. But William Penn wrote his
philosophy to the Indians prior to his coming:

> I have great love and regard towards you; and desire to win and gain
> your love and friendship, by a kind, just and peaceable life; . . .I have
> sent my commissioners to treat with you about land, and to a firm league
> of peace; let me desire you to be kind to them, and the people, and
> receive these presents and tokens, which I have sent you, as a testimony
> of my goodwill to you, and my resolution to live justly, peaceably and
> friendly with you." [15]

Israel Pemberton, leading Friend of Philadelphia, could write
sixty-seven years later, "Is it not a consideration worthy of thankful
remembrance, that on all the desolation on our frontiers, not one
Friend we have heard of, has been slain or carried captive, and we

have reason to think, both from their conduct in places where Friends were exposed as others and from their declarations to us, they would never hurt Friends if they knew us to be such."

There were a few exceptions to this policy on the part of the Indians. The five persons who were killed and few who were taken captive, lived in New England or areas where Friends had no controlling voice in shaping the Indian policy.

JUSTICE FOR AMERICAN INDIANS

Only a few instances of Quaker action in behalf of the American Indian can be cited here. Philadelphia Yearly Meeting in 1709 put a clause in its book of discipline prohibiting members from purchasing Indian slaves. In Pennsylvania, law after law was passed to prevent individual whites from making private land purchases from the Indians or from encroaching upon unpurchased territory. Friends developed the custom of attending treaty-signing ceremonies in order to safeguard the rights of the Indians. In 1757 the great Delaware Chief, Tedyuskung, refused to negotiate a treaty unless the Quakers were present. At the urgent request of the Indians a delegation of Friends attended a treaty conference in Sandusky, Ohio, in 1793.[16] A year later Friends sat in on the conference with the chiefs of the Six Nations at Canandaigua, New York, which drew up the Pickering Treaty of 1794. The story of this treaty and its violation by the building of the Kinzua Dam is told in a later chapter.

In 1867 Friends from various Quaker yearly meetings began activities in behalf of the Indians which led to the organization in 1869 of the Associated Executive Committee of Friends on Indian Affairs.

The Indian Rights Association was started in 1882. The Association is a nonpartisan organization and, like the Associated Executive Committee on Indian Affairs, does not major in active lobbying. Many of its officers and staff over the years have been Friends. These two organizations have carried on countless visits to the Indians and have publicized their problems and achievements, and the Indian Rights Association in particular has reported on measures in Washington for improving the lot of the Indians.

In 1869, two delegations met with President-elect Grant and laid before him the grave concern of Friends for a more peaceful and Christian policy toward the Indians. The outcome of these visits was an invitation from the President to nominate people to serve as Indian agents and the assurance that any attempts to improve the conditions of the Indians would receive from the President "all the encouragement and protection which the laws of the United States will warrant him in giving." Unfortunately there was a greatly changed policy under a new Commissioner of Indian Affairs ten years later, so as a result, Friends sent a note to President Hayes resigning all further responsibility to the Government for the management of the Indians.[17] During the Hoover Administration two able Friends were appointed to head the Bureau of Indian Affairs. Charles J. Rhoads was named commissioner and J. Henry Scattergood was appointed as his associate.

The Friends Committee on National Legislation has published an Indian Newsletter when it has had the necessary resources. The Committee has lobbied for many Indian causes, including appropriations, better education and sanitation. The FCNL has advocated that there shall be no termination of their status as wards of the Government without adequate preparation and that no change of tribal status should take place without the consent of the Indians involved. One of the brighter pictures was the generous settlement of the Alaskan Natives land claims related in a later chapter.

Indians have often been relegated to reservations where the land was poor, the water supply deficient, and where there were few opportunities for economic security. In 1973 the plight of Indians is still acute, as was evidenced by their sit-in in the Bureau of Indian Affairs and the confrontation with the Government at Wounded Knee, South Dakota.

Full justice for many Indians is a long way from fulfillment. People of good will are challenged to do more than is now being done to secure the rights and opportunities to which the Indians are entitled.

THE FRIENDS WAR PROBLEMS COMMITTEE

The coming of World War II in 1939 began to crystallize a more continuous concern on the part of many members of the two Philadelphia Yearly Meetings* regarding their relation to govenment. First, each yearly meeting appointed a draft committee to counsel young men in case military conscription was adopted by Congress. These activities led to the formation of the Friends War Problems Committee comprised for the most part of Friends from the two Philadelphia Yearly Meetings, and a few from a wider area.[18]

---

* The term "yearly meeting" denotes a body of Friends, usually in the same general area, who meet once a year for worship and for transacting business. Some yearly meetings are independent, others are grouped in associations such as the Friends United Meeting and the Friends General Conference. A monthly meeting is the local unit for worship and business.

The War Problems Committee met some fifty times in Philadelphia between July 26, 1940, and May 27, 1943.

Before it was expanded to form the Friends Committee on National Legislation in 1943, the main thrust of the War Problems Committee was for the rights of conscience in legislation proposed in Congress. Of particular concern was the original draft measure — the Burke-Wadsworth Bill — which finally became law on September 16, 1940. Their second objective was opposition to a whole string of proposed conscription bills, including total mobilization, draft of labor, draft of women and draft of 18- and 19-year-olds. None of these proposals became law during this prewar and early U.S. war era, but they were actively promoted by their supporters, and presented an almost constant threat during that period.

During this period, the War Problems Committee stimulated a considerable migration of Friends to Washington to visit Congress. Thomas A. Foulke during the war gave unstinted time to wartime Quaker concerns. During the three years of the War Problems Committee, he rotated as chairman with Harold Evans and in addition served as chairman of a local lawyers' committee for counseling on the draft.

In early 1940, the Race Street Draft Committee undertook to list all Friends of draft age and to encourage the overseers in the local Friends' groups to give these young Friends their full moral support in opposing conscription. By the end of the summer, fifty-four meetings had sent in lists of men between eighteen and thirty-five. State Selective Service officials were visited in Pennsylvania, Maryland and Delaware, as well as the governor in Rhode Island.

"How Meetings Can Help Their Members Meet War Problems" was the theme of a conference on April 30, 1940, attended by members of the Friends Peace Committee and delegates from all but ten of the eighty-six monthly meetings of the two Philadelphia Yearly Meetings as well as others from New York and New Jersey. Hope was expressed that the United States could keep out of war.

As the pressure for enacting a draft law was building up, a National Conference on the draft was held in Richmond, Indiana, July 2-4, 1940, which drew people from twenty-two of the twenty-five yearly meetings. Emphasis was placed on supporting young conscientious objectors in home communities and not letting them down as had been done in 1917, in opposing conscription in any form, in working to keep the United States out of war and in pressing for a negotiated peace.

The findings of the conference highlighted the religious roots of the Friends' peace testimony and outlined the case against military conscription. Some excerpts from the conference statement follow:

> We believe that the light of Christ leads all men into ways of peace and that no emergency can release us from the way of love. . . . We are absolutely opposed to the intervention of our nation in the wars now raging in the world. . . . Keeping out of war, however, is only the beginning of the responsibility of the United States. No country can be safe from the peril of war until the world is effectively organized for peace and justice. Friends must not be satisfied with relieving part of the misery caused by war and militarism. They must also bear an increasingly active part in developing the will to peace, the conditions of peace, and the institutions of peace. . . . Modern totalitarian war is only possible through conscription of life and property, and its elimination depends in part in depriving all States of the right to conscript their citizens for total war. . . .   [19]

The first intensive and sustained effort of the War Problems Committee was the attempt to amend the conscience provisions in the Burke-Wadsworth Bill which fastened conscription on the United States. This conscription bill was passed as a temporary emergency and has been with us for more than thirty-two years with the exception of a lapse of less than a year in 1947-48. Some cynics in the nation's capital say there are few things more permanent in Washington than a "temporary emergency."

Actual conscription for the armed forces stopped in 1972, and the authority for induction expired June 30, 1973, but the Selective Service System and the registration of 18-year-olds continue.

Paul French and I were asked to go to Washington in June 1940 when hearings opened on the bill which had been introduced by Senator Edward R. Burke of Nebraska and Representative James W. Wadsworth of New York. We spent most of the next nine weeks in active lobbying.

The six main things which those of us working on the legislation tried to get accepted that summer were: to base classification upon personal conviction rather than upon membership in a pacifist sect; to broaden the basis of conscientious objection beyond "religious training and belief"; to grant complete exemption to the "absolutists" — those who were unwilling to register or give any cooperation with Selective Service; to provide for a register for C.O.'s; to place them under civilian rather than military control; and to provide them with opportunities to do "work of national importance" as an alternative to military service. Of these, we succeeded in getting the first and last objectives but control rested with the supposedly civilian Selective Service System headed by General Lewis B. Hershey and Colonel Lewis Kosch so it was military control in fact.

Unfortunately, there was little discussion, as it unhappily turned out, on issues of pay, dependency, disability and death, service outside the United States, or the implications of work of national importance before the conscription bill came into effect in September.

CHAPTER 2

The First Protestant Lobby [1]

Therefore, when we build, let us think that we build forever,
Let it not be for present delight, nor for
present use alone; let it be such work
as our descendants will thank us for,
and let us think, as we lay stone on stone,
that a time is to come
when those stones will be held sacred
because our hands have touched them,
and that men will say as they look upon the
labor and wrought substance of them,
"See! this our fathers did for us."
> — John Ruskin
> *Seven Lamps of Architecture*
> *The Lamp of Memory 1854*

Both sound morals and sound policy require that the State should
not violate the conscience of the individual. All our history gives
confirmation of the view that liberty of conscience has a moral and
social value which makes it worthy of preservation at the hands of
the State. . . . When one realizes the seriousness of their purpose and
the power of their influence, he can have no illusion that the mere
application of force to conscientious objectors will bring any solution
to the problem.
> — Attorney-General Harlan F. Stone, later
> Supreme Court Justice, writing about his
> experience in 1918 as a member of the
> Army Board of Inquiry investigating con-

scientious objectors. Quoted in Paul
Comly French, *We Won't Murder*, (New
York: Hastings House 1940), pp. 138-9.

In 1943 the world was locked in the most devastating war in
history.

There was no United Nations — only a wartime alliance and a
defunct League of Nations which the United States had never joined.
There was no UNICEF, no World Health Organization, no Food and
Agriculture Organization, no U.S. technical assistance or foreign aid
program, no Arms Control and Disarmament Agency, no Peace
Corps and no National Council of Churches.

There were no atom or hydrogen bombs; no satellites circling the
earth; no television industry bringing the day's events and weekly
body count into our living rooms. There were few, if any, food
surpluses; and racial segregation was the law in eleven states.

It was at this time — right in the middle of the Second World War
— that the Friends Committee on National Legislation was started.
On November 1, 1943, it became the nation's first full-fledged,
year-round legislative program on behalf of any Protestant
denomination. A ping-pong table was moved out of an alcove on the
ground floor of the Florida Avenue Friends Meeting House in
Washington, D.C., partitions were erected, three desks were moved
in, and the FCNL was launched into a turbulent and somewhat
uncharted sea.

In the next three decades, it would have a small but exciting role
to play in the continuing struggle for peace, for an organized world
and a just allocation of world resources, for racial justice and for
liberty of conscience.

Prior to 1943, there had been considerable discussion in and out of
the Friends War Problems Committee about a long-term presence in
Washington that would give Friends a more effective opportunity to
share their point of view on issues of war and peace with legislators
and government officials. In January 1943 Thomas Foulke, writing
on behalf of the War Problems Committee, addressed a letter to the
board of directors of the American Friends Service Committee,
asking them what steps they might take to forward this concern.

In a four-page letter to Thomas Foulke on January 9, I tried to set
forth the opportunity to build on the War Problems Committee
experience by establishing a more permanent and broadscale
national organization in Washington. Stressing the crucial period
ahead and the importance of the decisions then being made by the

government, the letter went on to say:

> I am not talking about pressure in the ordinary sense, although there are times when the full weight of the Society of Friends needs to be mobilized in behalf of some policies and considerations or thrown against some proposal. It is more a task of raising questions and pressing them for consideration, of sharing points of view, of encouraging men who are forward looking, of helping shape policies in discussion before they are irrevocable, of bringing to bear considerations which are not based on self or party interest, or number of votes, or hope of immediate or personal or group gain.
>
> A democracy can function effectively only if valid minority points of view are expressed and considered in a total picture. We need to be modest about our own lack of wisdom on complicated issues, the failure of our own society to live up to its historic testimony and declarations, and the difficulty of urging pacifist solutions upon a non-pacifist society. . . .
>
> After twenty-five years of trying to bail out a bottomless pit of suffering and dislocation due in large measure to war, I am sure a large number of Friends want to advance the timetable and seek also to add their influence toward the organization of peace, the search for justice, the evolution of international agencies and the prevention of war. If this concern is shared, certainly the organizational framework could be evolved or adapted to do it. [2]

As a result of these discussions in the War Problems Committee and in the AFSC, these two organizations joined with other Friends bodies in the spring of 1943 in convening a broadly based conference to exchange ideas and decide whether to proceed on a more formal organization.

ESTABLISHMENT OF THE FCNL

The conference which established the FCNL was held at Quaker Hill, Richmond, Indiana, June 11-12, 1943. It was a gathering of fifty-two Friends from fifteen yearly meetings which met to consider the responsibility of Friends with reference to governmental policies expressed in legislation. (See list of attenders in Appendix I.) They agreed that the Friends Committee on National Legislation should be organized and decided upon the basic organizational framework. The General Committee would be constituted of appointed representatives from the various yearly meetings willing to endorse the FCNL, plus members appointed at large, in order to make the governing policy body widely representative of Friends across the country. A smaller executive committee which could meet more often would make the interim and administrative decisions.

These critical times, (declared the Conference statement), are bringing home to us acutely the sweeping role which government is playing in shaping life, both national and international. The conviction has developed that we as Friends have a responsibility to contribute as best we may to the shaping of wise and right legislation in those areas in which our principles and the causes we believe in are closely affected. To this concern we in this conference have given our best consideration. We are convinced that it is right and sound. To give effect to it, the Conference has decided to establish a Friends Committee on National Legislation. [3]

Some areas of legislation were listed as examples, including military conscription, relief and reconstruction in war areas, relation of the United States to world organizations for peace and justice, international economic relations, racial justice, and religious and civil liberty. The first year's projected budget was $15,000.

Soon afterward I was asked to help launch the FCNL as its first executive secretary. My twelve-year association with the AFSC had been a strenuous but happy one, and I was not anxious to leave. However, after some discussion, the AFSC agreed to release me for two years, but not for more than three. The challenge of this new venture was attractive enough to outweigh the adjustments required, and I accepted.

Ray Newton, secretary of the AFSC Peace Section, with whom I had worked for twelve years, privately gave us two years to survive as an organization and several times during that period as we squeaked along from one financial stringency to another, I wondered whether he had not been unduly optimistic. But there was increasing support among Friends for the belief that they had a modern role to play in the democratic process of decision making on vital issues and that the FCNL should continue to expand its services.

"We ought to be under no illusion," I said in my letter of acceptance, "that many of the ideals of the Society of Friends will be fully acceptable in the period of hate and disillusionment which follows such a tremendous war as the one in which the world is now involved. We ought to be willing to work for causes which will not be won now, but cannot be won in the future unless the goals are staked out now and worked for energetically over a period of time." I told the Committee that we should not expect many legislative victories in the first ten years if we were working on the fundamental issues that the Society of Friends ought to be working on.

In fact, victory is hardly the right word to use. The words of Richard R. Wood have often been helpful to me when he said that we should look upon conflict as a problem to be solved and not as a victory to be won.

The original staff trio included Jeanette Hadley and John Kellam. Jeanette had been executive secretary of the Board of Christian Education of the Five Years Meeting of Friends and had a wide acquaintance with Friends across the country. Over the years with the Committee, she has been especially concerned with the outreach among our constituency, the frequently changing membership of the Committee structure because of appointments by yearly meetings and other Friends organizations, and the myriad administrative details of meetings and events that are part of a dynamic, ongoing organization. She turned out a prodigious amount of correspondence. Her service until retirement in June 1972 spanned the life of the Committee except for a leave of absence for nearly two years, 1968 to 1970, in Kenya working with the superintendent of East Africa Yearly Meeting and in helping train young Quaker religious leaders there.

John Kellam had been a junior planner with the Maryland-National Capital Park and Planning Office in Silver Spring, Maryland. He was released when they learned that he was a conscientious objector, and he joined us until his number was called.

The first meeting of the General Committee was held in Philadelphia, January 29, 1944, with Murray S. Kenworthy presiding as general chairman. It was agreed that important decisions on policy should not be made by any small inner group but by the Executive Committee or the General Committee. Later, it was also agreed that the General Committee would recommend legislative priorities at the beginning of each year to help direct staff efforts. The General Committee adopted a Statement of Policy to interpret what it hoped the Committee would do and to give guidance to the staff. The two main lines of endeavor would be, first, to give current and accurate information to individual Friends and Friends meetings to assist them in reaching judgments about issues and in making their influence felt; and, second, to help Friends confer with Senators, Congressmen and other officials on matters of national policy, interpreting to them the principles and spirit of Friends.

FIRST STATEMENT OF LEGISLATIVE POLICY

The statement on Policy said further:

The policy to be followed in pursuing these aims ought to be carried out in harmony with the spirit and practices of Friends as a religious, not a

political body. In approaching the task we should seek both prophetic vision and practical wisdom. . . .The Committee does not intend to press its concerns in the legislative field by the political pressure methods of lobbies maintained by groups working in their own narrow interests. It expects to work in the manner and spirit of Friends, presenting our point of view to individual members of the House and Senate, and, when occasion arises, to administrative officials, exploring with them the problems to be solved; endeavoring to win the assent of reasonable minds and enlist sympathies with the objectives sought. Moreover, the Committee will not be concerned wholly with achieving immediate results through the passage or defeat of particular bills. It will have in mind the values which may be gained by the slower process of interpreting to people in government over an extended period of time the moral and spiritual approach to the problems of government and law. . . . Friends should actively assist in the development of a world order which establishes justice, prevents war and provides for peaceful change. . . . During this period, we believe Friends have two obligations:
1. To work toward our goal of a non-military world order based so firmly on justice, spiritual unity, and voluntary cooperation that there is no place for war or armaments for war;
2. To view sympathetically steps toward the goal, such as increasing international cooperation, progressive disarmament, and the bringing of national force under the control of world organization, while mindful that these fall short of our ideal. [4]

Toward the end of 1943, the country was infected by atrocity stories, desire for revenge, racial animosity and war engendered hatred. The first *FCNL Washington Newsletter*, published just a few days after the office opened, dealt with the critical issues of that moment that were of deepest concern to Friends. Systematic relief was urgently needed for the countries hardest hit by the war. The House of Representatives had passed a repeal of the Chinese Exclusion Act, but only on a very limited basis. Bills for national service legislation to conscript labor and women and to provide for compulsory permanent postwar military training and service were temporarily inactive but posed a threat. The governments of the United States, Great Britain, Russia and China had signed a four power declaration in Moscow, November 1, providing for joint prosecution of the war and for establishing a general international organization open to membership by all peace-loving states, large and small. They further declared (shades of later default!) that "after the termination of hostilities they will not employ their military forces within the territories of other states except for the purposes envisaged in this declaration and after joint consultation, (and) that they will confer and cooperate with one another and with other members of the United Nations to bring about a practicable general agreement with respect to the regulation of armaments in the post war period." [5]

The next two newsletters examined a possible repeal of the poll tax, lotteries for revenue, Senate repeal of the Starnes rider preventing the service of conscientious objectors abroad, a letter decrying indiscriminate bombings, Congressional action needed to relieve the plight of Jews in Germany, and the request of funds for the United Nations Relief and Reconstruction Administration. By January 1944 the newsletter had been mailed not only to every Civilian Public Service camp and detached unit for conscientious objectors, but to peace committee chairmen, ministers and board members in the Church of the Brethren. A sample copy was sent to 1250 Councils of Churches and ministerial associations through the Federal Council of Churches.

Later, partly because of postal costs and regulations, the newsletter was placed upon a paid · subscription basis with complimentary copies going to members of Congress and to some key editors and columnists.

FCNL OVER THE YEARS — A BRIEF SUMMARY

The achievements of the FCNL through three decades of legislative efforts have depended on the cooperation of like-minded people in many other organizations. In 1944 the FCNL helped launch an eight-year campaign against Universal Military Training and the domination of the military mind over our youth. That dramatic crusade continued until UMT was defeated by a recommittal vote in the House of Representatives on March 4, 1952. The campaign had to be revived again in 1955 when there was a drive by the military for a compulsory reserve. However, conscription for military service has continued and, as the Supreme Court ruling in 1971 against selective objectors indicates, the endeavors by Friends and others to guarantee legal protection for the rights of conscience against war and conscription have been only partially successful.

The FCNL took an active lead in calling the first National Conference on Civil Liberties and Civil Rights which led to the formation of the National Civil Liberties Clearing House. The Clearing House has held twenty-two national conferences and has focused continuing attention on civil liberties issues.

The initiative was taken by the Committee in calling the first

National Conference on World Disarmament and World Development, which met during the same week as the inauguration of President Eisenhower in early 1953. FCNL took a leading role in the six succeeding conferences. The Committee launched the Disarmament Information Service that, in many informal lunches, brought together representatives from some forty organizations to explore solutions for the still unsolved problems of world-wide disarmament. The FCNL also wrote the first draft of the Senate Resolution on universal guaranteed disarmament which was sponsored by 34 Senators in 1953. The FCNL played a very active role in the establishment of the Arms Control and Disarmament Agency.

Some of the most dramatic chapters of FCNL history involved attempts to broaden the scope of Food for Peace legislation. In one five-day period, thirty-three Senators and sixteen assistants were interviewed in person by a small group of organizational representatives to expand the overseas use of American food. Edward F. Snyder and Frances Neely worked for more than a year trying to find a formula to get some of our surplus food to the people of Mainland China who had suffered the worst series of natural disasters in a century. The effort was carried to Congress, to the Departments of State, Treasury and Commerce, to Embassies at home and abroad, and even to President Kennedy in the White House when he met with a delegation of Friends on their concerns during a Washington vigil. The effort was unsuccessful. Was it Emerson who defined one kind of crime not as failure but low aim?

While the Peace Corps has had its difficulties and limitations, it has given thousands of young people an opportunity to invest two years or more in helping the people of other countries, through education and technical training to help themselves toward a fuller life. The FCNL shared its experience with Senatorial staff long before the Peace Corps idea was proposed. They picked it up actively when Congressman Henry L. Reuss of Milwaukee first introduced a measure for a study, helped arrange a remarkable day-long conference of organizations with some experience in using young people abroad, and finally pushed for enactment of legislation authorizing the Corps.

FCNL helped to arrange for a representative delegation from nongovernmental organizations to interview presidential candidates Eisenhower and Stevenson in 1952 and encouraged a fourteen-member delegation of churchmen to visit candidates Humphrey, Nixon and Kennedy in one day in 1960.

When two million dollars had been cut from the Senate appropriation bill for Middle East refugees in 1951, a call from the State Department swung the FCNL into action with the happy result that the cut was restored on the Senate floor less than twenty-four hours after the distress call had been received.

Edward F. Snyder was able to persuade the Congress to revise the matching formula for United States contributions to United Nations assistance programs, a revision which added over a million dollars a year to these constructive enterprises.

The FCNL was the only religious agency to testify on the proposed sale of wheat to the Soviet Union on the same concessional terms as to other countries and to urge that food as a weapon be taken out of the Cold War. It was the only organization to testify against the United States-Japan security treaty, when it warned Congress against the violent reaction to occupation troops that has since taken place in Japan and especially in Okinawa.

Some other questions on which the FCNL has been active include membership in, and financial support of, the United Nations and the specialized agencies, including UNICEF, the United Nations Children's Emergency Fund; revision of immigration legislation, a more generous welcome to displaced persons, and aid to refugees and the victims of war; family planning and measures to eliminate hunger at home and abroad; improvement of race relations and civil rights legislation for Blacks in the United States; basic rights for American Indians, Chicanos, Alaskan Natives, residents of the Pacific Islands under U.S. trusteeship, and compensation for evacuated Japanese-Americans.

The list includes economic aid and technical assistance, student and cultural exchange, more liberal trade arrangements, a guaranteed minimum income as one measure toward eliminating poverty in this country, civilian control of atomic energy, and reform of Congressional organization and procedures.

During the past three decades nearly one hundred fifty different witnesses have testified for the FCNL in Congressional hearings.

At the beginning of 1973, the staff of FCNL numbered twenty-one with a projected budget for calendar year of 1973 of $235,000. The Committee was housed in its fourth location at 245 Second Street, Northeast, on Capitol Hill, one-half block from the New Senate Office Building, and a ten-minute walk from the sessions of the House and Senate.

CHAPTER 3

What A Church Lobby Is Up Against

The obligation of the Christian to express his faith in the realm of politics springs not from a sense of noblesse oblige, not from a feeling that by so doing, he proves his moral sensitivity, but from his conviction that what happens in every area of life either assists or resists the will of God for mankind.

> — William Muehl, "Mixing Religion and Politics," excerpted from the Haddam House book, *Politics for Christians*, Associated Press, New York, 1958, p. 119.

Yes, the Church should engage in lobbying in Washington, operating openly under the proper mandate, with humility in error, and determination in the right. With James Adams we can agree that 'the most relevant thing a church lobbyist can do is to remind persons in high places that even nations stand under the judgment of God.'

> — J. Elliott Corbett, "Should the Church Lobby?" *Engage*, Vol. III, No. 4, October 15, 1970.

The role of a religious lobby in Washington is to seek to relate the principles and insights of religious faith to the decisions which government makes, particularly those of Congress.

Jeremiah heard the call of the Lord, "Go down to the house of the King of Judah, and speak there this word, . . .Thus saith the Lord: 'execute ye judgment and righteousness, and deliver the spoiled out of the hand of the oppressor; and do no wrong, do no violence to the stranger, the fatherless, nor the widow, neither shed innocent blood in this place.' "[1]

In a cruel world that needed compassion — and we live today in a cruel world that needs much more compassion — Jesus said in the parable of the final judgment: " 'I was hungry and you fed me, thirsty and you gave me drink; I was a stranger and you received me in your homes; naked, and you clothed me; I was sick and you took care of me, in prison and you visited me.' The righteous will then answer him: 'When, Lord, did we ever see you hungry and feed you, or thirsty and give you drink? When did we ever see you a stranger and welcome you in our homes, or naked and clothe you? When did we ever see you sick or in prison, and visit you?' The King will answer back. 'I tell you, indeed, whenever you did this for one of the least important of these brothers of mine, you did it for me!' "[2]

What Is Lobbying?

The Friends Committee on National Legislation has perhaps the most clear-cut mandate among Protestant organizations in Washington to undertake and encourage intensive personal interviewing of members of Congress by its staff and by its constituents who come to Washington for that purpose. These visits to members of Congress or key assistants usually total between five hundred and a thousand interviews a year. The FCNL is the only Protestant agency whose staff involved in interviewing members of Congress are registered under the Lobbying Act of 1946, and who file quarterly reports with the House and Senate.

While the Lobbying Act is poorly and vaguely drawn and has neither been enforced nor fully observed by some groups who seek to influence legislation, the FCNL believes that it is in the public interest to know who is paid how much and by whom for advocating legislative measures in Congress. In compliance with this act FCNL makes quarterly lobbying reports regarding legislation sought and expenditures made for that purpose. These reports are filed with the Secretary of the Senate and the Clerk of the House, and are therefore a matter of public record.

The *Congressional Quarterly* lists three meanings of the term lobbying:

> (1) . . .any organization or person that carries on activities which have as their ultimate aim to influence the decisions of Congress, of the state and local legislatures, or of government administrative agencies.

(2) . . .any person who, on behalf of some other person or group and usually for pay, attempts to influence legislation through direct contact with legislators.

(3) . . .anyone who is required to register or report on his spending under the terms of the Federal Regulation of Lobbying Act of 1946. . . . [3]

In essence, lobbying is expressing the views of citizens or organizations to members of Congress or other government officials and sharing genuinely in the process — and often the agony — of talking out questions until they are finally decided by legislative determination or executive action.

Lobbying should be a two-way process of sharing and learning, because being a religious lobbyist does not automatically endow one with the undiluted wisdom of God. The lobbyist has to dig as hard for facts and values as any one else. Members of Congress who take a prophetic stance ahead of the crowd are often lonely and need encouragement and support. Legislators often get fixed in their ways when they should be challenged to change their minds.

The legislative process in Congress is really set up *not* to pass legislation. There are usually fourteen hurdles to be overcome culminating in the President's signature on a measure which has finally passed both Houses in the same form. It is easier tactically to defeat legislation than to pass it, because, if blocked successfully at even one point, the legislation isn't enacted into law. [4]

Few people realize the long legislative history of most laws which we now take for granted. It took about a century to achieve so small a step as woman suffrage. [5] Forty-seven years elapsed from the time the women's equal rights amendment was first introduced until it got out of committee and was brought to the floor of the House of Representatives for a vote. The lobbyist must be dedicated and persistent in the face of interminable delays and patient, but not resigned, in defeat.

THE ROLE OF A RELIGIOUS LOBBY IN WASHINGTON

In a nation whose government puts undue emphasis on national interest, a religious legislative organization must champion what it believes is the real public interest. Congress is besieged all the time with pleas for special interests. Some of these interests are quite legitimate, but somebody should be viewing them with a concern for humanity as a whole. Such a lobby can seek to be a spokesman for those who have no representatives in Congress — the starving millions of people around the world, the refugees and the victims of war. Government should be challenged to view humanity as one human family under God.

In a world which worships military and political and economic power, justice is often forgotten or overridden. During the Second World War, children were being used as weapons against Hitler through a hunger blockade, and Friends were among those who spoke out strongly against such a policy. At a time in history when so much blood and treasure is poured out in war, there need to be insistent voices for peace. When there is so much fear and suspicion and hatred, the Church should be seeking paths of reconciliation, understanding, cooperation and forgiveness. At its best a religious lobby can cultivate a kind of pastoral relationship with members of Congress that includes warm friendship and encouragement and loving criticism. It is hard to be both pastoral and prophetic at the same time.

There is nothing in the Gospels which promises the followers of Christ either an easy or a comfortable time. John C. Bennett, in writing about the prophetic ministry of the church, said: "The life of the Church must be lived in a constant tension between this world and the coming age."[6] I have frequently said that it is the job of the churches to be from one to fifty years ahead of the Congress in their aims and goals.

THREE TASKS OF THE FRIENDS COMMITTEE ON NATIONAL LEGISLATION

The FCNL views its primary task as that of informing its constituency about issues that are, or ought to be, before Congress and urging citizens to become better informed to express their concerns through letters, phone calls or visits to their Representatives and Senators in their state and to promote active discussion in their local meeting, church or community organization.

A second aim of the Committee is to promote widespread travel by its staff among and outside the Society of Friends in order to discuss major issues before the nation and have an exchange of ideas and opinions. On the average, FCNL staff members participate in about seventeen Quaker yearly meetings each year and spend as much time as schedules will permit, not only in formal reports and addresses, but in informal conversations and personal talks. They take part in many conferences, seminars and meetings across the country. Nearly a hundred Friends come to Washington each year to participate in one of the two four-day Quaker Leadership Seminars which are held in conjunction with William Penn House and the Friends United Meeting.

The third task of the FCNL is direct interviewing, or "lobbying" in the narrower sense, by FCNL staff and visitors from its constituency on members of Congress or their legislative and administrative assistants, voicing concerns of the Committee, advocating or opposing legislation and pushing for action during the frequent and prolonged delays. Most of these visitors are given a briefing at the FCNL office before beginning their interviews. The Washington office of the Friends Committee is not designed to exercise the individual citizen's responsibility for him, but to help him or her be a more articulate and effective part of democracy, and then to supplement local efforts by doing in Washington those things the citizen cannot achieve himself in his own community. Big government and the complexity of issues to be dealt with require a group approach and a persistent follow-up to reinforce efforts by the individual citizen.

SHOULD THE CHURCH LOBBY?

There is a widespread "hang up" among many churches and among some Friends about the appropriateness and necessity of direct interviewing of members of Congress. Lobbying is as American as the Fourth of July or turkey on Thanksgiving. It is exercising the right of petition as provided for in the Bill of Rights in the United States Constitution. It should be done with humility, with respect for the Congressman, with appeals to his reason and sense of moral values, and with moral earnestness, not threats or efforts to intimidate.

Some think that the church should not "get into politics" or that the issues are too complex with which to deal. The organized church should not be a partisan in party politics, but it ought to be intimately concerned with the problems of peace and justice and freedom. Church members can inform themselves about the broad aspects of public policy if they are determined to do so.

Others say the churches should stay out of controversy, but since controversial issues are usually the important questions of human life, this seems to suggest that the church should not try to be relevant to the issues that really matter in the world around it. At least the churches can act on issues where there is considerable consensus, and use those questions on which there are serious differences of opinion as subjects for relevant religious education.

THE CHURCHES SHOULD DO MORE TO INFLUENCE NATIONAL POLICY

In a brief study which I made in 1954 of the seven most active

Protestant denominations in the field of social action (other than
Mennonites, the Church of the Brethren and the Friends —
commonly known as the three Historic Peace Churches), the amount
of their central budget spent for social action varied from four to
fifteen cents per member.[7] Only a small fraction of these modest
amounts was used to influence legislation directly or indirectly.
While there has been considerable increase in activities along this
line since 1964, most national church agencies at the present time are
facing serious cuts because of reduced receipts. None of them has an
adequate staff and budget for the program of education and action
which the churches should be undertaking.

The most encouraging development in recent years has been the
creation of the Washington Interreligious Staff Council (WISC).
WISC consists of approximately 65 representatives of some 23
Protestant, Catholic and Jewish agencies which relate to social
issues in Washington. In recent years this group has become better
organized and more effective in selecting priority areas for
concentrated attention and sharing information on current issues.
Closely related to WISC is an action arm, IMPACT, which was
organized in 1968 to communicate directly with individuals and
groups interested in social action from a religious perspective.
Currently there are more than 5000 persons on its mailing list. WISC
priorities, which also suggest the subjects of IMPACT mailings,
include: concern about the continuing fighting in Indochina,
reductions in military spending, integrity in government, national
health insurance, welfare reform, civil rights, and the prayer
amendment.

It is outside the scope of this study to review in detail the
activities of religious organizations in Washington, with most of
whom the FCNL cooperates on issues of common interest. The
pioneering work in this field is Luke Ebersole's *Church Lobbying in
the Nation's Capital* published in 1951.[8] James A. Nash wrote a
dissertation "Church Lobbying in the Federal Government: A
Comparative Study of Four Church Agencies in Washington," in
which he examines in some depth the scope of operations of the
Methodist Board of Christian Concerns, the United Church of Christ
Council for Christian Social Action Washington Office, the National
Council of Churches Washington Office, and the Friends Committee
on National Legislation. Nash commends the FCNL for its clear-cut
mandate for lobbying and its forthright position on lobby
registration. He declares that "churches have a moral duty to
lobby."[9]

In his book *The Growing Church Lobby in Washington*, James L. Adams presents a rather critical view of the activities of some of the churches and the National Council of Churches.[10] He deals mainly with three isues: the war on poverty and racial discrimination, especially the Delta Ministry that sought equal rights for Southern Blacks; support for the Elementary and Secondary Education Act of 1965, which, in his view, broke down the constitutional provision for separation of church and state by providing some aid to parochial schools; and, third, many of the church pronouncements on Vietnam which he found long on specifics and short on political relevancy and impact in regard to the decisions which governments have to make. "There is little evidence," Adams writes, "of church bureaucrats having made any impact on either the conduct or the shortening of the Vietnam War."[11] He is not equally skeptical about the implied infallibility of government. Religious lobbyists should not expect to be exempt from criticism, merited or otherwise. They should learn from their mistakes, seek to make their policies as carefully considered and as morally sound as they can and their activities in line with their high purposes.

Adams does give the churches and religious organizations credit for a decisive role in the passage of the Civil Rights Act of 1964. He sums up his evaluation as follows:

> I believe that the Church Lobbyist, when he is speaking for a broad spectrum of the church (no one demands unanimity) has an important role to play. He should add a moral dimension to issues, however, rather than resorting to power politics. Church representatives in Washington have an unparalleled opportunity to use their moral authority and expertise in the Seventies for the betterment of all mankind. [12]

TAX EXEMPTION

The question of tax exemption is one of the troublesome questions involved in lobbying by religious organizations, which do not want to endanger the tax-exempt status and tax-deductibility of the religious bodies they represent. This consideration is a major factor in the hesitation of churches to do active lobbying.

Par. 501 (c) (4) of the Internal Revenue Code of 1954 states that a civic organization may be *tax-exempt* if it is "not organized for profit but operated exclusively for the promotion of social welfare." Churches fit into this category. Even though organized for the purpose of influencing legislation, the income of the FCNL is tax-exempt as an organization because it is not organized for profit. But property taxes are paid on the building in which it is housed, sales taxes on the materials purchased, and so on.

However, individual contributions to the FCNL are not tax deductible on the tax returns of the individual donor. Nobody who contributes directly to the FCNL gets his or her earthly reward of tax deductibility from Internal Revenue Service for his part in financing the organization. Local, quarterly and yearly meetings can contribute modest sums to the FCNL as part of their regular budgets, since FCNL strives to forward the historic testimonies and current concerns of the Society of Friends.

Under the provisions of Par. 501 (c) (3) of the 1954 Act, a religious organization can receive tax-deductible status if "no substantial part" of its activities is devoted to carrying on propaganda, or otherwise attempting to influence legislation. The phrase "no substantial part" has never been precisely defined. In the *Seasongood* case of 1955, the Sixth Circuit Court of Appeals held "something less than 5 per cent" of the effort and time devoted to legislative activity did not fall under the heading of "substantial."

Although raising nontax-exempt money, especially in sizeable amounts, is very much more difficult than securing tax-exempt gifts — I believe we could raise perhaps three times as much tax-exempt money with the same expenditure of time and effort — yet, in practice, there are some real advantages in not being financed by a grant from a central church treasury. Such a grant can be given or withheld somewhat arbitrarily by a narrowly based decision in a church hierarchy. Since the FCNL has to appeal to individuals and local Friends meetings for sacrificial gifts, the contributors have to know enough about the FCNL and believe in it enough to give their hard-earned money for its program. Raising an annual budget is in effect a yearly referendum on whether the FCNL is responsive to the concerns of its constituency. It would be very nice if the staff could put in all their time strictly on legislative endeavors and not worry about finances, but the advantages of lacking tax-exempt status outweigh the disadvantages.

PROFESSIONALS AND THE LAITY

Charles P. Taft in his foreword to Adams' book on church lobbying says, "There is today a sharp division between the clergy and the laity in most Christian churches. . . .In a National Council of Churches poll, 58.6 per cent of the people questioned said the church should not become involved in social and political issues. . . .I wonder if it is the job of the clergy to be out in front in religious enterprises without securing real lay understanding and backing."[13]

While the FCNL has by no means solved this problem satisfactorily, there is a constant invitation to a wide spectrum of people in the Society of Friends (or outside the Society but congenial to its main emphasis) to support it financially, to participate in the democratic process of opinion making on legislative matters and to take part in legislative interviewing. The General Committee of the FCNL is composed of Friends appointed by 21 of the 27 Friends yearly meetings and by 10 other Friends organizations in the United States. The General Committee in its annual sessions determines legislative policies and recommends yearly priorities but leaves considerable latitude to the staff to adapt its program to the ever changing situation in Washington.

Many Friends meetings follow the historic pattern of silent worship with the vocal ministry supplied by members hopefully "moved by the Spirit," but without a paid ministry. D. Elton Trueblood, Quaker philosopher and author, would elevate the concept of the "priesthood of the laity" so that each Friend would be a minister. But in many parts of the country this original form of Quaker worship has been replaced by a pastoral system. Among the Friends churches with ordained ministers the situation is sometimes reversed — the laity may be ahead of the pastor, particularly if he or she has been trained in a non-Friends seminary and has made no serious study of Friends' history and principles. There are still many Friends, particularly in the evangelical wing of the Society, but also scattered throughout most of our meetings, whose interest and activity in the work of the FCNL is minimal or nil. One of the real difficulties which democracy faces in this country is that only a small percentage of citizens are willing to take the time and effort to become informed, are ready to undertake leadership, or even to follow, in building a better world.

RELATIONS TO ONE'S GOVERNMENT

Henry J. Cadbury has listed four major relations of an individual to his government:

1. To support his government when he believes his government is right.
2. To oppose his government when he thinks it is wrong.
3. To encourage government to do what it ought to do and could do, but has not yet undertaken.
4. To do those things outside of government which the individual or the group could do, and not ask or expect the government to do.

There are three basic attitudes which an individual or an organization may take:

1. The prophetic. To advocate a point of view believed to be true regardless of whether it is accepted at the time, or whether it seems politically relevant or achievable in any reasonable future. The world often hangs or imprisons or banishes its prophets. But without them the world would sink back into complacency or lethargy. Emerson said that the measure of a man's success was bringing the world around to his point of view twenty years later. The problem of this approach is to make this stand appear relevant to the legislator.

2. The politically relevant. This is essentially the role the FCNL seeks to play. While keeping the long-term goals before the Congress, it puts major emphasis on supporting or opposing the next politically achievable steps. This is seeking to influence "the establishment" from the outside. The temptation here is to sacrifice principles to expediency.

3. Working within the government. A friend of mine, who has spent his life, first as an employee of the League of Nations, and then of the Department of State working on trusteeship and the rights of colonial and dependent peoples, told me that he considered himself fortunate to be 51 per cent right 51 per cent of the time. Boxed in by the military and the rigidity of a foreign office, he had to compromise his desires and hopes. Yet he was honest in recognizing the compromises he had to make and judged his efforts by whether they promised to move toward the goals of freedom and justice which he was trying to advance.

These approaches are complementary and all are important, but a decision has to be made within which framework one chooses to operate. The big tendency today for many young people is to reject all of them as irrelevant or ineffective and "cop out" on the democratic process. They view the "establishment" as too corrupt and unjust to be saved. Political action does not do any good. Some advocate violent revolution — the bomb, the torch, the gun. But anarchy and violence are not the answer to the evils of today nor the way to the better world of tomorrow. If the democratic process is to serve us in this transition, we must use it effectively and work at it harder.

Some Dilemmas for a Religious Lobby

Various dilemmas confront a legislative committee. How much time should be given to reacting against immediate crises such as Vietnam and how much to working on more fundamental solutions, such as improving the United Nations? What proportion of effort should go to opposing conscription as contrasted with the search for international security through general world disarmament? The answer is both, but in what proportion? It is the writer's conviction that the pressures of the moment have meant that too little attention has been given by the FCNL to long time programs for fundamental solutions.

Another real dilemma is the extent of compromise. In 1953 after weeks of lobbying and many revisions, a bill was introduced by 34 Senators calling for U.S. leadership toward general disarmament and the setting up of measures for cushioning the economic effect in the U.S. of eventual reductions in military spending. The Senate Foreign Relations Committee sent the bill to Secretary of State Dulles for review. When it came back, it had been drastically revised and weakened.

The real purpose behind the weeks of lobbying for the introduction of the measure was not so much to pass legislation as to provide the opportunity for hearings in order to explore this whole question of international disarmament and get nongovernmental organizations on record in favor of the idea. No hearings were held. The original bill had been gutted. Should the shadow of what had been hoped for be supported? Should one take half a loaf when the whole loaf could not be obtained? The FCNL supported the compromise, but without much enthusiasm. The substitute was passed, unanimously, but I believe, by voice vote in the Senate after very little discussion. But the potential educational value of Committee hearings and of vigorous Senate debate had been lost.

It is not at all unusual for the FCNL to be cooperating with a Senator on one issue and opposing him on another at the same time. But it does put a strain on a legislative committee to be trying hard to get a member of Congress to do something on one issue and at the same time to be very vocal in criticizing him for his position on some other issue.

NEUTRALITY TOWARD EVIL IS TO ENCOURAGE IT

Many individuals and organizations would like to take the comfortable position of being "neutral" and avoid the hard decisions and dilemmas of modern life. But religious bodies should have a social conscience and a procedure for expressing and acting on it, and for them neutrality means that they are in fact acquiescing in a situation which needs to be changed. The forces of disintegration, of narrow self-interest, of privilege, of discrimination are always at work. Not to resist evil and injustice, when it is within one's power to do so, is to encourage it.

Lobbying Is Frequently a Cooperative Enterprise

One individual or one organization unaided, unless very powerful politically, is not likely to exert much influence on Congress. Organizations with a common point of view on a particular subject frequently join together for exchange of information through such bodies as the National Civil Liberties Clearing House or the Point Four Information Committee. At other times organizations plan joint strategy through such bodies as the Civil Rights Leadership Conference, the Coalition for Reordering our National Priorities, or the National Council To Repeal the Draft. Thus this brief FCNL history should be understood as one part of a much broader spectrum of organizations and activities which make up the democratic process of citizen participation in decision making of our Government.

CHAPTER 4

The Starnes Rider —
A Case History in Lobbying

What a few determined, prejudiced, strategically placed Congressmen can do to defeat remedial legislation is vividly portrayed in FCNL's four-year struggle to eliminate the "Starnes rider."[1]

In the House Appropriations Subcommittee, during the last few months of the fiscal year 1943, Representative Joseph Starnes of Alabama proposed a legislative rider, or amendment, to the War Department Appropriations Bill for the coming fiscal year. This bill, with the Starnes rider attached, was passed by Congress in June 1943, a few months before the FCNL office was opened in Washington. The rider prohibited the use of any military funds to facilitate the service of conscientious objectors outside the United States. While no allocated government funds had in fact been involved in the training, transportation or use of men on alternative service abroad, the technical effect of the rider would be to bar the use, however incidental, of any military personnel or property to facilitate such service. For example, it would prevent the Director of Selective Service, General Lewis B. Hershey, who is a salaried military person, from using his time to sign the authorizations needed to release men for alternative service abroad. The first contingent of CO's for assignment overseas, who had trained for ambulance service and had already embarked for China, were recalled from Durban, South Africa, and their passports revoked.

THE CHINA CONVOY

The men recalled from Durban were to have been assigned to the

China Convoy of the Friends Ambulance Unit. This unit was made up largely of British and Canadian objectors and a few Americans who at that time had not been called up in the draft. They ferried medical supplies over the Burma Road from Rangoon to the interior of China until that road was closed. Already the unit had lost four men: two by typhus and two who were lost at sea when their boat was mined or torpedoed. The unit in December 1943 totaled 95 members and was in urgent need of replacements and enlargement.

A year previous, the Chinese Ambassador and the Chinese Ministry of Foreign Affairs had endorsed the proposal to send out seventy additional Americans. This proposal was considered by the President and the Secretary of State who recommended that the men be released from Civilian Public Service. Their recommendation had been heartily approved by General Hershey, Director of Selective Service.

President Roosevelt wrote to Clarence E. Pickett, executive secretary of the American Friends Service Committee, on February 13, 1943, "I approve your request to obtain seventy volunteers from civilian work camps for medical relief, sanitation and public health work in China and I have taken the matter up with the Secretary of War."

Men were selected and trained and the first seven embarked for China in June 1943. The entire expense of this project in the United States was borne by funds administered by the American Friends Service Committee, and in China by British and American Friends agencies. The project did not seek one penny of appropriations, but the effect of the Starnes rider would be to restrict such overseas relief services and to limit the opportunity for religious groups (including the Mennonites, Brethren or others if they desired) to continue at their own expense humanitarian service which they had carried on for seventy-five years or more in wartime.

INFLUENTIAL LIST OF ADVOCATES FOR REPEAL

During the next four years, FCNL had the active or tacit support of a wide variety of people in its effort to repeal the Starnes rider. The list included President Franklin D. Roosevelt; Secretary of War Henry L. Stimson and Assistant Secretary John J. McCloy; General Joseph W. Stilwell in charge of the China-Burma-India theatre; Brigadier General W.E. Burgin and Brigadier General Claire Lee Chennault, who had served in China; General Lewis B. Hershey, Director of Selective Service; Arthur Burns, in the Foreign

Economic Administration and later Chairman of the Federal Reserve Board for President Nixon. Requests for the assignment for transporting medical supplies had come from Wei Tao-ming, Chinese Ambassador to the United States; Loo Chi Teh, Surgeon General of the Chinese Army; and from the Chinese Foreign Minister.

In the House of Representatives, Everett M. Dirksen of Illinois, later Senate Republican leader, vigorously advocated repeal. Other supporters included Christian A. Herter, later Secretary of State, Walter Judd of Minnesota, John M. Coffee of Washington, John Sparkman of Alabama, and James Wadsworth of New York.

Among the Senators favoring repeal were Harry S. Truman; Harold H. Burton, later Supreme Court Justice; Carl Heyden of Arizona who had seen CO's mistreated during the First World War; Elbert Thomas of Utah; Richard Russell of Georgia, who later became Chairman of the Senate Armed Services Committee, as well as many others.

First Attempt at Repeal: 1943

At the AFSC office in Philadelphia various strategies for circumventing the Starnes rider were considered and abandoned. One was to ask the Attorney General to make a ruling whether in fact it would prevent men from going abroad when paid for by private agencies. Another was to get the administration of conscientious objectors transferred from Selective Service to the Department of Interior, in which case the restrictions on military appropriations would not apply.

In October 1943, John Rich, AFSC staff member concerned with projects of overseas relief, went to see Senator George of Georgia at the suggestion of Felix Morley, president of Haverford College. He explained to the Senator the effect the Starnes rider was having upon the work of the Friends Ambulance Unit in China. The Senator appeared sympathetic and referred John Rich to Senator Elmer Thomas of Oklahoma, who was Chairman of the Subcommittee on Deficiency Appropriations. Senator Thomas, when interviewed by John Rich, promised to introduce an amendment to the Deficiency Appropriations Bill if it were prepared for him with a supporting brief. A Deficiency Bill is a catch-all measure for additional appropriations not fully covered in regular appropriations.

John Rich and I took to him the proposed wording, drawn up by Harold Evans, Philadelphia lawyer and former chairman of the Friends War Problems Committee. When we asked the Senator what we could do to help, he asserted that the committee members were usually inclined to accept his recommendation and that he did not anticipate any difficulty getting our amendment through the committee or through the Senate. Thus he did not open our way to visit members of his Subcommittee. When the Senator offered our proposed amendment to the Subcommittee, however, it was not accepted, and Mr. Thomas left Washington for a brief time.

I then went to see Senator Nye of North Dakota, ranking Republican on the Appropriations Committee. I told him that it was a crime for relief work abroad to be made the football of politics and that something must be done about the Starnes rider. The Senator agreed and said that he would move for reconsideration. When I telephoned him that night, he said the Deficiency Bill would go to the floor of the Senate very soon. Mr. Nye then inserted in the *Congressional Record* the same amendment that Harold Evans had drawn up for the Subcommittee on Deficiency Appropriations. Edward Evans, George Hallett, Thomas Foulke and J. Barnard Walton all came to Washington for FCNL to interview Senators and Congressmen. An effort was made to reach ten leading Senators, who, it was felt, should be informed about this measure before it came up for discussion on the floor.

On the day the bill was to come up for action, John Rich and I were in the Senate gallery. The expectation was that Senator Nye would defend this amendment on the floor since it was then under his sponsorship. But before the amendment was reached, the Republican Minority Leader announced that Senator Nye had been taken to the hospital and would not be back for some time.

We then contacted Senator Elmer Thomas, who agreed to present the amendment. In the meantime, I had put in his hands a brief supporting statement and copies of the letters from the President, from the Chinese Ambassador, from Surgeon General Kirk of the U.S. Army, and from the Surgeon General of the Chinese Army.

The repealer amendment passed the Senate on December 8, 1943. It read:

> Nothing contained in this Act or in the Act entitled 'An Act making appropriations for the Military Establishment for the fiscal year ending June 30, 1944, and for other purposes,' approved July 1, 1943, shall be construed to prevent or to interfere with the instruction, education, training, transportation, or service of class IV-E conscientious objectors within or outside of the United States, its territories and possessions, when such instruction, education, training, transportation or service is conducted and paid for by a religious or philanthropic agency for the

purpose of carrying out relief operations, or to prevent persons paid
from appropriations made by the said Acts from incidentally facilitating
the said instruction, education, training, transportation, and relief
services.

Since the House had already passed a somewhat different version
of the Deficiency Bill, the Senate bill as adopted went to the
House-Senate Conference Committee to iron out the differences.

Tom Harvey, Philadelphia industrialist, came down and worked
with me the day the Conference Committee met. In spite of five
attempts to see Senator Nye, I never did get the full story of the
Conference Committee action. We were told that the opposition was
led chiefly by Representative D. Lane Powers and J. Buell Snyder,
who, it was reported, opposed accepting the Senate repealer because
it would give undue recognition to CO's, would be destructive of
army morale abroad, would mean training the men in the lap of
luxury in places like Haverford College, and would grant them more
pay than the army in China; all false assumptions. Senator Henry
Cabot Lodge, who was on two different Conference Committees the
same day, did not even attend the discussion on this bill. Episcopal
Bishop D. Appleton Lawrence of Massachusetts had appealed to
Lodge to strongly support the Senate amendment in conference.

As for affecting army morale, the British had been sending
ambulance workers abroad for at least two years, and there had been
no reports to our knowledge about adverse effects on their army. As
for the charge that the men would be trained in comfort if not in
luxury at Haverford, the army was training men there. In regard to a
higher standard of living than the army in China, the Friends
Ambulance Unit received only maintenance, not pay, and lived
under very primitive and uncomfortable conditions.

The repeal was lost in the Conference Committee on December 15,
1943, in the closing days before Christmas. There had been 96
amendments offered to the bill and ours was number 71. Once the
conferees agree on a measure to go back to both Houses for final
passage, it is virtually impossible to amend it. A conference report
can only be voted up or down.

Starnes had been defeated in the primary and would not be back in
the new Congress in January 1945, but D. Lane Powers of New
Jersey continued as the implacable foe of any change in the
prohibition against using conscientious objectors for relief work in
any part of the war torn world. He was in the strategic position of
being a member of both the War Department and Deficiency
Appropriations Subcommittees, which would have to act favorably

on overturning the Starnes provision.

SECOND Effort at Repeal: 1944

When Edwin P. Brown, a Friend from Murfreesboro, North
Carolina, and president of the Riverside Manufacturing Company,
and I went to see Congressman John H. Kerr from North Carolina
early in 1944, he suggested that a hearing on the Starnes rider be
requested before the Subcommittee on Military Appropriations of
which he was a member. Kerr promised his active aid in setting up
such a hearing.

When I went to the hospital in April for an appendectomy, Josiah
P. Marvel, chairman of the Quaker Emergency Service in New York
City, came to Washington to carry on this campaign during my
absence. Altogether he spent many weeks in Washington during the
next two years. When Kerr went to North Carolina to campaign for
reelection, Congressman Engle promised Marvel that he would
arrange for a hearing.

The House Subcommittee on Military Appropriations did call
hearings, and Clarence E. Pickett in his testimony on May 17, 1944,
explained that what the AFSC wanted to do was similar to what was
done in the First World War:

> At that time we sent about 600 men to rebuild homes in France and
> restore ruined farm lands and combat typhus with antiepidemic
> teams. . . . Throughout the present war the British Government has
> permitted conscientious objectors to do relief work in war zones; thus
> distinguished services have been rendered in Greece, North Africa,
> China and Italy. [2]

The results of the hearing were definitely negative. The original
plan had been for Clarence Pickett to present the initial testimony
and for John Rich, who had recently returned from the Far East, to
answer questions on actual conditions and needs abroad. It turned
out that the hearing was scheduled on the same day that the Surgeon
General was to appear for his own budget and we were told, just
before the hearing, that there would be time for only one brief
statement and little discussion.

In the time available Representative Engle and Case did not feel
that their questions had been adequately answered. Powers and
Starnes were particularly hostile. Some of Starnes' extreme
statements were revised and toned down before printing.

John Rich had conferred with Chinese, American and British
authorities about the desperate need for additional personnel in

medical relief. He filed a supplementary statement with the Subcommittee, going into more detail concerning the need and the current operations.

He pointed out in his statement that during the Burma campaign, the Friends Ambulance Unit had assisted General Stilwell and had provided practically the only ambulance personnel. In the retreat from Burma sixteen conscientious objectors had accompanied General Stilwell in his notable march through the jungle to India. During the hazards of this journey, they rescued several wounded American officers and transported them to safety. In China three mobile surgical teams of field hospitals were established on the Yunnan front where fighting was active. FAU workers had established a typhus control station where troops were deloused and they were also combating malaria.

Rich's report went on to explain that the transport system covered more than 5,000 miles of roads, running from the Gobi Desert south to the Burma border and eastward almost to the outskirts of Shanghai, where Japanese military operations were going on. Along this route, FAU workers were hauling drugs and medical supplies to hospitals and to the civilians of interior China.

In its June 25, 1945, issue, *Time* magazine (p. 70) gave a later chapter in the story of the China convoy, which they described as one of the war's toughest jobs.

> They learned that ambulances could not evacuate the wounded because no roads ran to the front. They also discovered that lack of transportation was keeping China's tiny stocks of medical supplies bottled up in Kunming. The FAU promptly got hold of 25 trucks to keep the supplies moving to short-stocked hospitals. China's rugged mountains were more than a match for FAU's trucks and a single trip of 300 miles often took 40 days and nights. Through necessity, members of the Unit became expert mechanics. When gasoline got scarce, they laboriously converted their fleet to charcoal.
>
> Moving the precious cargo along China's bandit-infested roads meant constant danger. At night, the Friends slept near their cabs. Religious scruples forbid them to carry guns or travel with armed guards. One Friend's arm was so badly slashed when he tried to ward off a robber's sword that the nerves were severed. . . .The group is actually delivering 90 per cent of Free China's civilian medical supplies.

According to Rich's statements, other areas of Quaker service needing additional personnel included work with refugees in Algeria and Morocco, Lisbon, Madrid, Geneva, Cairo and Italy. The Friends Ambulance Unit had been called upon to administer relief to Bengal famine victims in India. This proposed work would include Brethren and Mennonites under their own direction. Other requests were being made for personnel to serve overseas. The Public Health Authorities of France had asked for an enlargement of the Friends civilian relief program there. General Fox of the Surgeon General's office had asked for two or three hundred civilians for antityphus work in Italy on the basis of what he had seen the FAU do in Egypt and Italy.

Rich concluded his statement to the Military Appropriations Subcommittee by summarizing the number of conscientious objectors in the United States and the great variety of services they were performing. This information illustrated the large pool from which qualified men could be recruited for difficult overseas assignments. For example, the Office of Scientific Research was supervising about 20 medical experiments using 134 IV-E men who volunteered to serve as guinea pigs.

Some men had carried lice on their bodies for a considerable time while different treatments were applied in an attempt to find the best method for destroying lice and thereby the spread of typhus. Another group at the Harvard Medical School was trying to discover methods of prolonging the lives of men adrift on the high seas with only limited supplies of water, food and equipment, and was also trying to ascertain the amount of sea water that could be taken without disastrous effects.

These were the types of urgent calls for humanitarian service overseas which the stubborn resistances of Starnes and Powers and their colleagues in the House prevented the conscientious objectors, with their dedication and training, from responding to under the administration and financing of religious agencies.

After this abortive hearing, each member of the Subcommittee except Joe Starnes was then interviewed again. When Gilbert White, later president of Haverford College and chairman of the American Friends Service Committee, and John Rich went to see Congressman Case, he said that on many occasions he had supported conscientious objectors and was not opposed to them now, but that he was concerned about adding certain safeguards. He would be willing to support an amendment to the War Department Appropriations Bill, but not a repeal of the Starnes rider. Accordingly, an amendment, based largely on the suggestions of Congressman Case, was drafted and put into the hands of each Subcommittee member by a group which included Paul French and Joe Weaver from the National Service Board for Religious Objectors.

When the bill was marked up (drafted and decided on in committee), Congressman Kerr had not returned from North Carolina. We were told unofficially that in the Committee discussion Engel and Case had favored our amendment while Starnes, Mahon, Powers and Snyder had either opposed it or remained uncommitted. In any event, it was not accepted. When Kerr was interviewed at some length again by Edwin Brown and myself, he promised to support the amendment in conference if it could be passed in the Senate. This would still leave the House line-up 4 to 3 against us.

Then Josiah Marvel, Margaret Frawley and I, with several others, began active interviewing in the Senate. Seventeen Senators were either on the Military Appropriations Subcommittee or ex-officio. Senator Elmer Thomas of Oklahoma, chairman of the Subcommittee, promised to introduce either a repeal or an amendment that we would draw up for him. Hayden was favorable but was leaving to campaign for reelection. Chavez was particularly cordial, having heard very favorable comments on the work of CO's during his visit to Puerto Rico. Truman, O'Mahoney, Bridges, Burton, Ball and Reynolds all expressed themselves favorably. Maloney was noncommittal. The assistants of the others on the Senate Subcommittee were interviewed at least twice, including Overton, Russell, Maybank, Gurney, Brooke, Thomas of Utah and Austin.

As soon as the War Department Appropriations Bill had cleared the House of Representatives with the Starnes rider still in it and without the modifying amendment by Case, a letter over my signature and enclosures were hand-delivered to the secretaries of all the Senators on the Military Appropriations Subcommittee except Hayden, who had already left town.

The letter stated that Senator Elmer Thomas, chairman of the Subcommittee, was willing to introduce an amendment along the lines suggested by Congressman Case. Projects using Class IV-E men abroad would require approval by the Secretary of War or someone whom he would designate.

No appropriation was asked for since the men were being supported by the churches and relief activities were financed by private agencies and public subscriptions to such funds as China Relief. The letter continued, "Now as millions are being added to the tragic toll of people uprooted from their homes by the war, we trust that some Class IV-E men might be released for helping meet this desperate human need."

Senator Thomas sent the proposed amendment to the Secretary of

War for his comment. A year before, Mr. Stimson, at the suggestion of President Roosevelt, had approved the idea and had written a letter accordingly. This time, the Secretary's office wrote a letter dated June 17, 1944, which was intended to say that the proposed amendment was a matter of policy for Congress to decide and that it was not something which affected the war effort directly. However, this letter was interpreted by Senator Thomas as expressing disapproval by the War Department, though it seemed to me to express qualified approval. A memorandum prepared by the FCNL had accompanied the letter to the Secretary, explaining the need for such overseas service. Secretary Stimson's letter, after recognizing that conscientious objectors were performing valuable service in the United States, said in part:

> . . .Their use in relief activities in China has been approved by the President who has authorized the Selective Service System to release from civilian work camps the required individuals for this purpose.
>
> I can understand the reaction of those people who feel that in these times, the Nation is entitled to the first call upon the services of its citizens. However, in a war of the immensity and complexity of this one, it is my feeling that much might be achieved for the national interest such as are discussed in the memorandum prepared by the Friends Committee on National Legislation. It was evidently from the same point of view that the President authorized the Selective Service System to release from civilian work camps the required individuals for this purpose.
>
> The War Department is of the opinion that enactment of the proposed amendment would have no material effect on the war effort. . . . [3]

When it was rumored that Selective Service might be opposed to this amendment, Josiah Marvel went to see Colonel Kosch and received his categorical assurance that Selective Service was not opposed to it. In fact, they were quite willing for such an amendment to be passed by Congress and were prepared to cooperate in trying to send some CO's abroad, as they had agreed to prior to the halting of such service by Representative Starnes. Marvel also conferred with General Fox, who spoke strongly of his desire to use at least 100 such men in antityphus work behind the lines in the Mediterranean area.

Near the close of the fiscal year, which ends June 30, legislation frequently piles up and many items get scant attention or none at all. On Monday, June 19, we learned unofficially that the House Subcommittee had said that they would accept any amendment which the Senate, in the crowded days of the last week, might put on the War Department Appropriations Bill, with the exception of the one regarding the CO's, in which case they would throw the bill into conference and hold out to the bitter end against such an amendment. Faced with this opposition from the House Subcommittee led by Starnes and Powers, the Senate Committee yielded. As far as we could find out, there was no opposition to our amendment on the part of the Senate Subcommittee, but under the threat from the House, they declined to act.

ANOTHER TRY: 1944

I believe it was Senator Ball who suggested that one more attempt might be tried on the Deficiency Bill. It seemed wise to find a Southern Democrat to lead such a move if possible. The Republicans with whom we talked tended to be favorable, but, in a Democratic-controlled Congress, felt they were at a disadvantage in securing affirmative committee action, though they would be willing to support such a proposal.

M. C. Lehman of the Mennonite Central Committee came to Washington and joined Josiah Marvel and me for three days in this effort. I tried to reach Senator Richard Russell of Georgia, but his office would not set up an appointment for me, because he was spending most of his time in the Capitol. He would not come off the Senate floor when I sent in my card because he was involved in a vigorous debate on legislation designed to set up a Fair Employment Practices Commission.

Therefore I stalked him for five hours from the Senate gallery to talk with him for two minutes. When I saw him leave the Senate chamber, I dashed down to the ground floor and caught him in the revolving door on the way out of the building. When asked if he would support such an amendment, he replied affirmatively. When I inquired if he would take the initiative as a key member of the Deficiency Subcommittee, he said that with all he had taken on legislatively he could not, but thought it was a good idea to attempt it, and that he would support it.

On June 21, Marvel, Lehman and I went to see Senator Chan Gurney of South Dakota, co-sponsor of the Gurney-Wadsworth Bill for permanent Universal Military Training. This again was an example of working with a senator on one measure and against him on another. Since his office was filled with visitors, we took only three or four minutes to present our case, but he said that he would be willing to submit an amendment to the Deficiency Appropriations Subcommittee which was meeting that afternoon. We then presented to him a shorter version of the proposed amendment, which had been worked out the day before.

Our amendment was accepted by the Subcommittee. A meeting of the full Appropriations Committee was called for 5 o'clock that same afternoon at which ten members were present. There was no opposition in the full committee among those present and the amendment was reported out. The Deficiency Bill, including the repeal amendment, passed the Senate on Thursday, June 22, in the early afternoon, less than four days after we had approached Senator Gurney.

Since a similar but not identical Deficiency Bill had been passed by the House, however, the Senate Bill would now be subject to review by a Senate-House Conference Committee. At the same time, then, that we were working to get the Senate Bill passed, we were trying to see members of both the Senate and House Deficiency Committees who might be conferees. Some were already out of town for the forthcoming Republican Convention or for other reasons. Senator Bridges was ill. Congressman Judd attempted to see every member of the House Committee. He was able to answer Taber's objections, but Powers told him he would have to oppose the amendment as a matter of principle.

Lehman and I saw Woodrum briefly, chief sponsor of Universal Military Training the next year. While he did not commit himself, he gave us a very good hearing. Ludlow said he would support us, but told us afterward that he had not been in the Conference Committee when this amendment was considered.

After waiting for an hour to see Senator McKellar, chairman of the Senate Deficiency Subcommittee, I caught his attention for just one minute as he was leaving for the Conference Committee. It was impossible to explain much about the measure or to get his real interest. He had opposed the measure to compensate conscientious objectors the previous year. Since many had given him their proxies to vote in the Conference Committee, he was in a very strategic position. We were told by McKellar's brother, who was his legislative assistant, that it was McKellar's intention to support the Senate amendment in conference. We never learned how willing he might have been to trade this amendment off in the rapid and often superficial bargaining that frequently goes on in these secret conference sessions.

For the conference report eliminated the Senate-passed amendment, and the effort was lost on the last day before recess after favorable action had been taken twice in the Senate. The measure was defeated primarily because of the opposition by Joseph Starnes and D. Lane Powers, though the opposition, particularly in the House, was much wider. It seemed unwise to try to upset the decision on either floor of the Congress because of the rush to adjourn and because of the determination of certain people to express their opposition to conscientious objectors in any way open to them.

This account can only suggest the immense amount of time and effort which went into the legislative proposals launched by the FCNL against the Starnes rider in 1943 and 1944. Nor can it adequately describe the very intelligent and devoted work which Josiah Marvel did during the eight weeks which he spent in Washington as part of the FCNL team.

ANOTHER EFFORT: 1945

Senator Harold Burton, later Supreme Court Justice, said that we would always be traded out in an amendment proceeding and urged us to get our own bill introduced in January after Mr. Starnes would no longer be a member of the House of Representatives.

As the war dragged on, opposition to conscientious objectors became more vocal. Representative Francis Walter of Pennsylvania introduced a bill to put Civilian Public Service Camps under military discipline. Bradley of Michigan wanted to close the government camps as a result of the difficulties at the Germfask C.P.S. Camp.

Hollis W. Peter, one of several volunteers who came to Washington to lobby with FCNL against continuation of the rider, called on Representative Powers on January 11, 1945. Peter had been classified for noncombatant service in the Army. He was bombed by one of our own planes in Normandy, was awarded the Purple Heart, and after spending six months in a military hospital, came to Washington to lobby.

As a wounded veteran wearing his uniform, he hoped he could prevail on Representative Powers to modify his position. He described the destruction in Normandy and the great need for relief and reconstruction on a large scale, both military and civilian. He explained how useful the noncombatant I-A-O's were proving in the Medical Department of the Army.

Hollis Peter told Powers of the generous treatment of CO's in England who had been given wide latitude in doing useful work as civilians and who had been allowed to do overseas work in various countries in the Friends Ambulance Unit.

Powers replied that "conchies" were anxious to be sent only to China and in any case, did only medical work, not relief and reconstruction. Neither statement was entirely true. If they wanted to, he said, they could be sent overseas to do medical work as I-A-O's, but they did not want to go any place but China. There was plenty of medical work in the U.S. in hospitals where American lives could be saved, and personally he would rather see one American life saved than twenty-five Chinese lives.

The previous year I had written to Frank Aydelotte, head of the Institute for Advanced Studies in Princeton, to inquire whether any of his constituents in Princeton could influence Congressman Powers. He replied that it would be worse than useless for him to take up the matter with Powers. "I was one of a group of conscientious citizens in Princeton (mainly professors of Princeton University and the Institute) who opposed his reelection two years ago," Aydelotte wrote me. "Powers resented this bitterly and published a long article in the *Daily Princetonian* in which he called us Communists, Parlor Pinks, and all the names he could think of.

Our Professor Earle replied as follows:

'To the Editor of the Princetonian:

May I congratulate you on publishing the full text of the statement by Representative D. Lane Powers concerning his critics in the Princeton community. As the self-portrait of a demagogue it approaches perfection.' "[4]

In December 1944 some of us appealed to the Budget Bureau and the War Department to delete the rider before the War Department sent over to Congress the requested appropriation bill in 1945 for the fiscal year ending June 30, 1946.

President John Nason of Swarthmore College telephoned John J. McCloy, Assistant Secretary of War, telling him about the memorandum from the President to Secretary Stimson and the hearings in the Budget Bureau and requesting an interview for Josiah Marvel and me.

McCloy received us very graciously on February 16, 1945. He commented with a smile that the War Department was not interested in making more conscientious objectors, but he indicated that they were concerned about basic rights for them and that he would do what he could for our cause. He asked us to send him further information and documentation and I later sent him a two-page letter outlining our case and nine enclosures including the letter from the President and a letter received from Brigadier General W. E. Burgin who had secretly recently returned from Chunking. Burgin had told the FCNL that we did not need to sell him on the work of the men in China because he had seen something of it.

As we sat in this beautifully paneled office on the river side of the Pentagon where we could see over Mr. McCloy's shoulder to the Potomac River and Washington beyond, I thought of the tremendous power in the hands of Pentagon officials who had nearly twelve million men under them, and of the objectors who confronted them with consciences that could not be coerced.

I wished every objector could have been there to hear the concern of the Assistant Secretary of War and to feel that each one had enormous power as a dissenter if properly used. The political battle for favorable legislation might not be won this year, I reflected, but some day the conviction that war is morally wrong will prevail and war will be outlawed. Since governments make war and conscript men to wage war, I knew that the power and the right to make war must be taken away from governments. The conflicts, real or imagined, that lead to war must be solved in some other way.

Following up on our conversation with Mr. McCloy, Secretary of War Henry L. Stimson wrote me on February 27:

I have your letter of 20 February 1945, addressed to the Assistant Secretary of War, Mr. McCloy, concerning that part of the Military Appropriations Act which prohibits the use of funds appropriated to the Military Establishment for expenses pertaining to class IV-E conscientious objectors.

This provision will be omitted from the War Department's draft of the military appropriations bill for the fiscal year 1946. Final action on the matter rests with the Congress and the President. I trust that the result will be satisfactory to your Committee. [5]

When the appropriations bill for fiscal 1946 reached the House Military Appropriations Subcommittee, the language of the rider was enclosed in brackets, the usual custom for designating provisions in a current law not recommended by an administrative agency for passage in proposed legislation.

The 1945 line-up in the House Military Appropriations Subcommittee was Snyder of Pennsylvania, Chairman, Kerr of North Carolina, Mahon of Texas, Norrell of Alabama and Hendricks of Florida on the Democratic side and Powers of New Jersey, Engel of Michigan and Case of South Dakota on the Republican side. We had a reasonably good talk with the Chairman, who at first seemed a little hostile. But, after discussing the whole range of Friends' work with us, he said that he was for us and would not do anything to hinder our efforts although he did not indicate that he would give us active support. Finally in June the new bill with the Starnes rider bracketed for exclusion was sent to the Congressional committees for consideration.

Case and Mahon refused to see us. Engel, who had been very cordial the previous year, was rather hostile to conscientious objectors now because his son was in a bomb disposal squad overseas. Norrell took the attitude that while he was not opposed to CO's serving abroad, he wanted more protection for the War Department written into the measure. Thus we still had no real champion in the Subcommittee, which would make most of the decisions. In fact, we had some very active opposition.

Henry Koch wrote Chairman Snyder on March 21, 1945, that "Representative Starnes said he had no respect for any man that refused to wear the uniform of his country. He probably had no respect because he thinks the CO is either a hypocrite, a fraud, a coward or a combination of these. Now I humbly propose that a man who refuses to kill is a man of principle and not a hypocrite; not a fraud when his case is approved by a Presidential Board comprised of five Army Colonels; not a coward when he is roughly abused when inducted or placed in prison."[6]

When the War Department Appropriations Bill came to the Subcommittee in June, Powers and Case insisted on the reinsertion of the Starnes rider. The Subcommittee yielded and the rider was reinstated. At that point, practically all the forty members of the full Appropriations Committee who were in the United States were interviewed in person by FCNL staff or visitors to Washington briefed by them.

When the appropriations measure came before the whole Appropriations Committee, Congressman Dirksen made a ringing appeal for the deletion of the rider but to no avail. After the episode was over, I wrote him to thank him for his efforts, saying "I was astonished and amazed when I heard the interpretation which Representative Powers had put upon our request as to motive and financing and character of work. It is so far from the truth that it is no wonder that the Committee acted unfavorably." Representative Powers fought for the continuation of the rider with all the vigor he could command and made a great many insinuations and misstatements of fact which were never sufficiently answered in the Appropriations Committee. He had the support of other influential members of the Committee, such as the Republican member, Representative Taber of New York. After conferring with friendly Representatives, it seemed unwise to take the issue to the House floor where all said it would be decisively beaten by demagogic speeches.

Over in the Senate, Senator Mead of New York presented an amendment to the War Department Appropriations Bill by adding the clause, "Except any service which may be necessary to effect the transfer of such conscientious objectors for authorized service on foreign service projects approved by the Director of Selective Service." Several spoke up approvingly including Hayden, Russell, Gurney, Burton and Ferguson.

Hayden advised us not to appear at the hearings on this bill because the members of the Appropriations Committee were too busy and because he thought they were all in agreement anyway. There might be one member opposed but he did not think that would make much difference. Bridges said he would do anything to help us if he found himself in a position to do so. Ferguson promised to support us in the committee, in the Senate and in conference. Ball, while very sympathetic, felt that we probably did not have much chance in conference because they would be even more rushed this year tnan last. Again a memorandum had been placed by FCNL in the hands of each of the Subcommittee members, giving the essential facts about the need for the services of objectors overseas, along with the story from *Time* magazine.

So the bill went to conference where Powers, who was to leave the Congress in a few days, apparently put up a strong and determined effort to get the rider reinstated in the conference report. Since the Senate conferees, while personally sympathetic to our position, did not consider it a sufficiently vital question to create unpleasantness in the Conference Committee, they yielded and the rider, reinserted in the House, stayed in the bill without the qualifying clause added by the Senate.

1946 — THREE DOWN AND ONE TO GO

"Four hundred million people in Europe and Asia are on the verge of starvation. . . . The historic peace churches for whom I speak this morning have been helping and like most Americans would like to do more." Thus began the plea in my testimony on June 4, 1946, asking the House Subcommittee to follow the recommendations of the War Department and the Budget Bureau and not insert the Starnes rider again. "Never before in the history of the world have so many people been hungry or homeless because of the devastation of war. Humanity needs a service of love wherever it can be expended. Whatever can be done by governmental or private agencies to restore health, provide food, or fight the epidemics that follow war should be encouraged." A copy of this testimony was sent to each member of the Appropriations Committee.

However, the House passed the bill with the rider in it. Before the end of July, the bill had passed both Houses and had become law again.

The spirit of prejudice and militarism had repeatedly prevailed in Congress over the pleas for humanitarian service abroad to the victims of war and man's inhumanity to man.

For most of this four-year campaign against the Starnes rider, the regular staff of the FCNL totaled three persons. These three were putting out a monthly newsletter to several thousand persons, fighting a continuous battle against the threat of peacetime universal military training, working for adequate relief for a starving world, and involving themselves in postwar planning and a host of other legislative issues.

I was the only regular lobbyist for the FCNL. My efforts were supplemented for several weeks by the work of Josiah Marvel and many Friends and others who came to Washington for a day or so. On April 18, 1945, I had gone as one of the Friends' observers to the San Francisco Conference where the U N was established, but I was recalled May 8 because the Woodrum Committee on Post War Military Policy was about to begin hearings on compulsory military training. Paul Comly French and the National Service Board for Religious Objectors were also active against the rider but they took a much stronger lead on the frozen fund.

Some Lessons Learned the Hard Way

Some lessons can be drawn from FCNL's long battle against the Starnes rider. One is that in attempting to influence legislation, much more work ought to be done in the districts of the men who compose the Congressional committees that make their decisions. A second related lesson is that more constituents in those districts ought to be brought to Washington to see their Representatives and Senators in person. This procedure was followed in the successful crusade against peacetime conscription.

Third is the need to find active champions in Congress for the legislation being sought — men who will take more than a passive interest but will lead an aggressive campaign. With the exception of Walter Judd of Minnesota and John M. Coffee of Washington and John Sparkman of Alabama, few had been willing to say anything in behalf of the rights of conscience on the floor of either House.

The most disturbing thing about the whole experience was not so much the opposition to conscientious objectors in wartime, which was not unexpected. Prejudice was widespread, but outspoken antagonism was centered in relatively few individuals. The greater tragedy was the indifference on the part of nearly all of the forty members of the House Appropriations Committee who, through the power of the purse, controlled UNRRA, foreign loans for reconstruction, and relief for war victims and refugees, including food for Japan and devastated Europe.

THE FROZEN FUND: 1943-1958

Because of limitations of space, a parallel case history of the frozen fund is merely telescoped here. This attempt to secure justice for men of conscience was thwarted time and again by the arbitrary power of one man or another, or a very few men, at a crucial time in the legislative process over a span of fifteen years.

The so-called "frozen fund" which accumulated a total of more than $1,300,000 was collected from wages earned by conscientious objectors, chiefly on detached service on farms or as dairy testers. After deducting medical and maintenance costs and about ten dollars a month for clothing and workmen's compensation insurance, the rest of the prevailing wage was paid to the National Service Board for Religious Objectors (NSBRO) for transfer to the United States Treasury. The money was put in a special account in the U.S. Treasury with the expectation on the part of the men involved that the money would be used for some purpose in line with their convictions.

This money was put in escrow under a ruling by the Comptroller General, Lindsay Warren, that the 1943 appropriation for Selective Service contained no authority for the plan of Selective Service to use the money for rehabilitation of war torn areas. He ordered that the money should be designated to the government and received into the Treasury in a special account unless and until Congress provided by law for some other disposition.[7] This is an example of administrative law which, on occasion, can be extremely arbitrary.

The National Service Board for Religious Objectors, assisted by the FCNL, tried to get this money appropriated to various causes, one after another, in line with the convictions of the men who had earned it. There had been a memorandum of understanding on the part of the Department of Agriculture, the United States Employment Service, the Selective Service System and the National Service Board for Religious Objectors that this money would be used for war rehabilitation work of some kind. One legislative objective was to help finance programs of relief and rehabilitation abroad under the auspices of the Mennonites, Church of the Brethren and Quakers who were financing and administering the Civilian Public Service Camps for conscientious objectors. The religious groups associated with NSBRO had active rehabilitation projects in more than 40 countries, including rebuilding of devastated areas, refugee relief and assistance, clothing, food, medical supplies, shelter, sanitation and the rebuilding of educational institutions.

Other legislative goals were: the Office of Foreign Relief and Rehabilitation; the United Nations Relief and Rehabilitation Administration;[8] the CARE Book Program in countries where libraries had been destroyed by the war;[9] and the United Nations Children's Fund.[10] Maurice Pate, director of UNICEF, testified that this sum would give one supplementary meal to 100,000 children for a year.

During the fifteen years between 1943 and 1958, nine measures had been introduced in the House and two in the Senate. The Cole Bill with the United Nations Children's Fund as the beneficiary had passed the House in 1947,[11] and the Sparkman-Saltonstall measure to appropriate the fund to the CARE Book Program had cleared the Senate in 1950,[12] yet neither had been accepted by the other House. The legislative game of musical chairs ended with Congress having blocked every effort to utilize the fund for relief or libraries abroad or pay or dependency of objectors here. The money stayed in what the men viewed as "Uncle Sam's War Chest."

This episode of the frozen fund illustrates the difficulty of getting affirmative action in Congress in behalf of war dissenters in wartime because one or a few legislators prejudiced by war psychology can block the passage of legislation. The failure was due in part to a lack of a consistent strategy on the part of the National Service Board for Religious Objectors and the administrative agencies of the Historic Peace Churches. Naturally, as one goal failed to win support, another was tried, but the signals were changed too often.

While neither the efforts to lift the Starnes rider nor to get the frozen fund appropriated for humanitarian purposes was successful, the scores of interviews involved did develop a lot more understanding and tolerance and sympathy for the rights of conscience both in Congress and in official Washington.

The *Washington Post* editorialized on July 8, 1946, on the government treatment of conscientious objectors as follows:

THE FROZEN FUND

Congress, in accepting the principle of freedom of conscience, when the Selective Service Act was first adopted, provided that conscientious objectors should be assigned to "work of national importance" under civilian direction. It also provided that such men should be paid for their work at rates not exceeding those paid the Army. None of these conditions have been met. . . . Although church groups administered most Civilian Public Service camps, the entire conscientious objector program remained under essentially military control and was subject to the whims of Selective Service.

Finally, not one cent was paid by the Government to conscientious objectors. Often they had to pay for their own support. They received no family allotments, no insurance, and often had inadquate medical attention. . . . Conditions under which men with differences of conscience have been forced to serve resemble slave labor to a realistic degree. The agency responsible for most of this shabby treatment of war objectors has been Selective Service. . . . Conscientious objectors do not in any sense merit favoritism, but they do deserve fair play and justice, and so far they have not had a great deal of both.

CHAPTER 5

The Battle To Feed the Hungry [1]

"Give us this day our daily bread"
Matthew 6:11

For two thousand years Christians have mumbled this petition while all too many of them have turned a deaf ear to the plight of half the human race, who, in a world of exploding technology, are still hungry or malnourished.

Does "give" mean that food should go to those who cannot pay for it, as well as those who can? Does "us" mean *only* my family, my country, or the whole of humanity? Does "this day" imply now or some future, far-off time? Does "our daily bread" imply a balanced diet of nourishing food ample for maintaining health and growth and energy for a good day's work? I believe that this petition does imply that the world should be fed and puts a divine obligation upon mankind to eliminate hunger.

The First World Food Congress held in Washington, June 4-10, 1963, brought together 1330 delegates from 104 countries to confer on what could be done to close the world's hunger gap. Levinus Painter and I were delegates from the FCNL and the Friends World Committee. President John F. Kennedy said in opening this conference:

> As long as freedom from hunger is only half achieved, so long as two-thirds of the nations have food deficits, no citizen and no nation can afford to be satisfied. We have the ability, as members of the human race. We have the means, we have the capacity to eliminate hunger from the face of the earth in our lifetime. We need only the will.

THE CHALLENGE OF HUNGER: 1943-1972

Indicative of the prolonged and intense interest in meeting the challenge of hunger, seventy-one of the first one hundred issues of the *FCNL Washington Newsletter* carried one or more items on food and relief. Over the years, *Newsletter* information has been supplemented by many interviews with members of Congress and officials in executive agencies, testimonies before appropriate legislative committees and reports and discussions in meetings and conferences across the country. During the first ten years, most of the FCNL activities against hunger were directed toward emergency situations or short-term programs. But increasingly the Committee emphasized the necessity of long-term programs and fundamental solutions, most of which are not yet achieved.

The task of abolishing world hunger is extremely complex. It involves halting the population explosion. It means industrial progress so that people moving off farms can be usefully employed. Most of the food people eat will have to be grown near where they live. The world will have to undergo in a short time the technological agricultural revolution which the United States has undergone in the last century. Improved strains and hybrid seeds; better breeds of livestock; irrigation, fertilizer, and pesticides that will control insects without polluting the environment; agricultural credit; cooperatives; improved farm machinery, storage, refrigeration, canning, transportation; more research; and creative adaptation of these general improvements to particular locations: these are a few of the parts of the puzzle to be put together. These advances will take time and money and ingenuity and a much greater determination to conquer hunger than has yet been exerted.

One of the essentials is general elementary education that will enable people to understand some modern science and read instructions given them on how to better their conditions. Agricultural experiment stations, coupled with county and home economics demonstration agents, have carried the benefits of research to the people in the United States. Much more emphasis will have to be placed on good nutrition and a properly balanced diet and the growing of crops for that purpose. The more developed and affluent countries will have to multiply their investment of money and personnel in less developed areas. The United States now has about 1100 agricultural technicians around the world. This number could be increased and more provision made for students to come to the United States or to other countries for specific studies.

The "green revolution" promises a huge increase in the use of new varieties of rice and wheat and probably other breakthroughs in the future. But the prospect of closing the hunger gap in the foreseeable future is dim.

This chapter reviews some of the highlights of the efforts of the FCNL to press for a much more adequate legislative program, usually against widespread apathy or deeply held prejudices. For years we had a weekly body count of Americans killed or wounded in Vietnam. There has been no weekly body count of men, women and children who have died around the world from the effects of hunger, malnutrition or preventable disease.

One of the excruciating aspects of the quarter century was the glacial speed with which Congress responded, if it acted at all, to the cries of the hungry. When a political crisis threatened in Lebanon in 1958, the Defense Department moved troops there from Italy in twenty-four hours. But on December 16, 1950, when India asked for two million tons of grain on favorable terms because of widespread starvation, it took Congress until mid-June before they finally completed action to loan, not give, $190 million for the purchase of wheat and sorghum, to be repaid as far as possible in strategic materials. India was to receive about half her request by the end of a year after she had asked for emergency help. I wonder how many Indians died while waiting for Congress to share our surplus or how many members of Congress lost a wink of sleep over their procrastination?

FOOD FOR OCCUPIED EUROPE: 1943-1944

Former President Herbert Hoover began in 1941 urging food for the children in Nazi-occupied Europe. Many churchmen in the United States, including some bishops, defended the blockade of Europe which was being enforced by the British. On February 11, 1943, Senators Robert Taft of Ohio and Guy M. Gillette of Iowa introduced S. Res. 100 designed to get relief to the women and children in Belgium, Holland, Norway and France, who in the name of military necessity were, in a sense, being used as weapons against Hitler.

The first *FCNL Newsletter* led off with a report of the hearings which began November 4, 1943. Three Friends played an important part in the hearings. Herbert Hoover testified in a packed Senate Foreign Relations Committee room that he believed that the problems of shipping of supplies, of money, and of effective neutral supervision could be solved and that it would be possible for arrangements to be worked out with the belligerent governments, including Germany, for the transportation and distribution of limited supplies of food for relief.

Clarence E. Pickett, executive secretary of the American Friends Service Committee, at the invitation of Senator Gillette, followed with a strong statement about the impossibility of building a stable peace on "the destruction of the innocent children of Europe" and spoke briefly on the experience of the AFSC in feeding women and children in Spain and France. He told of the pathetic pleas made to him by representatives of occupied countries for food immediately. Roswell P. Barnes, associate general secretary of the Federal Council of Churches, reported that whereas there had been a strong division of opinion regarding the urgency and practicability of such efforts, he was now presenting the unanimous action of the Executive Committee of the Federal Council.

Howard E. Kershner, former director of Relief in Europe for the American Friends Service Committee, 1939-1942, and the executive vice president of the International Commission for the Assistance of Child Refugees, was a later witness. He had written in *Collier's* magazine, July 31, 1943, that "the pathos of a generation of children perishing from hunger is indescribable. Do not look at a human being hideously swollen from starvation if you want to sleep that night. Do not go to the maternity wards and see the wrecks that starved women become by the time they give birth to babies of half the normal weight if you want to preserve your sanity."

The Senate passed the Taft-Gillette bill on February 15, and the House of Representatives on April 17, 1944. This was more than a year after the legislation had been introduced. At this time preinvasion broadcasts from London warning about the coming invasion of D-Day, advised the starving French people to store up food!

Parcel Service to Germany and Japan: 1946-1947

Suffering and death on account of war does not stop with the armistice and cessation of hostilities. In 1945, wishing themselves a Christmas present, some eight-year-olds in Berlin prayed for a whole loaf of bread which they could eat, one gulp after another, without stopping.

Eight months after the end of the war in Europe, 34 Senators had signed a petition to President Truman, according to the FCNL minutes of January 10, 1946, asking for resumption of mail service and increase of food rations for Germany. Four Senators followed up this petition by calling upon the President on January 8, without visible progress. They argued that the government should continue its authority to set aside food supplies for relief. In the view of the

FCNL, a more generous policy toward Germany and Japan would require a review of the Potsdam agreement of the previous summer with its emphasis on vengeance instead of reconciliation.

"There is no question of the terrible hunger that stalks Germany today," reported James M. Read for the FCNL, April 25, 1946, to the Senate Judiciary Subcommittee.[2] He had just recently returned from a visit to Germany for the AFSC. He explained that while shipment of parcels is much less efficient than bulk shipments, there was a great value in person-to-person sharing by friends and families and people of good will in meeting hunger situations. Nearly a year had elapsed since the end of the war in Europe. The average intake in American-occupied Germany in early 1946 was only 1800 calories a day or less. After conscientious objectors had been subjected to such a ration for six months in a guinea pig experiment, they looked as if they had emerged from a concentration camp with hollow cheeks and ribs showing, and their spirits and morale had sunk to unpredictable depths. It took months of high calorie feeding to build them back to normal, according to James Read.

By April 1, 1946, the food available in the French and British zones was down to 1050 calories per day, and in the American zone to 1275. These were the people in Germany, Japan and Austria whom the Americans were counting on to establish a more democratic society than the prewar totalitarianism that had led them into war.

The FCNL in company with other organizations pressed for legislation authorizing such parcel shipments as an important gesture of friendship and reconciliation, but in no sense as an adequate answer to the full needs of food for the victims of war. They called for the continuation of rationing in the United States in order to increase the available food that could be shipped abroad, because there were also famine conditions in India and China. That shipping space was available was indicated by the fact that civilians working for the American Military Government at that time were allowed to take their cars with them to Europe and enough furniture to furnish a four-room house.

On April 29, 1946, the Senate passed S. 2101 to permit the sending of food parcels, clothing, medicines or relief. This bill had been introduced April 22 by Senator Styles Bridges of New Hampshire. Action by the House followed and announcement was made on May 28 that food parcels not exceeding eleven pounds would be accepted for delivery to the United States zone in Germany. Only one parcel could be sent by one person to the same address per month. Contents were limited to essential relief items such as nonperishable foods, clothing, soap and medicines.

A year later, April 9, 1947, James Read was back on the witness stand before the Senate Civil Service Committee urging that the Trading with the Enemy Act be amended to permit larger parcels than 11 pounds to be sent because of the desperate need in occupied Germany and Japan. He believed that such a change could be made by administrative action instead of legislation. He also urged that procedures be set up for sending remittances of money. There were many German-Americans who wanted to send parcels and money to their friends and relatives.[3]

GRAIN FOR LIQUOR OR GRAIN FOR RELIEF: 1946-1948

In the postwar emergency period when wheat and corn were in short supply, it became a clear-cut choice of grain for beer and whiskey or grain for starving people abroad. Congressman Jerry Voorhis of California introduced a resolution in March 1946, which unfortunately was never voted on, to empower the President and the Secretary of Agriculture to prevent the use of grain for liquor or nonessential purposes and to channel such grain either into human consumption or into the feeding of livestock in the United States. Similar legislation had been introduced by other members of Congress.

The Government was facing a prospective deficit of more than 3,500,000 tons of grain in what Herbert Hoover believed would be required in Europe. Yet, in the eleven months from July 1, 1945, to May 31, 1946, the brewers had used more than 1,650,000 tons of grain for beer, and the distillers, with two and a half years supply of whiskey on hand, were using scarce grain at about the same rate.

President Truman had issued War Food Order Number 66, Amendment 15, which took effect March 1, 1946, curtailing the use of grain for brewing purposes by 30 per cent and for hard liquor by 70 per cent. During the next two years, the FCNL campaign to support these restrictions as a minimum, and preferably to close down liquor manufacture during the food crisis, was carried on through the *Newsletter*, interviews in Congress, and testimonies before the Department of Agriculture and three legislative committees in the ensuing two years.

Liquor production was very much increased just before the partial curtailment went into effect in March. In February the manufacture of beer was at the rate of 68,000,000 31-gallon barrels a year. Each barrel requires about 46 pounds of grain.

The brewing industry fought hard against these restrictions on their operations. After about 30 spokesmen for the brewing workers' organizations had insisted that the order be rescinded, James M. Read, on July 16, 1946, took the stand in hearings arranged by the Department of Agriculture, which was administering this curb on supplies to the brewers.

"I calculate that this measure alone has saved the lives of two million people," declared the FCNL witness. The savings by the end of July would amount to about six million bushels or approximately 200,000 tons of wheat. "For every ton of wheat approximately ten people are kept from starvation — therefore two million people were saved. . .It is women and children that suffer most in hunger situations." [4]

Former AFSC Foreign Service Secretary James G. Vail gave his views in behalf of the FCNL to the House Committee on Agriculture on August 2, 1946. He was vice president of the Philadelphia Quartz Company and president of the Institute of Chemical Engineers. He had visited most of the countries of Western Europe, North Africa, India and China. In his testimony Vail said:

> I have seen hunger and starvation first hand, and it does something to you which you never forget. With the basic shortage which confronts the hungering populations of Europe and Asia, any diversion of grain beyond our absolute necessities is a tragic failure of an abundantly nourished country to do its utmost for the victims of food shortage consequent upon the war and its interference with local production. . . .
>
> If the members of Congress could see the suffering people of Europe as individual persons or if by a further projection of human sympathy this same feeling could be developed toward the hungry hordes of India and China, they could not rest in comfort until everything possible had been done to apply American surpluses to the need. This has not yet been done, though any thoughtful consideration of the implications in terms of the American ideal of life or the peace of the world would give it urgent priority. [5]

Donald Gay Baker, testifying for the Friends Temperance Association, asserted that "In the United States there is more money spent annually for alcoholic beverages than for all educational and charitable causes combined. As a nation we drink each year in alcoholic beverages five times what we are willing to give to people who were our allies in the war whom we know are on the verge of starvation."[6]

The issue was still acute in early 1948, with emphasis on the distilling industry. The House Banking and Currency Committee was considering a series of bills, including a Senate-passed proposal to extend the President's power to control or stop the use of grain for whiskey for another month until the end of February. Another proposal was for extension of such powers for a year. The FCNL was given an anonymous gift to pay for two half page advertisements in the *Washington Post* appealing to the Banking and Currency Committee and the Congress for favorable action in providing statutory control of nonessential uses of grain.

Representative Jerry Voorhis had been defeated by Richard Nixon, but Congressmen Edward H. Rees of Kansas and Joseph R. Bryson took up the crusade for a one-year moratorium on whiskey manufacture. The distillers had made a tremendous spurt in production during the first 25 days of October, using 8,000,000 bushels of grain just before the 60-day reduction which had been ordered, and which would end on Christmas, 1947. The Secretary of Agriculture had offered an allocation of 2½ million bushels a month for 1948, but the distilling industry had turned it down.

In the hearings before the House Banking and Currency Committee Charles F. Brannan, Secretary of Agriculture, explained the need for such legislation and the inability or unwillingness of the distillers to agree on a quota of 2½ million bushels a month as a continuing restriction. He reported that, as of June 30, 1947, stocks of aged whiskey on hand were in excess of 464,000,000 gallons.

In my testimony before the House Banking and Currency Committee on January 27, 1948, I tried to portray how critical the European food situation still was and to emphasize that, in the face of this need, the world production of bread grains was down 13 per cent. The needed shipments from the United States would only be possible by reduced feeding of livestock and diversion from nonessential uses. With the estimate that one bushel of wheat will make 60 loaves of bread, the 2½ million bushel proposed allocation to the distillers would represent 150 million loaves of bread a month. The 2½ billion dollars a year in taxes paid by the liquor industry should not buy immunity from judgment regarding the use of feed grains in a period of acute food shortage.[7]

Another plea was made to the Subcommittee of the Joint Committee on Economic Recovery on February 6, by Stephen G. Cary, who had recently returned from 18 months' service in Europe as relief commissioner for the American Friends Service Committee. He pictured the despair at the lack of improvement in the hopelessly inadequate rations in Europe and a growing feeling that the United States was betraying these people of Europe by failing to live up to the promises of help. The failure to allocate sufficient quantities of grain for starving Europe was publicized in

Europe and did "great damage to America's reputation and played an important role in undermining the confidence of Europe's hungry in the leadership of the United States."[8]

Despite the efforts of the FCNL and other concerned organizations, no significant restrictions on the use of grain for the manufacture of alcoholic beverages were imposed after 1947, because the House Banking and Currency Committee at the end of January 1948 voted 12-9 not to extend the controls.

THE OCEAN FREIGHT AMENDMENT: 1947

Senator H. Alexander Smith of New Jersey introduced a freight amendment to the $350 million relief bill to ex-UNRRA (United Nations Relief and Rehabilitation Administration) countries in 1947 after three representatives of the American Council of Voluntary Agencies had waited upon him — one from Church World Service, one from the National Catholic Welfare Conference, and James M. Read from the FCNL. While gifts in kind were increasing, total shipments abroad by private agencies were declining.

Senator Smith's amendment provided that the government would pay the ocean freight on relief shipments sent abroad under the auspices of voluntary agencies.

It was argued that it was desirable to encourage nongovernmental philanthropy as far as possible as a valuable supplement to the more impersonal and often nonexistent or inadequate governmental aid. For example, if the farmers of Kansas or Iowa were to offer the American Friends Service Committee or Church World Service a freight carload of wheat or corn, they could not accept it unless they were able to pay the inland freight costs to the port of shipping and the ocean freight to the country of destination. Private agency representatives were quoted on the floor of the Senate as estimating that for every dollar of free ocean freight made available, ten dollars of relief supplies could be delivered (*Washington Newsletter* No. 41, May 24, 1947).

This freight amendment was adopted by Congress and has had a far-reaching effect in facilitating relief shipments ever since. The Agency for International Development, Operations Report W-129, stated that ocean freight to the amount of $570,086,000 was used to facilitate relief shipments to be distributed by voluntary agencies abroad between July 1, 1949, and June 30, 1970, under Title II of Public Law 480. Just in the fiscal year July 1, 1969, to June 30, 1970, the government spent $45,738,000 for ocean freight for government to government disaster relief, economic development grants and the

World Food Program under this same title authorization. This provision of ocean freight for voluntary relief was expanded in 1956 to cover government-to-government donations for disaster relief as related later in this chapter.

AGRICULTURAL SEMINARS: 1950 AND 1956[9]

Few if any FCNL projects have evoked such a favorable response as the two seminars for farmers and their wives held in 1950 and 1956. The first was jointly sponsored with the American Friends Service Committee and drew fifty participants from eighteen states and nineteen Quaker yearly meetings plus a few from other religious denominations.

The ten-day seminar met with Charles F. Brannan, Secretary of Agriculture; Willard L. Thorp, Assistant Secretary of State for Economic Affairs; Sir Herbert Broadly, Deputy Director General of the UN Food and Agriculture Organization; and about 20 other leaders from the Department of Agriculture, State Department, President's Council of Economic Advisors, House and Senate Agriculture Committees and the four major farm organizations. In the two years since 1948 the basic problem had changed from scarcity to surpluses.

Their recommendations included giving away the food we could not eat and could not sell to needy people abroad through the Food and Agriculture Organization or some international agency and encouraging the receiving countries to set up counterpart funds from the sale of such food to promote agricultural education and agricultural and industrial production. They urged an economy of abundance with international planning for effective distribution, much larger financial and moral support for the Food and Agricultural Organization, the United Nations, the World Health Organization and similar international agencies, and a vastly enlarged program of technical assistance. It was recognized that the world was in a desperate race between population, food supplies and distribution. There was emphasis on programs increasing the welfare of family size farms and low income farmers.

The 48-page report, by Ruth Smith of the AFSC, *American Surpluses in a Hungry World*, was widely circulated, including an initial request of 200 copies from the Food and Agriculture Organization. Several ideas discussed in the seminar were objectives of active lobbying later by the FCNL staff.

Among the recommendations of the second, even more representative, seminar in 1956, were that farm income rather than market prices should be supported, gearing any subsidy program to conservation practices. Maximum overall payments to any producer should be graduated downward as the size of the farm increases — a proposal partially adopted by Congress in 1970, fourteen years later. The seminars urged an expansion of the school milk and the school lunch programs and the extension of social security to farm people. The farmers called for freer international trade and extending trade relations in nonmilitary goods with all nations, including the Soviet Union, Communist China and other countries in the Soviet bloc. They urged the expansion of aid and technical assistance through United Nations agencies and the donation of more food to the needy abroad, where possible through voluntary, nongovernmental channels. The energy, resources and manpower now devoted to armaments should be transferred to programs of human welfare.

A Five-day Legislative Blitz: 1956

One of the most dramatic episodes in the record of the FCNL took place in about a week's time in March 1956. The aim was to enlarge the person-to-person distribution of surplus commodities abroad through 18 voluntary agencies to 70 countries. It was hoped that this aim could be accomplished by authorizing more payment of ocean freight and processing costs, and by raising the amount of commodities which could be distributed overseas under Title II of the Agricultural Act from $300 million to $500 million, at the same time providing ocean freight for these shipments. This Title dealt with disaster relief by governments and distribution of surplus commodities by nongovernmental philanthropic agencies.

The idea for this amendment came to me when the farm bill, which had passed the House of Representatives the previous year, was already being debated in the Senate. As the legislative clock was about five minutes to twelve, there was no opportunity for hearings or any protracted campaign. After drafting the proposal, I started out to get two sponsors, one Republican and one Democrat. Senator Humphrey agreed and I was on the prowl for a Republican sponsor when I met Democratic Senator Herbert H. Lehman of New York in the corridor and told him of my proposal. Although I had not asked him, he said he would like to co-sponsor the amendment. Since he had been director of the United Nations Relief and Rehabilitation Administration and knew more about relief than any other Senator, I gladly said "Yes," even though the amendment would lack the bipartisan sponsorship which I had wanted.

In less than a week, the five of us working on this project, including Edward Behre and me from the FCNL, either together or singly talked with 33 Senators in person and 16 legislative assistants. We conferred with the Republican and Democratic leadership in both Agricultural Committees so they would be prepared to accept this amendment when the bill would come to conference. We cleared with the general counsel of the Department of Agriculture, talked with President Eisenhower's assistant, former Governor Pyle in the White House, and asked him to see that the White House telephoned Senator George Aiken of Vermont, ranking Republican on the Senate Agricultural Committee, to assure him of White House support of the measure. We asked a member of the Republican National Committee for its help and arranged with the editor of the *Washington Post* for a favorable editorial on March 13, the day before the amendment was to be presented on the Senate floor.

I prepared material for the sponsors so that they would have the basic facts and arguments for presentation in the Senate debate, including the estimate of some men in the Department of Agriculture that it would cost less per pound in ocean freight to ship surpluses abroad for distribution to needy people than to pay the storage costs, which were approximately a million dollars a day, on the inventories of the Commodity Credit Corporation. The farmers did not want the food which was stored to rot. The Government could not eat it. Hungry people needed it. If the taxpayers were taxed to pay for this food, they wanted it utilized for human welfare. This method of distribution would not disturb normal trade channels. It would enlist the cooperation of foreign governments in the distribution to needy people who otherwise would not receive it.

A letter was prepared over my signature, along with an explanation of the amendment and a detailed justification. Arrangements were made with a letter company to have these documents on the desk of every Senator at nine o'clock Monday morning.

After the measure was discussed in the Senate it passed without opposition on March 14. But when the farm bill was finally passed by both Houses, it was vetoed by President Eisenhower! The veto was not aimed at our amendment, but toward other provisions of the bill. Because we had touched all bases even in this brief time, when the Administration bill was later presented, this amendment was in it intact and later became a law.[10]

During the next year I visited Japan, Okinawa, Formosa, the Philippines, Hong Kong and Korea, saw something of the distribution of American surplus food in each country and could appreciate firsthand some of the benefits of this legislation that FCNL had originated and had helped get through the Senate in less than a week.

VISIT TO HOKKAIDO: FEBRUARY, 1957

The snow was nine feet deep when our survey team arrived in Kuromatsunai, in southern Hokkaido, the northern main island of Japan. We had come as representatives of the American Friends Service Committee, Catholic Relief Services and Church World Service to observe the distribution of American surplus rice under the supervision of these agencies to some 53,000 farmers who had suffered from 70 to 100 per cent crop loss — the worst in forty years. After a late spring the summer had been unusually cold when the rice was in flower. The average head of rice which should have had about 100 grains had about 4 or 5.

It was extremely humbling to hear everywhere we went the deep and moving expressions of gratitude. One little third-grade girl, Takako Ito, wrote:

> Last year the cold days continued and our whole household worried about the crops which did not come up. Mother and Father became frantic as they faced the winter with no food. The snow began to fall, and day after day I could not go to school for there was no food for my lunch. But one day some rice came, sent by the people of America. How happy we were! Mother said it was the most important thing that had happened since I was born. Now I can go to school with my little brother because we have a lunch to eat and we are so happy. We are so happy, too, because we can study. Thank you, thank you, people of America. . . .

In the previous October, I had traveled through the northern three provinces of Japan with the vigorous 83-year-old Dr. Henry Taylor, the pioneer writer on agricultural economics in the United States, and his wife, visiting agricultural experiment stations and talking to farmers and government officials about the problems and prospects of agriculture in that rather inhospitable climate, especially for rice growing. Upon my return, I told the agricultural attache in the American Embassy in Tokyo that Hokkaido was headed for a serious food shortage and that I hoped the American Government would respond quickly with aid from our bulging surplus. He replied that the United States Government could not act without formal request from the Japanese Government and that it would be much better for voluntary agencies to take the initiative. It was a chilling reminder of the role that voluntary agencies could play in initiating relief which only the cooperation of private and government resources could meet.

Hallam C. Shorrock, Jr., director of Japan Church World Service, had seen the distress coming and had stockpiled a large quantity of American surplus rice in warehouses in Yokohama. The English language *Japan Times* newspaper put on an intensive campaign for inland freight costs. The American government supplied under P.L. 480 various commodities free — mainly rice. The money raised by the *Japan Times* covered the inland freight costs for 94 fifteen-ton freight cars by the end of January 1957, and more rice was sent later. The three Christian relief agencies cooperatively made the arrangements and provided oversight of the distribution by the Japanese National Council of Social Welfare.

Supplies went to the most needy in all fourteen districts in Hokkaido. American relief was being given in other parts of Japan, too, to the inmates of welfare institutions, to orphans, infants in nurseries, aged persons, lepers, tubercular and other patients in hospitals. As far as we could learn the distribution seemed equitable and fair, the accounting and records seemed meticulous down to the name of the family, the date, the amount received, and the recipient's name stamp. This was in contrast to what I saw in Korea and Hong Kong where there was some diversion of American aid to the black market, but often it was commodities like butter or vegetable oils which they were trading for something they wanted or needed more.

Our trip wound up with a day's conference with the governor of Hokkaido and several of his staff who spoke of the problems they were facing in the development of Hokkaido. In agriculture the shift needed to be made from rice to corn, hay and dairy farming in the far northern climate. The governor spoke very movingly in appreciation for American aid through these voluntary organizations. "It was the first aid received. It was spiritual aid also, for it gave us new courage, and helped make possible the large expression of aid from within Japan." It was also followed by rice shipments from Thailand and Burma. For every pound of relief supplies sent through the three American voluntary agencies, people in Japan responded with eight.

The snow was only two feet deep in the fishing village near Oshamambe, where the families of the fishermen were suffering because the gardens and the fish catch had been so poor. The men were out working on the road, but the women and children received us graciously and told us of their plight as we sat on the floor of the little one-room village hall. I had brought along a nice box lunch from the Japanese inn where we had stayed the night before. I passed it on to one of the women who shared it with the children near her.

Soon one of the women, who had been slipping in and out of the room, came in with a simple bowl of white potatoes and gave them to the visitors from America. It was the only crop the village raised that year. It was their way of expressing their thanks. I thought of Moses coming on the blazing bush in the wilderness (I wonder if it was an azalea in full bloom?) seeing in it the glory of the Lord and taking off his shoes in reverence. Japanese style I already had my shoes off. It was the most sacramental occasion of my life, and I still cannot think of this sacrament of food without tears.[11]

INTERNATIONAL COMMODITY CLEARING HOUSE: 1959

Lord John Boyd-Orr, first director of the United Nations Food and Agriculture Organization, proposed in 1946 a World Food Board aimed at maintaining minimum and maximum price levels for staple food products and creating a world food reserve for times of famine. His proposal was turned down, among others by the United States, because of the amount of supra-national authority such a board would require.

In 1949, the FAO asked a group of international economists to make another proposal. They recommended an International Commodity Clearing House with $5 billion capital which could operate to permit surplus-producing countries to keep their output high, without resort to restrictive measures, dumping, or destruction of crops. Through it, importing countries that could not buy as much food as they needed could take additional amounts — either paying the International Commodity Clearing House considerably reduced prices in the currency of the country which sold the product or paying it the full amount in their own currency. In other words, the proposal was to move surplus agricultural products to where they were most needed and let the Clearing House work out the problem of convertibility of currencies. The proposal was turned down by the United States in the Sheraton Park Hotel in Washington on Thanksgiving Day!

The FCNL lobbied actively for the general idea that some device was needed to facilitate the international movement of food. We insisted to our friends in the Department of Agriculture that, if the United States turned down this proposal because they did not think that it would solve the convertibility difficulties, they had an obligation to come up with a better idea. The result is that the U.S.

continues to sell its surplus unilaterally, and has been piling up counterpart funds in several countries, so an international solution still has not been found. A good friend of mine in the Department of State said to me one time, "What we need are some new ideas."[12]

Grain For India: 1951[13]

Less than four years after it had been granted independence, India had suffered one great catastrophe after another, causing unprecedented crop failures and food shortages. Earthquakes turned rivers from their courses, flooding once fertile crop lands. A deluge of rain inundated Kashmir, washing away villages and homes. Monsoon failures in the south for four successive years were followed by blighting drouth and plagues of locusts.

On December 16, 1950, the Government of India asked the United States for 2,000,000 tons of food grains on "special and easy" terms. It was after six months of wrangling in Congress over whether the aid should be a gift or a loan or nothing, that President Truman finally signed into law on June 15 the bill authorizing a loan of $190 million. Of this amount only half was appropriated for the first year.

During these six months the FCNL tried to portray the need to bring firsthand experience to bear and to advance the idea that under the circumstances of India's distress the grain should be sent promptly as a gift since food, when used for relief, is gone and does not bring in economic return like a steel mill.

E. Stanley Jones, one of the world's great Christians in my estimation, had spent many years in India. Annalee Stewart, legislative secretary of the Women's International League for Peace and Freedom, and I went with him on January 3, 1951, to confer with Charles F. Brannan, Secretary of Agriculture. The Secretary expressed his deep and genuine concern for generous aid to India and intimated that the President felt the same way. He had written the State Department that 1,200,000 tons of wheat and grain sorghum or milo could be spared without adversely affecting the supply available for domestic consumption. For the long struggle to close the world's hunger gap, I urged more wholehearted support for the United Nations Food and Agriculture Organization. Other interviews included the Director of the Office of Foreign Agriculture, the Economic Advisor to the Economic Cooperation Administration and the Minister of India at the Indian Embassy.

What the Indians were too polite to say to us was that, according to the *New York Times* of January 2, in the first nine months of 1950 the United States "gave away" $2,978,000,000 and lent another $341,000,000 for the Cold War and that Congress had appropriated during the same period between $42 billion and $54 billion (depending on what is added in) for the military, for civil defense, and for the war in Korea. Even $200 million given away would be a very small investment, compared with our other expenditures, in good will toward 400,000,000 people.

During the busy week we talked with Assistant Secretary of State George C. McGhee about the political and Congressional problems involved and reviewed a number of questions concerning Korea and China. We explored the Congressional outlook with various members of Congress including Senator John Sparkman and Senator H. Alexander Smith, who became one of the vigorous champions of aid to India.

William Stuart Nelson, in his FCNL testimony on February 22, told the House Foreign Affairs Committee some of his impressions after his ten months' service in India for the American Friends Service Committee. "The evil fruits of the low daily calorie value of food available to Indians I have seen with my own eyes. I have followed to the burning pyre the dead with life cut short, I am convinced, by lack of sufficient food. I have lived in Bengal and the city of Calcutta where in 1943 my colleagues before me and American soldiers witnessed the indescribable horrors of death and suffering on the part of millions from famine. . . ." Speaking of Americans as a religious people who for a long time have sent missionaries to India, he concluded, "We can in one act reveal the true meaning of our religion with an eloquence impossible in language."

C. Lloyd Bailey, FCNL legislative secretary, persuaded Methodist Bishop Pickett, who had recently returned from many years in India, to come to Washington and interview a number of members of Congress about the need for food as he had witnessed it firsthand.

The nineteen witnesses, including the Secretary of State, Dean Acheson, during the four days of hearings before the House Foreign Affairs Committee all supported aid to India, most of them as a gift. The Secretary of State said, "Credits for the acquisition of consumer goods such as foodstuffs required to meet an emergency situation are economically unsound as they provide no basis for the creation of income and foreign exchange to repay the credit. It is clear to me that our own interest and India's interest require that we provide the grain which India needs to supplement its purchase program on a grant basis."

Twenty-nine Senators, led by H. Alexander Smith of New Jersey, joined in a bipartisan bill, stipulating that the grain should be a gift, and in the House a group of Representatives introduced identical bills. The House Rules Committee bottled up the measure for weeks thus preventing a vote in the House on making this transaction a gift. Finally in an attempt to break the deadlock, Representative A.S.J. Carnahan introduced a bill providing that the grain should be a loan. In the final House vote on this measure the roll call was Yeas 255, Nays 82, and not voting 95. In other words there were 82 Congressmen who voted against even *lending* the money to India for the purchase of food in the United States.

The months' long debate in and out of Congress had been unusually bitter. Opponents charged that they were being called upon to spend money for India without immediate return, and at a time when India had both opposed our war policy in Korea and had been strongly critical of our relations with China. Charity, they contended, should come from individuals and not from taxpayers. It is useless, they charged, to send wheat because it would merely keep up the birth rate or be wasted in food for sacred cows. Moreover, India was hostile to Pakistan, which was a good friend of the United States. They contended such aid would not solve India's present nor future food problems. It would add to our national debt. Since Congress was asked to supply only 1/25 of India's needs for the coming year, a corresponding reduction in the average diet of India was nothing to be concerned about.

Proponents put up a vigorous case for sending grain to India. Representative Jacob Javits, now Senator from New York, characterized this proposal as far more important than at first sight — a key to our total foreign policy, the touchstone of the sincerity of our intentions, and a weathervane whether we would help the people of Asia. Jacob S. Potofsky wired Senator Connally, Chairman of the Senate Foreign Relations Committee, that the "CIO is convinced that a gift of this sort, free of political strings, would tremendously enhance American democratic prestige not only in India but throughout Asia. Millions of Asiatic people. . .would have tangible evidence that our American democracy is true to its tradition of friendship, tolerance and good will."

Supporters argued that a slight reduction in the amount of food available when so many were already on a starvation diet could mean death to a great number. Senator Hubert H. Humphrey, said on May 15, "Our country has waited for months to answer this cry of human suffering. It borders upon something that is shameful. We should act with dispatch and in such terms that no one in the world can for a single minute misunderstand what we do. . .As we have cast our bread upon the waters, it has come back to us a thousandfold, not simply a hundredfold or tenfold. With every bushel of wheat we give and the hope of life, we give something that is eternal, and people do not forget it."

The final action of Congress was to authorize $190 million for two years, or less than one half of one per cent of the proposed $50 billion defense budget, but only to appropriate one half for the ensuing year. The aid was to be a loan instead of a gift to a brand new nation burdened with almost insoluable problems and staggering under a widespread famine, while in a very few years the United States would be spending more than a million dollars a day just to store the wheat that we could not eat.

Grain For India: 1966-1967[14]

In 1966 severe famine threatened India once more. Her 500,000,000 people were suffering the worst drouth in 70 years. A fifth of the population was severely affected by shortages and some 11 to 12 million were in danger of death by starvation. UN Secretary General U Thant and B.R. Sen, Director General of the Food and Agriculture Organization, on March 11 issued a joint appeal to the world community. This was followed by an appeal from President Johnson to Congress to step up shipments of wheat, corn and vegetable oils to be paid for in rupees and for powdered milk to be donated from surplus Commodity Credit Corporation stocks. He recommended additional shipments, beyond what was being shipped commercially, of 3½ million tons of wheat, 200,000 tons of corn, up to 150 million pounds of vegetable oils, and up to 125 million pounds of powdered milk.

Frances Neely directed the FCNL efforts to get Congress to act promptly and favorably. In her appeal circulated in April, she pointed out that port facilities in India were limited and needed expansion, but that Congress had just approved 1.2 billion dollars for construction of port and other support facilities in Vietnam. Further, the part of the President's recommendations for donations would cost only about $24 million, or no more than five cents for each man, woman and child in India. At that time the United States was spending at least $29 million *per day* to wage the war in Vietnam.

Finally, Congress acted and shipments began under the new authorization, in the face of box car shortages, frozen Great Lakes seaway and crowded Gulf Coast facilities. Nine railroads cooperated in shipping grain in covered hopper unit trains. These unit trains could make the complete round trip from Minneapolis to the East Coast in 5 to 8 days compared with 23 days for a train of box cars. Port facilities in India were increased from 800,000 tons a month to 1.2 million tons a month.

As the crisis in India continued, there was a great deal of criticism in November and December that President Johnson was holding off further promises to send grain to India in order to bring pressure on other countries, including the Soviet Union, to furnish more food supplies. He had in fact suspended shipments for a short time in a move which the *New York Times* on December 22 described as "playing Russian roulette with the life of Prime Minister Indira Gandhi's moderate democratic government."

Richard W. Reuter resigned in December as Special Assistant to the Secretary of State serving as Food for Peace Director, in part allegedly because of the bureaucratic struggle between the State Department on the one side and the Agriculture Department on the other, and in part because of dissatisfaction with the lack of full commitment by the U.S. Government to an adequate Food for Peace Program.

By the end of 1966 the United States had shipped about 8 million tons of food grains out of the 10 million tons which India had imported. Four fifths had been wheat and one fifth sorghum grains. India's serious food deficit continued. The Indian Government in December had asked CARE, Inc., to manage a second lunch program for 14 million school children and mothers, a 30-fold increase over the current program.

A Congressional delegation comprised of Senators Walter F. Mondale of Minnesota, Jack Miller of Iowa, and Gale McGee of Wyoming and Representatives W. R. Poage of Texas and Robert Dole of Kansas visited India and brought back vivid accounts of the distress of the people.

Finally President Johnson on February 2, 1967, sent a long message to Congress saying that he had earmarked 2 million tons under Public Law 480, which did not require matching, to tide India over while Congress acted and that he was asking Congress for authority to ship an additional 3 million tons provided it was matched by other countries. He proposed that all nations make the new Indian emergency that occasion to start a continuing world-wide campaign against hunger.

Again the FCNL swung into action to support the

recommendation for food shipments but strongly urged that the terms be eased. Friend Herbert C. Fledderjohn, president of the International Cooperative Development Association, told the House Agriculture Committee in his testimony on March 2 that, "any permanent solution to the problem of hunger in India must ultimately come from greatly increased productivity in her own agricultural industry," and that such an increase would take time. In the meantime, "it should be basic to the policy of the U.S. Government that our aid in the fight against famine should be limited only by our capacity to help, and not contingent upon others providing their 'fair share.' " Since the estimate of need might be low, he urged that the limitation to 3 million tons be removed, and that consideration be given to help on transportation. He also suggested that the interests of the citizens of the United States "might be better served if this food were furnished as an outright grant rather than a sale." I sent these recommendations to key House members and Frances Neely alerted the various nongovernmental organizations and sought their earnest support. Congress did authorize 2.5 million tons and the Department of Agriculture negotiated with India for a commitment of 3.5 million tons during the first half of 1968, but I do not have a record of how much was actually delivered.

FOOD FOR CHINA: 1961-1962[15]

The night before the inauguration of John F. Kennedy in January 1961, Washington had one of the heaviest snowfalls in recent history. Soon after I got on the bus to go home, I noticed that its one empty seat was beside Representative W.R. Poage of Texas, Chairman of the House Agriculture Committee. Not averse to lobbying a captive Congressman for an hour as the bus inched along Pennsylvania Avenue, I sat down beside him and asked his opinion about trying to get food to Mainland China.

He said he had been thinking about this question a lot that day and had suggested that the United States load up three ships with wheat, send them to Hong Kong, and tell the Chinese Government that the wheat was available if they would let Americans come in and supervise its distribution. I told him the impulse was good but I was sure his procedure would not be acceptable to the Chinese and that his recommendations would not break the deadlock.

Press reports indicated that China had suffered a series of natural disasters which some observers called the worst in a century, coupled with the adverse effects of rapid collectivization, over-emphasis on industrialization, lack of fertilizer, and rapid population growth of about 16 million a year. For the next two years, FCNL staff, led by Edward F. Snyder and Frances Neely and working closely with Colin Bell of the American Friends Service Committee, tried to find a formula to get some of America's 4½ billion dollars burden of surplus food to the Chinese mainland. I cannot recall another issue in FCNL history where the psychological and political situation was so delicate and the difficulties so involved and seemingly insurmountable, in spite of intense effort to find a way through.

"The pathetic search by millions of people for wild fruit, herbs, chestnuts, waterweed stalks, arrowroot and other wild plants to supplement the shrinking supply of staple foods," was the way an eye-witness reporter for the *London Sunday Times* for March 18, 1962, described the plight of the Mainland Chinese a year later. As evidence of China's great need, she had bought from Canada in 1961 about seven million tons of wheat and barley, not all of which had been delivered yet, and two million tons of wheat from Australia.

In its simplest terms, the problem boiled down first to the unwillingness of the Government of the People's Republic of China to ask the United States for either a purchase or a gift (or even to admit publicly their inability to meet their needs) and second, to the understandable reluctance of the American Government to make an effort which, in a period of intense antagonism between the two nations, would probably be turned down. We found warm interest on the part of many U.S. officials to respond to the privation of the Chinese people if a way could be found, but we also found skepticism or hostility on the part of others. For example, a newspaper reporter characterized to us the attitude of Secretary of Agriculture Orville S. Freeman, after attending one of his press conferences. Freeman had said in effect, "Until they come over here on bended knee, we're not going to give them anything."

Various Friends made inquiries through diplomatic or other contacts in London, Geneva, Stockholm, Bern, New Delhi, Hong Kong, New York and Washington, some of which were plain rebuffs. I talked in New Delhi, in November 1961, to an Indian official in the External Affairs Ministry who had been in Peking from 1951 to 1957 and again later, and who had recently returned from a visit to the Chinese capital. Chinese officials had talked to him quite freely about the fact that they had suffered the worst drouth in the North and the worst flooding in the South in a century. He had seen the marks of serious malnutrition on people in the street and on the Chinese staff in the Indian Embassy in Peking.

In London the British Friends, who were pursuing this inquiry, were reminded that, after the 1954 Geneva Conference aimed at settling the Indo-China question, John Foster Dulles, the American representative, had said publicly that the only contact he had with the Chinese was that they had dried their hands on the same towel in the washroom. Later, when the Chinese delegates at the Laos Conference gave a reception for all the delegates, the American representatives had refused to come. "That is how the Americans feel about contact with the Chinese," was the retort of the Chinese official. By 1961 the growing hostility between some American and Chinese officials was a real barrier to any agreement that would make Amerian food available for the desperate needs of Mainland China.

Edward Snyder and I called on George McGovern just after his nomination by President Kennedy as Food for Peace Director. He had not yet been confirmed. He did not have an office, nor a desk, nor a secretary. We had become acquainted with him when he was a Representative in the House from South Dakota. He warmly welcomed the idea of aid to China if it could be arranged. This was the first in a series of many interviews with government officials that went all the way up to the President.

FOOD FOR China:
INTERVIEW WITH PRESIDENT KENNEDY AND ADMINISTRATION OFFICIALS

A six-member delegation visited President Kennedy on May 1, 1962, during a Quaker vigil in Washington, and food for peace was one of the several topics discussed.[16] The delegation included Henry J. Cadbury, Dorothy Hutchinson, George Willoughby, Samuel R. Levering, chairman of the FCNL Executive Council, Edward F. Snyder, FCNL executive secretary, and David Hartsough, who later joined the FCNL staff. As one of the participants recalls the interview:

> We urgently raised our concern that he should make food available to Communist China immediately. His reply was "Do you mean that you would feed your enemy when he has his hands on your throat?" We replied that we meant exactly that, and that we believed that this would be practical as well as good Christianity, and we said that we thought he as a Catholic would agree with the last part of the statement. He said that he did, and that he would propose making food available immediately if it were politically possible. But he pointed out the strength of the China lobby, and said there was no point in his marching up Capitol Hill to defeat, as Wilson had done. He asked how many Quakers were lobbying on Capitol Hill with Senators and Congressmen

that morning. We said about eighty. He said there are six of you here with me, and the proportion is about right. President Kennedy said that there was much work for us to do, and also for him, before real peace would be possible.

Edward Snyder followed up this interview with a letter to President Kennedy on August 1 in which he reviewed past instances when food was offered to those regarded as "enemies" and the appreciation with which such assistance was received. These instances included Germany, France during the blockade, Japan, East Germany, Czechoslovakia, and Hungary.

Among the officials that Edward Snyder, Frances Neely, and other people working on this issue interviewed were Carl Kaysen, Special Deputy Assistant for National Security Affairs; Arthur Schlesinger, Jr., Special Assistant to the President; James W. Symington, Deputy Director, Food for Peace Program; David Bruce, U.S. Ambassador in London; Lord Lindsay, formerly in the British Embassy in Chungking; Alexis Johnson, Deputy Assistant Secretary of State for Political Affairs; Edward E. Rice, Deputy Assistant Secretary of State for Far Eastern Affairs; Chester Bowles, former Congressman and later U.S. Ambassador to India. They conferred with key officials in the Department of Agriculture, Commerce and Treasury and many members of both Houses of Congress. A special 14-page staff study "Should U.S. Surplus Food Be Offered in Mainland China?" was sent to every Senator, and to more than half the members of the House of Representatives and was given wide circulation in official Washington and in the country.

LEGISLATIVE RESTRICTIONS ON AID TO CHINA
AND OTHER COMMUNIST COUNTRIES

Since the Communists came to power in 1949, the United States had maintained an embargo on all sales or gifts of food to Mainland China. In my testimony before the House Agriculture Committee on May 24, 1961, I had appealed to this Committee "that the sale or donation of foods should be as far removed as possible from the Cold War. Sharing our abundance should be considered on a humanitarian and economic basis. We should not put artificial and arbitrary prohibitions on the use of food for people who need it even though they are in countries with whose political beliefs we disagree. There is a New Testament injunction, 'If thine enemy hunger, feed him, if he is thirsty, give him a drink. By so doing this you will heap live coals on his head. Do not let evil conquer you, but use good to conquer evil.' " [17]

However, restrictions were continued in the basic food legislation, Public Law 480. In Title I, providing for sales in the currency of the recipient country, and Title III, providing for donations through voluntary philanthropic agencies, the legislation specifically prohibited any transaction with the "Union of Soviet Socialist Republics or any of the areas dominated or controlled by the Communist regime in China."

Under Title II, the President was given authority in emergency situations to make surplus commodities available to "friendly but needy populations without regard to the friendliness of their Government." Donations under this title would be distributed either to governments directly or through such intergovernmental organizations as UN Food and Agriculture Organization and the League of Red Cross Societies or through private agencies such as CARE and the American Friends Service Committee. Dollar sales or short term credit were allowable under U.S. law but were currently prohibited by Administration action. Therefore the FCNL took the position that so far as laws and regulations were concerned food could go to China if the Administration was determined to send it.

However, such a possibility was jeopardized by action in the Senate. How lacking in compassion Congress could be on occasion toward people living under the totalitarianism of Communist rule but suffering from the effects of bad weather was exhibited by the Senate during the period when food for China was a subject of widespread discussion. On June 6, 1962, by a vote of 57 to 24, the amendment to the Food for Peace Bill, P.L. 480, offered by Senator Frank Lausche of Ohio, was adopted. This amendment laid down the prohibition that "no assistance shall be furnished under this Act and *no commodities may be sold or given* under the Agricultural Trade Development and Assistance Act of 1954, as amended, to any country known to be dominated by Communism and Marxism" (emphasis supplied).

The next day Senators Mansfield and Dirksen secured a modification of Lausche's move by getting another amendment adopted by a vote of 56 to 34. The Mansfield-Dirksen amendment gave the President leeway in extending aid under three conditions:

1. That aid be limited to countries not promoting the Communist conquest of the world;
2. That the assistance furnished be in the interest of the national security of the United States; and
3. That the President notify the Senate Committee on Foreign Rela-

tions, the Senate Appropriations Committee, and the Speaker of the House, of his intentions.

At his first press conference on January 25, 1961, President Kennedy, in response to a question, said that the Chinese were exporting some food and that there had been no indication from the Chinese Communists that they would welcome any offer of food. He went on to say, "If there is a desire for food and a need for food, the United States would be glad to consider that need, regardless of the source."

There was a lively and prolonged debate in and out of Congress over the issue of aid to the People's Republic of China. Opponents called upon the country not to be duped through their traditional goodwill into supporting an abominable regime which would use our food for its own nefarious political ends and not feed the starving. Rather we should render the greatest humanitarian service to the Chinese by hastening the economic and political collapse of the existing system.

Critics objected to the fact that China was exporting some food. They neglected to point out that these exports were mainly to Hong Kong, that they served to fulfill trade commitments and to secure foreign currency for the purchase of industrial equipment, and that, in any case, the amounts exported were small compared to enormous Chinese food purchases from Canada and Australia.

Adversaries of aid stressed that there was little likelihood that China would permit any observers from the United States to see how the food was distributed. Moreover, the Chinese Government would neither ask for nor accept assistance for fear that it would be taken as a failure of the Communist system.

Even the usually generous Averell Harriman said at one time, "Let the Chinese stew in their own juice." Rear Admiral Luther C. Heinz, Far Eastern Director of the Pentagon's Office of International Security Affairs, commented that any transaction "would come as an incredible shock to friends of the U.S. throughout Southeast Asia." A letter to the *New York Times* from one of its readers complained that in the end the expenditures would be devoted to the acquisition of nuclear weapons, and that the Chinese peasants would not know that the grain was from us. Representative William H. Milliken opposed sending any food on the grounds that "a few wrinkles in their bellies will bring them to terms."

The FCNL, leading churchmen, and many others took the position that to withhold help from one quarter of the world's people, when our agricultural abundance was at record heights, would be a moral disaster for our nation. *Life* Magazine said on January 27, 1961, that the Chinese were now meeting natural adversities without parallel in the past 100 years. As of December 22, 1961, the Commodity Credit Corporation had 1.1 billion bushels of wheat in their inventory, 1.2 billion bushels of corn and 31.1 million bushels of barley.

We hoped such a move might create a new and more generous pattern of international behavior. Offering food to China might help in some degree to counteract the virulent anti-American Propaganda in China. The FCNL had worked persistently since 1950 for reciprocal travel, trade and diplomatic recognition, for UN seating of the People's Republic, and for their participation in disarmament negotiations and agreements. These strides in U.S.-Chinese relations would have to be made some time, and a generous offer of food now might be a small first step. China had given very high priority to increased agricultural production and had done a rather remarkable job of distributing what food she had available, according to visitors to China. An assurance to the Communist world, which is normally somewhat deficient in food supplies, that they would have access to these supplies through reasonable trade policies should remove any excuse for Communist territorial expansion based on the need for food. Chester Bowles, later Ambassador to India, expressed his support of sending food because a hungry enemy is the worst possible kind to have.

It was recognized that U.S. military support for Taiwan was a major barrier to improvement of relations. Colin Bell, executive secretary of the American Friends Service Committee and former member of the Friends Ambulance Unit in China, took the position from the beginning that offers of aid would probably not be accepted until there was a change in the political climate and some noteworthy shifts in American policy.

The Gallup Poll reported on March 20, 1962, that 53 percent of those queried approved sending some of our surplus food to Communist China, 32 percent opposed and 15 percent expressed no opinion.

One of the major issues was whether grain to China should be a sale or a gift. One suggestion was that a gift might be made through the United Nations Food and Agriculture Organization with the expectation that the Chinese might want to repay it at a later date when they might be in a position to do so and when some agricultural products might help some other country in distress. While humanitarian reasons would dictate a gift, we were inclined to support either if it could be worked out, but rather favored a sale on the practical grounds that it might be more acceptable to the proud Chinese.

I was rather surprised at the number of members of Congress who said to me that they preferred that food be sent as a gift. Senator George D. Aiken of Vermont commented, "I have never believed that you could starve people into democracy." The legislative assistant to Senator Proxmire was upset over FCNL support of a sale, because to him it was a perversion of all that Friends stand for, and would be made for all the wrong reasons. However, the deadlock was never broken. The American taxpayer continued to pay nearly a million dollars storage a day on food he did not need while millions of Chinese continued to suffer from hunger.

Frances Neely and the Mennonites tried to secure permission for sending food parcels to China as at least a small personal gesture. The Mennonites earlier had offered wheat from their farms in Canada, an offer which was not accepted. They ran a three months limited parcel service in Hong Kong at a time when Chinese in Hong Kong and elsewhere were shipping thousands of small food parcels to their friends and relatives in Mainland China. But Americans ran up against the restrictions of the Trading with the Enemy Act. Frances was told that such a program would have to be cleared at the highest level — which sounded very much like the White House.

On July 16, 1962, Bernard Llewellyn of the Oxford Committee for Famine Relief in England, wrote to Duncan Wood, Geneva representative for the British Friends Service Council, and the American Friends Service Committee, in regard to nongovernmental relief: ". . .I think we must accept the fact at the moment that there is no way in which we could give aid to people inside China, since there is no reliable agency through which we could channel funds or gifts in kind."

The *Washington Post* ran an editorial on May 22, 1962: "Hunger admits of no armistice, delays, treaties or compromises. Diplomacy has not a good answer for it. Science has no answer. Politics and diplomacy and science are all very complicated. Hunger is very simple, and there is only one answer to it. That answer is food."

WHEAT TO RUSSIA: 1963

In the "new lands" of south central Asia, the winter of 1962-63 was hot and dry, and in European Russia — the Ukraine and the North Caucasus — it was fierce and cold and the kill of winter wheat was high. For six weeks in June and July there was less than an inch of rain in the new lands. In the European areas, spring was cold and late, followed by little rain. Because of adverse weather the wheat crop was far below normal.

So the Soviet Union turned to Canada in September 1963 for a purchase of 228 million bushels of wheat for $500 million, and to Australia for another large shipment at a cost of about $100 million partly on credit. Even these huge purchases did not close the gap in Russia's short grain crop. This calamitous effect of weather was on top of the perennial difficulties of Soviet agriculture, including poor incentives for farmers under collectivization, inadequate capital investments, lack of fertilizer and machinery and parts, and the low emphasis on agriculture in Soviet planning.

Their next move was to approach the United States, which had a surplus on hand of more than 1.2 billion bushels, with an offer to buy at least a $100 million worth of wheat. This would call for a quick thaw in the partial freeze of general trade with the Communist bloc and provision for some kind of credit terms. One obstacle was that current law forbade credits to nations in default of debts and the Kremlin had not cleared up its lend-lease account from World War II. American imports from the Soviet Union were not large enough for a barter deal.

Opponents of a deal argued that the "hard cash" which we would receive would be Soviet gold, mined by slave labor in Eastern Siberia. "Each bushel we sell her, relieves her of the burden of improving her obsolete agricultural society. Each bushel we sell her, permits her to allocate more of her efforts toward cold war competition and subversion," wrote a Long Island resident to the *New York Times*. Since the Russians would be buying at or near the world price, this meant a subsidy of 72 cents a bushel by the U.S. Government to make up the difference between the higher domestic price and the world price of wheat. There was one more handicap and that was in order to obtain a license to export to the Soviet bloc countries, the U.S. required that at least 50 per cent of the commodities had to be moved in American ships with usually higher freight prices.

The Senate Banking and Currency Committee called hearings on short notice on the Soviet wheat purchase; I was the only witness for any religious organization. I testified on November 22, 1963, against S. 2310 which would have prevented the Export-Import bank from joining in guarantees for temporary commercial credits if they were convinced that the arrangements, the timing, the size of the transactions and other factors warranted such assurances. The FCNL was simply asking for the same credit concessions which would apply to any non-Communist buyer. That was no radical proposal.

The FCNL Statement of Legislative Policy said "The development of freer trade and the mutual exchange of goods and services are important factors in achieving economic and political stability, and in turn, world peace. . .We recommend eliminating special restrictions on non-military trade with Communist nations." Our appeal was basically a religious and a humanitarian one that we and the Russian people were all part of one human family.

In my testimony I referred to a comment by the well known columnist and writer, Walter Lippmann, who years before had characterized U.S. policy as predicated on the assumption that, if sufficient political, economic and military pressure were put on the Soviet Union and Mainland China, their regimes would either collapse or surrender. He said the evidence did not support either thesis and described this position on the part of our government not as a policy but the absence of a policy.

During the question period Senator Peter Dominick of Colorado asked me rather sharply whether the Soviet Union ever kept any treaties. I reminded him that the Secretary of State had furnished the Senate Foreign Relations Committee in August during the hearings on the test ban treaty a list of some 32 treaties which the Soviets had "generally kept." It would be appropriate for the United States to be a bit humble on the question of keeping treaties. I once heard an American Indian say, and I have never had a chance to check it out, that the United States Government had signed about 300 treaties with the Indians and he wondered if they had kept a single one of them. [18]

FOOD FOR FREEDOM ACT: 1966

The general thrust of FCNL efforts on food policy in the mid-sixties was summarized in my testimony before the Senate Committee on Agriculture, March 8, 1966, on the proposed Food for Freedom Act of 1966, the extension of P.L. 480, and other War Against Hunger proposals.

Picking up on the President's proposal of February 2 that the "United States lead the world in a war against hunger" and that we "look to a world in which no man, woman, or child suffer want of food or clothing," I urged that this goal be more explicitly stated in the legislation, and that the United States should seek to make a maximum contribution in a world-wide campaign. In Secretary of Agriculture Orville Freeman's 26-page testimony there had been no reference to international agencies.

I testified that considerable pride could be taken in what had been done in the last decade in food sharing with about one hundred countries, but that it had been largely a surplus disposal program. It was high time to settle into a long term program for a world-wide, concerted effort to increase agricultural production everywhere with a view to nutritional needs. Strong emphasis should be put on population control and family planning; otherwise there could be no closing the hunger gap. There needed to be closer correlation of food, aid and trade policies. More use of cooperatives would be desirable. Loan and grant policies should be reviewed. Where food is needed and the possibility of payment is difficult at best, it would be better to donate the food and write it off as legislative sharing. I stressed that we look upon the whole human race as one family and emphasized that food as a weapon should be taken out of the Cold War. The people of the Communist countries should be treated the same as needy people in other countries. The Agricultural Committee was reminded that the $14 billion spent on the war against hunger during the previous decade was only what the U.S. was spending every three months for the U.S. military establishment. A crash program was called for to aid India which was suffering from the worst drouth in recent history.[19]

ONLY A SKIRMISH, NOT A WAR ON HUNGER

Dr. Roger Revelle, director of the Center for Population Studies, Harvard University, has said, "The level of aid we are giving now, less than one-half of one per cent of our gross national product, is ridiculous. It ought to be five or ten per cent. . .We could easily spare it."

President Johnson on February 10, 1966, called for the United States "to lead the world in a war against hunger." Measured quantitatively the United States has been generous, but certainly not sacrificial. During much of the postwar period farmers have been paid to keep about 60 million acres of cropland out of production. In view of our surpluses, our capacity to supply food in the short and long run and our ability to aid in agricultural technology and agricultural production, our assault on world hunger has been a skirmish, not a war.

CHAPTER 6

I Was A Stranger [1]

DISPLACED PERSONS, REFUGEES, IMMIGRATION, NATURALIZATION

Give us your tired, your poor
Your huddled masses yearning to breathe free.
The wretched refuse of your teeming shores.
Send these, the homeless, tempest-tossed to me.
I lift my lamp beside the golden door.

Words by Emma Lazarus inscribed on the
Statue of Liberty in New York Harbor

The right of political asylum has brought to this country
many a man of noble character and elevated purpose
who was marked as an outlaw in his own less
fortunate land and who has yet become an
ornament to our citizenship and to
our public councils.

Woodrow Wilson

The bosom of America is open to receive not only the
Opulent and Respectable Stranger, but the oppressed
and persecuted of all Nations and Religions;
whom we shall welcome to a participation of
all our rights and privileges, if by
decency and propriety of conduct
they appear to merit the
enjoyment.

George Washington
December 2, 1783

"I Was a Stranger and Ye Took Me Not In"
Matthew 25:43

For more than a decade following World War II, the attitude of many members of Congress was one of cold hostility to the admission to the United States of any sizeable and appropriate number of the millions of refugees and people displaced by the war or by the revision of boundaries made by the peace settlement.

In its very first *Newsletter* the FCNL started to press for liberalizing the immigration policy of the United States, beginning with the repeal of the Chinese Exclusion Act of 1882. In 100 of the succeeding issues of the monthly publication during the following twenty-two years, the editors reported on the frequently discouraging developments in immigration legislation, pled for the repeal of the Japanese Exclusion Act of 1924 or kept hammering away for generous legislation to admit displaced persons and to modify our restrictive immigration policies. Twenty-three formal testimonies were presented to Congressional Committees by seventeen different witnesses over these years.

In behalf of refugees, the FCNL worked for adequate care in the camps in Europe, for support of the International Refugee Organization, for funds for the UN High Commissioner of Refugees, the attempts of his office to resettle refugees, and for the World Refugee Year in 1959. James M. Read, who was the first legislative secretary for the FCNL (1946-1947) and who worked hard on displaced persons legislation while on the FCNL staff, served as Deputy High Commissioner for Refugees in Geneva for nine years from 1951 to 1960. He kept us aware of the difficult and devoted struggle of that office to secure protective measures in countries where refugees were and to seek permanent settlement for them.

The FCNL made strenuous efforts, along with many other organizations, to achieve fundamental revision in the restrictive immigration legislation passed between 1917 and 1929 and to abolish the quota system. The Committee pressed for the right of naturalization for the Chinese, Japanese and other groups who had been denied the right of citizenship. Proposed legislation rejecting citizenship for those conscientiously unwilling to bear arms was turned back.

One of the brighter episodes occurred in June 1949, when a cut in funds for Palestinian refugees was restored by FCNL initiative.

Two Million Dollars in Twenty-four Hours

The telephone rang about four o'clock on the afternoon of June 1, 1949. The caller was a good friend of mine in the Department of State who reported that the requested appropriation for $16 million for Palestine refugees had been cut two million dollars by the Senate Appropriations Committee. The money was desperately needed. The measure would be up for consideration on the Senate floor the next afternoon.

The need for the whole $16 million appropriation had been vividly portrayed by a letter from Eldon Mills of the American Friends Service Committee to Senator Styles Bridges on May 11, 1949, three weeks before this incident.

At that time the AFSC was distributing UN relief supplies to about one third of the Palestinian refugees, and Mills was supervising this distribution. Mills had written:

> For four months I have seen at firsthand, so vividly that long days of frenzied labor to relieve suffering and hunger leave little time to sleep, the tragic plight of 250,000 displaced persons in the Negev, the chief city of which is the ancient Gaza. Here was a normal population of 60,000 in a little strip eight miles wide and 25 miles long, mostly desert, providing mere subsistence, which now contains 310,000 people with resultant devastated economy in the area. This refugee population represents only about 30 per cent of the total number of displaced Arabs, the rest being in the north and aided by the other two agencies. . . .
>
> We in the Quaker unit are feeding 800 tons of food weekly, equivalent to 1700 calories per person per day at a cost of two dollars monthly per person. Forty-eight members of the Quaker unit distribute food, supervise an efficient medical, clerical and hospitalization program, which so far has prevented epidemics, give one litre of milk daily to 100,000 children, nursing and pregnant mothers, provide recreation in camps and have set up 150 schools with 800 teachers from the refugees, providing for an attendance maximum of 70,000 boys and girls. [2]

Along with Eleanor Neff who represented the Methodists at that time, and whose office was in the same building as the FCNL, I hopped in a taxi to Capitol Hill and roamed the corridors of the Capitol and Senate Office Building, hoping to find a sympathetic member of the Foreign Relations Committee who might be persuaded to move a restoration of the cut. But the members of this Committee were closeted in a discussion on the international wheat agreement. The afternoon passed with no progress whatever.

That evening I was sitting next to Senator Hubert H. Humphrey at a civil liberties dinner. I told him what had happened and asked whether he would take the lead in moving to restore the full amount if we could not enlist a member of the Foreign Relations or Appropriations Committee. It was a left-handed invitation but he could easily see the point. A member of one of the committees which had handled the legislation would have the background to champion the restoration more easily. He agreed and asked me to meet him at his office at ten o'clock in the morning to report what progress I had made.

I called James M. Read in Philadelphia to come and help. He was at that time secretary of the AFSC Foreign Service Section and therefore familiar with needs in the Middle East.

In the morning I called back to the State Department and asked if they could get an immediate statement from Dr. Ralph Bunche, who had been UN negotiator in the Middle East and whose prestige was at its height. The reply was "No, but good luck to you, Raymond." Then I went to see Francis Wilcox, chief of staff of the Senate Foreign Relations Committee. "This is a foreign relations problem, and the responsibility for it should lie with the Foreign Relations Committee," I told him. He replied, "No, we can't do anything significant about it. We are up against an $800 million slash in the foreign aid budget and we have our hands full. But good luck to you, Raymond."

At ten o'clock with no progress so far, I went to Senator Humphrey's office. He was leaving with his coattails flying. "I'm supposed to be at three committees and chairing one, so come along on the way to the committee hearing." As we went down the corridor almost on the dog trot, I said to him, "I guess it's up to you." "All right, meet me at the Senate lobby at 11:45 and brief me," was his answer.

When I met Senator John Sparkman and asked his help, he said, "Raymond, you go and work on the Republicans and I will see what I can do with the Democrats." Both Senators Flanders and Aiken were already in committee, but their legislative assistants assured me that their senators would give this measure their active support. I rode down two floors on the elevator with Senator Paul Douglas so the conversation was short and to the point. He said "yes" but both he and Sparkman were involved in other matters that day and I did not see them again.

At quarter to twelve, James Read, who had joined me by this time, sat on one side of Senator Humphrey and I on the other in the

Senate reception room. The Senator was exceedingly quick in grasping the situation as we rattled off to him the history of the measure. The money had been pledged by the U.S. on condition of Congressional appropriation, the money was needed, the good faith of the U.S. was at stake. We reviewed the arguments for and against and put into his hands the pertinent documents from the House action, the decision of the Senate Appropriations Committee, and information about the refugee situation. "Thanks," he said, "I think I have the story now." As the Senate convened at noon, the Senator rose and went into the chamber to be ready when this item might be called up.

Jim and I rotated between the Senate reception room and the gallery. When I spoke to Senator Clyde Hoey of North Carolina, with his wing collar, flowing white hair and flower in the buttonhole of his long-frocked coat, he looked down his nose and said, "It is a very serious thing to go against an appropriations committee report," and disappeared into the Senate chamber. Mr. Republican, Senator Robert Taft, used almost the same words, "Mr. Wilson, it's a very serious thing to go against an appropriations committee, particularly if they are trying to save you money," as he faded out of sight.

Finally, as the afternoon wore on, the measure was called up for consideration. Senator Kenneth McKellar of Tennessee defended the Committee cut on the grounds that other nations had not fully pledged their 50 per cent share of the proposed total $32 million UN fund. Humphrey moved the restoration, pointing out that the United States had as much to do with establishment of Israel as any other nation. The agreement to pledge the $16 million had been made in November 1948, when Congress was not in session and could not be officially consulted.

Senator George D. Aiken, as his aide had promised, rose to say that he joined in the request, "on the basis of information I have personally received from persons who have firsthand knowledge of the situation and in whom I have implicit confidence; in fact, I have known them for many years." Apparently he was referring to Levinus Painter, a Friend who had been a neighbor of the Senator, and who was then involved in the AFSC relief program. "So far as I can learn, the Arab refugees in Palestine may perhaps qualify for the doubtful designation of being the most unhappy people on the face of the earth."

Senator Ralph Flanders, also from Vermont, chimed in, "It is a question of justice, it seems to me, because our government, our administration, was particularly responsible for the policy which set up the Nation of Israel and which dispossessed these Arabs of their homes and their lands." He argued that both self-interest and our responsibility as a nation should require us to supply this aid even "if no other nation gave a dollar to this fund."

James Read came flying down from the gallery saying that Senator Humphrey was in trouble for one set of facts and to get this material to the Senator immediately. You can not send in documents by the Senate pages but I caught Senator Langer of North Dakota by the coattail as he was going in the Senate door and asked him to put this information in Senator Humphrey's hands. By the time I got back up to the gallery the information had been placed in the debate.

Then an interesting development happened which I have seen in Quaker meetings but never before in the Senate. There was a little huddle of Senators groping for consensus, and Senator Bridges proposed their postponing further discussion on that item and then returning to it later that afternoon when the proponents of the amendment had a formula to propose.

In the meantime, Max Kampelmann, Senator Humphrey's legislative assistant, came out to James Read and me and said, "Would you accept a compromise that required other nations to match the $2 million?" I replied that I did not like to play arithmetic with human misery and that the United States had not asked for matching funds for the military aid granted to Greece and Turkey. But if that were the price for restoring the cut, the answer would be a reluctant "yes." An amendment to the amendment was drafted and in about an hour the Senate returned to this item. The motion for the restoration was agreed to, almost exactly 24 hours after the distress telephone call had come from the State Department.[3]

Displaced Persons — "All of Them Children of God"

This reinstating of funds was one of the very few encouraging incidents in an almost unrelieved series of defeats, delays and disappointments so far as hospitality to the uprooted millions of Europe and Asia was concerned.

World War II left in its swirling wake the most tremendous population dislocation in all recorded history. While some of the movement was in a sense voluntary, most of it was forced. Large groups of people were forced to move under the Nazi program of slave labor, other groups were swept before invading armies, others fled to escape hostile occupying forces, still others were fugitives from political oppression and religious persecution. The first of the major movements, before 1943, was due to Hitler's racial laws, slave-labor policies and German military advances. The second, after 1943, was occasioned by Allied victories. The third, after the end of the war, resulted from banishment or flight because of political and religious oppression, especially in Eastern Europe dominated by the Communists.

Estimates of the number of people uprooted by World War II and by the changes of boundaries afterwards ran between 20,000,000 and 30,000,000. Only a few of the 12,000,000 or more evacuated because of German occupation from European Russian areas to Asiatic Russia — German expellees as they were called — who filtered back to Western Europe ever became United Nations Displaced Persons. By VE Day, the Allied armies found about 8,000,000 displaced persons — persons liberated from the extermination camps, from concentration camps, prisoners of war, forced laborers brought into Germany and refugees who fled in front of the Russian armies.

By 1949, the great bulk of these people, about 7,000,000, were repatriated to their homelands by the efforts of the United Nations Relief and Rehabilitation Administration (UNRRA), its successor agency, the International Refugee Organization, and the Allied Armies. Three years after the end of the war, by the time the dillydallying Congress got around to serious attempts at displaced persons' legislation, 850,000 people were still either in refugee camps in Germany, Austria or Italy, or were awaiting settlement elsewhere.

Churches and voluntary agencies, including the FCNL, pushed for legislation that would admit at least half this remainder or from 400,000 to 425,000. A flood of bills was presented early in the Eightieth Congress in 1947, none of which were acted on. Congressman Stratton of New York on April 1, 1947, introduced a bill to authorize the United States to take its "fair share" of displaced persons. It would have authorized the admission of 100,000 persons a year for four years and would have been administered by the Departments of State and Justice. The Judiciary Committee did hold hearings, which included a strong statement by Frank Aydelotte for the American Friends Service Committee, but the bill languished in Committee for nine months and finally died there.

The opposition was led by the American Legion, the Veterans of Foreign Wars and other organizations on the grounds that the United States had already done its fair share in providing care and maintenance for these refugees and no further assistance was required or should be given. Many veterans were unemployed and the employment picture for new arrivals was not favorable. Moreover, the housing situation was acute with an inadequate number of low rental housing units available for veterans.

Proponents of such legislation claimed that these people, instead of being a burden on the American economy, would bring many skills and would provide employment for others by paying millions of dollars in taxes every year. But the main argument was humanitarian. The subcommittee, headed by John Vorys of Ohio, that considered the Stratton bill, said in its report:

> Throughout this report we have attempted to present this problem objectively with statistics, stressing economy for us and an austerity basis for the D.P.'s. We should not forget, however, that we are talking about 1,000,000 men, women and children, human beings, wise and simple, strong and weak, young and old, good and bad, sick and well, but all of them children of God, who are suffering deeply, in body and spirit, because they are uprooted, through no fault of their own, from the place that is dearest to all of us — home. . . . . [4]

On July 7, 1947, President Truman sent a strong plea to Congress reemphasizing the need for legislation directed toward the entrance of displaced persons into the United States. He declared that this was not a proposal for a general revision of United States immigration policy. The President observed that since statutory quotas for Eastern Europe were wholly inadequate, special legislation was necessary. These people had opposed totalitarian rule and "because of their burning faith in the principles of freedom and democracy" had suffered privation and hardships. There should be no problem in assimilating the relatively small number to be admitted.

A year later a bill finally was passed during the last two days of the session and was signed by President Truman on June 25, 1948. The President maintained that elements of the bill "form a pattern of discrimination and intolerance wholly inconsistent with the American sense of justice." The *New York Times* called the measure "shameful."

The *FCNL Washington Newsletter* for July 23 summarized some of the features of the bill. The bill was to expire in two years. Instead of 400,000 or more, only 205,000 persons would be admitted during the next two years, including 3,000 war orphans and 2,000 Czechs. There were many discriminatory features which operated against

Jewish displaced persons. Those who were not in refugee camps by December 22, 1945, were not eligible, and most of the Jewish groups did not arrive until 1946 or later. Agricultural labor was given 30 per cent of the representation; 40 per cent of the total would go to those countries which were annexed by a foreign power — Eastern Poland, Latvia, Lithuania and Estonia. Fifty per cent of the normal German and Austrian immigration quotas available during the two years would go to the Volks Deutsche, or persons of German ethnic origin who were born in Poland, Czechoslovakia, Hungary or Rumania. One of the worst features of the bill was that future quota numbers would be mortgaged by half the number admitted from any one country. (By 1957, 50 per cent of the regular Greek quota was mortgaged until the year 2017, the Lithuanian quota until 2019 and the Latvian quota until A.D. 2274.) There were grave questions whether the bill would be administratively workable. This was the American answer to distressed and displaced humanity, *three years* after the close of the war!

One of the more constructive items in the measure as passed was the creation of a Displaced Persons Commission which was charged with the responsibility of expediting the flow of displaced persons to the United States.

Immediately organizations such as the FCNL began working for reforms in the legislation and for extending the length of time and the number of people who could be admitted.

After a long period of wrangling on June 7, 1950, Congress finally passed H.R. 4567 which extended the 1948 act to June 30, 1951, and made eighteen changes in the original act. The eligibility date was changed from December 22, 1945, to January 1, 1949. Visas were increased from 205,000 to 341,000, but all those under quota were "mortgaged" to future years. Authorization was provided for the admission of 54,744 German expellees. Every person 18 years of age or over was required to take an oath upon arrival at port of entry that he was not a member of a communist or other subversive organization. Only United States' planes and vessels were authorized for use in transporting to this country persons whose admission was provided for by the United States. Three days before the Act expired it was extended another six months to December 31, 1951.

The history of displaced persons legislation and what was accomplished under it is well told in *The DP Story: The Final Report of the United States Displaced Persons Commission*, published in 1952. This commission was able to process, to transport and to visa some 370,000 persons by the target date, with a total expenditure of only $19 million in the four years of its existence.

This widespread program under the Displaced Persons Commission was terminated all too soon. On June 10, 1953, on behalf of the American Friends Service Committee, Clarence E. Pickett told the House Immigration Subcommittee that further emergency legislation was needed and supported President Eisenhower's request for authority to receive 240,000 more special immigrants in two years. He spelled out the variety of groups needing asylum in the United States and spoke of the generally favorable experience the AFSC had in sponsoring 234 families of displaced persons and those of Volks Deutsche origin.

Another refugee bill, introduced by Senator Arthur V. Watkins of Utah, as finally passed, would admit 290,000 refugees, expellees and escapees during the ensuing 3½ years, but with rather serious restrictions in procedure and qualifications. However, this legislation was either so restrictive or was administered so badly that between August 1953 and March 18, 1955, only 764 refugees, escapees and expellees, 543 orphans and 14,541 relatives had been admitted.

Although the FCNL was not equipped to give much effective aid on individual refugee or immigration cases, our files contain the stories of 34 individuals or families who turned to the Committee for advice and counsel. Some were of a nature which required a private bill through both Houses of Congress for redress of their particular difficulties.

CUBAN PRISONERS

One example of unrealized efforts on specific legislation was the attempt to rebuild some bridges with the Cuban people in 1961.

Congressman Frank Kowalski of Connecticut was a member of the House Armed Services Committee. He was a veteran of 33 years in the Army where he rose to the rank of colonel. In June 1961, at his request, Edward F. Snyder, Frances Neely and Stuart Innerst of the FCNL staff, worked with him in drafting House Resolution 315, which read:

> Resolved, that it is the sense of the Congress that the United States should offer to explore the possibilities for some exchange, through the United Nations or the Organization of American States or otherwise, which would result in the freeing of the captives and political prisoners, and at the same time show the Cuban people in Cuba that the United States is willing to supply them with nonmilitary equipment, health or

technical assistance programs, school lunches, or milk for children, or other programs which will contribute to the well being of the Cuban people as a whole.

This was after the abortive Bay of Pigs invasion, into which the Central Intelligence Agency had poured more than $45 million. This invasion had been approved by President Eisenhower and not countermanded by President Kennedy. More of the Bay of Pigs story is told in Chapter 13, "Wars, Revolutions and Interventions."

However, in the Cold War climate of that period, this proposal was too generous and humane a piece of legislation to get through Congress. It was aimed at maintaining contact and friendship with our Cuban neighbors in their social revolution from the Batista days without implying approval of the Castro regime.

In these few pages I have been able to give only the merest glimpse of this heartbreaking story — the cruel delays, the various arbitrary provisions that cut off so many people from consideration, the limitations on the number of people whom the United States could have absorbed relatively easily, the failure to include an appropriate number of Jews from those who had survived persecution and extermination. The reader has escaped most of the bitterness of the debate in both Houses of Congress, and has not had portrayed in detail the earnest labors of the FCNL and other public-spirited organizations for a humane policy toward the victims of war.

The Middle East

There have been four wars in the Middle East and at this writing no permanent peace settlement. How might history have been changed if the United States had been willing to admit a greater number of Jews after World War II? Perhaps the thousands of Jews suffering from persecution and war in Europe would have created a smaller homeland in the Middle East and not felt compelled to establish the State of Israel — at the expense of still more refugees — if a greater number had been allowed to emigrate to the United States. Here they could have been readily absorbed and they would have contributed their great abilities at a critical time in the history of this country.

Captain Liddell-Hart, England's great military historian, says in his book *Why Don't We Learn from History?* that what we learn from history is that we don't learn from history!

I wish the story of refugees could end with the settlement after

World War II. But that war was followed by the upheaval of people in the separation of India and Pakistan, the refugees caused by the conflict between India and Pakistan, which led to the independence of Bangladesh, the civil war in Nigeria, and the massive displacement of the unfortunate victims of the Indo-China War in North and South Vietnam, Cambodia and Laos (summarized briefly in Chapter 15 on Vietnam).

The World Refugee Report 1970, issued by the United States Committee for Refugees, calculates that in the 25 years following 1945 there have been 75 wars. Primarily from wars and political upheavals there were in 1970 an estimated total of 17,318,320 refugees, not counting the dead and wounded, nor the uncountable casualties of the fighting itself. *"In any event, the shocking number of refugees on every continent is tragic evidence of man's inability to manage himself, his religion, his politics and his hunger with due concern for his fellowman."*

REVISION OF IMMIGRATION AND NATURALIZATION LAWS: 1953-1965

The Chinese Exclusion Act, originally passed in 1882, was repealed in the measure signed by President Roosevelt, December 17, 1943. A bill to admit 100 each from India and the Philippines finally cleared Congress June 25, 1946. The Japanese Exclusion Act of 1924, deeply wounding the pride of a proud and sensitive people, was one of the root causes of the Japanese attack on Pearl Harbor which brought the United States into World War II.

The provision for immigration and naturalization of Japanese, and for citizenship for non-native-born Japanese living in this country, was one of the few commendable features of the original McCarran-Walter Immigration and Nationality Act of 1952 passed over President Truman's veto by only one vote on June 27, 1952. Of the McCarran-Walter Immigration Act the *FCNL Newsletter* said that it "looks on paper as if it will be an insensitive, exclusionist, racist, arbitrary, undemocratic measure." Staff members of the FCNL were in frequent consultation with drafters of a bill proposing fundamental revision of the McCarran-Walter Immigration Act. Senator Herbert H. Lehman and seven other Senators introduced S. 2588 on August 3, 1953. The same bill was introduced the same day by 24 Representatives. From that time until 1965, twelve years later, FCNL efforts to secure thoroughgoing revision of the McCarran-Walter Act were many and varied.

Until 1921 there had been no numerical limitation on immigration into this country. An act in 1921 placed the first maximum ceiling upon immigration at 357,800. An act in 1924 placed further restrictions which by 1929 had become the pattern for the next twenty-three years. This measure provided for the admission up to 153,714 immigrants based on a total of 150,000 plus minimum quotas of 100 for all countries. In addition to these, nonquota immigrants could come in including alien spouses and natives of independent nations of the Western Hemisphere.

The McCarran-Walter Act of 1952 set a maximum authorization of 154,657 but was even more highly discriminatory than the legislation it replaced. The figure was based on a flat one-sixth of 1 per cent of the white population in the 1920 census, excluding Blacks, Indians and other nonwhite persons in the population. Out of this number 2,990 were allocated to all of Asia, 200 to all of Africa and 126,131 to Northern and Western Europe.

President Truman established the President's Commission on Immigration and Naturalization by executive order and required it to make a final report not later than January 1, 1953. This 300-page report, entitled "Whom Shall We Welcome," was a remarkably good summary of the immigration situation with detailed recommendations for revision of legislation. It argued that the United States could absorb 250,000 quota immigrants annually. This report was a very helpful guide to citizen agencies concerned with fulfilling America's opportunities for a fairer system of receiving settlers from around the world.

FCNL POSITION ON IMMIGRATION AND CITIZENSHIP

Beginning with its first annual meeting in January 1944, the FCNL started proposing more generous provisions for asylum for refugees and liberalization of immigration and naturalization laws. By 1955 the Committee issued a very comprehensive statement based largely on recommendations of the National Committee on Immigration and Citizenship. "The first and foremost need. . .is to change our negative attitude of fear, suspicion, and restrictiveness to a positive attitude of welcome toward immigrants, recognizing that while this country has much to offer them, it also has much to gain from them." The following is a paraphrase and condensation:

> The first principle would abolish the quota system and eliminate any implication of superiority among peoples because of race, nationality or religion. The main criteria should relate to individual qualifications. While the number of immigrants to be admitted must be limited, it should be measured by the absorptive capacity which, we believe, is

larger than the present provisions, and by the dynamic needs of our country, with flexibility to meet changing needs and emergency situations.

There should be provisions for adequate appeal and review procedure, without undue delay, on decisions concerning the issuance of visas. Native-born citizenship should be an inalienable right subject to revocation only upon voluntary renunciation. Loss of citizenship should not be a penalty for the commission of a crime.

Naturalized and native-born Americans have equal responsibilities under the law, and should have equal rights. Resident aliens should be given the protection and benefits accorded to United States citizens, except for the right to vote and hold elective office. Fraud in securing admission should be the sole basis for deportation. Deportation should be limited by a reasonable statute of limitations and subject to a system of fair hearings and appeals.

The admission of foreign visitors for travel, conferences, business and other purposes should be encouraged, and regulations governing the admission of such visitors should permit as free an exchange of persons as possible without endangering the nation's security.

Responsibility for administering our immigration and citizenship policies should be vested in a single government agency, concerned solely with these functions and specifically charged to administer these policies in a humane and considerate spirit.

Democracy will not be preserved primarily by the exclusion of those who may espouse different ideologies but rather by the vigorous application of democratic principles at home and abroad. In common with freedom of speech and other principles of democracy, this kind of immigration policy involves some risk, but less risk to our country than the opposite policy.

No person should be prevented from becoming a naturalized citizen because of conscientious convictions against participation in military service. Conscientious objectors should not be denied naturalization because they are unwilling to work in war industry. [5]

Between July 29, 1953, and July 14, 1960, sixteen different amendments to previous refugee legislation or to the McCarran-Walter Act were passed by Congress. With the exception of the provision for the admittance of approximately 32,000 Hungarian refugees out of 179,000 who had fled to Austria in 1956-57, the enactments were minor. They provided for

sheepherders, for orphans, for tubercular relatives, and for a limited
number of refugees under the mandate of the UN High
Commissioner for Refugees.

FCNL WORKS FOR LIBERALIZED IMMIGRATION

Trevor Thomas, secretary of the Northern California Friends
Committee on Legislation, came from San Francisco to testify on
December 1, 1955, in behalf of the Bay Area Committee for Revision
of the Immigration and Nationality Act of 1932. This committee was
composed of more than 60 organizations in the San Francisco area.
He cited many injustices of the McCarran Act.

The next year, when President Eisenhower proposed some
far-reaching changes, Action Bulletin No. 1 was sent February 10,
1956, to more than 2,000 key people, urging letters to Congress. The
President had recommended pooling unused quotas in four areas,
eliminating the mortgaging of quotas, giving the Attorney General
discretion in individual cases instead of the current practice of
having to submit private bills, and an increase in the total quotas
from 154,657 to 220,000. This legislation was not enacted.

In 1956 and 1957 the plight of Hungarian refugees was a center of
concern, as well as continued striving for general immigration
reform. Edward Snyder arranged for Edward Myerding, former
member of the Quaker Mission in Austria, to talk to the Vice
President's staff, with Senator Watkins of Utah, one of the sponsors
of the Administration bill, and with Warren Unna, feature writer for
the *Washington Post*, who wrote a two-column story. Senator
Watkins told the Senate about his conversation with Myerding and
read the Unna story into the *Congressional Record*.

On August 9, 1957, Edward Snyder appealed to the Senate
Immigration Subcommittee for nondiscrimination in immigration
and commented that no measures before the Subcommittee proposed
all the changes that would be desirable. A bill was passed to alleviate
some of the hardships but effected no far-reaching change.

Sarah Swan asked the Senate Judiciary Subcommittee on January
18, 1959, for return of the confiscated German and Japanese private
property which had been seized during and after the war. She cited
the case of Ryu Sato Oyaizu, graduate of Bryn Mawr College, who
had been given $5,000 under the terms of the will of David G. Alsop,
a Philadelphia Friend. The income of this was to be paid to Mrs.
Oyaizu, but had been withheld for eighteen years under the Trading
with the Enemy Act. Her husband had been an invalid for

twenty-three years and the money was much needed.

As the end of the World Refugee Year approached in 1960, FCNL and others worked with Senator Humphrey and Administration officials who were supporting an increased U.S. contribution. Ultimately the Administration made available an additional $1.5 million for a total sum of some $5 million for the World Refugee Year. I alerted other organizations and Senators to restore cuts made by the Senate Foreign Relations Committee in regular refugee programs. In conference $1.2 million of the $3.4 million was restored. In 1961, Oliver Stone, legal counsel for the FCNL, voiced the Committee's objection before the Senate Foreign Relations Committee to proposed legislation circumscribing the rights of aliens threatened by deportation or exclusion proceedings. FCNL staff joined church leaders from 27 denominations and member units of the National Council of Churches for a Conference on Immigration Policy in Washington, April 13 and 14, 1961. The closing message stated:

> We are critical and ashamed of the present basis of our immigration quota system resting upon the national origin of our white population as per the census of 1920, and strongly urge the abandonment of that system or a drastic revision of it in a direction that will exclude any racial or regional discrimination among those who seek to enter our land. [6]

Immigration policy continued to be an FCNL priority in 1964. Richard Smith, an American Friends Service Committee specialist on immigration and refugees, pressed the House Subcommittee on Immigration and Nationality to eliminate the national origins quota and to set up a permanent program for admission of refugees. On June 21 he attended a special meeting with White House Staff. At Thanksgiving time FCNL chairman Charles Darlington urged the President to stress the need for immigration revision in his forthcoming State of the Union message.

The year 1965 marked the culmination of twelve years' struggle for significant changes in the McCarran Act when Congress agreed to the phased elimination of 41-year-old discriminatory national origins quota system. In support of this legislation, two Action Bulletins had been sent to 2700 people. James Read had appeared before both the House and Senate Committees. The amendment which he proposed for softening the deportation regulations was later incorporated in the legislation approved by the House. Telegrams were sent to members of the House Immigration Subcommittee on July 30, urging them to support the Administration bill with amendments for fairer treatment for refugees. A special telegram campaign was launched in uncertain areas and 45 Congressmen were asked to be on the floor for the House vote.

The national origins quota system had allowed three Northern European countries to supply 70 per cent of all the immigrants to this country. The new bill put a ceiling of 120,000 immigrants from the previously unrestricted Western Hemisphere and a 170,000 limit on quota immigration from outside the Western Hemisphere to be effective in July, 1958. These quota numbers were to be distributed under a new priority system which placed major emphasis on family reunion. The vote in the Senate was 76 to 18 and in the House 318 to 95. By 1965 it was 21 years after the FCNL had called for liberalization of our immigration laws in its first statement on legislative policy in 1944. The 1965 bill was by no means perfect, but it was a long step forward.

Dolliver Bill To Deny Citizenship to Pacifist Immigrants

"Such a bill would deny citizenship to men like Dr. Harry Emerson Fosdick, Dr. George A. Buttrick, former president of the Federal Council of Churches, and Rufus M. Jones, former chairman of the American Friends Service Committee; to Jane Addams, William Penn and other men and women who have given distinguished services to America. Such legislation seems to me to violate the fundamental principles of religious liberty which have been an ideal of the United States from the days of Roger Williams."

This was part of my contention in a letter to Representative Brooks Hays in a dialogue on the bill H.R. 2286, introduced on February 27, 1947, by Congressman James I. Dolliver, Iowa, at the instigation of the American Legion. This bill would exact a promise on the part of an applicant for naturalization, male or female, to swear "if required, to bear arms in support and defense of the United States." Dolliver, who descended from Quaker ancestry, teamed up with Ed Gossett of Texas and Frank Fellows of Maine to push this measure through the immigration subcommittee and then the full House Judiciary Committee over the objection of Congressman Emmanuel Celler of New York, Chairman of the Judiciary Committee.

"We are not concerned about this primarily from the standpoint of Quakers," I assured Representative Brooks Hays. There are only a few Quakers outside the United States and England, and only a few of them emigrate to the United States. We are much more concerned about groups like the Mennonites and Brethren who have been subject to severe persecution in countries like Russia, Holland and Germany. . . . Opposition to combatant military service is by no means restricted to the historic peace churches. . .there were men from approximately 125 religious groups in CPS camps during the last war, as well as a good many who claim no definite membership in a religious body."

FCNL worked energetically against this proposed legislation. President Samuel D. Marble of Wilmington College, Ohio, wrote his representative Clarence J. Brown: "The oath for admission to the Bar, for holding office, etc., customarily follows the wording of the naturalization oath and this would mean in effect depriving Quakers of the opportunity to practice law, hold office, and would in general make them second-class citizens. As a result they are at considerable distress because of the implication of this legislation." Many of the members of the House Judiciary Committee were interviewed by Friends visiting Washington.

The *American Bar Association Journal*, Vol. XXXIII for February, 1947, carried an article in favor of the principles of the Dolliver Bill. As part of the argument it was asserted, in reviewing the regulations which had been used to require such an oath in the past, "No rights were denied, no freedom restrained. Aliens have no inherent right to citizenship. It is offered on certain conditions as a favor. They can take it or leave it."

Julien Cornell, attorney from New York City, in speaking for the FCNL and the American Civil Liberties Union, presented a spirited case against the bill in his testimony. He referred to some of the Supreme Court decisions bearing on this question and called the *American Bar Association Journal* article "replete with fallacies, and actual misstatements of fact." Cornell believed that one of the most successful colonies in this country was founded by Quakers under William Penn who were pacifists. If the Dolliver Bill had been on the statute books of George III, Pennsylvania would not have come about.

William C. Dennis, president of Earlham College, explained the implication of the Dolliver Bill in a letter to his Congressman, Ralph Harvey. For more than a hundred years, he wrote, we have used our present oath of allegiance and until recently there was no thought that it barred Quakers and others conscientiously opposed to bearing arms from becoming American citizens. In 1929, however, a split decision in two Supreme Court cases, the Macintosh case and the Rosika Schwimmer case, ruled that all applicants for citizenship must swear an oath to bear arms, if required. Absurdly enough,

Rosika Schwimmer was a woman 49 years old.

Chief Justice Hughes, Mr. Justice Holmes and Mr. Justice (later Chief Justice) Stone, were among the four who dissented on the ground that Congress had made no such requirement and that the requirement should not be implied "because such a construction is directly opposed to the spirit of our institutions and to the historic practice of the Congress."

Dennis went on to observe that the 1929 decisions aroused great criticism. Then in 1946 in the Girouard case the Supreme Court reversed itself and restored the construction of the oath which had previously been used and which Justices Hughes, Holmes and Stone had held was the proper construction. The Dolliver Bill sought to overthrow this latest decision of the Supreme Court, according to President Dennis.[7]

The Dolliver Bill was amended, reported out by the House Judiciary Committee, put on the unanimous consent calendar, called up four times and passed over because of objections. Then it was put on the regular calendar but never voted on by the House. Possibly because of the opposition it aroused from groups like the FCNL, the Dolliver Bill never came to a vote in either the House or Senate.

CHAPTER 7

What Liberties
Should A Person Have? [1]

I have sworn upon the altar of God eternal hostility against every form of tyranny over the mind of man.
> — Thomas Jefferson

> *Our ideal of limited government is founded upon respect for civil liberties. These liberties in turn are based in part upon a religious emphasis on the worth and dignity of each individual and on his right to a large measure of freedom and privacy. . . .*
> *We cannot remain silent at a time when individual liberties are under attack. We oppose all totalitarian ideologies. We are aware that even the most democratic governments are sometimes tempted to use totalitarian methods. Therefore, a free people must be continually concerned with the means employed to preserve their government, lest these means undo the rights they seek to protect. We believe that fair rules of procedure and due process of law can never be dispensed with — in fact, must be even more jealously cultivated in times of crisis. . . .*
> — From Statement on Civil Liberties
> and National Legislation by the
> FCNL Executive Committee,
> April 8, 1954

Men are qualified for civil liberty in exact proportion to their disposition to put moral chains upon their own appetites. . .Society cannot exist unless a controlling power upon will and appetite be placed somewhere. . .It is ordained in the eternal constitution of

*things, that men of intemperate minds cannot be free. Their passions
forge their fetters.*   — Edmund Burke

*If there is any fixed star in our constitutional constellation, it is that
no official, high or petty, can prescribe what shall be orthodox in
politics, nationalism, religion, or matters of opinion or force citizens
to confess by word or act their faith therein.*
                    — From the opinion of the Court delivered by
                      Mr. Justice Jackson in *West Virginia State
                      Board of Education v. Barnette*

In Washington parlance, *civil liberties* are those rights of the individual against arbitrary, unjust or tyrannical acts of government. In common usage, *civil rights,* discussed in the next chapter, refer to the relations of one group to another and include such questions as segregation and discrimination, equality of opportunity and voting rights, and justice for minorities. At this stage in the evolution of our society both still require eternal vigilance and constant effort to maintain and expand them. The specific issues may vary from year to year, but the struggle is unceasing. Legislation in Congress and in the state legislatures plays a key role and often the political and psychological obstacles to justice for the accused or to new and more just laws are enormous.

This chapter can give only a few samples of FCNL efforts to maintain and expand civil liberties in a turbulent and fear-ridden quarter century. Largely passed over are the excesses of the government loyalty-security program and the blight of the Joe McCarthy years, when the Wisconsin Senator thundered about Communists in the State Department but never produced one.

There was the case of William Martin, who was fired from his post as a senior Senate page by a Republican Personnel Committee because he had signed a letter in behalf of the Young Friends in Washington to high school seniors in the District of Columbia area pointing out that rights for conscientious objectors were contained in the Selective Service law. We asked most of the Republican Senators in person if it were impossible to question or discuss or explain a law which they had passed and charged that it was they, not Bill Martin, who were on trial.

Missing from this account is the story of state and local loyalty oaths, special provisions in the Defense Education Act, and a whole string of actions against conscientious objectors or dissenters. Nor is there an examination of the civil liberties issues raised by vigils, demonstrations and other protests against the Vietnam War. Also not dealt with is the broad area of surveillance, government dossiers, and other devices of government control.

FCNL POSITION ON CIVIL LIBERTIES

The basic position of the FCNL in regard to civil liberties was spelled out in a statement adopted by the Executive Committee, April 8, 1954 (with two dissents), which amplified the recommendations approved by the General Committee at its annual meeting on January 8, 1953.

> As citizens of the United States we do not lightly assume the duties and privileges of citizenship. We have a daily duty to respect those rights of individuals inherent in men and to discharge the obligations of individuals to the peace and well being of society. . . . [2]

According to this statement, the liberties guaranteed in the First Amendment against "abridging the freedom of speech or of the press; or the right of people peaceably to assemble and to petition the Government for a redress of grievances" must be zealously asserted and supported.

The statement criticized the procedures of some Congressional investigating committees (without naming the House Un-American Activities Committee) and declared, "We are opposed to Congressional investigations of persons as to their opinions and beliefs except in cases involving Senatorial confirmation of appointments." Even where Congressional inquiries are appropriate,

> We would urge that fair standards of procedure be established to safeguard individual rights or personal integrity, privacy and freedom of thought. . . .Nothing shall abridge the right of a person to testify in his own behalf; to present additional evidence in his own behalf; to subpoena witnesses, both for and against him; to confront and cross-examine his accuser within reasonable limits; to file a statement in his own behalf; to have the opportunity to be accompanied and advised by counsel; and to receive advance notice of the charges against him, insofar as possible. [3]

The Committee upheld the right of dissent and the privilege against self-incrimination under the Fifth Amendment.

> . . .The right of political dissent, if it is to mean anything, must extend to the ideas we loathe, as well as to the ideas we cherish. . . .

> We oppose any legislation calculated to deny to any individual the privilege against self-incrimination, in exchange for immunity, in matters involving political associations and belief, afforded by the Fifth Amendment. . . .This privilege was placed in our Bill of Rights after centuries of bitter experience with inquisitions relating to religious and political beliefs, and the brutal treatment of suspected criminals. . . .
> We oppose any and all wiretapping. A law to legalize wiretapping would seem to be contrary to the spirit of the Fourth Amendment in the Bill of Rights which provides that 'The rights of the people to be secure in their persons, houses, paper and effects, against unreasonable searches and seizures, shall not be violated. . . .' [4]

In regard to special loyalty oaths, the Committee believed that loyalty cannot be coerced or compelled; it can only be earned and merited.

> The general promise one makes when becoming a public official 'to support this Constitution' is all the Constitution requires (Art. VI, 3) and should be adequate. We oppose required loyalty oaths whether Federal, State, local or private. . . . It implies that he is disloyal unless he repeatedly swears his loyalty. The fruits of these oaths have been resentment, confusion and waste. . . . [5]

Apprehension was expressed about the growing size and power of the Federal Bureau of Investigation. In 1953 the FBI spent about 2½ times the amount of the appropriation for the entire federal court system which it was to serve. (The appropriation in calendar year 1972 for the FBI was $353 million.)

The statement closed with the comment that, in keeping with the finest American tradition, encouragement should be given to the expression of widely divergent opinions and beliefs to the end that truth may prevail in the market place of ideas.

> Both as members of the Society of Friends and as Americans, our concern is to open the channels of inquiry and communication so that the market place may be a vital, active, even turbulent forum where error may in fact be vanquished when truth is left free to combat it. . . . [6]

CAPITAL PUNISHMENT

One night while riding on the train between New York City and Washington, I struck up a conversation with a Black minister in the seat in front of me. He had been reading a religious magazine containing articles defending war and capital punishment. When I asked him if his mind were made up on these two issues, he replied: "No." I replied:

> I would like to leave two questions for you to answer in due time. In regard to war, do you know any Christian way to kill a man? As for capital punishment, do you know anybody wise enough to play God and take another's life?. . . .

The Northern California Friends Committee on Legislation took a strong lead against capital punishment for many years. Trevor Thomas prepared a pamphlet, *This Life We Take*, which was given wide circulation over the United States and which formed the basis of an article in the *New York Times* on the Chessman case. In the special session of the California legislature called to consider capital punishment in 1960, Coleman Blease, FCL advocate, as the issue approached a vote in the Senate Judiciary Committee, urged complete abolition. The bill to abolish the death penalty was defeated in committee 7 to 8, much closer than had been expected. Later, Michael Ingermann worked with the American Civil Liberties Union and others in getting an injunction against further execution in California for a time.

Friends were active in New Jersey, Virginia, Pennsylvania and Indiana against the death penalty. J. Stuart Innerst testified for FCNL before two Congressional committees and before a committee of the Virginia House of Delegates. In his Virginia testimony Stuart Innerst pointed out that "executing a person doesn't undo the evil he had done, but multiplies it. It adds violence to violence by the individual. It cheapens life and brutalizes society."[7]

William Graves carried the issue to the Democratic Convention Platform Committee. The *FCNL Newsletter* urged support for abolition bills by Congressman Abraham Multer of New York and Senator Philip Hart of Michigan.

The most noted case was that of Caryl Chessman, who had been on death row in San Quentin, California, for years. Governor Edmund Brown granted Caryl Chessman a 60-day reprieve from the gas chamber and urged the State Legislature to abolish capital punishment. The fateful character of one vote was illustrated in what happened. As already pointed out a legislature committee rejected the Governor's request 8 to 7. The State Supreme Court recommended against clemency 4 to 3.

The Southern California FCL office played an important role in supporting the Governor's program. They secured the signatures of

Eleanor Roosevelt, Harry Golden, Aldous Huxley and many other Americans to a clemency petition. A wide circulation of the petition in California netted 1000 additional signatures. Invitations were received from television channels and radio stations to explain the FCL position. Newspapers gave generous coverage to FCL efforts and statements. In Washington some of us worked up to the moment of execution trying to get a Supreme Court Justice to halt the carrying out of the death penalty which was scheduled for May 2, 1960. The revulsion over the execution was a considerable factor in delaying further executions in California and elsewhere.

In England in 1802 the number of crimes punishable by death was 223. In 1968 capital punishment was abolished in England. A United Nations study, released in April 1972, reported that only six countries — Argentina, Austria, Colombia, Ecuador, Uruguay and Venezuela, had completely abolished capital punishment and nineteen more had eliminated the death penalty except in exceptional circumstances. Within the United States the last execution was in Oklahoma in 1966. According to the *New York Times* of May 4, 1971, there were 648 men and women on death row, of which 557 were sentenced for murder. Rhode Island abolished the death penalty in 1852. Alaska, Hawaii, Iowa, Maine, Michigan, Minnesota, North Dakota, Oregon, Vermont, West Virginia and Wisconsin have done so since.

In 1972, the Supreme Court ruled 5 to 4, that the death penalty, as presently imposed in the United States, is unconstitutional. In a three-way decision the majority held that the punishment had been meted out in a random and unpredictable and discriminatory manner. The decision left the option open to the states to pass laws exacting the death penalty "by providing standards for juries and judges to follow in determining the sentence in capital cases or by more narrowly defining the crimes for which the penalty is to be imposed." As of March 1974, twenty-two states have reinstated the death penalty for certain prescribed crimes. On March 13, 1974, the U.S. Senate passed a capital punishment bill by a vote of 54 to 33, which now goes to the House where action is uncertain this year.

The case against capital punishment was well summarized by Justice Brennan in his dissenting opinion.

The punishment of death is inconsistent with. . .four principles: Death is an unusually severe and degrading punishment; there is a strong probability it is inflicted arbitrarily; its rejection by contemporary society is virtually total, and there is no reason to believe it serves any penal purpose more effectively than the less severe punishment of imprisonment. . . . [8]

WIRETAPPING: "DIRTY BUSINESS"

The subcommittee hearing ran on long after the lunch hour as the informal dialogue continued between the FCNL witness and the chairman in company with the committee counsel. The Attorney General had asked for authority to legalize wiretapping under certain safeguards and William H. Rahill was arguing against any such sanction before Senator Welker of Idaho, Chairman of the Senate Judiciary Subcommittee. As the hearing concluded this exchange took place:

Mr. Rahill. . .You and the other members of Congress are under the burden of passing the kind of legislation which in your judgment, not mine and not my brother's, will do the best job of making this nation secure. I am here today on behalf of the Friends Committee on National Legislation only to suggest a point of view that we hope you will be aware of.

We realize it is a minority point of view and we hope that it may have more validity than the number who adhere to it because it is based on not just our experience but on our religious beliefs and our efforts to live according to the Sermon on the Mount and the life of Jesus Christ.

Senator Welker. . . . I have already heretofore paid my respect to your great religious body. I want to say to you that I have examined hundreds and hundreds of witnesses since I have been in the Senate — 3½ years. I have never enjoyed more the examination of any other witness than you because you have been profound, sincere, and I know you have made a great study. We may differ as reasonable minds will always differ but I certainly respect you and I commend you very highly, sir. . . .
Mr. Rahill. . . . It has been a pleasure to me, Mr. Chairman. [9]

Wiretapping is only one component in a growing technology of interception which no longer relies entirely on physical tapping of wires but can pick up conversations by other electronic means. And eavesdropping is only one part of an expanding surveillance system on the part of the government that has alarmed many people and has been the subject of extensive hearings in 1970 and 1971 in Congress by the Subcommittee on Constitutional Liberties headed by Senator Sam Ervin of North Carolina. The issue of wiretapping has been in controversy during most of the life of the FCNL.

William Rahill in his testimony quoted from the FCNL statement on Legislative Policy adopted January 8, 1953. "We condemn treason or spying or any disloyal act. At the same time we highly value free thought, free speech, and free association. These are essential to the elimination of error or wavering loyalty. Government can deal with sabotage, espionage, and subversion, and judge the competence of persons in government service, without infringing upon these basic rights."[10]

Proponents of wiretapping have argued that it is necessary for apprehending persons guilty of kidnapping, subversion, espionage and threats to national security. Laws in the different states vary, and there has been a great argument over the admissibility of wiretap evidence in court cases and criminal trials.

The kidnapping of Charles Lindbergh's son was an infamous crime, but statistics show that the number of kidnapping cases in the United States is very small. Were wiretapping confined to major organized crime, the case for it would be more convincing.

Opponents recall that Mr. Justice Holmes in 1928 called the use of wiretapping by government "dirty business." Justice Brandeis found wiretapping an unreasonable search and seizure contrary to the Fourth and Fifth Amendments to the Constitution. The views of Justice Brandeis have been supported by Chief Justice Stone, by Justice Butler, by Justice Murphy, by Justice Frankfurter and by Justice Douglas. Experience has shown that, once authority is granted for wiretaps by police or investigation officials, it is very difficult to limit their number or control their use.

Admittedly, wiretapping is one of the many sticky and controversial questions with which the FCNL has tried to deal. But you do not maintain civil liberties by giving them up. The line is not always easy to draw between the rights of the individual and the claims of society, between individual freedom and the welfare of society and the nation.

The revelations in 1973 in the Watergate scandal and in the Pentagon Papers case of Daniel Ellsberg and David Russo have unveiled gross misuse of wiretapping and have tended to reinforce the position of the FCNL against any and all wiretapping which has been subject to great abuse by various government agencies.

The FCNL has tried to maintain, not only on wiretapping but on other civil liberties issues, in testimonies before committees in both Houses of Congress, in *Newsletters*, and *Action Bulletins* and other literature, a constant and consistent stand for the legitimate rights of individuals and groups under the First, Fourth and Fifth

Amendments to the Constitution, which are essential articles in our Bill of Rights.

LAUNCHING THE NATIONAL CIVIL LIBERTIES CLEARING HOUSE

Late in 1947 a few of us were talking together about the almost unbroken pattern of segregation in Washington, D.C., and the general attitude of repression and fear which characterized the postwar years in the nation's capital. In the group were Philip Schiff of the National Jewish Welfare Board, a warm friend and close colleague of mine until his untimely death a few years later; Lillian K. Watford from Pittsburgh, representative of the Northern Baptist Convention; Fern Colburn from the Presbyterian Church Department of Social Education and Action; and Thomas B. Keehn, legislative secretary for the Council for Social Action of the Congregational Church, now the United Church of Christ.

This group, along with others, organized a day-long National Citizens Conference on Civil Liberties which was held at the Washington Hotel, a block from the White House, on April 14, 1948. This was one of the first fully integrated conferences held in the Capital. It was well attended with a lively program that went off without incident.

Growing out of this conference was a meeting of individuals and organizations on May 12 and June 2, which formed what later became the National Civil Liberties Clearing House. From that time until it was laid down May 15, 1971, for lack of funds, the Clearing House met about once a month to exchange information and alert organizations about the various threats to civil liberties and to discuss ways and means to meet these challenges and expand the basic American freedoms.

The Clearing House addressed itself to four main areas.

1. The various questions involved in civil liberties, including the government loyalty-security program, legislation and attacks on civil liberties from the House Un-American Activities Committee and the Senate Internal Security Committee or from members of Congress like the Mundt-Nixon Bill, the McCarran Act, and the irresponsible antics of Senator Joe McCarthy.

2. Civil rights and economic justice for Blacks, Japanese-Americans, and other minorities. In more recent years the Leadership Conference for Civil Rights has largely pre-empted this field in cooperative planning for strategy.

3. Academic freedom from the arbitrary action of school boards,

citizen's groups and superpatriotic societies.

4. International human rights such as UN conventions and the Universal Declaration of Human Rights.

For 22 years there were annual two-day conferences in Washington which drew attendance and participation from many Government agencies and more than a hundred organizations. The Clearing House brought together representatives from some forty organizations for sharing information and ideas and discussing strategy. The Clearing House did not issue statements or action proposals in its own name but provided a process whereby such groups as wished to take action on a given question were free to do so. It helped nongovernmental organizations build up a body of knowledge and well considered positions on many controversial subjects.

I was asked to serve as chairman during the first three formative years and members of the FCNL staff have been on the steering committee or planning committee or otherwise active participants in the organization throughout the years. Mary Alice Baldinger provided able and dedicated leadership almost throughout the life of the Clearing House.

The *Washington Post* said editorially on the occasion of its tenth annual conference, "In the decade of its energetic existence. . .the National Civil Liberties Clearing House has rendered service of exceptional value not alone to its constituent organization but also to the cause of American freedom. . . . It is a pleasure to congratulate the Clearing House on a decade of significant accomplishment and to wish it a robust future as a sentinel of freedom."

All too often I have been given credit for what my colleagues in the FCNL have done or what was essentially a team effort. One of the many examples was the letter in 1954 from Mary Alice Baldinger to me, "I think you know how grateful I am personally, and the Clearing House is officially, for all the time and thought and energy you have expended upon it over the years. And I think it is quite indisputable that without you there would *be* no Clearing House."[11]

The Mundt-Nixon Bill

The Mundt Bill, H.R. 5852, was designed to outlaw the political activities of the Communist Party. In 1948, a month after the National Citizens Conference on Civil Liberties, the following telegram was sent to Joseph W. Martin, Jr., House Speaker; Charles A. Halleck, House Republican Majority Leader, and Sam Rayburn,

Democratic Minority Leader. It was signed by six of us representing organizations, and six who signed as individuals.

> As non-communist organizations and invididuals we are very much concerned about the deeper implications of the Mundt Bill, H.R. 5852, because we believe it violates the constitutional provisions for freedom of expression and political activity and that it places unneeded and unjustified restrictions upon political dissent.
>
> It is our belief that the Mundt Bill, while it does not purport to outlaw the Communist party, would do so in effect because of the penalties which would tend to drive Communists underground and make martyrs of them.
>
> Public education and progressive political action are much more appropriate and effective means of dealing with Communist ideas than suppression and outlawry. . . .
>
> We associate ourselves with the following statement by the commission on governmental invasion of civil rights at the National Conference on Civil Liberties held on April 14: 'Opposed as the commission is to the Communist party, its principles and its aims, it concluded that in the interest of freedom of all Americans there should be no resort to totalitarian methods in dealing with this minority. The commission opposed the enactment by Congress of any legislation either outlawing or curtailing any political movement on the basis of its beliefs and objectives.' [12]

This was in line with the Jeffersonian philosophy of opposition to any form of tyranny over the minds of men by government and a differentiation between ideas and opinions, and overt acts which might be considered criminal. The telegram pointed out, in the section deleted from the excerpt above, that there were laws on the statute books designed to give protection against overt acts that seriously threaten the national security.

The main features of this bill were still around two years later in the companion bill in the House of Representatives sponsored by Richard Nixon, H.R. 7595. Harrop A. Freeman, secretary of the Cornell Law School, and one of the sharpest minds in the Society of Friends, gave his views in behalf of the FCNL before the House Un-American Activities Committee. He said that in regard to the Quakers, "I suppose they outrun this committee in being against violence and the violent overthrow of government. . .The religious philosophy of the Society of Friends is based on the concept that you cannot coerce people in their beliefs, and the only way we can have a democratic form of government is by persuasion."

As a lawyer, Harrop Freeman believed that the statute was of questionable constitutionality:

> As of the present time, the Supreme Court has said that the Communist Party is a legal party and Congress could not legislate them out of existence. What is attempted here is to do indirectly what the Supreme Court has said you could not do directly. I am aware of the problem you have, but if what we are trying to do is to preserve the kind of government we have here, the attempted cure for subversive activity may be worse than the disease. [13]

This and similar bills were designed to compel registration by "Communist political organizations" and "Communist front organizations" and to impose criminal sanctions on individuals for various "subversive activities," whether or not in connection with such organizations.

On March 30, 1950, a four-page statement against such legislation was released over the signatures of 18 organizational representatives including the FCNL. Among the several reasons given against such measures was the argument, "If this proposed action is taken against Communists today, a dangerous precedent is created for extending it tomorrow to progressives, socialists, or trade unionists." They might have added, "or Quakers."

Another reason advanced was that "it would inflict serious penalties on individuals, criminal sanctions, social and economic ostracism and character assassination — merely on the ground of association with certain organizations whose natures are not themselves defined with sufficient precision, and would thus inevitably restrict inquiry and thought, belief and expression."[14]

Kermit Eby, dynamic Church of the Brethren leader, wrote in *The Messenger*, July 28, 1953, "Communism will certainly never be overcome by surrendering civil liberties on the idolatrous altar of anti-Communism."

The bill was not called up for House Action.

THE POOL BILL, H.R. 12047

One of the few legislative proposals to emerge from the House Un-American Activities Committee and an unfortunate sample of their unwholesome activities, was the bill sponsored by Representative Joe R. Pool of Texas. This bill would have heavily penalized the shipment of any relief supplies to the victims of American bombing in North Vietnam.

The Executive Council of the FCNL approved a statement at their meeting in Washington, September 10-11, 1966, which said in part:

> We oppose this legislation especially on the ground that it punishes acts of compassion and humanitarianism by harsh fines and imprisonment. Members of the Religious Society of Friends, along with many other Americans, are appalled by the increasing barbarity of the Vietnam conflict. The American Friends Service Committee is already aiding refugees and other victims of the war in South Vietnam. Friends have historically attempted to give relief to all sides in a conflict, and many Friends, including the AFSC, have wanted to extend medical and relief supplies to *all* the parties involved in the Vietnam War. . . .

> It is clear that many of the victims of this war are innocent men, women and children. We grieve when terrorist bombs explode in Saigon killing and maiming bystanders. But we are haunted also by the knowledge that the bombs and napalm which our tax money has helped to purchase are killing and maiming thousands in North Vietnam and the Vietcong-controlled areas of South Vietnam.

> We feel a religious compulsion to try to help these and other war victims. Existing laws and regulations already provide nearly insurmountable barriers to humanitarian efforts to establish human contact and succor across military lines. The proposed bill would absolutely prohibit any such contact and punish it by severe fines and imprisonment. We strenuously oppose this governmental interference with humanitarian efforts to help those in need in other lands. . . .

During a tumultuous four days of hearings 50 people were arrested including 12 witnesses. Senator Dirksen commented that this "spectacle can do Congress no good." The bill, amended to make it somewhat less objectionable on freedom of speech grounds, and aiming it more against obstruction of the Armed Forces, passed the House by a vote of 275 to 64, after a very lively debate. Senators Dirksen and Mansfield expressed strong opposition to the bill, and after Representative Pool was arrested for drunken driving, little more was heard of the measure. No action was taken by the Senate.

THE CASE OF DR. EDWARD U. CONDON, 1946-1954[15]

One of the distressing examples of character assassination was that of Dr. Edward U. Condon during the days of Senator Joe McCarthy, with its atmosphere of virulent anti-Communism and the fear of Russian espionage. He was hounded during his job as Director of the U.S. Bureau of Standards, and then in 1954 was in effect forced from his position as Director of Research for the

Corning, N.Y., Glass Works.

There had been sporadic attacks in 1946 and 1947 including a very biased and inaccurate article in the *Washington Times-Herald* for July 17, 1947, which Congressman Chet Holifield answered point by point in a House speech on July 22, 1947. Again, on March 9 and April 22, 1948, Holifield replied to the critics of Dr. Condon. The concentrated drive against Dr. Condon by some of the members of the House Committee on Un-American Activities began on March 1, 1948, when from his sick bed, Congressman H. Parnell Thomas of New Jersey, Chairman of the House Un-American Activities Committee, released a seven-page statement calling Dr. Condon "one of the weakest links in our atomic security." This statement was released in behalf of the subcommittee including Representatives Thomas, Richard B. Vail and John S. Wood. So far as the FCNL could find out, it was not submitted to, nor authorized by the full committee.

Congressman Adolph Sabath of Illinois said on the House floor on March 9, 1948, in the debate on this release by the Un-American Activities Committee:

> Every time that the funds of the Committee on Un-American Activities are about exhausted, a new propaganda is started to rile the American people and to create prejudice and fear in their minds as to dangers to our democratic form of government. The last propaganda leveled by the Committee, chairmanned by the gentleman from New Jersey, Mr. Parnell Thomas, but dominated by the gentleman from Mississippi, Mr. John E. Rankin, are the charges against Dr. Edward U. Condon, Director of the National Bureau of Standards.
>
> . . .These investigations were largely carried on without regard to the rights of these persons and in violation of our Constitution and the Bill of Rights. . . . [16]

It was at this point that Lilian K. Watford, Northern Baptist Convention legislative representative in Washington, asked me to go with her to see Richard Nixon, who was an active member of the Un-American Activities Committee. She knew Mr. and Mrs. Condon better than I did, and while it was recognized that they were strong individualists and outspoken, she was convinced that they were loyal and responsible American citizens.

We did not assume that Richard Nixon had anything to do with the release of this statement, but we told him bluntly that releasing such unproven charges was a shabby way to treat anybody and that the Committee had a responsibility to call Dr. Condon before them in a full and fair hearing at which he could clear himself or at which the Committee could prove beyond a doubt that Condon should be removed from his post.

Nixon did not defend Thomas' action. He said that he did not believe that Condon was subversive but was not sure whether he might be a security risk.

On March 18, Condon insisted on a hearing and said he had nothing to conceal. Finally one was scheduled without explanation, more than four years later when Condon was given a hearing in Chicago on September 5, 1952. Chairman Thomas did not attend the hearing, having in the interim served a sentence in a Federal penitentiary for alleged kickbacks from his staff. There were political overtones in the hearings because Representatives Vail and Velde — past and present members of the House Un-American Activities Committee — were present and both coincidentally up for re-election in Illinois districts. The *Federation of American Scientists Newsletter* commented, "It appeared that it was too late to repair the damage done him and that other purposes were being served by the belated hearings in this election year." The *Christian Science Monitor* on September 9 reported that Dr. Condon, who had testified under oath, had answered all questions and "at the end he was free of any charges against him."

There is not space here for a summary of all the charges and the answers by Condon, nor the strong support given on the House floor by Representative Chet Holifield, who had served with him in the President's Evaluation Board for Operation Crossroads at Bikini observing the atom bomb tests.

Dr. Condon had a distinguished scientific career which began with a full professorship at the University of Minnesota at the age of 27. In the fall of 1940 he helped organize the government-sponsored radiation laboratory at the Massachusetts Institute of Technology. At that time he was associate director of research for the Westinghouse Electric Corporation. In 1941 he was put in charge of that company's research program of microwave radar. His genius as a theoretical physicist was recognized when he was chosen among the dozen people of science initially assigned to the historic task of producing the first controlled release of atomic energy.

Some of his friends thought that part of the criticism of Dr. Condon stemmed from his expert work with Senator McMahon and other members of Congress in the drafting of the Atomic Energy Act in 1946 which provided, in theory at least, for civilian control of atomic energy and which disappointed some like Dr. Leslie Groves, former head of the Manhattan Project, who were more favorable to military control.

He was elected to membership in the National Academy of Sciences and to the presidency of the American Physical Society. The American Physical Society sent a letter to the President and to House Speaker, Joseph W. Martin, Jr., vigorously assailing the action of the House Un-American Activities Committee.

Nine Nobel Prize winners and 123 notable scientists sponsored a dinner in New York on April 12, 1948, to express their confidence in Dr. Condon. The executive board of the Washington Association of Scientists summarized their study of "The Condon Case and Its Implications" by saying that the implications of this attack were "dangerous and ugly." Later Dr. Condon was elected president of the large American Association for the Advancement of Science. All of these actions spoke eloquently of the respect with which his scientific colleagues held him.

Dr. Condon had received four security clearances. The first came as a result of his work on atomic energy and the development of microwave radar including a brief period as associate director of the Los Alamos Laboratory. The second was made at the request of Condon after 2½ years of controversy initiated by the attack of J. Parnell Thomas, Chairman of the House Un-American Activities Committee. The third clearance was made by the Atomic Energy Commission which announced on July 15, 1948, that it had cleared Dr. Condon after a thorough study of his records including the results of two F.B.I. reports.

When Condon came to the Bureau of Standards from Westinghouse, he did it at a sizable cut in salary in order to devote his talents to government work. In October 1951 he resigned from the Bureau of Standards and became director of research at the Corning Glass Works.

On February 10, 1953, the Army-Navy-Air Force Security Board lifted Dr. Condon's security clearance and he appealed. In the meantime he worked on nonmilitary projects for Corning. On July 12, 1954, but not announced then, the Eastern Regional Industrial Security Board granted industrial clearance. This was Condon's fourth clearance. This clearance was suddenly suspended by Secretary of Navy Thomas on October 21, 1954, under circumstances considered by a *Washington Post and Times-Herald* editorial of October 23 as "very curious." When questioned, Secretary Thomas was unable to give explicit answers to reporters about the origins of Dr. Condon's recent difficulties or about the handling of the case.

In the *New York Times*, October 24, 1954, the story of the Vice President's western trip datelined Cheyenne, Wyoming, October 23, under the headline "Nixon Links Reds to Left-Wing Foes," reported. . .Mr. Nixon said this morning that he had intervened in the security clearances of Dr. Edward U. Condon before starting this final campaign trip. "Before I left Washington I asked that the Dr. Condon matter be reexamined, he said. . . ."[17]

In an item in the same paper the same day, in the News of the Week section, a reporter declared ". . .From Butte, Montana, where Vice President Richard Nixon was campaigning, there came a suggestion that politics had something to do with the suspension. Mr. Nixon declared that he had taken a strong hand in the revocation of Dr. Condon's clearance. The Vice President said he felt all the facts in the Condon case were not known and the full record should be reviewed before any clearance was given."

Although Condon's last clearance had been granted on July 12, 1954, it was not until October 19 that the *Washington Post and Times-Herald* reported the clearance.

Science Service in a wire story on October 22 stated, "Some scientists are saying privately that the sudden action must have resulted from recent newspaper publicity concerning the granting of Dr. Condon's clearance. They question if the reversal would have been made on such short notice if elections were not less than two weeks off."

It was right after this that Dr. Condon came to see me in Washington. His face was wan and drawn and he was visibly deeply shaken. He asked if there was anything I could do with either the Vice President or his staff. I had been told that one of the Vice President's speech writers had resigned because he was unhappy about the conduct of the campaign. I had to confess that I did not have any measurable influence on the Vice President or his staff at that time.

On December 13, Dr. Condon announced his resignation as research director of the Corning Glass Works and withdrew his application for clearance stating that he did not feel "there is any possibility of my securing a fair and independent judgment. . .I am now unwilling to continue a potentially indefinite series of reviews and reviews."

On December 15, Secretary Thomas denied outside influence on the case. "The Vice President never talked to me directly or indirectly; or through any person, about this case. . .the people in my office said I should take a look at the file. I did and withdrew clearance." Sometime I wish somebody would tell me how things happen in Washington through complete coincidence![18]

While in Washington, Edward U. Condon joined the Florida Avenue Friends Meeting in Washington, September 16, 1947. At the testimonial dinner given for him on April 12, 1948, he asked: "Will we improve conditions of life everywhere in world brotherhood? Or will we live in a state of suspiciousness, mistrust, fear and hate, in a state of constant dread of the outbreak of another war in which atomic bombs and bacterial warfare are as commonplace as blockbusters and incendiary bombs were in the war just passed? Will we live in a constant state of anxiety, devoting so much of our energy to preparation for war that there is little left for material or spiritual improvement in our way of life?"[19]

It was some time after his resignation before Edward Condon was invited to teach at Washington University in St. Louis and he was able to return to academic life. Dr. Condon died in 1973. Many others in government, in teaching, and in the ministry, were driven from their positions on flimsy grounds in this period of fear and suspicion and hysteria. Most of them had been denied the due process spelled out as the heart of the FCNL position on civil liberties.

CHAPTER 8

A Matter of Justice

AMERICAN INDIANS, ALASKAN NATIVES, JAPANESE-AMERICANS,
BLACKS AND OTHER MINORITIES

*Ours should be a society where human beings are accepted on their
merits and not discriminated against because of race, color, or creed.
The demands of racial justice call for drawing upon every spiritual
resource — Faith that all mankind is one family under God and
should live together in respect; Love to overcome the hatred and
bitterness engendered by centuries of slavery, oppression, and
discrimination; Earnestness to move with more than deliberate
speed; Penitence on the part of those holding special privilege and
readiness to ask forgiveness and extend the hand of friendship;
Courage to supplement the law with heroic determination to help
right the wrongs in our own communities; Dedication to the
principles of nonviolence as the moral and truly effective method of
social change. Law can and must increasingly provide the framework
of justice, but law is harsh and sterile without the spirit of love and
reconciliation.*

From 1957 FCNL Statement
on Legislative Policy

For nearly three decades the FCNL has struggled to achieve
justice for disadvantaged groups of American citizens, including the
American Indians, Alaskan Natives, Japanese-Americans, Blacks
and other racial minorities. The story of this struggle reveals
frequent callousness and inhumanity on the part of the American
Government, including Congress, and on the part of the dominant
white community. It also demonstrates the need for religious and
other citizens' groups to work with people of good will in and out of

Congress and other branches of government toward righting the wrongs under which so many of our fellow Americans have suffered.

AMERICAN INDIANS

Two Friends seminars in 1956 and 1960 brought together Quakers from different parts of the United States who had firsthand experience with many Indians. The second seminar included representatives from 19 yearly meetings and 18 Indian tribes. These seminars threshed out guidelines for Indian policy which have shaped the philosophy and legislative program for the FCNL under the leadership of Edward F. Snyder and Frances Neely.

The seminar urged that the distinctive Indian culture should be preserved "so that we who so often feel the imbalance and unimportance of our lives may draw wisdom and inspiration from the sensitivity, serenity and spiritual wholesomeness found in so many Indian lives."

The seminar further recommended that "At the present time the goal of the Bureau of Indian Affairs and the Indian Health Division of the Public Health Service should be to provide health, education, welfare and expanded economic development programs which will place Indians on an equal footing with other Americans. Such programs should continue until such time as Indians themselves ask that federal control and special services to them be discontinued."[1]

Two key actions of the seminar were to express opposition to the termination without preparation and consent, and opposition to the construction of the Kinzua Dam.

The FCNL has worked for Indian rights in the field of legislation and administrative policy by testifying before Congressional Committees and by lobbying with members of Congress in their offices and in the halls of Congress. It has given support to bills, including vocational training programs, sanitation, and appropriation measures for health, welfare and educational programs of the Bureau of Indian Affairs and the Public Health Service.

THE KINZUA DAM CONTROVERSY

An American Indian said to me in New York some years ago that the United States Government had made over three hundred treaties with the Indians and had violated every one of them. The incident of the Senecas and the Kinzua Dam is one glaring example of broken promises. See Charles J. Kappler, *Indian Treaties, 1778-1883,* Reprint, Interland Pub., N.Y., 1973, 1099 pp., which gives all the texts of Indian treaties without comment. In the foreword, the compiler says, "Soon, however, the Indian treaties became little more than real estate conveyances, by which the Indians ceded almost any land the United States wanted, for the price it was willing to pay."

In 1794 a treaty was negotiated between the United States and the Iroquois Confederacy. This treaty, signed by George Washington, assured the Seneca Nation of certain lands in Western New York State in perpetuity. The text of the Pickering Treaty included the following provision:

> Now, the United States acknowledges all the land within the aforementioned boundaries, to be the property of the Seneka nation; and the United States will never claim the same, nor disturb the Seneka nation, nor any of the Six Nations, or of their Indian friends residing thereon and united with them, in the free use and enjoyment thereof: but it shall remain theirs, until they choose to sell the same to the people of the United States, who have the right to purchase. [2]
>
> From Article III,
> Pickering Treaty of
> November 11, 1794

When George Washington asked the Indians to meet with Timothy Pickering in Canadaigua, New York, to make a treaty, the Indians asked the Philadelphia Yearly Meeting of Friends to send delegates to advise them and give them some reassurance that the United States Government would keep such a treaty. Four friends, two of whom kept journals, made the difficult journey, eight days on horseback, through much wild country, and participated in the negotiations lasting seven weeks.

The Quakers listened to both parties, and assuming the integrity of the United States Government, they advised Red Jacket, Cornplanter and their associates to sign the treaty. One of the Quakers, William Savery, recounts in his journal on October 21, 1794, that Colonel Pickering "gave them assurance of his desire to promote the happiness and peace of their nations, and told them that they might depend upon one thing at least, which was, that he would never deceive them. . . ." Two days later Savery wrote:

> . . .Captain John, an Indian Chief, visited us, and had much to say about the many deceptions which had been practised upon them by the white people; observing, that however good and honest white men might be in other matters, they were all deceivers when they wanted to buy Indian lands. . . . [3]

In 1957 Congress authorized the building of a dam that would violate the Pickering Treaty by flooding the Seneca reservation and driving about 800 Senecas from the land which their tribe had held for more than one hundred and sixty years. The plan for the Kinzua Dam was worked out by the Army Corps of Engineers and was designed for flood control on the Allegheny River to protect Pittsburgh and for water conservation.

In protesting this action, the Second Friends Seminar on Indian Affairs, February 4-7, 1960, said in part:

> It is important that the Government of the United States, which is interested in promoting good faith among nations in the world today, should keep faith with the Seneca Indians. . . .

Arthur E. Morgan proposed an alternative plan which would divert the flood water through a swamp north to Lake Erie and which he believed would give total protection at a probable saving of more than $100 million. This Conewango alternative would save the Seneca reservation and avoid disturbing their ancient settlement. Arthur Morgan, a Friend, was the first chairman and chief engineer of the Tennessee Valley Authority. He designed the dams above Dayton, Ohio, which saved that low-lying city from perennial flooding. He had acted as consultant in the field of water control in India and Africa, so his recommendations were that of an experienced civil engineer.

However, the Senators from Pennsylvania and Representatives from Western Pennsylvania had been sold a bill of goods by Pittsburgh commercial interests. The Army Engineers refused even to survey the proposed alternative proposal. Bureaucracy and Congress rode roughshod over the sacred treaty rights of the Senecas, unilaterally, without negotiation.

Arthur Morgan's revised Plan Six was examined only by the Chief of Engineers, who rejected any impartial study of Plan Six on the spurious grounds that, following such study, there would be "Plan Seven" and "Plan Eight," etc. The Indians had agreed to the building of the Kinzua Dam *if* an alternative route was proven completely unfeasible, but no attempt was made to find another solution.

Apart from authorizing and financing an engineering plan, Congress has never specifically acted to abrogate or revise the Pickering Treaty. Its indirect action has been termed "treaty abrogation by legislative erosion."

Arthur Morgan was attacked by the proponents of the Kinzua

Dam as being a paid engineering consultant for the Seneca Indians. However, two thirds of his time in the employ of the Seneca Nation was not charged for, except for expenses. The remainder of his services were provided at half the usual consulting rate. When he began he told them that, if the Kinzua Dam was found to be essential to the protection of a great city like Pittsburgh, in his opinion they should not object.[4]

In regard to the impartiality and infallibility of the Corps of Engineers, there were many critics. Clarence Cannon, long-time Chairman of the House Appropriations Committee, said in presenting the request of the Engineer Corps for 1960 funds:

> . . .The Corps of Engineers were invariably in favor of the largest expenditures the Committee could be prevailed upon to make. Much of their testimony was wholly unreliable. When they were consulted on the cost of a proposed project they invariably underestimated the cost. . .It is impossible to escape the conclusion that they were either incompetent or deliberately misleading. [5]

Former Secretary of the Interior Harold Ickes said:

> No more lawless or irresponsible federal group than the Corps of Engineers has ever attempted to operate in the United States, either outside or within the law.

Yet it was the Corps of Engineers and not the Senecas pleading for their ancient treaty rights, nor the chief engineer of the T.V.A. with his alternative plan, nor the voices of the FCNL and many other organizations, that Congress responded to when it voted to break the solemn promises of three presidents.

It was argued that the property rights of the Senecas would be protected by eminent domain proceedings. Throughout our history few Americans have understood the American Indian concept of land. It seems eminently fair to most Americans to take land as long as it is paid for. To the Senecas, land is not compensable. "The land is your mother. You do not sell your mother."

George Heron, president of the Seneca Nation of Indians told the House Subcommittee on Indian Affairs in 1960:

> . . .the thought that we would freely give up the lands of our ancestors, which we pledged to hold for our children yet unborn, is so contrary to the Seneca way of life that it is not even considered seriously. . . . To lose their homes on the reservation is really to lose a part of their life. . . . My people really believe that George Washington read the 1794 Treaty

before he signed it, and that he meant exactly what he wrote. For more than 165 years we Senecas have lived by that document. To us it is more than a contract, more than a symbol; to us, the 1794 Treaty is a way of life. . . .

President George Washington, in replying to the speeches of the Seneca leaders in 1790, said:

Your great object seems to be, the security of your remaining lands: and I have, therefore, upon this point, meant to be sufficiently strong and clear, that, in future, you cannot be defrauded of your lands. . .the sale of your lands, in future will depend entirely upon yourselves.

A letter issued by the War Department to the Seneca and Onondaga Nations by authorization of President Thomas Jefferson, March 17, 1802, said:

. . .All lands claimed and secured to said Seneca and Onondaga Nations of Indians by treaty, convention or deed of conveyance, or reservation lying and being within the limits of the said United States, shall be and remain the property of the said Seneca and Onondaga Nations of Indians forever, unless they shall voluntarily relinquish or dispose of the same. . . .

During the 1960 election campaign, John F. Kennedy made a personal promise in a letter to Oliver LaFarge, president of the Association on American Indian Affairs, that ". . .there would be no change in treaty or contractual relationships without the consent of the tribes concerned. . . .Indians have heard fine words and promises long enough. They are right in asking for deeds. . . ."

Yet I do not find evidence that Kennedy when President intervened to challenge the Kinzua Dam development and he signed the bill appropriating the money for constructing the dam which meant the "abrogation of the treaty by legislative erosion." The *Christian Century* of May 31, 1961, said, "Since preliminary construction has started under the Army engineers, only President Kennedy can postpone proceedings until an impartial study is made."

The FCNL in cooperation with other Friends organizations opposed the construction of the Kinzua Dam from early 1957 onward. A press release was sent to 60 Pennsylvania papers in January 1957 and to New York papers, on behalf of the FCNL, the Association on American Indian Affairs (New York), the Indian Rights Association (Philadelphia), and the Indian Committees of the

New York and Philadelphia Yearly Meetings of the Society of Friends, supporting the Seneca Nations in their opposition to the Kinzua Dam. Those same organizations petitioned the Governor of New York State, W. Averell Harriman, who appealed to the Army Engineers on behalf of New York State's Indian citizens "to take a new look" at this area "to determine whether other flood control measures might solve the problem without forcing the Indians to leave their homes."

These efforts were followed up by the appearance of Robert Phair on May 10, 1957, before the House Appropriations Public Works Subcommittee, who reiterated FCNL opposition to the appropriation of $1 million as a start on the projected $100 million to complete the project.

The FCNL, the Indian Committee of Philadelphia Yearly Meeting, the American Friends Service Committee, and many individual Friends worked hard trying to get the Morgan plan considered on its merits and to prevent faithless uprooting of the Senecas.

Levinus Painter submitted testimony before both the House and Senate Appropriations Subcommittees on Public Works on April 13, 1960, and before the Subcommittee on Indian Affairs of the House Committee on Interior and Insular Affairs on June 24 on behalf of the FCNL and the Indian Committees of New York, Philadelphia and Baltimore Yearly Meetings. His grandparents had served as heads of one of the early Indian schools in the Middle West a century ago and Levinus had been a teacher of Bible in the Thomas Indian School on the Cattaraugus Reservation near his home and had been a guest in the sessions of the Seneca National Council. He spoke from a lifetime of interest in Indian rights.

He quoted from the text of the letter by the War Department authorized by President Thomas Jefferson and told these three subcommittees:

> If the treaty is abrogated or set aside by the courts or by Congress, it means that the United States has not kept faith with the Indians. Such action would also be a great disappointment to present-day Quakers who want their government to maintain honorable dealings with the Indians.

Prior to the President's decision, *FCNL Newsletter* readers were urged to write or wire the President regarding the need to abide by the treaty. On June 12, FCNL and AFSC mailed 1655 *Action Bulletins* to concerned individuals asking them to call for a reappraisal of the Kinzua Dam project. FCNL staff also joined with other Friends groups and various Indian interest organizations in a cordial discussion with Interior Secretary Stuart Udall and a special Department of Interior Task Force charged with reviewing Indian policy.

Then on August 9, 1961, President Kennedy announced that "it is not possible to halt construction of the Kinzua Dam currently underway."[6] This announcement brought to an end the Seneca Indians' long and unsuccessful fight to preserve their homelands in the Allegheny River Valley.

The battle for the Senecas then shifted to issues of relocation and compensation. By 1964 the deadline for moving the Senecas out of the area to be flooded was rapidly approaching. Walter Taylor was representative to the Seneca Nation from the Indian Committee of Philadelphia Yearly Meeting of Friends. He testified on March 2 before the Senate Subcommittee on Indian Affairs that the two bills before them for relocation should be passed promptly but that one of them, H.R. 1794, was deficient in many ways. For example, it failed to provide a sufficient amount of substitute land in place of the ten thousand best acres on the reservation. It did not protect the Seneca Nation from having more land taken for a limited access expressway further dividing the remaining land. Three bridges were replaced by only one. The amount of compensation originally for the Williamsburg-type tourist program had been reduced by 72 per cent.

This testimony was followed by a strong letter March 5 from Walter Taylor to the Subcommittee Chairman, Senator Frank Church of Idaho, vigorously protesting projected cuts in appropriations for rehabilitation and reconstruction projects designed to help place the Senecas on a sound financial base. He compared the proposed appropriation of $20,150,000 with the $20,000,000 settlement given to the Pennsylvania Railroad three years previously in return for their 28-mile right-of-way in the same area; one that was failing and scheduled by the railroad to be discontinued.

For months the Senate and House conferees were deadlocked but finally Congress voted 15 million dollars for damages and the expense of relocation, which was 6 million dollars less than the House-passed version. Senators Church, Clark and Dominick argued that this was a generous settlement. Senator Hugh Scott of Pennsylvania denied that it was "generous" and declared, "The original recommendation of the Interior Department was that Congress approve a 29 million dollar fund, and we have fallen far short of that mark."[7] Senator Jacob Javits of New York expressed his disappointment: "The whole record of the United States' dealing with the Senecas in the Kinzua Dam is a sorry one. From the breaking of the treaty to this inadequate settlement, we have never yet dealt fairly and generously with Chief Cornplanter's descendants."

OTHER ENDEAVORS FOR FAIR PLAY TO INDIANS

In 1962, in conversations with Congressmen, opposition was expressed to the construction of the Knowles Dam in Montana, since the dam would destroy Indian resources and violate other Indian treaty rights.

Two other examples of efforts to protect Indian lands — other than the monumental case of Alaska Native Land Claims dealt with later in this chapter — were the testimony filed in 1949 against giving the squatters title to land in the Pyramid Indian reservations and the testimony by Theodore B. Hetzel in support of S. 3085 to restore some 50,000 acres around Blue Lake in Arizona to the Taos Indians as a sacred religious area which the Taos have used from time immemorial for religious purposes. Hetzel said, "Our forebears crossed the ocean to achieve religious freedom; let us not deny it to those who were already here."[8]

One of the most controversial issues for the Indians has been that of termination policy. The FCNL has stressed repeatedly that there should be no major changes of government policy of Indian status without both consultations with the Indians and their consent.

The statement of the Second Friends Seminar on American Indian Affairs, in reviewing the problems of termination of Federal wardship, said in part:

> We suggest that the word "termination" and the policy of imposed "termination" be abandoned as confusing and misleading to all and frightening to American Indians.... At the present time the goal of the Bureau of Indian Affairs and the Indian Health Division of the Public Health Service should be to provide health, education, welfare and expanded economic development programs which will place Indians on an equal footing with other Americans. Such programs should continue until such time as Indians themselves ask that Federal control and special services to them be discontinued. ....[9]

In April 1961, the Menominees in Wisconsin were deprived of their reservation status as wards of the federal government without adequate preparation for their economic survival. Chester Graham, secretary of the Illinois-Wisconsin Friends Committee on Legislation, sought generous provisions for this transition. Looking back on this episode from the vantage point of June 14, 1971, John J. O'Connor, commenting in the *New York Times* on the documentary put together by the National Education Television, said that what had happened since"can hardly trigger an outburst of national pride." I think it is fair to say that the result of this abrupt termination was a disaster for many of the Menominees. Earlier, Melvin Laird, Republican House leader from Wisconsin, had described this deplorable experience of the Menominees, citing increased taxes, low income, unemployment, substandard education, critically substandard housing and poor health.

Chester Graham's efforts for justice to the Menominees are dealt with more fully in Chapter 17 on lobbying on the state level.

REPORT ON INDIAN LEGISLATION

For four and one-half years, from February 1964 to October 1968, Louise Farr, a Washington attorney and graduate of the Yale Law School, edited *The Report on Indian Legislation* which the FCNL printed and circulated to organizations and key individuals particularly concerned with the rights of the American Indians.

Its 34 issues were packed with pertinent information on bills introduced, committee hearings, House and Senate action, budget requests and news about the Bureau of Indian Affairs. This Indian newsletter was suspended for three years because of the loss of its volunteer editor but was revived in November 1971 under the authorship of Richard Thompson. The Indian newsletter was suspended again a year later when Richard Thompson left for volunteer service in Vietnam for the AFSC.

This brief account does not adequately portray the many idealistic officials in the Bureau of Indian Affairs or in Congress who wanted to do the decent thing. The Indians suffered from the incompetence or greed or apathy on the part of men in and out of government who constantly sought to take advantage of them. Because of severe limitations of money and staff, the FCNL has never been able to do nearly all that many Friends wanted it to do in behalf of American Indians.

ALASKA NATIVE LAND CLAIMS

"Do They Expect Us To Live on Snow?"

At the height of the Senate debate over Alaskan Native Land Claims, Senator Edward Kennedy, in a speech on the Senate floor February 9, 1971, recalled that:

In 1885, Helen Hunt Jackson, surveying the past hundred years of relations between American Indians and the government of the United States, observed that we had generally mistreated Indians, had seldom kept our agreements with them, and could look back on our efforts to deal with Indians as reflecting dishonor on our Government. Her book was entitled *A Century of Dishonor*.

It had been over a century now since the United States acquired Alaska from Russia. At that time, and in the Organic Act of 1814, the United States recognized Native rights to the land and Congress provided that the Natives. . .'Shall not be disturbed in the possession of any lands actually in their use or occupation or now claimed by them.' [10]

Congressional debate over claims of the Alaskan Natives began to heat up as early as 1948. Senators Hugh Butler of Nebraska and Arthur V. Watkins of Utah introduced a bill to take away six land reserves totaling more than 1,500,000 acres from the Alaskan Natives. The bill would not only have taken back without compensation, but would have prevented any future grant or confirmation of Indian titles to lands in Alaska. The story was carried in the February 26, 1948, *FCNL Newsletter*, urging thorough consideration to determine what forces were behind this move.

Amy Hollingshead, president of the Alaska Native Sisterhood Grand Camp at Petersburg, Alaska, wrote on December 19, 1947, "The men in Washington who are supposed to be our protectors say that the big corporations can take over our trees, our minerals, and all our lands without asking our permission or paying us. . .We are wondering if they expect us to live on snow and to keep warm in winter by burning ice?"[11]

In the March 30, 1953, *Washington Newsletter*, readers were warned that the Indians of Alaska needed help. For two years there had been measures in Congress providing that, if the Natives proved ownership in lands within the exterior boundaries of a national forest, the court could force them to take a money judgment in lieu of the land. The Forest Service was insisting that the Indians not be given title to any of the timber because divided ownership of the timber would discourage pulp mills from operating in Alaska. One of the bills introduced would have further required the Natives to take cash in lieu of any right they might prove to waters below the high watermark. Since the native economy is based in great part on fishing rights, no cash compensation could equal the value of fishing rights. The bill was not passed, but it was one more in a long series of attempts, all too often by government bureaucrats, to take away land and other things which the Indians regarded as their natural rights.

One of the major strengths of the FCNL has been the number of dedicated supporters from its constituency who have traveled to Washington to express their concerns in person to members of Congress. An excellent example was Irene Heine, from the Pittsburgh area, who came twice in 1970, after considerable research and writing on Alaskan Native Land Claims, to support the request of the Alaskan Natives for a generous settlement of this complicated question.

Irene Heine's visit, March 16-20, occurred when the bill, S. 1830 — a totally inadequate proposal to settle the land claims — was before the Senate Interior and Insular Committee. She and Edward F. Snyder visited 16 of the 17 offices of the members of the Senate Committee that week. There were numerous contacts with the representatives of the Alaska Federation of Natives and the Association on Indian Affairs. She came back for the week during and after Senate passage in July to seek a favorable climate for House consideration. Despite repeated efforts by native groups and interested organizations like the FCNL, the House merely held some preliminary hearings but took no further action. As a result this bill died with the adjournment of the Ninety-first Congress. The FCNL, to back up these direct legislative efforts, issued a legislative memo and two position statements as well as publicity in the *Washington Newsletter.*

In 1971, ten Senators, led by Senator Fred Harris of Oklahoma and Senator Edward Kennedy, introduced S. 835 on February 17, 1971, which provided for acknowledging most of the claims of the Alaska Federation of Natives. Edward Snyder and Irene Heine submitted testimony for the FCNL supporting in principle the Native requests including a land settlement of 60 million acres. They pointed out that the Natives "seek an equitable settlement of their land rights. We believe you understand that the Natives are not asking to be given anything. They are requesting legal title for the lands they retain, and compensation for what they relinquish."[12] The Natives had asked for a $500 million cash settlement to augment the land grant. The cash settlement and the land grant would enable them to begin their development program without delay.

A third Native request was for a two per cent royalty or revenue-sharing provision in perpetuity. And a fourth was that the Natives should have primary responsibility for the Native Corporations and for the Regional Associations which were to be set up.

While 60 million acres, even of Arctic wilderness, seems like a lot of land, it was only about 20 per cent of what the Aleuts, Indians and Eskimos felt was rightfully theirs. They believed this much land was necessary to sustain them in their historic practice of fishing, hunting and trapping for subsistence living.

At issue has been not only the amount of land — the Senate bill passed in 1970 specified 10 million acres — but whether the Natives would be given under-surface mineral rights and how much acreage would be set aside for right of way for the proposed 900-mile Alaska oil pipeline. Oil companies have already bid $900 million for the rights of exploration on the Prudhoe Bay Reserve on the Arctic Slope.

The century-old claim by Alaskan Natives was settled December 14, 1971, when Congress cleared H.R. 10367 granting them $962.5 million and 40 million acres of land. This Alaska Native Claims Settlement Act provided that the estimated 53,000 Eskimos, Aleuts and Indians would receive $462.5 million over an eleven-year period in federal grants and $500 million from anticipated state and federal mineral revenues, particularly oil. The Act also allowed the Federal Government to claim an additional 80 million acres for national parks, forests or refuges.

The 40 million acres of land would be divided among native villages and twelve regional corporations. This legislation extinguished all aboriginal titles to Alaskan land and all claims based on such titles. It specified that, if the Secretary of the Interior sets aside a utility and transportation corridor for the projected 900-mile Alaska pipeline, neither the State of Alaska nor the Natives may select lands in that corridor.

Representative Elford A. Cederberg of Michigan said, "That we are going to give 40 million acres of land and $900 million to approximately 50,000 people, the size of my hometown, in my opinion, is absolutely an unreasonable settlement for the taxpayers of this country to be saddled with." On the other hand, Congressman John H. Kyl of Iowa commented, ". . .we will have at least taken a step in the right direction to solve the problem of aboriginal people in one of our states, and ultimately we will find the cost is very much less than it has been per capita for the natives in the lower forty-eight. More than that, we give these people their birthright of individuality, of freedom and dignity."[13]

While generous on the face of it, the settlement left many questions unanswered. Will this settlement provide sufficient range for hunting and fishing, which is the present major source of food and income for the natives? What economic and ecological effect will the projected oil field exploitation and the proposed pipeline have on the elk and reindeer and other animals in the region and on the hunting practices of the inhabitants?

Let us hope that this will prove a much fairer settlement than most of the Indians in the other states have received.

THE JAPANESE-AMERICAN EVACUATION: 1942

The authors of *Prejudice, War and the Constitution* conclude that the wartime evacuation of more than 110,000 aliens and citizens from the West Coast in 1942:

> . . .looms as a great and evil blotch upon our national history. The whole vast, harsh, and discriminatory program of uprooting and imprisonment — initiated by the generals, advised, ordered, and supervised by the civilian heads of the War Department, authorized by the President, implemented by Congress, approved by the Supreme Court, and supported by the people — is without parallel in our past and full of ominous forebodings for our future. [14]

These writers viewed the failure of the Supreme Court in its unique position to rule against the discriminatory and forced evacuation as "the greatest failure of all. For the military is preoccupied with war, not with the Constitution and men's rights. . .(The Supreme Court's) self-arrogated and perhaps inherent function is to strike the governmental balance between motion and stability, between new action and old doctrines, between the powers of the nation and men's rights."[15]

JAPANESE-AMERICAN EVACUATION CLAIMS COMMISSION

At its annual meeting in January 1947, the Friends Committee on National Legislation called for the setting up of an Evacuation Claims Commission to make restitution to those who were evacuated by our government. Homer L. Morris filled in the picture in his FCNL testimony, May 28, 1947, before the House Judiciary Subcommittee for speedy enactment of H.R. 2768 to set up an Evacuation Claims Commission.

As a staff member of the American Friends Service Committee, he was on the Pacific Coast from May 19 to September 1, 1942, while the evacuation was going on. Later he was responsible for the organization and management of Japanese relocation hostels in Chicago, Cincinnati and Des Moines. He received the official reports from AFSC representatives after they had visited all the relocation centers.

The evacuees were usually given seven to ten days' notice of the time when they would have to report, with only what they could carry, to a railroad station, with no idea where they were going, how long they would be excluded from their homes, whether they would ever be permitted to return, or whether they might be deported to Japan. This meant that they must sell, lease, rent, loan, store, place in custodianship or dispose in some way of all tangible property.

During the hectic days after evacuation orders were issued, Homer Morris visited many homes of the evacuees. He saw secondhand dealers and competitors buy articles at ridiculously low prices — five to ten dollars for a good electric refrigerator, $400 to $500 for $1500 trucks. Growing crops in the field were sold either at nominal prices or left to be harvested on the shares from which nothing was usually realized. Homer Morris protested the denial of due process and the flagrant disregard of basic civil liberties.

Another eyewitness account was given by Paul B. Johnson to the Senate Judiciary Subcommittee a year later on May 21, 1948. He told one case after another of gross exploitation of the unfortunate victims of the evacuation orders.

The Japanese-American Citizens League under the very able leadership of Mike Masaoka put in strenuous efforts for this legislation. The FCNL kept in close touch with the JACL, followed this bill from its introduction, interviewed Congressmen and Senators and encouraged letters and telegrams from its constituents, and kept plugging for the passage of an evacuation claims commission in the *Washington Newsletter*. In 1947 a revised bill, putting the responsibility for settling claims in the hands of the Attorney General, passed the House on July 23 without a dissenting vote. During 1948 the Senate passed a claims measure so that the process of settling claims could begin.

The sad, sad story of the evacuation claims settlement is briefly summarized in the book *America's Concentration Camps* by Allan R. Bosworth.[16] About 24,000 claims were filed before the 1950 deadline. Because the procedure became bogged down in administrative and technical difficulties, the Japanese-American Citizens League proposed an amendment, authorizing compromise settlements, which became law.

The Attorney General was allowed to compromise and settle claims "up to $2,500 or up to three-quarters of the amount of the claims, whichever was less."[17] By 1955 more than 20,000 claimants had settled for that amount or less. Taking into account the shrinking value of the dollar, the actual settlements amounted to about 5 per cent of the estimated value of property lost on account of the evacuation. Bosworth comments:

> Payments for property losses suffered by the evacuees were still being made seventeen years after legislation was passed authorizing the U.S. Attorney General to receive and adjudicate such claims. The average rate of the settlement was 10 per cent of the amounts asked, based on the 1941 dollar. Nobody was ever paid a cent for losses due to death or personal injury, personal inconvenience, physical or mental hardships, or suffering. Neither was anyone ever compensated for the money he might reasonably have been expected to earn from business profits or gainful employment during the period of detention.

> In 1942, the Federal Reserve Bank of San Francisco estimated that the total loss to the evacuees would approximate $400 million. How closely the 10 per cent rate of settlement followed this estimate is shown by the fact that when the last claim was adjudicated on October 1, 1965, the Government had authorized payment of $38,000,000 to 26,560 claimants. [18]

Such a sum was only a small fraction of the cost of the evacuation. The cost of constructing the assembly centers and ten relocation centers was approximately $70 million. Estimates of the cost of maintaining the evacuees during the three years of detention was around $150 million. So the direct cost, not counting the loss to the evacuees or to the country for what might have been produced, was on the order of $350 million.

One can only regret that the Japanese-American Citizens League and the Friends Committee on National Legislation and the others who worked on compensation were not more persuasive with Congress for at least a fairer settlement for the injustices done.

The *Washington Post* said on October 9, 1965, "The injustice done to the Japanese-Americans will remain forever a stain on American history." And Bosworth concludes, "Today, twenty-four years after the fact, nearly everybody agrees that the mass removal of the Japanese-Americans from the West Coast was militarily unnecessary, that it was a tragic and expensive blunder, and that it accomplished little more than an all-around waste of manpower and gave the Axis Powers excellent, ready-made propaganda material that proved Democracy did not always work."[19]

CIVIL RIGHTS FOR BLACKS AND OTHER RACIAL MINORITIES

Two landmark dates stand out in the century-old struggle, since the Emancipation Proclamation, for simple justice for the Blacks in the United States. On May 17, 1954, the Supreme Court handed down in the case of *Brown vs. Board of Education* its long-awaited but unanimous decision outlawing segregation in public schools. The second landmark was the passage of the Civil Rights Act of 1964, which became law July 2, 1964. Bayard Rustin describes this decade "as the period in which the legal foundations of racism in America were destroyed."[20]

Had justice really operated in the South, segregation would have been abolished by democratic procedures in local school boards, churches, county governments and state legislatures. It should never have been necessary to refer this question to the Supreme Court for a decision.

The Supreme Court decision of 1896 allowing "separate but equal" facilities legalized segregation. In 1954 seventeen Southern and border states still had segregation laws on their statute books and three others allowed local option.[21] While the 1954 decision did not solve the problem, it did put law on the side of integration and made it possible for civil rights advocates to work *within* the law for its implementation.

"You work particularly on the Midwestern Republican Senators" was the assignment given Richard W. Taylor, FCNL Friend-in-Washington in the cooperative effort organized by the Leadership Conference on Civil Rights which mapped the strategy that led to the passage of the 1964 Act. During a 1963-64 sabbatical from Coe College in Iowa, Richard Taylor came to Washington hoping to work largely on issues involving the United Nations, but was soon drawn into the civil rights battle.

Richard Taylor had more than 130 interviews on Capitol Hill during the first six months of 1964 and carried on extensive correspondence with people and organizations in 28 states. He participated in an almost split-second schedule of 14 community meetings set up by the Iowa Council of Churches for ministers and key lay leaders in October 1963 since Bourke B. Hickenlooper and Jack Miller of Iowa were two of the strategic Senators whom we hoped to influence both on cloture and on the bill itself.

For the first time in history, the Senate, on June 10, 1964, voted to close off debate on a civil rights filibuster. The vote for cloture was 71-29. With all 100 Senators present and voting, 67 votes were needed. The filibuster had already lasted 74 days. Since 1938 eleven previous attempts to shut off debate on antilynching, antipoll tax, Fair Employment Practice Commission and literacy test legislation had failed.[22]

The Commission on Religion and Race of the National Council of Churches sponsored a Church Assembly on Civil Rights each morning for about two months prior to the passage of the Civil Rights Act at the Lutheran Church of the Reformation, one block from the Capitol, for worship and daily orientation, in which Richard Taylor took part. More than 1000 clergy and lay leaders from 44 states came at their own expense to attend the services and visit their Senators to stress the moral issues involved.[23] The leadership in charge of the bill in the Senate credited the religious forces of the nation with having played a decisive part in the passage of this bill.

Helen E. Baker from Baltimore testified before the Special Subcommittee of the House Education and Labor Committee on April 20, 1964, on behalf of the American Friends Service Committee and the Friends Committee on National Legislation in support of the Economic Opportunity Act. Representative Edith Green of Portland, Oregon, in the discussion which followed said: "It is good to see you again, Mrs. Baker. I have said many times that I know of no group that is affiliated with any religious organization that shows anywhere near the interest in legislation that the Friends do on Capitol Hill. So, again, my hat is off to you.[24]

Senator Hubert H. Humphrey, who with Senator Everett M. Dirksen had been floor leader on the bill, wrote to Richard Taylor:

> This is just a brief note to express my deep appreciation for your splendid efforts during the civil rights debate in the Senate. Without the unremitting support of the Leadership Conference this bill could never have become law.
> Although we have been engaged in this struggle for many years, the victory has now been won. But this is a victory that presents each of us with the larger task of implementing the law with justice, courage and compassion. . . .

Twenty of his colleagues in the civil rights movement signed a letter, June 12, 1964, expressing their appreciation to Richard Taylor:

> For giving voice, applying intelligence, and providing organization in the legislative struggle to guarantee the Constitutional rights of equal protection of the laws to all Americans. For using his inexhaustible powers of persuasion and intimate knowledge of the legislative process to increase support for enforceable and comprehensive civil rights legislation. . . . [25]

The Civil Rights Act of 1964 contained eleven titles which required that the same standards be applied to all individuals seeking to register and vote; forbade discrimination in public accommodations; authorized the Attorney General to bring a civil suit to compel desegregation of any publicly owned or operated facility; extended the life of the Commission on Civil Rights; required federally assisted programs to eliminate discrimination; and set up an Equal Opportunity Commission and established a Community Relations Service. Even this comprehensive bill did not satisfy the civil rights advocates, and not only was further legislation needed, but implementation and enforcement had to be sought from executive agencies.

There had been "mild" and very inadequate bills passed in 1957 (the first civil rights bill in 82 years), in 1959, and in 1960. But even in 1965 the Senate narrowly rejected an outright ban on poll taxes by a vote of 49-45 and approved instead, 60-20, a Congressional declaration that poll taxes infringe on the constitutional right to vote. The Voting Rights Act of 1965 provided for: (1) suspension of literacy tests or similar devices; (2) appointment of Federal examiners to require local registration of qualified individuals; and (3) challenges by the Attorney General on the constitutionality of local poll taxes.

THE POLL TAX

The FCNL began its almost continuous crusade for civil rights legislation in the second newsletter, December 1943, with a three-page presentation on the pros and cons of the poll tax. The injustice of the poll tax was well stated by Herbert Agar, editor of the *Louisville Courier-Journal*, in his testimony before the Senate Judiciary Subcommittee. He said:

> The poll tax is a symbol of undemocracy in a world which must stand or fall by its fidelity to the democratic creed. The result of a poll tax is to keep the poor from voting, or keep the Negroes from voting, or both. If you keep the poor from voting, you make a joke of Jefferson. If you keep the Negroes from voting, you make a joke of Lincoln. If you do both of these things at the same time, you make a joke of the American idea. . .[26]

The devastating effect of the poll tax and other restrictions on voting, such as the grandfather clause, unfair literacy tests and outright intimidation, is revealed by the mathematics of how many reactionary Congressmen and Senators from the Southern states got elected, stayed in power, inherited important committee posts by seniority and retained their conservative influence.

votes than were cast in electing one Illinois Congressman (Leonard W. Schuetz). In 1942 the average vote cast in a poll tax Congressional election was 10,500 or three per cent of the population. In the average nonpoll tax district, seven times as many persons voted — 77,800 persons or twenty-five per cent of the population. Of the seventy-nine poll tax Congressmen, sixty had no opposition in the 1942 election. Eight Representatives from the states of South Carolina, Georgia and Mississippi were elected by a vote of only one per cent of the population in their district. "Cotton Ed" Smith of South Carolina received the votes of only two per cent of his constituency to assure his re-election as a Senator in 1938 for the sixth time.[27]

Senator James O. Eastland of Mississippi has been chairman of the powerful Senate Judiciary Committee since 1956 and has used his influence many times to obstruct fair and progressive legislation. In figures released on voting in Mississippi by the U.S. Commission on Civil Rights for June 1, 1962, only one Black in Clarke, Chickasaw and Amite Counties was registered, and only two in Panola and Walthall Counties. There were none in Lamar County. In Franklin County out of 3403 eligible whites, 3731 were registered, and in Marion County out of 8997 eligible whites, 9540 were registered (which must have included many laid to rest in cemeteries).[28]

The Mississippi Freedom Democratic Party issued a report on "Statistics of Negro and White Voter Registration in the Five Congressional Districts of Mississippi." According to this summary the percentage of whites county by county who were registered to vote ranged from a low of 46.5 per cent to a high of 100 per cent. But for adult Blacks in the five Congressional Districts which sent representatives to Congress (and who opposed voting rights legislation to overcome this disparity), the percentage of Blacks registered was 2.4, 2.97, 5.8, 2.64 and 11.5.

Congress submitted to the states the Twenty-fourth Amendment to the Constitution on August 27, 1962. The thirty-eighth state to ratify, and thus put the Amendment in effect, was South Dakota on January 23, 1964. At that time only five still had poll taxes as a requisite for voting. After the passage of this amendment, legislatures of four of those states, Alabama, Mississippi, Texas and Virginia set up "dual election" systems in which all citizens could vote for federal officials without payment of a poll tax, as provided by the Twenty-fourth Amendment, but only those who had paid a tax could vote for state and local officials.[29]

LYNCHING

When I stepped off the boat train from LeHavre in Paris on my first trip to Europe in 1930, what caught my eye first was a magazine cover depicting a lynching in Marion, Indiana. Lynching has been defined in most proposed federal antilynching legislation as an act of mob violence which results in the death or maiming of a person or persons in the custody of a peace officer, or suspected of, charged with, or convicted of, a serious crime, often one punishable by death.

Byron Haworth filed testimony on February 4, 1948, for the FCNL with the Subcommittee of the House Judiciary Committee in support of a federal antilynching act, based on his thirteen years of active practice in the Criminal Courts of North Carolina. Byron Haworth later served many years as a judge. He was also named presiding clerk of the Friends United Meeting from 1966 to 1969, the highest office in that branch of the Society of Friends.

As a Southerner, he gave illustrations of gross miscarriage of justice. In his testimony he declared:

> Every citizen of a democratic society has a right to physical freedom and to security against illegal violence. These rights are not now secure for all Americans and will not be so long as communities in which lynchings occur are unwilling to apprehend and punish the lynchers. . . . [30]

Byron Haworth asserted that lynching ought to be declared a federal crime and that it should be the duty of the Federal Government to assume responsibility when local government abdicates to mob rule and terrorism. Local government and local law enforcement officials who, because of a failure to use diligence, permit a lynching to occur should respond in damages to the victim of a lynch mob or to the family of the victim. He concluded his statement by saying that "it should be the concern of our Federal Government to take whatever steps are necessary to bring about equal justice before the law."

Lynching has been outlawed in practice by public opinion, rather than by Federal or State Legislation. Statistics compiled by the Tuskegee Institute indicate that between 1882 and 1962, there were 4736 lynchings, of which 3442 were black and 1294 white. Twice in 1938 the Senate voted against closing debate to even permit a vote on antilynching legislation, once by 51 votes and another time by 46. [31]

THE THOMPSON RESTAURANT CASE

One evening at Howard University, I was introduced to an elderly

Proponents of antipoll tax legislation in 1943 estimated that the poll tax disfranchised 10 million American citizens. It permitted the seating of 50 representatives who were elected by a total of fewer Black woman. "Do you know who I am? I'm the Thompson Restaurant case." I asked Mary Church Terrell to tell me her story.

She was rocking in her rocking chair one day when she said to herself: "Mary Church Terrell, why don't you do something?" She called up David Scull, a Friend in Virginia and printer for the FCNL, and said "Let's do something." So three people went to the Thompson Restaurant on Pennsylvania Avenue in Washington, D.C., to eat. Because two of them were Black, they were refused service.

C. Lloyd Bailey, legislative secretary for the FCNL, wrote the Attorney General on September 28, 1950, urging the Department of Justice to file an *amicus* brief in favor of reversing the decision of Municipal Court Judge Meyers which upheld discrimination. A thirty-six page *amici curiae* brief was filed in the Municipal Court of Appeals for the District of Columbia by eighteen organizations including the Friends Committee on National Legislation.[32] The case went on up to the United States Supreme Court, which handed down a decision on June 8, 1953, outlawing discrimination in restaurants in the District of Columbia. Twenty organizations, including FCNL, followed this decision up on September 26, 1953, by an appeal to the D.C. Board of Commissioners asking them to prohibit racial discrimination in hotels, theaters and other licensed places of public accommodation in the city of Washington. Anticipating the Supreme Court's decision nearly a year later against school desegregation on October 16, 1953, the FCNL, the American Friends Service Committee, and the Joint Social Order Committee of the Friends Meetings of Washington, united with fourteen other organizations in the District of Columbia in an appeal to the D.C. Board of Education. They said in part:

> Whatever decision is made by the (Supreme) Court one thing is and will remain unaltered: the Constitution forbids all discrimination on grounds of race or color. Racial segregation, we are firmly convinced, is both immoral and unconstitutional, and in practice always discriminatory. The "separate but equal" doctrine has been for too long a thin disguise for discrimination. . . . [33]

Mary Church Terrell was more than eighty-five years old when she took the initiative which finally lead to the outlawing of racial discrimination in the capital city. She died in 1954 at the age of ninety.

"The Bank of Selma Welcomes You"

On March 6, 1965, as Cecil Thomas looked up through a cloud of tear gas which overwhelmed the marchers who were demonstrating against the denial of justice to Blacks in Alabama, he saw a sign "The Bank of Selma Welcomes You." And how! He was profoundly interested and active in civil rights and served as Friend-in-Washington from January through May, 1962. He was back in Washington as the moving force behind the organization of the big conference on United States-China relations in Washington in 1965. Later he helped organize the Committee on United States-China Relations which held several important conferences in New York City.

Cecil is remembered by those of us who worked with him as a genial, driving, dynamic personality whose enthusiasm was contagious. One vivid memory is of Cecil sitting at his desk soaking his aching feet in a pan of hot water after walking the marble halls of Congress or marching for justice in the South, with his papers spread out on the floor in a ten-foot radius.

His untimely death from an automobile accident in Africa, August 16, 1969, was a great loss to the peace and civil rights movements in the United States. The FCNL Executive Council said in a memorial minute,

> We are united in a deep sense of sorrow in the loss of this beautiful spirit, strong in the stand for truth, dedicated to energetic work for world peace and understanding, and so full of a deep love of life. . . . We give thanks for his sparkling light and life. . . .

Civil Rights Crusade Intensifies

The FCNL General Committee at its annual meeting in January 1968 raised the area of human and civil rights to a high priority and approved the employment of special staff. Edward T. Anderson began work on July 8, 1968. During the two years before he transferred his activities to Common Cause, he closely monitored the programs of the Department of Health, Education and Welfare, the Department of Housing and Urban Development and the Department of Agriculture.

FCNL concerns on behalf of excluded minorities and lower income groups included welfare reform, meaningful family assistance, plans for a minimum guaranteed income, the elimination of poverty, food stamps and adequate nutrition for the poor, decent housing for the underprivileged, voting rights, civil liberties and opposition to preventive detention and "no-knock" provisions. Emphasis was placed on enforcement and adequate funding of laws already on the books, and fair and equitable administration.

Ed Anderson was in demand as a speaker from Florida to California and testified before three sections of the Republican Platform Committee in 1968 in Miami Beach. He organized six luncheons and dinners during 1970 for Black members of Congressional, agency and departmental staff.

The Poor People's Campaign, led by Ralph Abernathy and the Southern Christian Leadership Conference, brought hundreds of people to Washington in June 1968, when they built Resurrection City on the Mall to dramatize the needs of the poor and the minorities in the United States. Charles H. Harker, associate secretary of the FCNL, accompanied the first 100 leaders to arrive in Washington for a visit to the State Department. Appeals to Dean Rusk were made by the Blacks, Appalachians, whites, American Indians, Mexican-Americans and Puerto Ricans, to improve the conditions of the poor in the United States. Because of its convenient location and facilities for both housing and meetings, the William Penn House, a Quaker conference and seminar center near the Capitol, provided about a thousand overnight accommodations, served more than twenty-five hundred meals, and conducted 25 meetings.

When William G. Lunsford became FCNL program secretary and lobbyist in March 1971 in the area of civil and human rights, *Congressional Quarterly* indicated that his was the twenty-first registration for the Friends Committee since 1946. Edward Anderson and William Lunsford were the second and third Black lobbyists to be registered (and the first for a religious organization) after the dean of them all — Clarence Mitchell of the National Association for the Advancement of Colored People — who has been a close colleague to the FCNL for many years.

William Lunsford's active participation in the Campaign for Adequate Welfare Reform Now, was another example of the intricate relationships with other organizations which characterize the role of the FCNL in Washington. CAWRN was a coalition of church and social interest organizations seeking an adequate assured income for the twenty-five million Americans now below the poverty level. After a very insufficient bill passed the House, it became stalled in the Senate Finance Committee. Major efforts were concentrated on trying to get a good bill through Congress. The Nixon Administration abandoned the drive for a minimum income program, the Senate Finance Committee remained opposed to an adequate bill and in 1973 no measure putting a floor under income for the poverty-stricken millions of Americans had reached the President's desk.

After William Lunsford left the FCNL staff, Harold B. Confer became program secretary in May 1973 for domestic issues including civil rights and civil liberties, assured minimum income and health legislation.

More than one hundred *Newsletters* prior to 1972 carried information or exhortation on some aspect of needed legislation. There were thirty-six testimonies before Congressional committees by twenty-seven different witnesses on the issues referred to in this chapter. The struggle has hardly begun for equality of opportunity in jobs, education, housing and income for disadvantaged groups in this country.

CHAPTER 9

Involving the U.S. in the UN

"Throughout history, it has been the inaction of those who could have acted, the indifference of those who should have known better, the silence of the voice of justice when it mattered most, that has made it possible for evil to triumph."

> Haile Selassie, Emperor of Ethiopia, at the United Nations Security Council meeting, Addis Ababa, Ethiopia, January 28, 1972.

A well-upholstered American, so the story goes, who had been dashing around Europe in the mid-1930's scooping up what information he could on the run, was dining in Geneva after a day's sightseeing there. He turned to his dinner companion and asked, "If a tiny little country like Switzerland can have a League of Nations, why can't a great big country like the United States have one?"

The United States now has a United Nations headquarters in its midst, and how has our country supported it? — for more than twenty-five years in a great variety of ways but unfortunately not nearly as vigorously as it should have. In nearly a hundred testimonies before Congressional committees or in communications to the President, the FCNL has encouraged more support for, and more active participation in, the development of an organized world.

The FCNL goal has been a world federation with sufficient enforceable world law to provide the moral and political authority and power to settle disputes and maintain peace, to achieve general and world-wide disarmament, and increasingly to provide the machinery for international cooperation for working on the major unsolved problems of mankind.

Even a catalog of FCNL activities in this direction would make a long list. FCNL supported moves during World War II which were made in Congress to commit the United States in advance to join the world organization that would emerge after the war.

Continual emphasis has been placed on making the United Nations the cornerstone of U.S. policy and not by-passing it as the U.S. did, for example, in the Vietnam War, and in its military intervention in the Dominican Republic. Delbert and Ruth Replogle, who had been in charge of AFSC relief operations in the Middle East and who had witnessed the crucial importance of the supplies furnished by the United Nations Children's Emergency Fund, came down to champion the continuation of UNICEF when a California Congressman, Donald L. Jackson in 1949, was pressing for its termination. This was a crucial time for the Children's Fund because the United States contribution was about sixty per cent of its budget. (Later, Delbert Replogle was chairman of the FCNL General Committee and Ruth was a lead-off witness on the first round of hearings considering the establishment of the Peace Corps.)

There were sustained efforts to provide more U.S. financing for the UN, including the Food and Agriculture Organization, the World Health Organization campaign against malaria, technical assistance programs, and the UN bond issue of $100 million in 1962.

Difficult questions of FCNL policy were raised by the UN actions in Korea (dealt with in another chapter) and the Congo and by the economic boycott of Rhodesia because of her racial policy.

Frances Neely and Edward Snyder were each released to serve at different times on a Quaker UN Program team so that they could contribute their Washington background and could benefit from the interviews and firsthand observations of United Nations personalities and activities.

INTERVIEWS WITH MIDDLE POWERS ON
PROPOSED UN CHARTER

In April 1945, as the San Francisco Conference was about to convene and after the Dumbarton Oaks Charter proposals had been widely discussed, a group of Friends arranged interviews with officials of some of the middle-sized powers about the role which they might play in the final shaping of the United Nations Charter. Interviews were held in Washington with key officials, most of whom were going to San Francisco, from Australia, Belgium, Brazil, Canada, France, Mexico, the Netherlands and the Philippines. Friends who participated in one or more of these interviews were

Anna Cox Brinton, Edward W. Evans, Roy McCorkel, Richmond P. Miller and I.

The response on the whole was surprisingly cordial. We explained that we had come as representatives of the Society of Friends and that we were deeply concerned about the possible establishment at the San Francisco Conference of a world organization. As members of the Society of Friends, which had a long and devoted concern for peace, we primarily had at heart not only the details of a constitutional charter but more the broad and basic spiritual and moral principles which should underlie the peace.

These officials were reminded that there was a large body of opinion in the United States which hoped for a substantial improvement over the original proposals in the place and power of the General Assembly and in the stressing of justice and human welfare and peaceful change. No nation should set itself above the law and constitute itself a judge in its own case. Stress was laid upon reducing the burden of armaments, the abolition of conscription as a national and international policy and the need for making the Charter easier to amend. We felt the middle-sized powers had an important opportunity to see that the conference was not dominated by the big powers.

We left with them: *1*] the statement of the London Yearly Meeting for Sufferings, March 2, 1945, which had also been approved by the Board of the American Friends Service Committee, April 4; *2*] the statement of the Cleveland Conference of the Federal Council of Churches as representative of widespread sentiment in the churches for improvements in the Charter; *3*] the statement on the Dumbarton Oaks proposals issued by the Friends Committee on National Legislation; *4*] fourteen recommendations for amendments or changes summarized in the April *FCNL Newsletter* drawn from government and private sources.

In a critical appraisal of the Dumbarton Oaks draft Charter, Edith Wynner, in an article in *Common Sense*, December 1944 (page 422), said "Dumbarton Oaks offers the form of international government without the reality. . .Its Assembly cannot legislate, its Court is a shadow, and its Council of great powers can act only against the weak. . .It is limited to enforcement of peace by means of war."

SAN FRANCISCO CONFERENCE

Seven members of the Society of Friends, who were appointed to attend the San Francisco Conference as observers from various Friends organizations, sent a memorandum to all the fifty delegations urging twelve points for consideration in the final text of the Charter.[1] Those who signed the memorandum were David E. Henley, Eleanor Stabler Clarke, Joseph W. Conard, Esther Holmes Jones, Richard R. Wood, Horace G. Alexander, and I.

The memorandum follows:

Justice and Welfare
In the Statement of Principles recognition should be given to the fundamental place of justice and human welfare as the goal of international relations and the basis for extension of international law.

Easier To Amend
The Charter should be easier to amend in order to keep it adaptable to new situations and responsive to the democratic will of the people.

Review of Treaties
It should be made explicit that the general international organization has the power to review, under reasonable safeguards, treaty arrangements.

Universality of Membership
All nations willing to accept the purposes and responsibilities of the organization should thereupon be made members of the organization and a uniform procedure established whereby nonmembers may be admitted.

Strengthening Peaceful Settlement
Provision for resolving conflicts before they become critical should be strengthened by requiring submission of all justiciable disputes to the world court; and by establishing a court of equity, conciliation boards and other agencies competent to dispose of all other disputes.

Human Rights
Provision should be made in the charter for a declaration of fundamental rights and for a commission which should work to secure for all people without discrimination, such rights as freedom of religion and conscience, speech, assembly, and communication, and to a fair trial under just laws.

Abolition of Conscription
Provision should be made for the abolition of conscription for military service, in order to prevent the youth of the world from being brought up to accept as natural and inevitable the use of armed force as an instrument of national policy, and to give reality to the belief expressed in the eighth point of the Atlantic Charter and reaffirmed in the declaration of the United Nations "that all of the nations of the world, for realistic as well as spiritual reasons, must come to the abandonment of the use of force."

Limitation of Armaments
To secure the progressive subordination of force to law, definite

provision should be made in the world organization for limitation and reduction of national armaments and for the control of the international traffic in critical raw materials necessary to wage war.

Dependent Territories

A special commission of the world organization should be charged with the responsibility for promoting the rapid development of all dependent territories to full cultural, economic, and political autonomy within the family of nations. The commission should supervise the administration of all territories not yet able to govern themselves without assistance. It should be interracial in membership, with a majority from countries without colonies.

Enlarged Responsibility of the Assembly

In order to give all nations a full chance to share in the decisions of the world organization, the General Assembly should have the authority to consider any issue raised by any member of the organization including those issues before the Security Council.

Social and Economic Council

In order to increase the usefulness of the Economic and Social Council, we recommend that it be in continuous session.

Development of the Organization

Provisions should be made for a commission under the General Assembly to consider and make recommendations for the development of the international organization by the further delegation of sovereignty in those areas of international activity which are essentially concerns of the world community. [2]

LOBBYING FOR A BETTER UNITED NATIONS CHARTER

There were many nongovernmental consultants and observers at the Conference, representing a wide spectrum of private organizations. Some were more equal than others, which aroused some criticism, because forty-two organizations were given preferential consultant status with supposedly easier access to the U.S. official delegation. Each of the forty-two organizations of national scope was invited to appoint one consultant and two associate consultants. No Friends organization was in the special consultants' group.

At least thirty-nine Protestant religious leaders, representing a great many different churches and other organizations, were present. O. Frederick Nolde and Walter Van Kirk, for example, who were consultants from the Federal Council of Churches, were effective in enlarging the emphasis in the final Charter on human rights and fundamental freedoms. These consultants and observers had considerable influence, not only with the official U.S. delegation, but with delegates from other countries, in pressing for amendments and improvements in the Charter. And when they returned home they could interpret from firsthand observation what had happened at San Francisco.

In regard to the twelve recommendations in the Quaker memorandum of April 30 by the Quaker observers, the Charter as adopted is not easy to amend formally, although some interpretations have changed. There is a provision for a review conference after ten years, but the political climate has not been propitious for such a review. In one draft of the League of Nations Covenant there had been a recommendation for the international abolition of conscription but it did not survive later revisions. No action was taken on conscription at San Francisco, nor since by the United Nations. Among the issues which we did not deal with in the memorandum was the question of the veto, perhaps because voting procedure had not been reached in the deliberations until then. A case could be made for the veto so long as the enforcement provisions envisioned war as the last resort, as in Korea.

Much more was said in the final Charter about human rights than in the Dumbarton Oak versions. An impressive Declaration of Human Rights has been adopted. Various Human Rights Conventions have been drafted and signed but most of them still await ratification by the United States Senate. Less stress on disarmament was evidenced in the UN Charter than in the League Covenant.

A great deal has been done on behalf of dependent territories by the Trusteeship Council. Most of the colonial empires have collapsed since 1945. Most of the former colonies have been freed. UN membership as of September 1973 comprises 134 countries. However there are still many areas of repression, such as Angola, and the right of petition is still circumscribed. The United States still retains unilateral control of the Pacific Trust Territories because of their alleged security importance.

The General Assembly was given more authority than in the Dumbarton Oaks draft. The power of the Assembly was increased later, in part through the initiative of the United States, by the "Uniting for Peace Resolution" in 1958 but it still does not have legislative or taxing powers.

After twenty-eight years the two great weaknesses of the UN remain. In its shadow, but not under its auspices, have been negotiated the limited nuclear test ban treaty and the nuclear nonproliferation treaty, yet there has been no major progress toward general and complete disarmament. While the UN has prevented several small wars, it has not been able to prevent either four Middle East wars or the Vietnam War. The United Nations is a register of the willingness of the Great Powers to cooperate at a given time on a given issue. If the United Nations is weak, and it is, the United States and the Soviet Union have helped to make it weak.

No Full-time Lobby for the UN

In a consultation in New York sponsored by the Carnegie Endowment for International Peace some years ago, I called attention to the fact that there was no full-fledged lobby in Washington to keep the needs and problems of the United Nations before Congress. As a tax-exempt organization, the American Association for the United Nations, now the United Nations Association — U.S.A., is not free to engage in extensive legislative action and has not set up a nontax-exempt affiliate to do round-the-calendar legislative action. For many years this organization had yearly foreign policy conferences in Washington that were extremely valuable to the participants from peace, church and other agencies. The United World Federalists, and more recently the Members of Congress for Peace through Law, have been active on many aspects of developing a more effective world organization to achieve and maintain world peace.

Since the United States plays such a powerful role in the United Nations because of its size and resources, the Congress ought to be much more aware of and much more dedicated to expanding the usefulness of the UN. Much as it has done, and some might say the FCNL has been the most active lobby for the UN, there is much more interpretation that needs to be made.

For example, some years ago I was talking to Senator Frank Carlson of Kansas. He had been governor of his state, representative in Congress and then Senator, and for years a member of the Senate Foreign Relations Committee. He had never even visited the United Nations! I passed on this information to the State Department, and not long afterwards, he was appointed as one of the U.S. delegates to the General Assembly where he would have the experience of participation in the Assembly. I have no way of knowing whether my suggestion had anything to do with his appointment. I wonder if more than half of the members of Congress have even visited the United Nations headquarters in New York or have any deep understanding, appreciation and concern for what goes on, or does not go on, there.

Throughout its history the FCNL has tried to take a realistic but hopeful view of the UN and to give it support wherever support seemed justified. In the four-page supplement to the *Newsletter* No. 21, July 4, 1945, analyzing the provision of the Charter, I wrote:

> So as the Unites States joins the United Nations Organization it is evident that machinery will work only as there is the will and the spirit to make it work and to improve it. We can face earnestly the long process ahead to develop a democratic and effective world system and begin now to build public opinion for the additional steps that need to be taken and the revisions that should be made. There is the gigantic task of transforming a league of victors into a democratic world organization. Even Switzerland and Sweden were not invited to attend the San Francisco Conference nor to be among the original signatories. . . .Both the United States and Britain seem to be planning gigantic increases in armaments over prewar levels instead of campaigning for world-wide reduction and international abolition of conscription. . . .The claim of the U.S. Navy for unilateral control over such strategic areas as it may desire seriously weakened the Trusteeship Council and gave the Russians, for example, too much moral justification for their actions in manipulating their borders and their neighbors for strategic and security reasons. . . .

FCNL PROPOSALS TO WHITE HOUSE CONFERENCE ON
INTERNATIONAL COOPERATION: 1965

On behalf of the FCNL, Edward F. Snyder submitted six proposals for strengthening U.S. support of the United Nations and the process by which nations and peoples should work together, to the White House Conference on International Cooperation in November 1965. The National Citizens Commission on International Cooperation had invited the FCNL and other organizations to respond to President Lyndon B. Johnson's request to "search, explore, canvass, and discuss every conceivable approach and avenue of cooperation that could lead to peace." The recommendations included:

1. Ratification by the Senate of the four UN Conventions on Abolition of Slavery and of Forced Labor, the Political Rights of Women, and Prevention and Punishment of Genocide.

2. Repeal of the "self-judging" reservation to the World Court treaty, popularly known as the Connally Resolution from its author, former Senator Tom Connally of Texas. If it repealed this reservation, the United States would no longer retain the authority to judge whether a dispute was within its domestic jurisdiction but would accept the compulsory jurisdiction of the International Court

of Justice. This action would go far in upholding a slowly growing system of international law.

3. Creation of a special nongovernmental committee to recommend specific East-West Cooperative projects. These projects could involve international economic development, scientific cooperation and an intensified attack on world hunger to close the world food gap.

4. Traveling international exhibits of arts and crafts. Representatives of every nation should participate in their planning and execution, thus increasing international cooperation and ensuring the best possible exhibitions. This project could be done under the auspices of the United Nations Economic and Social Council.

5. Exchange of parliamentarians between the United States and the Soviet Union.

6. Conversion of the U.S. bacteriological warfare plants into a world health center as an initiative toward peace, starting with Fort Detrick near Frederick, Maryland. Research at Fort Detrick under the World Health Organization might then become part of a large-scale cooperative research drive against such diseases as cholera, malaria, tuberculosis, smallpox, yellow fever and other plagues of mankind. Ratification was urged of the Geneva Protocol of 1925 prohibiting the use of chemical and bacteriological weapons in wartime.[3]

President Nixon announced on October 16, 1971, that the biological warfare facility would be converted into a cancer research center. The government claims that only research on defense against biological warfare and the necessary stocks of biological agents for defense are being maintained by the military.

The ratification of the 1925 Geneva protocol has been held up in the Senate because of the insistence of the Nixon Administration that it wanted to retain the right to use herbicide defoliants and tear gas. More than 90 nations — including the Soviet Union and every major power except the U.S. — have ratified the 1925 prohibition against first use in combat of "asphyxiating, poisonous or other gases and all analogous devices." More on recent developments in chemical and bacteriological warfare (CBW) is related in the chapter on disarmament.

Tenth Anniversary of the United Nations: 1955

One day as I was working at home, the telephone rang. It was Edward Snyder reporting that Representative Frances Bolton from

Cleveland, Ohio, had just been in touch with him. She was ranking Republican member of the House Foreign Affairs Committee and former delegate to the United Nations General Assembly. She wanted suggestions for a peace message from Congress to the San Francisco Tenth Anniversary of the United Nations. The text was to be not too long, not too controversial, appropriate to the occasion and one which could pass both Houses within the following week.

I drafted a resolution, Edward improved it a little and took it over to her; she modified it slightly and introduced it as House Concurrent Resolution 157 which passed on June 13. A companion resolution (S. Con. Res. 38) sponsored by Senator H. Alexander Smith went through the Senate the following day. President Eisenhower used this resolution in beginning his address at the opening meeting of the Tenth Anniversary observance in San Francisco on June 20, 1955.

Hope deferred is one of the realities of a lobbyist's life. But hope is better than despair. The resolution began with this paragraph.

> . . .it is the hope and prayer of the American people that peace will be established among all the nations of the world, thus avoiding the carnage and destruction of war, making possible the lifting of the burden of arms and thereby freeing the energies of mankind to work more effectively to overcome the ravages of hunger, disease, illiteracy, and poverty. . . . [4]

UNITED NATIONS TWENTIETH ANNIVERSARY: 1965

As the twentieth anniversary of the United Nations approached, Edward Snyder encouraged Representative Don Fraser on the House Foreigns Affairs Committee and Senator Frank Church to introduce resolutions commemorating the UN Twentieth Anniversary and urging Congress to provide a Congressional delegation to participate in the White House Conference on the International Cooperation Year. The House resolution was co-sponsored by Dante Fascell of Florida, Frances Bolton of Ohio, and Peter Frelinghuysen of New Jersey. Church's co-sponsors were Senators Fulbright, Hickenlooper, Clark, Aiken and Cooper.

The resolution declared that "Congress rededicates itself to the principles of the United Nations and to the furtherance of international cooperation within the framework of law and order." If Congress had taken this resolution seriously, they would not have acquiesced in what has happened in Vietnam since 1965.

This joint resolution further urged the executive branch to "1) review with a high sense of urgency the current state of international peacekeeping machinery with a view to making specific suggestions for strengthening this machinery; 2) review other major elements of international community and cooperation with a view to making specific suggestions to promote the growth of institutions of international cooperation and law and order, and 3) review urgently the status of disarmament negotiations with a view to further progress in reducing the dangers and burden of competitive national armaments." In regard to reducing the burden of armaments Congressional appropriations for military activities have risen from $54 billion in calendar year 1964 to $80 billion in 1968, and $83 billion in 1972. This is progress in reverse.

Four spokesmen for religious action groups addressed a letter to President Lyndon B. Johnson on June 17, 1965, urging several points for consideration in his address at the twentieth anniversary meeting in San Francisco. The letter was signed by Herman Will, Jr., Associate General Secretary, General Board of Christian Concerns of the Methodist Church; Rabbi Richard G. Hirsch, Director, Religious Action Center, Union of American Hebrew Congregations; Homer A. Jack, Director, Department of Social Responsibility, Unitarian Universalist Association and Edward F. Snyder for the FCNL.

At a time when there is much criticism, the letter said, that the United States has not acted sufficiently through international channels, a strong statement of faith and confidence in the future of the UN can have a most salutary effect on the American public and on world opinion. Hope was expressed that he might meet the Secretary General there. Tribute might be paid to the largely unknown but important UN social and economic development programs. The President was urged to try to resolve the impasse over Article 19 on peacekeeping operations. The writers of the letter said they believed in regard to Vietnam "that the UN can play an important role in bringing about a cease fire and beginning the process of negotiation. We urge you to ask the Secretary General to use his good offices in this direction. . .It might in fact be the crucial element in achieving a cease-fire before the United States becomes so fully engaged in a land war that it cannot extricate itself without vast cost." How prophetic this recommendation was and how sad that it was not accepted!

UN Bonds: 1962

On U.S. China policy, the FCNL was a strong dissenter on the position of the State Department and of the Presidents over the years. But on the UN bond issue, the Committee went all out on the side of the President's proposal for meeting the UN financial emergency.

It costs money to fight a war. It also costs money to avert one. When the Congo became independent in July 1960, it became a potential arena of conflict among outside powers. Belgium's troops returned in an attempt to restore order. The Soviet Union sent arms, trucks and planes to the Congo at the personal request of Premier Patrice Lumumba. There was great danger of a major military confrontation between the Soviet Union and the United States.

To head off a showdown situation the United Nations, with U.S. Government support, sent in 20,000 troops. It also sent large numbers of teachers, engineers, doctors, dentists, lawyers, business and trade experts, agricultural specialists, road builders, mechanics and communications and transportation experts. Because of these actions in the Congo and the UN Emergency Force in the Gaza strip in the Middle East the United Nations faced a deficit of $200 million. As a result, a bond issue was proposed to tide the UN over, partly because of the failure of France, the Soviet Union and some other countries to pay their share of these "peacekeeping" actions. The United States was asked to subscribe one half of the amount, or $100 million. As Norman Cousins said in a *Saturday Review* editorial, February 10, 1962, in supporting the idea, "It is less than one-fifth of one percent of the cost of putting a man on the moon. Finally, it is less than it cost to fight a war in Korea for only one week."

There was intense debate in Congress over whether the money should be granted as a short-term loan, which would have left the UN in about the same morass in two or three years' time, or a loan to be repaid over twenty-five years from regular assessments. The long-term loan idea finally won out.

President Kennedy in his State of the Union message in January 1962 made a strong plea for Congressional support of the bond issue. Congress was very reluctant to grant this authority, in part because they were concerned over the growing power of the UN General Assembly and resentful of the irresponsibility of UN members who vote for special programs but refuse to help pay the bill. Many members of Congress insisted that whatever the United States did should be matched by other countries. Others took the position that the United States should do what seemed the right thing regardless of what other nations were willing to do and not reduce its actions and its leadership to the lowest common denominator.

Negotiations over these issues were long and involved and the

FCNL participated in various ways, part of which are enumerated here. The staff worked very closely with other nongovernmental organizations in rallying support for the President's proposal. Throughout the year, representatives from a dozen organizations met frequently to share information, plan strategy and confer with State Department representatives.

An FCNL staff member and a representative of the National Council of Churches met with Senator George D. Aiken of Vermont, whose criticisms of UN financing had been stimulating increased opposition to the President's proposal. When it was learned that the FCNL was the only nongovernmental organization which had asked to be heard by the Senate Foreign Relations Committee on the bond issue, the staff telephoned other interested groups, warning them that hearings had been scheduled. On February 14, fourteen nongovernmental witnesses appeared before the Committee.

When the bill in support of the $100 million bond issue was before the Senate, FCNL kept a running record of the position of Senators for the benefit of all groups that were trying to rally support for the proposal. Later an "Estimate of House Attitudes on UN Bonds" was compiled and was widely used as a lobbying guide by other nongovernmental bodies and Government officials.

When the Senate bill reached the House, FCNL cooperated with other organizations in urging leading citizens to sign a joint letter in support of the UN bond purchase. The letter was drafted by FCNL and signed by Rabbi E. Balfour Brickner, Norman Cousins, Oscar A. de Lima, Clark M. Eichelberger, Ernest A. Gross, Murray Gross, Mrs. Charles Hymer, Arthur Larson, Murray D. Lincoln, James G. Patton, Walter P. Reuther, Herman W. Steinkraus, James J. Wadsworth, Paul W. Walter and E. Raymond Wilson. It was submitted to 65 newspapers across the country and carried in the letters-to-the-editor columns of such papers as the *Washington Post* and the *New York Times*. Copies were sent to the House leadership.

In a related endeavor, Denise O'Connor prepared a study on "Who Supports UN Bonds?" quoting Dwight D. Eisenhower, Harry S. Truman, Henry Cabot Lodge, Dean Rusk, Eugene Black, Adlai E. Stevenson, John J. McCloy and James J. Wadsworth. The publication also listed 23 organizations which supported the U.S. purchase of UN bonds. It was distributed to each member of the House, just before the debate began, by volunteers representing nine nongovernmental groups.

Close contact was maintained with the Executive Branch throughout the extended debate. In addition to regular strategy meetings with State Department representatives, Cecil Thomas, Friend-in-Washington, went to New York in January to discuss the bond issue with Ambassador Philip M. Klutznick of the U.S. Mission to the UN. In August Edward Snyder warned the White House of various Congressional criticisms and of the need to bring some Congressional members into any future sessions on UN financing so that Congressional-Executive Branch antagonisms might be reduced.

Testimonies were presented to both House and Senate Foreign Relations Committees. I told the Senate Committee on February 19 that:

> You can appreciate the fact that the UN Congo military operations present some difficulties to us as Friends. What many of us want is a world system of security, disarmament and law where enforcement procedures would operate upon the individual by true police action under established law. The Congo operations represent a great advance over the Korean War, but are not the ideal toward which the world should strive in the peaceful settlement of disputes.
>
> We support the Administration's request for funds for UN bonds because it is obvious that the United Nations must become financially solvent and continue in existence if it is to grow into a truly effective instrument of law and order in a disarmed world. . .$100 million is actually a very small sum. . .Last year the United States gave the Republic of China, Italy, Japan, Korea and Turkey more than $100 million each in military aid.
>
> One Polaris submarine costs about $105 million; a Forrestal class super type aircraft carrier, about $118 million. Regular city police services are also expensive. Policing activities in the city of New York cost $161 million in 1960. [5]

Elton Atwater, head of the Department of Political Science at Pennsylvania State University, testified on July 18 before the House Foreign Affairs Committee from the background of two years as representative of the Friends World Committee at the UN. Not only did he support the bond issue but spoke at length on the value of channeling more economic assistance through UN agencies. Then he took up the need for more adequate and assured financing for the United Nations in the future. He mentioned three new possible sources of revenue, among others: exclusive authority to tax outer space traffic and communications; royalties from natural resources found in the oceans or under the ocean floor beyond the territorial jurisdiction of national governments or resources and transportation routes in the polar regions; and third, a small tax on each passport or visa issued. He urged the committee to undertake a study of independent sources of revenue for a more reliable long-term system of UN financing.

The March, May and June *Washington Newsletters* reminded friends of the UN that Congressmen needed to receive more letters. In March a special memo was sent to *Action Bulletin* subscribers in nine states where one or both Senators were undecided. Special Action Bulletins were mailed out April 18 and August 1, suggesting immediate efforts. North Carolina Yearly Meeting sent telegrams to all 12 North Carolina Representatives, and the Peace and Service Committee of New York Yearly Meeting sent letters to 57 Representatives.

After the bill authorizing the UN Bond was finally passed, Assistant Secretary of State Harlan Cleveland wrote to the FCNL: "We in the administration are warmly aware of how much you helped to give effective bipartisan support for the UN."[6]

A compromise measure was finally approved September 19 requiring matching by other nations. The Senate approved a more liberal bill 70-22. A motion to kill the bond bill entirely was beaten down in the House by 48 votes. The bill was finally passed 216-134. Other UN bills died in Committee: a proposal to eliminate the "Connally reservation" on the World Court, two bills to authorize the Treasury to float UN peace bonds for sale to the general public on which the FCNL had done considerable work, and a bill by Edith Green of Oregon to permit citizens to deduct contributions to the UN from their income tax.

SEATING OF THE PEOPLE'S REPUBLIC OF CHINA

For 22 years preceding the momentous reversal in 1971 of U.S. policy toward the People's Republic of China by President Nixon, the FCNL had been campaigning for such a change. It was not sympathy for Chinese communist idealogy, but a belief that international disputes should be brought to the conference table and resolved by procedures of the UN Charter, that led FCNL to champion Chinese membership in the United Nations.

"We are not so much against you, we are merely ahead of you," was a frequent comment of mine to State Department officials in briefings when some of us would take a completely opposite point of view to the adamant position of the administration and of the Department of State. We kept telling the State Department bureaucracy that we knew they knew that they would have to make a U-turn and that we would like to hurry up that turn.

At first there were very few of us — Philip Schiff of the National

Jewish Welfare Board, Annalee Stewart of the Women's International League for Peace and Freedom, Norman Thomas of the Post War World Council and I. We persistently argued for universal membership in the United Nations. Gradually we were joined by others.

A slight thaw began under President Johnson and Vice President Humphrey when it was announced that certain scientific and health and medical personnel might be given passports to go to Mainland China. At one time the U.S. Government was willing to grant passports to newsmen, hopefully on a reciprocal basis. But since the Chinese wanted at that time to admit only journalists who would report news favorable to the Communist regime, no arrangements for such an exchange were concluded. For years the Friends in the United States wanted to send a goodwill mission to China, as the British Friends had done in 1955, but the Chinese government did not respond favorably until 1972.

Issues of the *FCNL Washington Newsletter* for September 1953, October 1958, August 1961, and February 1966, were devoted to a consideration in depth of the issues involved in restoring trade and diplomatic relations with one quarter of the human race and in seating the People's Republic of China in the UN.

After more than two decades of cultivated hostility on both sides, President Nixon on January 10, 1971 ended the trade embargo. On July 15 came a surprise announcement that the President would visit Peking in 1972. Faced with probable defeat in the UN General Assembly, the Nixon Administration declared on August 2 that the United States would support the seating of the People's Republic of China coupled with a retention of a UN seat for Taiwan. The General Assembly seated the People's Republic and expelled the Taiwan Nationalist Government.

In 1973 the People's Republic of China is an active member of the UN Security Council and of the UN General Assembly. Diplomatic missions, short of full Embassy status, have been exchanged. Many American groups have visited China, and it is reported that hundreds of thousands of U.S. citizens have applied for visas or expressed an interest in going to China. No serious discussions on disarmament have been undertaken with the Chinese, nor have the Chinese been invited to join the SALT disarmament talks between the United States and the Soviet Union, nor have they participated in the Eighteen Nation disarmament talks in Geneva.

SUPPORTING THE UN: 1963-1970

The FCNL urged government officials to concentrate less on the relatively small amount the UN costs the United States and to pay more attention to ways of strengthening the UN so that its potential could be realized as keeper of the peace and supporter of the weak and needy.

In 1963, when the House Foreign Affairs Committee was marking up the foreign aid bill, there was some indication that the Committee might add two anti-UN amendments which would 1) limit U.S. contributions to all UN voluntary aid and relief programs to one-third of their budgets, instead of about forty per cent for some and 2) prohibit any contribution to international organizations that aid Communist nations. Constituents were contacted in some of the home districts of the Congressmen serving on the House Foreign Affairs Committee and were urged to ask their Congressmen to oppose these amendments when they were offered in the Committee. The Committee did adopt an amendment prohibiting contributions to any international organization that gave economic aid to Cuba, but this amendment was eliminated in conference. The United Nations Development Program under Paul Hoffman was helping Cuba in diversifying her agriculture and in other training programs.

The amendment to limit U.S. contributions to one-third of the UN budgets was not added by the Committee, but it was narrowly defeated on the House floor, 157-168. Prior to the vote, Edward Snyder expressed FCNL's concern to Representative Durward Hall of Missouri who sponsored the amendment, and to Gerald Ford, leading Republican. He provided materials to Representative Dante Fascell, who led the opposition to the amendment.

When a House Appropriations Subcommittee cut the budget for U.S. contributions to UN technical assistance, relief and peacekeeping activites some 24 per cent below what the United States had already agreed to pay, FCNL joined other nongovernmental organizations in urging leading Congressmen to press for a restoration of these funds on the floor of the House. Two efforts to restore all or most of these funds were rejected 105-149 and 89-149. About half the amount was restored in conference.

In 1964, another national election year, as always, planks were prepared for presentation by the FCNL to the party platform committees. Urging a high priority on international affairs, the FCNL plank stated, "The United Nations should be regarded as the cornerstone of foreign policy in our relations with other states in negotiations, in the settlement of continuing problems as well as in crisis situations, and in economic and social development programs."

On June 30, FCNL telephoned 77 members of the House, asking them to take leadership in defeating an amendment by Otto Passman of Louisiana to cut $15 million out of the $134 million budgeted for UN technical assistance. It was not cut. Letters were written to three Senators and Secretary of State Dean Rusk at the end of June, urging them to give favorable consideration to establishment of the UN Training and Research Institute proposed by Secretary General U Thant.

In mid-August, FCNL encouraged a number of Representatives to oppose H.R. 5990, which as originally proposed would have limited solicitation in the District of Columbia to programs that promote the health, welfare and morale of the District itself. This meant that solicitations could no longer be conducted for such organizations as CARE and UNICEF. The bill was liberalized on the floor.

Steps which were taken in 1965 to celebrate the Twentieth Anniversary and the International Cooperation Year have already been outlined in this chapter. In another effort to stress public concern and support for the UN, FCNL joined in circulating a petition, initiated by the United World Federalists, calling upon the President to help save and strengthen the United Nations when it was under severe attack. Edward Snyder and Sanford Z. Persons of the United World Federalists presented a sampling of the petitions to the White House, June 15.

Experts on the Quaker United Nations Program were invited to act as witnesses before Congress. Robert Cory, program associate, and later co-director of William Penn House in Washington, testified April 20 on the UN Charter amendments enlarging the UN Security and Economic and Social Councils. William Huntington, director of the Quaker UN program, testified for the FCNL and AFSC May 11 on the planning for peace resolution submitted by Senator Joseph Clark of Pennsylvania and 25 other Senators.

A letter was sent in early March 1965 to the House Foreign Affairs Committee supporting the President's request for $365 million in new authorization for U.S. bilateral technical assistance and contributions to UN relief and development activities and making suggestions for improvement of the foreign aid program. Congressional and nongovernmental representatives were called together June 16, to hear Chief Adebo, head of the UN financing team, discuss the UN financial crisis. Staff members met with UN Ambassador James Roosevelt in New York, November 5, to discuss liaison between Congress and the United Naitons, the human rights conventions, UN assistance programs and China and Vietnam policies.

In 1967, the Senate ratified only one of the Human Rights Conventions, the Supplementary Convention on Slavery. As part of years of campaigning for the various UN conventions by the FCNL, James M. Read, president of Wilmington (Ohio) College and former Deputy High Commissioner of Refugees, urged the Senate Foreign Relations Committee to report out the UN Human Rights Conventions on Slavery, Forced Labor and Political Rights of Women and implored the United States to "stand up and be counted with a recommitment to human rights."

Senator Mark O. Hatfield of Oregon developed a great interest in the possibility of the United Nations' using volunteers like the Peace Corps. On November 2, he met at William Penn House with leaders of organizations which sponsor volunteers abroad to explore the problems involved in such an undertaking.

UN peacekeeping was emphasized in 1968. When the Senate was considering a resolution calling for U.S. support for a permament UN peacekeeping force, Robert Cory brought Barry Tackeberry, former officer in charge of Canadian-UN peacekeeping forces, to Washington April 30-May 1 for conversations with Congressional staff and with organizations preparing to testify at the Senate Foreign Relations Committee hearings. Dorothy Hutchinson spoke on behalf of the Women's International League for Peace and Freedom on May 2 in support of a permanent UN peacekeeping force.

The January 1969 *FCNL Newsletter* suggestion that voluntary personal contributions be sent to Congressmen for the UN Development Program brought many responses. Paul G. Hoffman, UN DP Administrator wrote the FCNL an appreciation letter.

A group of Friends with extensive experience in international assistance programs drafted a four-page document on "Encouraging International Development — Challenge to the Conscience and Common Sense of America" which was adopted as a policy statement at the FCNL annual meeting, January 18, 1970. The statement dealt with establishing priorities, the sharing of skills, the need for social development to keep pace with economic development, adequate capital, trade and investment, family planning and population control and food. On channels for international development, the statement recommended:

The need for assistance is so great that all possible channels must be used — multinational, bilateral, public and private. Each can play an important role in individual situations. We see special advantages in using international channels which strengthen international institutions, reinforce the concept of international cooperation, and are able to draw upon resources and personnel from a wider range than bilateral or national programs. Hence we strongly support the work of the "family" of UN development programs such as the United Nations Development Program, the Specialized Agencies, the World Bank and its affiliated International Development Association and regional economic commissions. [7]

This was read into the *Congressional Record* (p. 9731) by Representative Jonathan B. Bingham of New York on March 26, 1970, with the comment:

. . .All too many Americans believe that we can ignore the increasing gap between the rich nations and the poor nations. . .Revolutions, civil wars, wars of national liberation, all feed on the discontent caused by the abject poverty of much of the world's population. Fortunately, groups like the Friends Committee on National Legislation, whose policy report is included below, are aware of this need to build a stable community in which the distribution of wealth more closely approximates that of equals than of clients and masters.

Robert Cory was a witness May 12, 1970, for the FCNL and AFSC before the House Subcommittee on International Organization and Movements, which was evaluating the first twenty-five years of U.S. participation in the United Nations and preparing suggestions for its future. He spoke in behalf of: 1) research and training on the processes of mediation; 2) the establishment of a UN voluntary service; 3) more adequate funding for work with refugees; and 4) the use for international development of international Monetary Fund drawing rights. [8]

The United Nations reached its twenty-fifth anniversary in 1970 with many noteworthy achievements in international cooperation but with a long way to go before fulfilling the hopes of the world as a fully effective instrument for preventing war, maintaining peace and achieving general disarmament. The Vietnam War was winding down, the Middle East was still a tinder box, and the arms race was unchecked, although the Strategic Arms Limitations Talks (SALT) were still going on in an atmosphere of secrecy and guarded optimism.

For some time Robert Cory had been specializing in possible rights of the UN to the resources of the seabed. He attended a meeting of the UN Committee on the Seabed in Geneva on August 10, 1970, and kept in touch with Robert Dockery, the observer for the Senate Foreign Relations Committee who was dealing with the proposals of President Nixon for an International Seabed Resources Authority. The FCNL is pursuing this concern on ocean resources under the leadership of Samuel and Miriam Levering.

SAVE OUR SEAS

A very important new initiative in developing the reign of law was undertaken by the FCNL in 1972-73 with the launching of the Save Our Seas legislative project under the direction of Samuel Levering, who has been serving as "Friend-in-Washington." Miriam Levering is secretary of the separate Ocean Education Project. The Leverings are an outstanding husband and wife team who have given active leadership in many Quaker activities. For sixteen years Samuel Levering had been chairman of the FCNL Executive Committee until undertaking the SOS program.

President Nixon said on May 23, 1970:

> The nations of the world are now facing decisions of momentous importance to man's use of the oceans for decades ahead. At issue is whether the oceans will be used rationally and equitably and for the benefit of mankind or whether they will become an arena of unrestrained exploitation and conflicting jurisdictional claims in which even the most advantaged states will be losers. . . .The stark fact is that the law of the sea is inadequate to meet the needs of modern technology and the concerns of the international community. If it is not modernized multilaterally, unilaterial action and national conflict are inevitable.

The aim of the Save Our Seas Program is to encourage the United States to exert its maximum influence toward making the projected UN third Law of the Sea Conference, which opens June 1974 in Caracas, Venezuela, a landmark in protecting the huge resources of the oceans for the benefit of humanity as a whole, without exploiting them for the profits of a few nations or corporations.

One major problem is to iron out the conflicting claims for exclusive jurisdiction for fishing or mineral rights or for navigation. The historical three-mile limit has been expanded to a claim of two hundred miles by Ecuador, for example.

Eighteen percent of the world's petroleum already comes from the seabed and it is estimated that 2200 billion barrels could be secured which would make the oceans the largest oil potential. The estimated $18 billion fish catch constitutes an important part of the world's scarce protein. Some fish stocks have already been wiped out by overfishing, and others are threatened. Another rich resource is the estimated one and a half trillion tons of manganese nodules which contain nickel, copper, and cobalt — ores whose land sources are rapidly being used up.

The policy of the administration, for the most part, has been liberal and forward-looking. Major legislative efforts have included initiating and helping to get good resolutions passed, by both houses of Congress, and assisting in bottling up legislation aimed at enriching U.S. mining corporations at the expense of the rest of the world.

A big question before the Conference will be what will happen to the "common heritage"? In 1970, the United Nations unanimously adopted a declaration that seabed resources beyond national jurisdiction are the common heritage of mankind to be governed by an International Authority, with revenues to be used for international community purposes, and particularly for developing nations.

Among the goals for the Law of the Sea Conference are:

1. Agreement by the end of 1975 on a new and just law of the sea.
2. The agreement should be viewed by the developing nations as fair and just with substantial revenues for the international community and especially for developing nations.
3. Standards and controls over pollution and protection for the environment.
4. Freedom of the seas for navigation, scientific research and enjoyment.
5. Effective conservation of fish and other marine life.
6. Provision for compulsory settlement of disputes and the creation of an effective International Seabed Resources Authority.

A prestigious United States Committee for the Oceans has been organized with former Supreme Court Justice Arthur J. Goldberg and Governor Russell W. Peterson as honorary chairmen. Miriam Levering spent several weeks in Geneva in 1973 attending preliminary meetings and talking with representatives of many nations under the auspices of the educational affiliate, the Ocean Education Project.

These programs of education and of legislation were launched with the generous financial support of William Fischer and Barton Lewis, who were deeply concerned about the strategic opportunity now to think of the good of humanity as a whole before the last remaining great natural resources were gobbled up by private interests.

CHAPTER 10

The Birth of Two New Organizations: 1960-1961

. . .I want you to know that my Government and indeed the people of Botswana deeply value service which the Peace Corps have provided in this country. . . . When I read and hear of the growing disenchantment in the developed nations over external aid and technical assistance, when I learn of the international resources which are being consumed in military confrontations, I cannot help wishing that there were a few more people who could recognize the impact which fifty-two young men and women are capable of making in a country such as mine. . . .

> — Seventh Annual Report of the Peace Corps, June 30, 1968, excerpt from a letter to U.S. Senator E.L. Bartlett from Q.K.J. Masire, Acting President of Botswana and Minister of Development.

During 1961 two forward-looking governmental agencies were launched with energetic FCNL support — the Peace Corps and the Arms Control and Disarmament Agency (ACDA).

SUMMARY

The Peace Corps held great promise of utilizing the idealism of American youth in overseas projects. Hungry, illiterate, diseased people in disadvantaged countries wanted a better life and could benefit from the warm, hearty cooperation of young people. In the legislative history of the Peace Corps, Congressman Henry Reuss credited the Friends Committee with having tipped the scales in Congress for reporting out a bill to study the idea of a Peace Corps and for its enactment.

Humanity was threatened with being poisoned by nuclear fallout or exterminated by nuclear war. Through scores and scores of Congressional interviews and nation-wide appeals, the FCNL clamored for an organization in the government to challenge the spiraling arms race. Large nations were obsessed with the power struggle and fearful of being outclassed in armaments or of being drawn into war because of military weakness. The Arms Control and Disarmament Agency was designed to work on these most difficult and baffling problems in order to make progress toward general disarmament. There had been a few people in the State Department who had concentrated on disarmament since the end of World War II, but it was not until the creation of the ACDA that a sizeable staff and sustained attention have been directed toward the unsolved problems of ending the arms race.

In their accomplishments to date, the Peace Corps and the ACDA have not fulfilled all the great hopes and expectations with which they began. Indispensable goals remain to be achieved in helping disadvantaged people overcome their handicaps and in beating swords into ploughshares.

Origin of the Peace Corps

The basic concept of youth serving humanity in other countries had been under considerable discussion for a decade, but the Peace Corps idea was dramatically and politically crystallized on Wednesday, November 2, 1960, less than a week before the Presidential election. At the end of a frenetic day of campaigning, John F. Kennedy called on his 25,000 tumultuous supporters in the Cow Palace in San Francisco to help establish a pool of "talented young men willing to serve. . .in the underdeveloped world." He appealed for "Ambassadors of Peace" who "could work, building good will, building the peace." His suggestion was hailed on television and radio and front-paged on countless newspapers. Thirty thousand people wrote in to support the idea.[1]

Back in 1957 the idea for such a program had struck Congressman Henry S. Reuss of Milwaukee while on a foreign aid tour of the jungles of Cambodia. He was impressed by the respect and love which the native population had for four young American school teachers who were going from village to village setting up elementary schools. Whenever he outlined his proposal for a "Youth Corps" to college audiences, the response was enthusiastic.

Thus, in January 1960, Reuss had introduced legislation calling for an appropriation of $10,000 to study the feasibility of a Point Four "Youth Corps." Senator Richard Neuberger of Oregon introduced a companion bill in the Senate. Ruth H. Replogle, testifying in March before the House Foreign Affairs Committee on behalf of FCNL and the Board on Peace and Social Concerns of the Five Years Meeting, was the first witness before Congress to endorse the Reuss Bill. FCNL witnesses appeared before three other Committees on a similar mission. Later, I testified before both the House Appropriations Subcommittee and the Senate Appropriations Committee in favor of the proposed study and sent a strong letter to twenty-one Senators urging an appropriation.

In the meantime Peter Grothe had been compiling a review for Senator Humphrey of the experiences of organizations, such as the American Friends Service Committee, the Brethren Service Commission and the Mennonite Central Committee in sending young people abroad in service projects. FCNL provided what information it could and encouraged Senator Humphrey to press for action by Congress. On June 15, 1960, Humphrey offered a bill in the Senate to establish a Peace Corps. He insisted that enough was already known about such a program to proceed without the recommended study. The Humphrey bill envisioned a 500-man corps the first year, growing into a 5,000-man corps after five years. Although it was not acted on by Congress, this proposal gave significant impetus to the general discussion of a possible Peace Corps.

Within a week after the introduction of the measure by Senator Humphrey, FCNL hosted a two-hour strategy session composed of a dozen people, including representatives from the Congressional offices of Humphrey and Reuss, International Voluntary Service, the American Friends Service Committee, Americans for Democratic Action, and the National Council of Churches. The proposal, which had been included in the foreign aid bill, by Congressman Reuss for a $10,000 study had been defeated on the House floor June 10, five months before Kennedy made his speech at the Cow Palace. Participants in the strategy session laid plans for urging the Senate to restore the authority for the study and, if passed by the Senate, for assuring that the provision was accepted in conference with the House. Then consideration turned to the advantages, feasibility and difficulties of the projected Peace Corps.

A Peace Corps project would have the advantage of teaching by example the dignity of common labor to people in underdeveloped countries where often those who have the greatest privilege and opportunity for leadership look down upon manual labor. The project would also provide an outlet for the idealism of young people in our country and for their desire to serve.

Many suggestions for meeting the expected problems were drawn from the experiences of the International Voluntary Service, which had 125 people overseas in 1960, and of the American Friends Service Committee, which had supervised hundreds of young people in work camps, peace caravans and other projects in the United States and in other countries.

Finally, in September Congress approved the Reuss proposal for a Peace Corps study as part of the Mutual Security Act. The $10,000 appropriated was awarded to the Colorado State University Research Foundation at Fort Collins under the direction of a Friend, Maurice Albertson. The Foundation was given a February 15, 1961, deadline for legislative proposals and a May 1 deadline for a final report.

After the 1960 election the Peace Corps project gained momentum. Edward F. Snyder chaired a three and one-half hour round-table discussion of this idea at the National Point Four Conference on December 16. Congressman Reuss and Edward Snyder drew up a list of organizations to be invited to an all-day meeting on December 20 in the House Office Building with Maurice Albertson and two of his staff. The Congressman invited me to chair both the morning and afternoon sessions. Present were eighty-eight people representing six government agencies, thirty-eight nongovernmental organizations, eight colleges or universities and seven Congressional offices. Among the organizations who sent staff members to this consultation were the American Friends Service Committee, the National Catholic Welfare Conference, the National Jewish Welfare Board, Future Farmers of America, the Ford Foundation, the U.S. Chamber of Commerce and International Voluntary Service.

The problems involved in carrying out a satisfactory Peace Corps program served as the theme of the day's discussion. Drawing upon their extensive experience, participants in the meeting made recommendations for the recruitment, selection, training and supervision of young people in overseas projects.

A preliminary report recommending the establishment of a Peace Corps was issued by the Colorado group on February 27, 1961. In a special message to Congress on March 1, 1961, President Kennedy launched the Peace Corps as a temporary pilot project, at the same time recommending that it be established on a permanent basis. In late March more than 600 students from colleges across the country came to Washington for a three-day conference on the opportunities for service in the Peace Corps. U.S. Ambassador to the UN, Adlai Stevenson, urged the UN Economic and Social Council to consider a UN Peace Corps at its Geneva meeting.

Finally, in September, the President's request to establish a permanent Peace Corps passed the Senate by a voice vote and the House by a vote of 289 to 97. The President had requested $40 million for the first fiscal year. FCNL lobbied for the full amount, and on the day final action was to be taken, I stalked the Senate Appropriations Committee, which was meeting in closed session. When the meeting adjourned, I was among the first to learn that the first year's appropriation for the Peace Corps had been cut to $30 million.

Since the establishment of a permanent Peace Corps, volunteers have performed a myriad of tasks. In a world where half the people are illiterate, many have taught English or helped others learn to read and write in their own language. Some have built roads, water systems, bridges and irrigation ditches. Technically-trained volunteers have increased rice production by introducing new varieties or better methods of raising and storing this food staple. Wheat has been introduced where it has never been grown before. Nearly 2000 volunteers have worked in agricultural development in countries where hunger is a fact of everyday life for millions of people. Some have served as home economic demonstration agents, stressing balanced nutrition. Health, sanitation, nursing and medical projects have been undertaken.

The Peace Corps is aimed at a real people-to-people level of genuine sharing. Volunteers go to countries where they are invited by the government and welcomed by the people. By April 1971, Peace Corps volunteers had served in more than seventy countries, although for various reasons programs had been terminated in sixteen countries. Over a billion dollars has now been spent on Peace Corps projects.[2]

After the first volunteers had completed their two years of service with the Peace Corps, Representative Robert McClory remarked on the low administrative costs at that time. There were seven Peace Corps Volunteers in the field serving the cause of peace for each administrative employee, whereas the military requiried thirty-five persons behind desks for each man in the field in uniform.[3]

In 1971 President Nixon merged the Peace Corps with five other programs in a conglomerate entitled ACTION. This unwieldly agency now includes Foster Grandparents, Service Corps of Retired

Executives (SCORE), the Active Corps of Executives (ACE), University Year for Action and Volunteers in Service to America (VISTA). The latter, the domestic little brother of the Peace Corps, has about 4,000 volunteers and a budget for fiscal 1973 of approximately $39 million. The Peace Corps at one time received appropriations of $113.1 million. In 1972 it enrolled 7,000 volunteers. The appropriation for fiscal 1973 was $81 million, the result of a long history of money problems with Congress.

It is ironic that our government can bail out the inefficient Lockheed Corporation, with its hundreds of millions of dollars of overruns on defense contracts, but that for fiscal 1974, the Nixon Administration drops the boom on the Arms Control and Disarmament Agency by cutting the request for fiscal 1974 to a paltry $6,700,000, a cut of $3,300,000 from the estimated expenditures of fiscal 1973. It doesn't make sense to talk about a "generation of peace" and then to up the asking for military appropriations by approximately seven billion dollars and gut the agency charged with seeking the alternative to an arms race by slashing its budget more than a third and reducing its staff accordingly.

The request for the Peace Corps for fiscal 1974 was $78 million or a cut of one-third from its high point for young people helping other people help themselves.

Greater emphasis is now placed on technical skills that will enable volunteers to share more with the host country than youthful enthusiasm. Older volunteers are being accepted in greater number.

On balance, the virtues and benefits of the Peace Corps far outweigh its shortcomings. It has been a useful web binding together people deeply divided by language, color, custom, income and prejudice. It has been a living expression of humanitarian concern for people in other countries from a nation which still worships too much the god of nationalism and measures success too much in materialistic terms. Perhaps the greatest value has been in changing the lives of many of the volunteers who have now returned to enrich our own country.[4]

ESTABLISHING THE ARMS CONTROL AND DISARMAMENT AGENCY

In February 1960 a journalist in the Senate press gallery tipped me off that Senator John F. Kennedy was preparing a major address in which he would propose a disarmament agency. I telephoned Meyer Feldman in the Senator's office and requested an opportunity to confer with him. Feldman replied, "I would rather talk to you after I get a draft of this speech completed." I countered that I would prefer to talk with him *before* he finished the speech. So Feldman graciously yielded, "All right, come on over now." Our office was only a block away.

Edward Snyder and I went over for an hour's earnest discussion. The Senator and his staff were thinking creatively about mobilizing the best brains they could recruit for a real attack on the many tough problems in the disarmament field. They were toying with the possibility of spending between one and two hundred million dollars on such a venture if Kennedy became President.

Presidential Candidate Kennedy made his maiden speech on disarmament March 7, 1960, at the University of New Hampshire at Durham. His proposals were pared down — not at our suggestion — from the time we had talked with Feldman, but they were still very forward-looking. "Peace," observed the Senator, "like war, raises tremendous economic and social problems." He proposed the establishment of an Arms Control Research Institute which:

> . . .could undertake, coordinate and follow through on the research, development and policy planning needed for a disarmament program. . . .The Institute would act as a clearing-house for peace proposals . . . .Here in one responsible organization — guided and directed by the White House — would be centered our hopes for peace. . . .It will need strong leadership, imaginative thinking, and a national priority of attention and funds. [5]

The FCNL distributed 16,000 copies of the speech. As a nonpartisan organization, we would have been delighted to do the same for Kennedy's political rival, Richard Nixon. But, to our disappointment, Nixon did not speak at length on disarmament.

In the summer of 1960 the FCNL witnesses made a strong plea to the Republican and Democratic Platform Committees for including in the platform a recommendation that the "Executive Branch greatly expand its staff and activities in the field of disarmament and undertake technical, political and economic studies on disarmament."[6]

After Kennedy became President, the idea of a peace agency or a disarmament agency began to gain momentum. The Kennedy Administration bill for such an agency was sponsored in the Senate by Hubert H. Humphrey and fourteen other Senators and in the House by Foreign Affairs Committee Chairman Thomas E. Morgan and sixty-four other Congressmen. There were no opposition witnesses at the hearings. The fact that so many members of

Congress sponsored this or similar legislation was no accident. Part of this response was due to the very active role which the FCNL played that year in working for disarmament legislation.

Diminutive Marion Krebser, whose home was in the Washington area, gave a marvelous demonstration of what a full-time FCNL volunteer could do. With the zeal of a true crusader, she interviewed seventy-two Representatives, six Senators and some ten members of President Kennedy's staff in behalf of legislation to establish a disarmament agency. Since members of the House cannot co-sponsor the same bill, she asked representatives to introduce similar measures on their own (which explains why so many bills were introduced). She plugged hard for prompt and favorable action.

FCNL threw what weight it could behind the establishment of such an agency. Friend-in-Washington J. Stuart Innerst conferred with eighty members of Congress. Edward Snyder not only talked with many Congressmen but encouraged Friends to come to Washington to tell their Congressmen about the need for such an agency. The Friends Committee called together some sixty members of national organizations for a luncheon meeting of the Disarmament Information Service. Representative Robert Kastenmeier and two members from the staff of Presidential Disarmament Advisor John J. McCloy reported at this luncheon on the outlook for passage of the bill for 1961.

Samuel R. Levering told the Senate and House Foreign Affairs Committees that the need for such an agency:

> . . .should be apparent to all. The advent of nuclear, chemical and bacteriological weapons of unparalleled destructive power has made imperative the abolition of war in our generation. The prophet's dream cannot become reality merely by wishing for it. It will take a firm commitment to the goal of world disarmament, hard, clear thinking and planning, and the carrying through of policies in the face of strong countervailing pressures. [7]

The Arms Control and Disarmament Agency was finally approved by Congress in September 1961. The legislation provided for an independent agency authorized to undertake research on different aspects of disarmament either by its own staff or by contract with private organizations. An important responsibility was to undertake negotiations with other nations for arms limitation agreements. The head of the agency was to serve as an advisor to the President.

After eighteen years in Washington in fighting the military-industrial complex with its tremendous political power and the military mind with its prejudices and fixations, the Friends Committee was not particularly starry-eyed about the prospects for ACDA. But I, for one, was not fully prepared for the delays, frustrations, difficulties and relative impotence of the Agency in securing agreements for drastic disarmament.

Burdened by all the handicaps placed on it, the ACDA could not be the prophetic, crusading agency needed to lead us out of the morass of war and the rivalry in arms. Many members of Congress did not want it to succeed. In fact, fourteen senators and fifty-four House members had voted against even making a serious try at disarmament. After ACDA was approved, some members strove to eliminate the agency altogether. In 1963, Congressmen James B. Utt and Robert Sikes introduced bills to abolish the agency, HR 3613 and HR 5528 respectively, but no action was taken on either proposal.

Nor was the agency ever adequately funded. Congress, which shoveled out money for arms — sometimes even beyond the President's astronomical requests — churlishly trickled out funds for ACDA with an eyedropper. The first year's request for $3.9 million was cut back to $2 million. The next year the agency did receive $6.5 million for the first full year of operation, including $4 million for research contracts. Never were more than $10 *million* dollars a year appropriated for ACDA; yet its job was to work toward a disarmed world. Armament expenditures around the globe were estimated in 1971 as exceeding $216 *billion* a year.[8]

ACDA's personnel were subject to severe security checks which discouraged recruitment and adequate staffing from civilian agencies and the universities. Research was heavily concentrated on the technical and scientific questions of arms control and elimination, while the agency's authority to study the social and psychological aspects of disarmament and the economic consequences of substantially reducing the present heavy spending was scarcely exercised. As the ACDA was being organized, I had recommended to the general counsel, George Bunn, that a study of nonviolent alternatives to war would be an important project since it would help the President choose from among a greater range of responses in a crisis situation. Studies of the solution of conflicts through the UN, the World Court, mediation and mobilization of world opinion were among those that I suggested. Mr. Bunn replied that, although such a study was within ACDA's authority, it was not within their budget.

The agency was not even given permanent status. FCNL made a

concerted effort to extend ACDA's life expectancy beyond the year-to-year effort needed to keep it alive. On September 11, 1963, Elton Atwater spoke for FCNL in strongly urging the House Foreign Affairs Committee to approve a permament authorization for the ACDA comparable to that which exists for other regular governmental agencies. He felt that it would be

> unfortunate to give any impression that we are temporizing with the disarmament program, or hesitating to make a long-range commitment to it. . . .This is not the way to treat either our interest or our responsibilities on anything so important as disarmament. The achievement of disarmament will require many years of patient, persistent effort, and there should be no uncertainty about our willingness to stick with it. [9]

Congress responded by extending ACDA's year-to-year existence to a biennial requirement for authorization.

Congressional opposition prevented the agency from carrying its story to the country in any dynamic way. Only a paltry sum was allowed for publications. Although the Defense Department spends millions and millions of dollars on "public relations" and propaganda, an amendment to the 1963 two-year authorization for ACDA provided that none of the Agency's funds should be used to pay for "propaganda concerning the work" of ACDA. In part this restriction grew out of an erroneous impression that the strong public support for ACDA in 1963 was solicited by the Agency. This action might be compared to the lack of Congressional concern over Senator Fulbright's charge that the space agency had asked for $6 million the previous year for "public relations to go around the country with space-mobiles and drum up support."[10]

Thus, during its twelve years of life, the ACDA has been boxed in by the Defense Department, the Congress, a State Department which for the most part has crusaded for defense pacts and negotiations from strength and usually a President with only a peripheral interest in disarmament. The Agency has not been free to speak with a clarion voice and to stump the country in support of heroic measures to end an arms race. The trumpet was muted.

This is certainly not to impugn the motives nor the aspirations of many dedicated public servants who have been or are in the ACDA. They have always welcomed members of Quaker seminars who visited them for briefings and have always been gracious and attentive to FCNL staff members who have gone to confer with them about disarmament problems and prospects.

EIGHT DISARMAMENT TREATIES RATIFIED

A main purpose of the ACDA was to prepare for and to play its part in carrying out international negotiations on different aspects of disarmament. To date, the ACDA has played a major role in the achievement of eight treaties between the United States and the Soviet Union.[11] The Antarctic Treaty, 1959, prohibited the establishment of military bases and the testing of any weapons in Antarctica and included provisions for inspections. The Hot Line, 1963, established two direct communication circuits between Washington and Moscow to lessen the danger of war resulting from error or misunderstanding.

The Limited Test-Ban Treaty, 1963, on which the FCNL worked for nearly a decade, banned nuclear weapons tests in the atmosphere, in outer space and underwater. Unfortunately it did not outlaw underground tests, largely because of the lack of agreement on verification through on-site inspection. The Outer-Space Treaty, 1967, provided that the moon and other celestial bodies should be used exclusively for peaceful purposes. It prohibited the installation of weapons on celestial bodies and the placing into orbit of any objects carrying nuclear weapons.

Having demilitarized the South Pole, the moon and outer space where nobody lives, the next step for the two nuclear giants was the Treaty for the Prohibition of Nuclear Weapons in Latin America, which was signed in 1967. The U.S. and the U.S.S.R. were apparently willing to disarm other nations. In 1968 emerged the Non-Proliferation Treaty to which 76 nations have now adhered. The NPT provided that states having nuclear weapons would not transfer them to any states having none. The latter agreed in turn not to acquire such weapons.

The Seabed Arms Control Treaty, 1971, disarmed another unsettled region of the world by prohibiting the emplacement of nuclear weapons and other weapons of mass destruction on the seabed and ocean floor beyond a twelve-mile coastal seabed zone. This treaty left for later action the frightful race between this country and the Soviet Union in Polaris-type submarines, with their increasingly destructive capacity.

After nearly three years of prolonged negotiations in the Strategic Arms Limitation Talks (SALT) in Vienna and Helsinki, two accords were finally reached in May 1972 at the time of President Nixon's visit to Moscow.

In addition to a treaty, which requires Senate ratification, and an executive agreement, which is usually not submitted to the Senate for action, there are eighteen "agreed understandings." The treaty limits each side to two sites with 100 antiballistic missiles each — one around the capital and the other some 800 miles away around an offensive missile site. The executive agreement puts limits on the number of land-based and submarine-launched offensive missiles in each arsenal.

The treaty limiting the number of ABM's was ratified by the Senate August 3, 1972, by an 88-2 roll call vote. Approval of the five-year interim agreement was delayed six weeks because of a bitter debate on an amendment offered by Senator Henry M. Jackson of Washington. The Jackson amendment specified that any future treaty on offensive arms must assure each country numerical equality in intercontinental strategic forces. The Jackson amendment was adopted 56-35 after the Senate had voted to end a filibuster.

It would appear that the hard-liners are in control in the Kremlin and in the Pentagon. Each side seems determined to match the other side in weapons of terror and overkill. An example of the U.S. hard line was when President Nixon asked the Congress for ratification of the Moscow package of agreements and almost simultaneously requested more funds for weapons systems not covered by the agreements. Secretary of Defense Melvin Laird tried, in effect, to blackmail the Congress by threatening to oppose the ratification of the Moscow treaties unless his requests for additional weapons systems were voted by Congress.

One of the results of the Cold War has been that for nearly twenty years a growingly expensive military program has been sold to Congress on the claim that the U.S.S.R. and China were a serious military threat to the United States. Now, fortunately, that fear is fading under the impact of time and events, as indicated by President Nixon's visits to Peking and Moscow in the spring of 1972 and the visit to Washington of Communist Party General Secretary Leonid I. Brezhnev in June 1973.

In the communique issued by President Nixon and General Secretary Brezhnev on June 25, 1973, after their historic summit meeting, they reaffirmed "that the ultimate objective is general and complete disarmament, under strict international control." These leaders agreed to work toward removing the danger of war, especially nuclear war, and toward further limitation of strategic arms. They called the prospects for reaching a permanent agreement on more complete measures limiting strategic offensive armaments "favorable." They also pledged continued effort to conclude agreement on chemical weapons.

Let us hope that the effect of these encouraging conversations may be to remove the ludicrous anomaly of 1972. Instead of the 1972 arms control agreements resulting in the reduction of military spending, Pentagon spokesmen insisted that it was necessary to spend *more* than ever so that the U.S. would have more bargaining chips in the next round of negotiations and more weapons to agree not to produce or deploy.

In giving qualified support to some parts of the SALT agreements as a possible beginning to a significant disarmament program, Edward Snyder, in his testimony before the Senate Foreign Relations Committee on June 30, 1972, advocated that the Congress and the public have a larger role in future negotiations. Such participation would help avoid the current situation in which the President reaches an agreement in secret sessions and then presents it to Congress and the public on a take-it-or-leave-it basis.

Snyder suggested four goals for the next round of discussions:

1) Dismantle even those ABM's which are now being constructed or are in place.
2) Establish a permanent limitation on launchers.
3) Initiate a comprehensive ban on all nuclear weapons testing.
4) Withdraw nuclear weapons from bases outside national boundaries of the nuclear powers. This action should be coupled with a no-first-use agreement.

In his plea to the Foreign Relations Committee for a greatly changed national policy, Edward Snyder commented in part:

These agreements enshrine the balance of terror as national policy. . . . (However,) we are glad to note that the preamble to the ABM Treaty states the parties' "intention to achieve at the earliest possible date the cessation of the nuclear arms race. . . ."
The most effective way to assure that these will be more than mere words on paper is to cut the military budget, not increase it. Some progress toward world disarmament can come by agreement, but, in our opinion, more rapid progress will come by example, interlaced with occasional agreements on key points. [12]

In a world whose resources of manpower, money and materiel should be used to meet basic human needs, the ACDA still has its main tasks before it — by agreement or by example to achieve drastic steps toward general disarmament and the elimination of weapons of mass destruction. To achieve this goal, the ACDA needs a President not obsessed by the fear of losing wars; who wants such a program more than power and prestige; a Congress and a country that demand world government under law; and an international system of security not based on bombs and battleships.

CHAPTER 11

Fighting Militarism for Thirty Years

The question is nothing less than whether the most essential rights of personal liberty shall be surrendered and despotism embraced in its worst form. . . . They may be put on any service at home or abroad, for defense or for invasion, according to the will and pleasure of government. . . .

Is this, Sir, consistent with the character of a free government? Is this civil liberty? Is this the real character of our Constitution? No, Sir, it is not. . . . The people of this country. . .have not purchased at a vast expense of their own treasure and their own blood a Magna Carta to be slaves. . . .

> — Daniel Webster on the Draft,
> House of Representatives, July 9, 1814

I would go so far as to say that while the Great Powers are allowed to raise conscript armies without hindrance or limit, it would be vain to expect the lasting preservation of world peace. If the instrument is ready for use the occasion will arise and the men will arise to use it. I look upon conscription as the taproot of militarism; unless that is cut, all our labors will eventually be in vain.

> — Prime Minister Jan Smuts
> December 16, 1918[1]

. . .I came to see also, that the greatest contributory factor to the Great Wars which had racked the world in recent generations had been the conscriptive system — the system which sprang out of the muddled thought of the French Revolution, was then exploited by Napoleon in his selfish ambition, and subsequently turned to serve

the interests of Prussian militarism. After undermining the eighteenth century 'Age of Reason,' it had paved the way for the reign of unreason in the modern age.

> Major General B. H. Liddell-Hart, *Why Don't We Learn from History?* (London: Allen and Unwin Ltd., P.E.N. Books, 1946), pp. 23-4.

Militarization of the United States

We reiterate our determined opposition to universal military training, to the Selective Service System, to the increasing militarization of America through military training in the schools, to the military control of scientific research and atomic development, to the military domination of American foreign policy, and to the large proportion of federal expenditures which go for military purposes.

> — From the FCNL Statement on Legislative Policy for 1950

The campaign against the adoption of universal military training (UMT) was probably the most intensive and sustained effort in FCNL history. The military drive to enact UMT began January 11, 1944, when Chairman Andrew J. May of the House Military Affairs Committee introduced a bill (H.R. 3947) to require one year's military training for every young man at age seventeen plus eight years in the reserve. The FCNL then began to organize the opposition. FCNL efforts reached their peak before the temporary defeat of UMT by a recommittal vote in the House of Representatives on March 4, 1952, but had to be revived in 1955, when there was a new drive to pass a universal training and compulsory reserve plan.

The convictions of many Friends crystallized at the National Conference on Conscription at Richmond, Indiana, November 1-2, 1944. Members of the conference concluded:

> If it is argued that peace must be preserved by military conscription, is it not perpetuating war rather than achieving peace? We believe conscription to be an unwise public policy. Many of our staunchest citizens came to this country seeking liberty, and freedom from military conscription.
>
> . . .military conscription is no guarantee of peace and freedom from attack as evidenced by the experiences of Russia, Poland, Holland, Belgium, and France. Security can come only through good will and confidence leading to an organized and cooperative world. [2]

FCNL sought to implement Friends' concerns by maintaining an active program against the persistent effort to increase the power of the military. Accordingly, it worked against the nurses' draft, the drafting of doctors and dentists, proposals to draft eighteen- and nineteen-year-olds, the continued drive to enact some kind of universal military training, and attempts to extend the Selective Service draft every time its authority was about to expire.

Universal military training was to involve a period of six months' to a year's military training for every able-bodied young man. The trainees were not to be part of the Regular Army or Navy and were not to be liable for overseas military service while in UMT. *Conscription or military service,* on the other hand, had been in operation since the passage of the Conscription Act in 1940. With the exception of a fifteen months' lapse from March 1947 to June 1948, men whose draft numbers have been called have been liable for military service wherever sent. This chapter deals both with the campaign against UMT from 1945-1955 and with the efforts during the entire history of the FCNL to defeat Selective Service or the military draft for service anywhere.

Legislatively, UMT and extension of the Selective Service draft were very much intertwined in the decade between the end of the war in 1945 and 1955. In 1955, a universal military *training* program was defeated for a second time and a modified compulsory reserve was enacted for those being released from service in the military establishment. Faced with the decision between six months' *training* and two years' military *service* anywhere, the promilitary forces, since they were unable to get both, chose the continuation of Selective Service. Many Americans believe that the prolonged involvement in the Vietnam war would have been unlikely if the President had not had a conscript army to send into combat.

MARSHALING THE OPPOSITION AGAINST UMT

FCNL opposition involved not only a disproportionate amount of regular staff time in the immediate postwar years and a great deal of space in the monthly *Washington Newsletter*, including twenty-four issues devoted largely or entirely to UMT and conscription. It involved also special extra-budgetary funds in 1947-48, 1950-51 and 1954-55, with total receipts approximating $57,000 — a sum less than the Defense Department spends every thirty seconds around the clock — and the recruitment of additional staff to specialize in UMT.

Hundreds of people flocked into Washington to interview Congressmen and Senators from their region after up-to-the-minute briefing by the FCNL on the legislative situation and Congressional attitudes. For example, in the first four months of 1951 more than 300 people from nineteen states came to Washington as the result of a special effort. In January and February 1952 visitors from twenty-seven states were briefed. The campaign was directed primarily toward the House of Representatives because our polls indicated that it would be difficult, if not impossible, to defeat UMT in the Senate. But the Senate did not want to vote on the question until after the House had acted.

The FCNL was the major coordinator of legislative strategy in this cooperative effort which was characterized by considerable division of labor. The FCNL recruited opposition witnesses and, where possible, talked over with them suggestions for effective testimony and discussed points to be stressed or avoided. Between 1945 and 1955, FCNL opposition to UMT or a compulsory reserve was voiced by eleven different witnesses appearing before the House or Senate Armed Services Committees or the President's Commission in thirteen rounds of hearings. Several times there were prolonged negotiations to get the right of certain witnesses to be heard, or to extend the hearings so that the opposition would have a fair chance.

One example of seeking to neutralize the influence of testimony in favor of UMT was when, after weeks of negotiation with members of the House Committee on Military Affairs, the Willard Straight Post of the American Legion in New York City was finally scheduled to appear. Its witness was followed by the spokesman of the American Legion, the chief advocate of UMT, who used up much of his time denouncing the independent stand of this one liberal Post. Thus, the main thrust of the American Legion's position was largely offset.

FCNL Committee members and staff did a great deal of visiting with members of Congress and, of course, worked closely with those Representatives leading the opposition, like Dewey Short of Missouri. A constant flow of information was printed in the monthly *Newsletter*, or in special memos and publications. House and Senate roll call votes on conscription between 1940 and 1946 were printed and widely distributed. Numerous interorganizational strategy conferences were arranged.

In October 1944 I was in a panel with Warren Atherton, former National Commander of the American Legion, and others, discussing the question of peacetime military training over the NBC radio network. On February 17, 1952, John Swomley, director of the

National Council Against Conscription, and I confronted Lt. General Raymond S. McLain, Comptroller of the Army, and Maj. General Lewis B. Hershey, Director of the Selective Service System, on the American Forum of the Air in discussing the subject, "Do We Need UMT Now?"

The American Friends Service Committee deployed a number of traveling workers to stimulate meetings and discussions and to encourage the passage of resolutions and appropriate action. The National Council Against Conscription had the dynamic team of John Swomley and Marjie Carpenter, who put out 262 issues of *Conscription News* for community leaders and prepared and printed much of the literature used in the campaign. The Women's Committee Against Conscription, with Mildred Scott Olmsted as director and Annalee Stewart as chief lobbyist, trained their efforts against the nurses' draft, as well as against UMT and other forms of military conscription.

One of the first, if not the first, organizations to pass a resolution opposed to peacetime universal military training was the Educational Policies Commission of the National Education Association. But by mid-1947, most of the major religious, farm, educational and labor groups had gone on record against universal military training, and many of these nongovernmental organizations took a very active part in building public opinion against UMT among their own constituents.

Religious groups included the Federal Council of Churches of Christ in America, United Council of Church Women, the National Catholic Welfare Conference, and the Synagogue Council of America, and most of the major Protestant denominations. The three leading farm organizations were on the list — the American Farm Bureau Federation, the National Farmer's Union and the National Grange. Among the labor groups were the Congress of Industrial Organizations, the Executive Council of the American Federation of Labor, the United Mine Workers, and the American Federation of Teachers. The two major educational groupings — the National Education Association and the American Council on Education — opposed UMT, as did the National Congress of Parents and Teachers, the American Association of School Administrators and the National Catholic Education Association. Both the American Veterans' Committee and the Catholic War Veterans lined up with the opposition.

In 1947 Guy Solt and I took to Senator Robert Taft (often called Mr. Republican and a very influential Senator) a collection of 236 resolutions against universal military training which had been passed in the preceding two years by religious, labor, farm and educational groups, national, state or local. He was much impressed and promised to send a copy with a letter to each of the other ninety-five Senators, if we would have this compilation printed.[3] According to our records, the ultra-conservative American Council of Churches, led by Carl McIntire, was the only religious group to support UMT, and the Teamster's Union was the only labor organization to do so.

Intensified Anti-UMT Effort

Fred Burdick, who put out a personal sheet called *Capitol Gist* for distribution to members of Congress, made many polls of Congressional attitudes, supplemented by FCNL's reports of Congressional interviews and correspondence. Among those traveling for the FCNL were Alexander and Annalee Stewart, Mrs. Clyde Matheny, and Dutton Peterson, who visited religious groups; Chester A. Graham, who traveled among farm organizations in the Middle West; George Loft, who worked with church, educational and farm groups in strategic Congressional districts in Pennsylvania, Ohio, West Virginia, New Jersey and New York. George A. Walton and William Rhoads Murphey were among Friends recruited for a few months to work largely in the FCNL office.

In December 1954 a six-room apartment across the street from the FCNL office was rented for the special anti-UMT staff headquarters. It was promptly dubbed "Turmoil," which was a fairly accurate description of the maze of activities which centered there in opposition to draft extension and to the enactment of a UMT measure coupled with a compulsory reserve. This thrust was a supplement to renewed efforts by the regular FCNL employees.

William Fuson, on leave from Earlham College, took over the preparation of special action sheets. Milton and Freda Hadley spurred Friends to write letters and visit Congressmen from the many states. Marie Klooz monitored hearings, kept records up-to-date on attitudes of members of Congress and left a sixty-two page summary of the seven months' intensive effort. Six other special staff members helped in special mailings, meeting visitors, answering the phone and the other myriad activities involved in an intensive campaign.

The proponents of UMT included many well-known individuals, such as President Truman, General Eisenhower, General George C. Marshall, later Secretary of State, and Dr. Karl T. Compton, President of Massachusetts Institute of Technology, and Governors Warren and Dewey. Organizations promoting UMT were the American Legion, the Citizens Committee for Military Training for Young Men, many spokesmen for the War Department, the Disabled American Veterans, the United States Chamber of Commerce, the General Federation of Women's Clubs and the Business and Professional Women's Clubs, the Reserve Officers Association, the National Guard Association and other military and patriotic groups.

Much of the press favored putting every boy in uniform. Only once do I remember that an anti-UMT story was printed on the front page of the *New York Times*. One bill after another was introduced in both Houses of Congress. President Truman in 1946 appointed a nine-member Commission on Universal Training, hoping the prestige of the appointees would help get UMT accepted. Congress authorized a National Security Training Commission in 1951, which issued a report advocating six months' compulsory training and seven and a half years in the reserves.

The Defense Department, the Administration, the Veterans groups and the promilitary organizations pushed for their objective in fifteen different hearings before one or the other Armed Services Committees. When fairly conducted, the pro and con discussion by various witnesses makes committee hearings a very important part of the democratic process of shaping up legislation for consideration on the floor of Congress. These hearings played a key role, not so much in changing the minds of the members of the Armed Services Committees, as in getting organizations on record and in rallying public opinion for or against the militarization of the youth of America.

Frequently these proceedings, because of the bias of the committee chairman, were loaded in favor of the proponents of the military in time assigned or in the conduct of the hearings. Sometimes there was a long delay in printing the hearings or only a limited number of copies printed so that the opposition story would not get wide distribution.

But the opposition arrayed against putting every young man under military indoctrination never gave up. The opponents of UMT believed that true national security and peace depended on attempts to resolve the basic causes of war rather than on building up military strength. Because of the earnest and prolonged activities of religious and other nongovernmental organizations, it took seven years for the proponents of universal military training to bring the question to a vote in the House of Representatives, and then, in March 1952, UMT was turned down.

THE INTERNATIONAL ABOLITION OF CONSCRIPTION

The first full scale hearings on universal military training (UMT) or peacetime conscription were held June 4-19, 1945, by a specially appointed Select Committee on Postwar Military Policy under the chairmanship of Representative Clifton A. Woodrum (D) of Virginia. Various opposition witnesses stressed the need for eliminating conscription world wide. D. Robert Yarnall, testifying June 7 for the FCNL and the AFSC, insisted that the U.S. should: "Discourage every step toward nationalism, militarism and imperialism at home and abroad."

Norman Thomas, speaking before the Select Committee as chairman for the Postwar World Council, was more explicit:

> It is our business to do all in our power to make an end to military conscription throughout the world, not merely for the glorious cause of universal peace, but in our own selfish interest. . .the greatest single help to peace would be a movement toward the total abolition of military conscription and a policy of progressive disarmament following the disarmament of Germany and Japan. A movement like this could not fail if the two most powerful nations, the Soviet Union and the United States, should institute it. . . . Perhaps a beginning could be made by proposing a 5- to 10-year arms holiday in which there should be no conscription. . . . Conscription which goes back to the French revolution and the first Napoleon never prevented any war or guaranteed victory to any nation in war. Indeed it made war more likely because it created great vested interests in the rivalries, fears, and hates that lead to war. . . . Not only has conscription tended to make wars more likely in the world; it has contributed directly to the coming of the totalitarian state. [4]

With the encouragement of the anticonscription forces, Republican Speaker of the House, Joseph W. Martin, Jr. of Massachusetts, and Democratic Senator Clyde R. Hoey of North Carolina took the initiative in 1945-47 in pressing for Congressional action in favor of the international abolition of conscription through the United Nations.[5] The Martin resolution asked for the President, the Secretary of State and the U.S. representative to the United Nations "to work unceasingly for an immediate international agreement whereby compulsory military service shall be wholly eliminated from the policies and practices of all nations." Although worded slightly differently, the Hoey resolution had a similar purpose. Senator Hoey told me with considerable satisfaction that he had received letters of commendation for his proposal from thirty-three states — one small evidence of the value of mail to members of Congress.

The nation's leading military analyst, Hanson W. Baldwin, said, "The Martin resolution deserves enthusiastic support." In his column in the *New York Times*, February 27, 1946, he wrote:

> Though there seems to be little chance that Russia would agree to any such proposal, the attempt should be made, if only to lessen the strain and growing tension of the international situation. Conscription cannot possibly be interpreted as a constructive measure, philosophically, economically or politically. The only justification for it in this country, where its peacetime perpetuation would mean a sharp break with all American concepts and tradition, would be the military security of the nation.

In support of these two resolutions, the FCNL and other anticonscription organizations spurred letters to Congress, rallied testimony and urged favorable action by the two Armed Services Committees, but neither Committee reported out such a measure. Unfortunately, this move by two important members of Congress was not supported by the Administration. Both President Harry S. Truman and Secretary of State John F. Byrnes opposed the attempt to secure international abolition of conscription.

Attempts to secure an international agreement to abolish conscription date back to the end of World War I. Harrop A. Freeman, Friend and dean of the law school at Cornell University, pointed this out when he testified in favor of the principle of international abolition and against the constitutionality of peacetime conscription[6] before the House Select Committee on Postwar Military Policy, June 5, 1945, and before the House Committee on Military Affairs on February 27, 1946.

In his 1946 testimony on the Martin resolution, Freeman reviewed the historical attempts between 1915 and 1935 to outlaw conscription — the most comprehensive summary of that effort which was made during the ten-year series of UMT hearings between 1945 and 1955. His summary provides a useful perspective on the moves made in the period between the two World Wars for abolishing compulsory military service.

According to Freeman, Prime Minister David Lloyd George in January 1918 called compulsory military service a blot on our civilization "of which every thinking individual must be ashamed." During his electoral campaign later that year, Lloyd George expressed the hope that the League of Nations would establish a world order "under which conscription will not be necessary in any country."

General Jan Smuts, who represented South Africa at the Paris Peace Conference, called conscription "the taproot of militarism; unless that is cut, all our labors will be in vain. . . ." In his famous plan of December 16, 1918, the forerunner of the Covenant of the proposed League of Nations, he urged the abolition of conscription, the limitation of armaments and the nationalization of munitions production.

It was Jan Smuts and David Lloyd George who encouraged President Woodrow Wilson to include the outlawing of conscription in his drafts of the proposed covenant. As the Paris Peace Conference got underway in January, 1919, after World War I, Wilson drew up his first and second Paris drafts, in which Article IV contained the following paragraph:

> As the basis for such a reduction of armaments all the powers subscribing to the Treaty of Peace of which this Covenant constitutes a part hereby agree to abolish conscription and all other forms of compulsory military service, and also agree that their future forces of defense and of international action shall consist of militia or volunteers, whose numbers and methods of training shall be fixed, after expert inquiry, by the agreements with regard to the reduction of armaments referred to in the last preceding paragraph. [7]

Because of the objections of Italy and France, the language in Wilson's third Paris draft was changed to "inquire into the feasibility of abolishing compulsory military service and the substitution therefor of forces enrolled upon a voluntary basis and into the military and naval equipment which is reasonable to maintain."[8]

Some of Wilson's colleagues had collaborated with him in preparing these drafts. But even this mild version was not accepted by the negotiators at the Paris Peace Conference. There was no strong protagonist for the idea of doing away with compulsory military service. The French implied that the obligation of military service was a corollary of universal suffrage. The Italians thought such a prohibition would work a hardship upon the poorer powers because the rich powers could afford to pay their standing armies. The abolition idea was not pressed in the Peace Conference. It was not defeated; it was abandoned.

When it came to the settlement with the defeated powers, Lloyd George proposed the abolition of compulsory military service in Germany, Austria and Hungary, as one of the conditions of real peace. Strange as it may seem, this proposal was opposed by the French and Italian military men — Foch, Desgoutte, Weygand, Cavallero — but was approved by Clemenceau. Foch was most vociferous. His opposition seems to have been based upon the fact that, if Germany had no large army, France would have no excuse for a conscript army, and he could not look with equanimity on the destruction of the French military machine to the building of which he had given his life. Germany kept insisting between the two wars that, according to the Treaty of Versailles, German disarmament should only be the prelude to general disarmament.

Nine years later, at the fourth session of the Preparatory Commission for the Disarmament Conference of the League in 1927, Russia presented a far-reaching plan, not merely for the abolition of conscription but for the dissolution of all land, sea and air forces.

Only Turkey and Germany supported the Russian plan; the opposition was led by Italy, France, Japan and Great Britain, all of whom questioned Russian motives, arguing that the League Covenant prevented total disarmament and called the plan visionary. In February 1932 at the General Disarmament Conference, the German delegate, von Nadolny, urged "the general abolition of compulsory service, and failing this, the inclusion of trained reserves in the general limitation."[9] But by this time, Japan had invaded Manchuria, and Hitler was soon to come to power. The General Disarmament Conference failed to abolish conscription or to arrive at a disarmament agreement.

Noting the failure of governments to outlaw conscription, outstanding citizens of fourteen countries signed a manifesto in 1926 calling for:

. . .some definite step toward complete disarmament and the demilitarizing of the mind of civilized nations. The most effective measure toward this would be the universal abolition of conscription. We therefore ask the League of Nations to propose the abolition of compulsory military service in all countries as a first step toward true disarmament.

It is our belief that conscript armies, with their large corps of professional officers, are a grave menace to peace. Conscription involves the degradation of human personality and the destruction of liberty. .[10]

Signatories included Norman Angell, H. G. Wells, and Bertrand

Russell of England; Henri Barbusse, Georges Duhmel and Romain Rolland of France; Albert Einstein and several military men, including General Von Deimling, of Germany.

But the political efforts by governments and individuals over the years to abolish compulsory military service internationally failed because they were not sufficiently tied in with an acceptable system of international security and because the major powers were unwilling or unable to agree on a program of genuine disarmament.

Had the attempts to secure the international abolition of conscription succeeded, then the ten-year drive against UMT and the thirty-year struggle against compulsory military service in the United States would not have been undertaken by the FCNL and others who advocated the end of military compulsion. Since these moves did fail, however, the Pentagon and the Administration continued their efforts in support of compulsory military service, particularly in their all-out drive for universal military training.

President Truman put his power and influence behind UMT by the appointment of the President's Commission on Universal Training in 1946 and of the National Security Training Commission in 1951.

PRESIDENT TRUMAN'S COMMISSION ON UNIVERSAL TRAINING

President Truman's nine-member Commission, chaired by Karl T. Compton, was to hold off-the-record hearings and make a report. At the invitation of the Commission, the American Friends Service Committee appeared on January 24, 1947, with Harold Evans, Clarence E. Pickett and myself as spokesmen. Clarence Pickett explained that the AFSC at that time was carrying on relief work in fifteen countries. Across his desk flowed a stream of correspondence expressing earnestly and constantly a fear on the part of many people in these countries of the economic power and military might of the United States, which could be exerted without a corresponding sense of responsibility. It was time for our country to give suffering humanity a basis of hope.

Harold Evans spoke of the difficulty of successfully going in two directions at once. The choice which the U.S. would make on UMT was essentially a decision of whether the U.S. was going to support the United Nations with our confidence and determination or not.

I urged concentration on finding ways to abolish war, compared the estimated cost with what had been spent for international agencies, the TVA, and education and health services, and presented sixteen questions which I asked the Commission members to face squarely before they reached a conclusion.

Among the questions which I posed to the Commission were the following:

What obligations do we have under the United Nations Charter, the Disarmament Resolution adopted by the U N General Assembly, the Atlantic Charter, and the Four Freedoms to press for general disarmament, the international abolition of conscription, and no compulsory military training in the United States?

In view of the State Department's assertion of January 16, 1947, that "for the foreseeable future there can be no adequate military defense against atomic weapons," should not the government be spending its energy and an amount comparable to the billion dollars or more required for universal military training on finding a way to abolish war?

What has been the effect of conscription in France, Germany, Europe, Japan, Russia and other countries?

What would universal military training mean to the orientation of education, the academic freedom of professors and students, the militarization of our educational system, and the subsidization and control of our schools and colleges?

What have been the official actions of church, farm, labor and educational organizations, and do any of them support compulsory military training?

The attitude of the Commission was cordial, attentive, respectful and easy, and the discussion lasted about an hour and a half — much longer than originally scheduled. When our testimony was finally over, the door in the White House opened and in walked quite a number of generals in uniform with their charts and maps. They had been kept waiting by our extended discussion. Clarence Pickett said to the Commission in a stage whisper, "Does it take a dozen generals to offset the testimony of three unarmed Quakers?"[11]

Since all the members of the Commission, with one possible exception, had gone on record in favor of UMT, nobody expected an objective study and recommendations. It seemed obvious that fear of Russia was an overriding consideration. The hearings were never published. The report, which was unanimously in favor of UMT, alleged twelve benefits, including the grotesque assertion that "the adoption of universal training would reassure the peace-loving countries of the world and enhance the influence and authority of the United Nations." The National Council Against Conscription, with a foreword signed by twenty well-known Americans, issued a widely circulated analysis containing an item-by-item rebuttal of the Commission's claims.[12]

The report of the President's Commission became the basis for legislative proposals and a renewed drive by the pro-UMT forces to get a UMT program enacted, but anti-UMT forces prevented the passage of such legislation. Four years later another high-level Commission, apparently committed in advance as individuals to support compulsory training, was authorized by the Congress and appointed by the President to repeat the cycle.

THE NATIONAL SECURITY TRAINING COMMISSION

The bill to extend the Selective Service Act as passed in 1951 included universal military training but with the requirement that Congress would have to give it further consideration. It also authorized the appointment by the President of a National Security Training Commission to propose a plan for a Universal Military Training Program. James W. Wadsworth was named chairman. The members of the Commission either had long time records of favoring peacetime conscription or were members of the national military establishment.

Their 124-page report,[13] issued on October 29, 1951, would have drastically changed the character of our democracy and undermined the chances of preventing a third World War. The report was based on the assumption that (a) war is inevitable, (b) we are living under conditions of immediate danger, which "will be of long duration," (c) the only way out is to frighten aggressors by a "foreign policy based upon adequate strength," and (d) adequate strength depends upon a permanent program of eight years of Universal Military Training and Service for every boy. This would entail six months military training and seven and one-half years in the active reserves. There was no mention of the United Nations or international negotiation or world disarmament, nor the need for trying to solve the problems and conflicts which might lead to war.[14]

The Commission said, "We regard the approval of UMT as. . .tangible evidence that the ultimate obligation of citizenship — the bearing of arms in defense of the community — shall now be explicit." (p. 4) Thus one of the central issues in the long debate over UMT and other forms of military conscription was joined. Should the United States abandon its historic tradition against conscription in peacetime and follow the European tradition of compulsory military service, which had neither prevented wars nor guaranteed victory in them? Thousands of people had emigrated from Europe to the United States to escape such military regimentation. Will a nation indoctrinated with the inevitability of war lead the world to peace or seriously explore some of the essential avenues to peace, such as disarmament, an improved United Nations, the possibility of world government, and effective cooperation in removing the causes of war?

The Commission Report makes clear that a main purpose of UMT was military indoctrination of the nation's youth. "Too often their early education has failed to impart to them a clear awareness of their implicit obligation to bear arms, to pledge their lives to duty and country." (p. 5).

The Cost of UMT

Cost estimates varied widely both as direct and indirect costs, depending on whether the length of training would be six months or a year. The military estimate in 1945 of the direct cost of training approximately 750,000 men annually amounted to $1,750,000,000 per year. To this must be added the indirect cost of the training program as a whole, which Rainer Schickele and Glenn Everett estimated would divert a potential amount of goods and services worth $2,500,000,000 from civilian use.[15]

Hanson W. Baldwin, writing in the July 1947 *Reader's Digest*, (p. 105) said: "The advocates of peacetime universal military training say it will save money and make a large professional army unnecessary. This is the worst kind of deception and the most fallacious argument offered." He reported the estimates as ranging from three to five billion dollars annually.

In 1951 the National Security Training Commission, as contained in the Commission report, estimated the first year's cost to be $4,187,600 for six months' training of 800,000 men per year and the annually recurring cost at $2,158,746,200 for a fully implemented program. Even this higher military estimate was open to serious questioning.

The December 1947 *FCNL Washington Newsletter* outlined one of the many attacks on UMT costs. In referring to the cost of UMT in addition to the regular military establishment, it was reported that $27,200,000 was being spent *every day in the year* by the United States Army and Navy while only $25,000,000 was spent *in a whole year* by fifty-five countries for the General Budget of the United Nations. The total amount spent by Federal, State and local agencies on public elementary and secondary school education during the school year 1944-45 for 23 million children was only $2,638,665,908. Total appropriations for the U.S. Public Health Service amounted to $192,348,000. At that time, the United States was putting only $10 million into the General Budget of the United Nations.

OPPOSITION TO THE DRAFT

The defeat of universal military training, after a decade of intensive effort, was a small, but important, step in the difficult and tortuous transition from a militarized and war-making society to one adequately organized for making and maintaining peace. It still left the uphill and longer task of eliminating the draft, which began with the passage of the Burke-Wadsworth bill on September 14, 1940, as a temporary emergency measure. There are few things in Washington as permanent as a temporary emergency.

The draft was adopted originally for one year. The extension squeaked through the House in August 1941, by a vote of 203 to 202 because America's historical opposition to military conscription was still very strong. But the Japanese attack on Pearl Harbor and the entrance of the United States into the Second World War fastened on this nation the system which has continued for more than thirty years, except for the brief lapse in 1947-48, the halting of inductions for a few months in 1971, and the termination of inductions in 1972.

On September 22, 1945, almost as soon as the war to crush German and Japanese militarism was over, and the Allies were beginning to disarm the defeated countries, President Truman asked for indefinite extension of the Selective Service System and the authority to draft men for two years of military service. Reports were prevalent that the Army wanted 1,200,000 troops for overseas service.

The draft was extended nine times by Congress between 1946 and 1971. At every feasible time the Friends Committee pled for ending the draft and pressed for investing the necessary energy and brains in preventing wars, and strengthening the United Nations and voiced the crucial importance of general disarmament. Between 1955, when the threat of UMT was over, and 1971, ten witnesses for the FCNL appeared before the House or Senate Armed Services Committees to oppose continuation of the draft.

RECENT EXAMPLES OF OPPOSITION TO THE DRAFT

In 1964 the FCNL helped to gather materials for a major attack on the draft by Senator Gaylord Nelson of Wisconsin. A Congressional resolution was encouraged calling for shifting to a voluntary military force, and various reprints were sent out to the entire FCNL mailing list. By 1965 the escalation of the Vietnam War dampened the Congressional drive to halt the draft.

President Johnson appointed a twenty-member Commission on Selective Service under the chairmanship of Burke Marshall, former Assistant to the Attorney General for Civil Rights, to evaluate Selective Service and to make recommendations regarding the draft and proposals for national service. Edward F. Snyder, FCNL executive secretary, wrote a letter to the Commission on October 19, 1966, urging strongly that the draft be terminated and that our government dedicate itself to the task of abolishing war. Snyder wrote, "There is a growing recognition that world peace must rest on a system of international law and order, world disarmament, a rapid closing of the gap between the haves and have-nots and a cooling of ancient antagonisms based on race, religion and national origin." Later Snyder met with Commission staff members to discuss the proposals. In spite of widespread surveys and analyses, the Commission did not agree that the time was ripe for abolishing the draft.

Beginning in 1968 Charles H. Harker, acting FCNL executive secretary during Ed Snyder's appointment by the AFSC to Southeast Asia, helped to organize, and served as chairman of, the Executive Committee of the National Council to Repeal the Draft. This was a coalition of a dozen religious and civic organizations to plan a common strategy and pool their efforts for terminating the draft. Their goal was to end the whole Selective Service System rather than merely halting inductions and retaining a standby draft. After Harker left the FCNL, Edward Snyder replaced him as executive committee chairman.

General Lewis B. Hershey, Director of Selective Service, was visited in October, 1968, by Charles Harker and four members of the Quaker Action Group to explain why so many young people were resisting the draft and to ask for fairer treatment by draft boards, which often seem to act arbitrarily. Hershey said that he respected people with sincere convictions but that he was not aware of any need to bring about better understanding of this problem on the part of the local draft boards. The next year representatives of FCNL and NCRD called upon eighty-five Congressmen to try to get open debate on the draft in the House and and to urge support for outright repeal of Selective Service.

Although hearings had been promised by Committee Chairman Rivers in the House and Stennis in the Senate, the draft lottery was pushed through in the waning days of 1969. In 1970, no hearings were held. It was clear that the military did not want to give draft opponents a forum for the swelling dissent led by Senator Mark Hatfield and others. President Nixon's Commission on an All-Volunteer Armed Force, headed by former Secretary of Defense Thomas Gates, recommended in February that basic military pay be increased, that the transition to a volunteer army be made by June, 1971, and that a standby draft system be established to be activated by Congress upon request of the President.

Senators Hatfield and Goldwater introduced the Gates Commission recommendations to the Senate in August in the form of an amendment to the Selective Service Act, without benefit of Committee action or hearings. Senator Hatfield read into the *Congressional Record* on August 10 the testimony by Ralph Rudd for FCNL and a letter by Edward Snyder, expressing FCNL's support for the Commission proposals in general, but requesting total repeal rather than a standby draft. Snyder pointed out that, had the Hatfield-Goldwater amendment been in force at the time of the incident in the Gulf of Tonkin, "The President would have been required to ask Congress for authority to reinstitute the draft, and Congress would have had to take affirmative action to involve the nation deeply in a war in Southeast Asia. "

ENDING THE POWER TO INDUCT

The crucial year for the draft was 1971. Although Congress finally extended the President's induction authority after a six-month battle, the difficulties encountered by the Pentagon in Congress on the draft helped pave the way for an end to the President's induction authority in 1973. FCNL was in the thick of this battle. It helped initiate an interreligious lobbying effort, "Wednesdays in Washington," with twelve other organizations, including the National Council of Churches and the U.S. Catholic Conference. Ed Snyder worked closely with Jim Bristol of the AFSC and Sandy Kemp of the National Council To Repeal the Draft, which was the spearhead, broad-based coalition group. It included organizations ranging from peace and civil liberties groups to the Young Americans for Freedom. FCNL cooperated closely with AFSC's Visitation on the Draft which brought in eighteen people from key districts over a five-day period. They visited some 230 Congressional offices. FCNL also played a key role in arranging Congressional participation in the March 17 Emergency Convocation To Repeal the Draft. Lyle Tatum was the witness before both the House and Senate Armed Services Committees in 1971 for FCNL, AFSC and the Friends Coordinating Committee on Peace.

In the Congressional struggle FCNL cooperated especially closely with Senators Mark Hatfield, Oregon, and Mike Gravel, Alaska, and Representatives William Steiger, Wisconsin, and Spark Matsunaga, Hawaii. The constant threat of a filibuster by Senator Gravel kept the draft bill on the Senate floor from May 6 to June 24 and delayed consideration of the Conference Report until September, resulting in an unprecedented situation in which there was nearly a three-month hiatus in the President's induction authority. During 1971 the draft bill was also a vehicle for a number of crucial debates on a massive pay raise for first-term servicemen, withdrawal of United States troops from Europe, and ending U.S. involvement in Indochina.

The struggle to end conscription continued through the transitional year of 1972. The FCNL did work with Senator Hatfield to secure a vote on August 1 to end the draft in 1972. The vote failed 25-64, but provided a reading on attitudes of Senatorial candidates in the November elections.

As 1973 began, FCNL and the National Council To Repeal the Draft geared up to oppose an expected Administration proposal to extend the President's induction authority, at least on a standby basis, when it expired July 1, 1973. This confrontation never occurred because President Nixon did not ask for a renewal of authority. The struggle then shifted to an effort to reduce funds for the Selective Service System. John Hancock, who had come to Washington from California to head the antidraft efforts in 1973 for NCRD, led the fight on funding. The Administration had originally asked for $55 million. The House cut this to $47.5 million, the Senate to $35 million. But as so often happens in promilitary conference committees, the final figure was "compromised" at $47.5 million.

The struggle must still go on, however. Only the President's induction authority ended in 1973. The Selective Service System is intact. Registration continues and conscientious objectors are still being sent to prison for refusing to register. Therefore the efforts led by Senator Hatfield to repeal totally the Selective Service System must be supported. He has been joined by Senators Cranston, Calif., Gravel, Alaska, Proxmire, Wis., Stevenson, Ill., Abourezk, S.D., Hughes, Ia., Bayh, Ind. In the House total repeal bills were sponsored by Representatives Matsunaga, Hawaii, Abzug, N.Y., Mitchell, Md., Helstoski, N.J., Sieberling and Vanik, Ohio, and Stark, Waldie, and Brown, Calif.

NATIONAL SERVICE

There have been sporadic proposals over the years to institute a program of national service for all young men; some advocated such obligation for women also. National Service was generally conceived as two years' service of all young men.though not necessarily in the military. In theory individuals could choose from among a limited set of alternatives, such as the Peace Corps and the Army, but in all probability the military would want to be certain that the quota for the Armed Services was filled.

The FCNL has voiced constant opposition to the principle on various grounds. Such a program would be a distortion of democracy, which is based on a great deal of voluntarism; mandatory national service is coercive and involuntary. The cost would be astronomical. The Gates Commission used the figure of a minimum of $16 billion and perhaps as much as $40 billion for a two-year National Service program, involving about 4,000,000 young men, or twice that number if women were included. The administrative personnel and problems would be enormous. It would probably also be unconstitutional as involuntary servitude under the Thirteenth Amendment. While various bills were introduced, national service never developed into a serious threat legislatively.

THE CONSCIENTIOUS OBJECTOR UNDER CONSCRIPTION

Bertram Russell put the importance of respecting the rights of conscience in these words: "The reason why the State ought to respect the claims of conscience, and why the individual ought to follow its dictates, is not that conscience cannot err, . . .but because the determination to live according to conscience is itself of infinite value." (*Pacifist Handbook*, Philadelphia: AFSC et al, 1939, p. 7.)

Under a system of military conscription, there is no satisfactory solution to the problem raised by conscientious objection to war. For the objector, there are only different modes of compromise with the system, some of which, however, are better than others. The FCNL has tried unceasingly to achieve two goals, among others, which the Friends War Problems Committee had attempted to secure in 1940. These were equal consideration for the nonreligious objector and provisions for the "absolutist" — the conscientious objector who would not cooperate even to the point of registration or assignment to some kind of alternative service.

The British provided for complete exemption from any required military or civilian service as one of the alternatives which the tribunals could recommend. Where granted, this exemption gave the absolutist his own choice of what he would do in a wartime situation. When I was in England in May 1940 about eleven percent of the conscientious objectors were given complete exemption, but that percentage dropped as the war intensified. We were never able to secure this option in the United States for the nonregistrant or the noncooperator. Had this been possible, it would have given some of the most sensitive and earnest conscientious objectors something more socially useful to do than spending their time in jail at considerable expense to the government both for prosecution and for maintenance in prison.

In the case of Daniel Andrew Seeger, the Supreme Court somewhat broadened the Selective Service interpretation of the language of the 1940 conscription act regarding "religious" training and belief. The Court said in effect that, instead of requiring a rather strict belief in a "Supreme Being," the test of belief in relation to a Supreme Being "is whether a given belief that is sincere and meaningful occupies a place in the life of its possessor parallel to that filled by the orthodox beliefs in God of one who clearly qualifies for the exemption."[16] But even this slight easing of the criterion for classifying C.O.'s still left out those whose claims were based primarily on sociological or philosophical grounds.

A sweeping change in the handling of conscientious objectors was provided for in the revision of the Selective Service Law passed by the Senate on June 1, and by the House on June 7, 1951. This change in the law, due in part to the leadership of Senator Leverett Saltonstall of Massachusetts, provided for individual assignment by local boards to work in the national interest with prevailing pay for the work performed. The law clearly stated "such employment will not be performed through the establishment of, or assignment to, national work camps." Individual assignment gave a man some choice in recommending acceptable type of work to the local draft board, and removed his dependency upon either church agencies or the government for his upkeep, but it did not eliminate many inequities and miscarriages of justice on the part of some local draft boards.

When the House Armed Services Committee in 1967 recommended that conscientious objectors be placed under military jurisdiction, FCNL and other church-related groups made a concerted effort to prevent this recommendation from becoming law. Talks were held with many key Congressmen, and a letter was sent to the entire House membership. When the bill finally came to the floor, the House Committee members asked if they could withdraw their recommendations, and the wording that would have placed conscientious objectors under military jurisdiction was stricken from the bill.

THE SELECTIVE OBJECTOR

As the Vietnam war lengthened and created more and more opposition, the problem of the "selective objector" became acute — the young man who opposed this particular war, but was not ready to declare his opposition to every conceivable war that might arise. Actually one war is about all any conscientious objector ever faces. The language covering C.O.'s in the original conscription act limited consideration to anyone "who, by reason of religious training and belief, is *conscientiously opposed to war in any form.*"

The military establishment is essentially a totalitarian set-up and does not look favorably on deviation or opposition. The Selective Service System tended toward a strict interpretation of conscientious objection and refused the claims of the selective objector.

In testimony for the FCNL before the two Armed Services Committees in 1967, Ralph A. Rose strongly urged an end to the draft. He declared that if the draft were extended, the Friends Committee would recommend not only broadening the definition of religious objection, but would ask for:

> Recognition of similar rights for those opposed to a particular war declared or undeclared. We believe the Nuremberg and Tokyo war crimes trials asserted an inescapable responsibility of individuals for their own acts, even when under orders from government or military authorities. [17]

Chairman Richard B. Russell, in commenting on Rose's testimony, which was followed by spirited questioning, said, ". . .the Friends. . .are always very clear in their testimony. . . . I do want to congratulate them on the fine spirit that they have shown in living up to the principles which they espouse."[18]

Many other organizations made similar requests for recognizing the right of selective objection, including the Methodists, the National Council of Churches, the Jewish Peace Fellowship, the American Civil Liberties Union, the Church of the Brethren, and the United Church of Christ.

On June 8, 1971, Senator Philip Hart of Michigan called up an amendment to the Selective Service Act which would have provided for the recognition of the right of conscience for those opposed to "all wars or a particular war." In defending the proposed amendment, the Senator argued:

I believe it is now time to re-examine our own consciences and grant selective conscientious objection the same protection as the total pacifist, providing the former's objection is based on sincerely held moral conviction central to his personal beliefs. . . .One proud element of our free society is the willingness to recognize individual conscience as worthy of respect by the Government and, where possible, to permit fulfillment of society duty in ways which do not offend it. . . .We recognize that asking a man to participate in the killing of other human beings against the dictates of his conscience is the harshest demand society can impose on anyone. 19

Senators Nelson, Tunney and Gravel supported the amendment, but Senator Stennis, Chairman of the Senate Armed Services Committee, objected. After a brief debate, only twelve Senators voted for recognizing selective objectors, and fifty voted against it. So any affirmative consideration for a man who objected to the war he was actually faced with, but was not ready to affirm that he was opposed to all wars past and future, awaited the termination of compulsory induction in 1972.

CHAPTER 12

Dare the World Disarm?

We must recognize that we cannot rely on governments or officials to initiate the novel and far-reaching measures which will alone suffice. Let it be understood that in all probability the necessary ideas must come from the people themselves. . . . Our salvation is not primarily or mainly an affair of Presidents, Prime Ministers or Foreign Offices, but must proceed from ourselves.

. . .Those who seek disarmament and peace must, in practice, work through their respective governments. . . . While those in authority cannot normally be expected to initiate the necessary measures, they will readily adopt them if and when there is sufficiently strong and intelligent public opinion in their support.

> Grenville Clark, Message to the First
> National Workshop on World Disarmament,
> January 14, 1953

More than one true thing may be said about the causes of the war, but the statement that comprises most truth is that militarism and armaments inseparable from it made war inevitable. Armaments are intended to produce a sense of security in each nation — that was the justification put forward in defense of them. What they really did was to produce fear in everybody. Fear causes suspicion and hatred; it is hardly too much to say that, between nations, it stimulates all that is bad, and depresses all that is good.

> Sir Edward Grey, British Foreign Secretary,
> *Twenty-five Years* Vol. II, (New York: Frederick
> A. Stokes Co., 1925), p. 53

During World War II, the noted American philosopher-mathematician Morris R. Cohen wrote:

*We are adopting the things which made our enemies powerful, and
incidentally the things that made them our enemies. The first result
of any war is that the adversaries exchange vices. Our danger is that
we shall copy the militarism that corrupted Germany and Japan.*

The achievement of general and complete disarmament is probably
the most difficult political step which the human race has attempted.
For nearly thirty years the FCNL has worked actively for that goal.
Because of the complexities, difficulties and fears involved in
securing international agreements on disarmament, relatively little
progress has been made. The concept of security through mutual
terror and huge armaments must be replaced with political
settlements, the development of the institutions of peace and
peaceful change and international disarmament. If mankind is to
survive without destruction and bankruptcy, that transition has to
come.

Since 1940 the United States has spent much more than one
trillion dollars for war and other military purposes that have brought
neither peace nor security. World military expenditures mounted to
an estimated $204 billion in 1970, the equivalent in dollar value to
the total income of the poorer half of the world's population. That is
only part of the cost of an unresolved arms race.[1]

Some FCNL Actions for Disarmament

The FCNL has supported efforts for international and civilian
control of atomic energy and pressed for the total elimination of
atomic and hydrogen bombs and weapons of mass destruction. For
ten years FCNL labored to secure a comprehensive nuclear test ban
treaty, but so far only a partial test ban has been achieved.
"Questions and Answers about Nuclear Tests," a pamphlet by
Trevor Thomas, secretary of the Friends Committee on Legislation
of Northern California, in 1957, received a distribution in excess of
21,000 copies. Finally, a nonproliferation treaty and a beginning
SALT agreement to halt the spread of Anti-Ballistic Missiles
(ABMs) and intercontinental ballistic missiles were ratified.

The Committee took the initiative in calling the first of seven
national conferences on disarmament and played an active part in
arranging and promoting all of them. I was asked to serve as general
chairman or chairman of the arrangements committee for five of
them.

Various other conferences, including one on the Politics of
Disarmament, were launched on different aspects of peace and

disarmament. For five years FCNL did the staff work in securing speakers and arranging luncheons of the Disarmament Information Service for representatives of some forty national organizations who met for discussion of different issues related to disarmament.

Much time was spent in drafting and soliciting support in 1953 for the Flanders-Sparkman resolution (S. Con. Res. 32) calling for the United States to seek international agreements for enforceable universal disarmament. This resolution was co-sponsored by 34 Senators, more than one-third of the Senate. After the Senate Subcommittee on Disarmament was authorized, with Senator Hubert Humphrey as chairman and Betty Goetz as staff director, time and again it had to be given another breath of life through further appropriations, with the FCNL dashing to its rescue. Betty Goetz displayed remarkably fine staff leadership for the Disarmament Subcommittee and gave cordial cooperation to the representatives of nongovernmental organizations concerned with halting the arms race.

"Disarmament and Your Job," published in 1958, was one of the very first popular publications to assert that, with adequate planning by government, industry and labor, cutbacks in military spending and eventual disarmament need not result in a serious depression nor widespread unemployment. Encouragement was given to Senator George McGovern who tried year after year to get adequate federal machinery in the Defense Department and other agencies to plan for the transition from huge military spending to a civilian economy.

Intensive and largely unsuccessful attempts were made to cut back defense spending and to eliminate military aid from the foreign aid program.

FCNL and five other sponsoring Friends organizations held a four-day national disarmament conference in March, 1958, at Germantown, Ohio. Friends came from California to Maine to Texas from twenty-one Yearly Meetings and Associations of Friends. The conference statement was given wide circulation and attenders were urged to put on one-day workshops in their own communities.[2]

On March 26, 1958, seven persons from the AFSC, the FCNL and the Women's International League for Peace and Freedom delivered to the White House an AFSC-initiated petition protesting nuclear tests. The petition carried 47,000 signatures. The group was unable to see President Eisenhower. On the same day, however, he accepted a tray from a representative of the press. The year before, the President accepted a silver replica of the millionth baseball on the same day that the WIL was refused an opportunity to present to the President or his staff a petition carrying 10,000 signatures.[3]

More than 200 Friends descended on Washington during the first week of August, 1958, in response to a call to consider "Our Obligation to Tomorrow" issued by the Peace and Social Order Committee of the Friends General Conference. Many conferred with their Congressman and Senators after FCNL briefing. More than 100 Friends walked to the White House with a request for a smaller group to see President Eisenhower. Later, Frederick Fox, Presidential liaison with religious groups, met with a delegation. Others met with John A. McCone, Chairman of the Atomic Energy Commission, and urged an end to nuclear testing. On Hiroshima Day four Friends carried a bouquet of flowers and a letter of regret to the Japanese Embassy. The letter said "we rededicate ourselves. . .to the task of insuring that such massive destruction will never recur."[4]

It seems almost like a bad dream to reflect back on the civil defense fiasco when the government was urging the building of fallout shelters and some citizens were arming themselves with guns to shoot their neighbors who might want to crowd in on a nearby shelter. It was an incredible period of near hysteria and naive belief that somehow the citizen could protect himself in a nuclear holocaust. The FCNL argued that the money and energy would be better spent in trying to prevent a nuclear war.

While the FCNL is a legislative and educational organization, and does not make it a practice to organize or sponsor major demonstrations, it did join in sponsoring a Quaker Peace Witness. More than a thousand Friends circled the Pentagon in a silent vigil on November 14, 1960, as a rededication to the Friends peace testimony.[5] Nearly two years later the Friends Witness for World Order convened in Washington, April 28-May 1, with 1073 registered, 780 of whom were Friends, representing yearly meetings. Over the ensuing ten years, staff members briefed hundreds of participants who came to Washington in a long series of demonstrations against the Vietnam War about whatever current legislative opportunities were open at the time.[6]

An appeal was made to President Eisenhower, Prime Minister MacMillan and Premier Khrushchev to "exert vigorous, constructive and constant leadership to find a way to end the arms race." Interviews were held with the successive advisors to the President on disarmament and with the top officials of the Arms Control and Disarmament Agency.

Opposition was voiced to German rearmament. I testified against the U.S.-Japan Security Treaty and the Okinawa Reversion Treaty which permitted the retention of so many U.S. military bases on foreign soil.

Thousands of copies were circulated of the 1950 speech by Senator Brien McMahon, calling for a two-thirds cut in military expenditures (see the chapter on memorable interviews), and the address of Senator Millard E. Tydings in 1946 for a world conference to seek agreements on world disarmament. In this speech Tydings proposed disarmament down to rifles by 1950. Also mailed out in large quantity was the 1960 proposal by Senator John F. Kennedy for an arms control institute, which evolved into the Arms Control and Disarmament Agency after he became President.

Uncounted hours were spent in interviews with members of Congress and in collaboration with other organizations having a general or peripheral interest in disarmament. Out of this cooperation has evolved the Coalition for Reordering National Priorities, of which Frances Neely is vice chairman, which seeks to co-ordinate the activities of more than thirty national organizations working to curtail military spending and upgrade much needed domestic programs. Former Senator Joseph Clark has served as chairman.

Reviewed in other chapters of this book are the appeals in person to Eisenhower and Stevenson and Kennedy for more active leadership toward world disarmament and for opposition to the arming of Greece and Turkey and to the Truman Doctrine of military intervention. Other chapters trace the evolution of the Arms Control and Disarmament Agency and the SALT talks, and the prolonged campaign against universal military training and the Selective Service System of conscription for military service.

APPEAL TO PRESIDENT TRUMAN TO OUTLAW THE ATOMIC BOMB AND WAR

On August 20, 1945, within two weeks after the dropping of the bombs on Hiroshima and Nagasaki, 34 religious and educational leaders appealed to President Truman "to take immediate steps to discontinue its production and to press for commitments by all nations outlawing the atomic bomb and also war, which has developed the technology of mass destruction." Rufus Jones, Clarence Pickett and I were the signers from the Society of Friends.

The statement called the bombings "an atrocity of a new magnitude" which "violates every instinct of humanity. . . . Its reckless and irresponsible employment against an already virtually beaten foe will have to receive judgment before God and the conscience of mankind. It has our unmitigated condemnation."[7]

Scientists began making much the same outcry. Dr. Harold C. Urey, who helped develop the atom bomb, was quoted in *Collier's* for January 5, 1946, "as a scientist, I tell you: *there must never be another war*. . . . I have never heard — and you have never heard — any scientist say there is any scientific defense against the atomic bomb."

INTERNATIONAL AND CIVILIAN CONTROL OF ATOMIC ENERGY

Beginning with the September 1945 *Washington Newsletter*, soon after the atom bombing of Hiroshima and Nagasaki and the end of World War II, the FCNL advocated the abolition of atomic weapons and the abolition of war. This was similar to the recommendations of scientists like Albert Einstein and Leo Szilard. In company with many other organizations the FCNL kept calling for international control of atomic energy and within the United States civilian rather than military control. However, for much of the time between 1945 and 1952, the major emphasis of the Friends Committee was directed toward the defeat of Universal Military Training.

The following summary vastly oversimplifies the intense struggle over atomic policy during the next three years. Representative Louis Ludlow introduced a resolution on September 5, 1945, urging the President, the Secretary of State and the U.S. Representative to the United Nations to seek an "agreement by the United Nations to ban the bomb forever as an instrument of war."[8] No action was taken on this resolution.

In the Senate, Brien McMahon took the lead toward establishing the Atomic Energy Commission designed to insure domestic civilian direction and government ownership of all fissionable material and its production. He was strongly opposed by Major General Leslie R. Groves, who had been in charge of the Manhattan Project which developed the atom bomb, and by Congressman Andrew J. May, Chairman of the House Committee on Armed Services. After prolonged hearings and debate and revision, the proposal for the AEC became law on August 1, 1946.[9]

Although it set up a commission of five civilians to be appointed by the President to direct the use of atomic energy, the Act did not stop or outlaw the continued production of atomic weapons. Some of the comments in the Senate Report No. 1211, accompanying the proposed legislation, were quite prophetic. According to the report no real military defense against the atomic bomb had been devised, and none was in sight. The real protection against the atomic bomb lay in the prevention of war. "Since the only real solution to the whole problem lies in continued world peace, legislation should be directed in specific terms toward that end. . . ."[10]

The importance of public opinion created by civic organizations was well illustrated in this legislation. The *New York Times* reported that nearly 71,000 letters had been received by members of Congress endorsing the McMahon Bill in principle and only about a dozen letters opposing it. The May Bill for military control was opposed in more than 34,000 letters and the Vandenberg Amendment in 24,800.[11]

On January 28, 1946, Senator Millard E. Tydings of Maryland, a ranking Democratic member of the Senate Armed Services Committee, proposed that the President call a world conference, outside the United Nations, to be charged with the single duty to seek agreement for world disarmament on land, sea and air, by January 1, 1950, except for occupying forces and for international and internal policing.[12] He argued that failure of the U.S. to take the lead would result in the weakening of the United Nations similar to the way the League of Nations was weakened in the 1930's by nations arming themselves to the teeth and failing to use the League as a means of solving disputes. Unfortunately Congress took no effective action on this important and prophetic proposal.

One time during the hearings on Universal Military Training before the House Armed Services Committee, Robert Hutchins, Chancellor of the University of Chicago, was on the stand. As I recall the dialogue, during the question period, Leslie Arends, House Republican Whip, turned to Hutchins and said: "You know something about the atom bomb, don't you?" "Yes," replied Hutchins, "the principle of it was worked out on the University of Chicago campus."

"Tell me, Mr. Hutchins," Arends asked, "is there any defense against the atom bomb?"

"No," replied Hutchins, "except not to be there when it goes off."

"The more I listen to you, the more I think of my farm down in Central Illinois," countered Arends.

With a smile, Hutchins cracked back, "Give us scientists ten more years and we will take care of you and your farm, down there in Central Illinois."

The hearings under the chairmanship of Representative Chet Holifield on "The Nature of Radioactive Fallout and Its Effects on

Man" before the Special Subcommittee on Radiation of the Joint Committee on Atomic Energy in 1957-59 proved that there was no place to hide in the U.S. or elsewhere.

FAILURE OF INTERNATIONAL CONTROL

One of the major tragedies of the postwar era was the failure to reach international agreement on the outlawing of atom and hydrogen bombs. The Acheson-Lilienthal Report was drawn up in 1946 by a committee appointed by the Secretary of State and aided by a board of consultants headed by David E. Lilienthal of the Tennessee Valley Authority. Their unanimous report recommended international action to further the exchange of scientific information, to assure that atomic energy would be used only for peaceful purposes, to eliminate atomic and other weapons of mass destruction and to provide effective safeguards at every stage.

Bernard M. Baruch became the official U.S. spokesman for a modification of the Acheson-Lilienthal Report. The Baruch plan proposed international ownership and control of atomic energy, the elimination of atomic weapons and punitive sanctions which would not be subject to Great Power veto.

Blame for the inability to evolve an agreement rests heavily on both sides. The Russians did not want to give up the veto in the UN Security Council and did not trust the Western world, which originally had a monopoly on nuclear energy, to give the Communist world their fair share of this potentially great new source of power. The problem of inspection has dogged all disarmament discussions during the last quarter of a century, but is receding in importance with the development of spy satellites and more sophisticated electronic detection devices.

Later the Russians countered with a proposal in the UN General Assembly for a general limitation on all armaments. Secretary of State Byrnes and Baruch construed Molotov's proposal as a political maneuver to confuse the plan for atomic energy control with the general disarmament issue, which would force the U.S. to reveal its rate of bomb production.

The intensity of the Cold War, increased by the Truman Doctrine, which began with the unilateral military intervention in Greece and Turkey in 1947 and the North Atlantic Pact in 1949, made any kind of political or disarmament agreement difficult.

Baruch was adamant in his views and unwilling to compromise. The U.S. wanted to retain its monopoly until there was truly effective and enforceable control. The Baruch plan proposed that the transition to international ownership and control would be by stages, another of the ideas which the Russians were unwilling to accept.[13]

On December 14, 1946, by unanimous vote, the UN General Assembly passed a resolution for general disarmament which implied something of a Russian shift. A middle group consisting of Dutch, French, Australian and Canadian delegations in the UN Atomic Energy Commission tried to work out a compromise plan. However, Baruch and later Frederick Osborn, insisted on all the essential features of the U.S. plan and the deadlock was never broken. Instead of outlawing the atomic weapons, the emphasis later shifted toward halting the testing of nuclear weapons, a process which culminated in the 1963 partial test ban treaty.

SEVEN NATIONAL CONFERENCES ON DISARMAMENT AND DEVELOPMENT: 1953-1961

The FCNL took the initiative in proposing the first of seven national conferences on disarmament and was very active in the promotion, arrangements and conduct of all of them. These conferences illustrated the necessity of wholehearted cooperation among nongovernmental organizations if a national impact is to be made on public opinion on a question as difficult as disarmament.

Not many private organizations had defined their position on disarmament. The invitation to the first conference or workshop, as that one was called, was signed in a personal rather than an official capacity by a top officer, either president or secretary, of twelve national organizations. They were drawn from a wide range of groups including the American Veterans Committee, the National Council of Jewish Women, the National Grange and United Church Women. The first conference was held in Washington, January 16-17, 1953, right after the inauguration of President Eisenhower.

Norman Thomas, the lead-off speaker, called for a world-wide crusade for complete disarmament under the United Nations coupled with political settlements and adequate inspection. Merze Tate, professor of history at Howard University, examined the obstacles to disarmament from the viewpoint of history. Quincy Wright, professor of international law at the University of Chicago, dealt with the political barriers that would have to be overcome. The efforts of the U.S. Government were reviewed by Ambassador Benjamin V. Cohen, Deputy U.S. Representative to the United Nations Disarmament Commission.

That the United States could disarm without a serious depression and unemployment if sufficient planning and action were undertaken was the thesis of the address by Kenneth Boulding, economist from the University of Michigan. The outlook in Congress was examined by Senator Ralph Flanders of Vermont and Congressman Brooks Hays from Arkansas.

Grenville Clark drafted the Conscription Bill in 1940. Later he focused his attention on the problems of world order and revision of the United Nations Charter. He was unable to accept our invitation to speak in person but sent a twelve-point message (quoted at the beginning of this chapter). He stressed that disarmament must not only be universal and enforceable, but also complete, right down to the level of strictly limited and lightly armed forces for internal order. Disarmament must be coupled with the development of effective world institutions.

Follow-up conferences were held in New York City in 1954, Chicago in 1955, San Francisco in 1956, Baltimore in 1957, and Washington again in 1959 and 1961.[14] The Seventh National Conference was co-sponsored by 43 religious, farm, labor, civic, veterans and scientific organizations. It drew an attendance of almost 400 people from 78 organizations and eighteen states.

President John F. Kennedy sent greetings to the last conference in which he said that "...It is most encouraging to know that so many organizations are taking such a vital interest in the disarmament problem — a matter which is so directly concerned with world peace and security...I wish to assure you that we will vigorously pursue our quest to find effective and reliable means of controlling and limiting armaments...."[15]

This last conference wrestled with the problems of a test ban, the difficulty of negotiations and political settlements with the Soviet Union, inspection, the lack of progress in UN efforts, the question of deterrence as a means of keeping the peace or as an obstacle to disarmament, the economics of disarmament and what organizations and citizens could do to further the elimination of armaments. Each delegate was supplied with a substantial packet of material on different aspects of disarmament. Some 20,000 copies of a 24-page summary were distributed after the conference.

In my opening address as conference coordinator, I remarked:

Financially, we prepare for war like elephants and for peace like amoebas.... In this revolutionary age, our genius as Americans is not to fashion ever greater bombs to blast our fellow-men into indescribable oblivion or to brandish those bombs to preserve a peace of fear. Our genius should be to build the fabric of peace, to erect schoolhouses instead of missile bases, hospitals instead of bomb shelters, to blaze skyways for trade and travel and trust, to construct governments based on the consent of the governed, to achieve freedom within a system of law and disarmament. [16]

Rather than continue more national conferences it was decided to encourage regional and local meetings as a means of reaching more people.

SENATE RESOLUTION ON ENFORCEABLE, UNIVERSAL DISARMAMENT: 1953

The first National Disarmament Conference had recommended that efforts be made to secure legislation committing the United States to work for general world disarmament. Annalee Stewart, legislative secretary of the Women's International League for Peace and Freedom, and I were asked to take the initiative in drafting legislation, securing sponsors and pushing for enactment of such a measure.

Republican Senator Ralph H. Flanders of Vermont and Democratic Senator John S. Sparkman of Alabama agreed to be chief sponsors if we would do the work in securing additional senators to back such a measure. We reviewed all the resolutions on disarmament introduced since World War II, worked out a draft which the two senators agreed to and began asking other senators to join in supporting such a move. The language was revised eight times before S. Con. Res. 32 was introduced on June 3, 1953, co-sponsored by thirty-four senators. Annalee Stewart interviewed sixty-six senators in person, and I talked to many. We could have had more Democratic sponsors but had agreed to seek an even number from each party. In introducing this resolution Senator Flanders read into the *Congressional Record* statements on disarmament by twenty-seven organizations including the Friends Committee on National Legislation and the American Friends Service Committee. More than fifty representatives led by Brooks Hays of Arkansas introduced similar measures on the House side.

The bill provided that the declared purpose of the United States be to obtain, within the United Nations, agreements by all nations for enforceable, universal disarmament, down to those arms and forces needed for the maintenance of domestic order under UN inspection and policing. It recognized the need for effective control and elimination of atomic and other weapons of mass destruction. The President would be asked to develop a program to transfer the resources and manpower now being used for arms to constructive ends at home and abroad toward overcoming hunger, disease, illiteracy and despair.[17]

Our goal was not so much to get legislation passed as to encourage hearings and public and Congressional debate. Not many nongovernmental organizations had taken a firm position in favor of general disarmament. It was important to develop informed, articulate public opinion. Unfortunately, the whole process was short-circuited.

The Senate Foreign Relations Committee sent the resolution to Secretary of State John Foster Dulles for his comments. When the proposal came back and was reported out of the Senate Foreign Relations Committee without public hearings, the original language had been gutted. All reference to planning for economic conversion to cushion the shock of reduced military spending had been stricken from the resolution. Instead of proclaiming the goal of enforceable, universal disarmament the new resolution (S. Res. 150) merely asked the United States to seek agreements by all nations for enforceable *limitation* of armaments.

This presented a real dilemma for those of us in nongovernmental organizations who wanted a far-reaching measure which would be vigorously debated in Congress. Do you settle for half a loaf? Under the circumstance we reluctantly decided to support this resolution as better than nothing.

Senator H. Alexander Smith of New Jersey brought the resolution to the floor on July 29, saying that there was "nothing startling or new about this resolution" but that it was in line with the desire of the American people to be freed from the crushing burden of armaments expenditure. It would also be an implementation of the hopes for limitation and reduction of armaments expressed by President Eisenhower on April 16, 1953, in his speech before the American Society of Newspaper Editors.[18] The President called for a "new kind of war. This would be a declared, total war not upon any human enemy but upon the brute forces of poverty and need." Senator Smith referred to the President's statement that for the price of a heavy bomber we could have a modern school in more than thirty cities, or two fine and fully equipped hospitals, or fifty miles of concrete highway. It was in this address that President Eisenhower said:

> "Every gun that is made, every warship launched, every rocket fired signifies, in the final sense, a theft from those who hunger and are not fed, those who are cold and are not clothed." [19]

Senator Paul Douglas of Illinois reminded the Senate of the

necessity of making adequate plans for conversion and told his hearers that defense expenditures by the leading industrial nations were about equal to the total national income of all the underdeveloped countries.

After a relatively brief discussion, the resolution was agreed to by the Senate without expressed opposition or a roll call vote.[20] The action reflected a consensus without much conviction because it had been taken without thorough discussion and debate. The resolution passed while the country still remained in the shadow of the Korean War for which there was as yet no political settlement, although a truce had been arranged.

APPEAL TO EISENHOWER, MACMILLAN AND KHRUSHCHEV: 1959

The staff drafted an appeal which I mailed, with twenty-one other co-signers, to President Dwight D. Eisenhower, British Prime Minister Harold Macmillan and Soviet Premier Nikita Khrushchev, urging them to "exert vigorous, constructive and constant leadership to find a way to end the arms race." The letter, dated January 30, 1959, called for the governments to "secure an agreement to end all nuclear weapons tests." The signatories, signing as individuals, included Mrs. Franklin D. Roosevelt; Edwin T. Dahlberg, president of the National Council of Churches; Norman Cousins, editor of *Saturday Review*; Augustus H. Fox, chairman, Federation of American Scientists; and Ralph Lapp, atomic scientist. The letter was given widespread press coverage.

Gerald P. Morgan, Deputy Assistant to the President, replied for President Eisenhower with thanks for the letter. In regard to discontinuing nuclear weapons tests, he brought up the inspection question. The United States "will continue to insist on a fully effective control organization whose day-to-day operations are not subject to veto or obstruction. If the Soviet Union is prepared to accept such a control system, it should be possible to arrive at a stable and lasting agreement to end the testing of nuclear weapons." The acknowledgement from the British Embassy was brief and noncommittal.[21]

Khrushchev replied in a long letter that the Soviet Government attached great importance to the conclusion of an agreement on the cessation of nuclear tests. But the letter was very critical of the attitude of the British and American governments over the control system. The Russians had proposed that control posts and inspection groups be staffed by mixed international personnel including specialists from the U.S.S.R., the U.S.A., Great Britain and other countries. The U.S.A. and Great Britain insisted, he declared, that the staff of the control posts on U.S.S.R. territory should not include a single Soviet specialist.

To this proposal Khrushchev countered, "Such staff of the control posts could be used for giving false evidence, for inciting totally ungrounded suspicions. It is our deep conviction that under these conditions the control system would only lead to deepening distrust and to continuing the arms race." The letter concluded with the hope that the Western powers would at last take a constructive position which would allow for reaching agreement.[22]

In March I addressed a letter to Indian Prime Minister Nehru with seventeen co-signers, many of whom had signed the previous appeal. This message asked Nehru to speak out again about the urgency of a nuclear agreement. "We believe that the peoples who are not represented at the conference table in Geneva have as much at stake in the survival of mankind as those who are."[23]

THE PARTIAL TEST BAN TREATY: 1963

The appeal to the four heads of state for an end to nuclear testing and for substantial progress toward disarmament was only a tiny fraction of a decade of labor in behalf of stopping the poisoning of the air by strontium 90 and other effects of nuclear fallout.

Cecil Thomas, Edward Snyder and I talked with Glenn T. Seaborg, Nobel prize winner in physics and Chairman of the Atomic Energy Commission in February 1962. He listened attentively when we tried to express the very wide apprehension about the dangerous effects of nuclear fallout and the desire of so many American people for a test ban. He replied to us that the American Government did not decide political questions from public opinion polls, but that he was hopeful that a test ban treaty could eventually be achieved.

At one time in the long negotiations the U.S. government proposed 180 inspection stations around the globe just to monitor nuclear tests. This proposal is one of many examples of how far out and unrealistic governments can be. With the improvement of detection instruments including spy satellites, the inspection problem began to narrow down to on-site inspections for alleged underground tests. One of the difficulties was to differentiate between earthquakes and underground explosions. Finally the gap narrowed to a demand by the U.S. for at least seven on-site inspections per year, while the Russians were at one time willing to grant three. The gap was never closed.

In 1963, agreements were reached for stopping nuclear tests in the atmosphere, in outer space and under water, but not underground. Back of that 1963 agreement, the culmination of five years of negotiations, lies a lot of interesting history which can only be scratched here. At one time we were told that the White House mail over a period of seventeen weeks had run anywhere from two to one to twenty to one in favor of a test ban or continuing the halt in nuclear testing. The President's mail during the second week in February 1962 ran sixty letters and 10 cards for resuming nuclear testing and 2000 letters and 350 cards against. At the same time there were 115 letters and 100 cards for disarmament and four letters against.[24]

The break in the negotiations deadlock came with the June 10 commencement address by President John F. Kennedy at American University in which he held out the olive branch to the Russians and received an encouraging reply.[25]

The President dispatched former Ambassador to the Soviet Union, W. Averell Harriman, to Moscow and told him to come back with a treaty. Usually information on international negotiations circulates rather widely in the State Department. This time circulation of such information was narrowly restricted. The President kept in touch with Harriman by phone and soon a treaty was drawn up and signed. This is an example of my oft-stated thesis that in the search for peace and disarmament there is no substitute under our form of government for strong affirmative leadership by the President and the Secretary of State. Such leadership has been in very short supply much of the time over the last thirty years.

When some of us from the FCNL were in the Pentagon early in 1963, Arthur Barber, Assistant Secretary of Defense for International Security and Disarmament, said to us that the Defense Department was not opposed to a test ban — in fact, it was strongly in favor of it. If a test ban treaty were achieved, he predicted that Defense Secretary McNamara would be the first person on Capitol Hill to testify in favor of ratification. McNamara followed Secretary of State Dean Rusk as the second witness in the Senate hearings in August.

The FCNL and other peace groups put on an intensive crusade for ratification by the necessary two-thirds of the Senate. James J. Wadsworth, former U.S. disarmament negotiator, headed a prestigious Citizens Committee for a Nuclear Test Ban Treaty.

Before the treaty was agreed upon, the FCNL circulated an article by Adrian S. Fisher, Deputy Director of the Arms Control and

Disarmament Agency, to counter the attacks on the nuclear test ban negotiations. Ben Seaver, in testimony before the Senate Foreign Relations Committee on April 10, 1963, urged that the ceiling on ACDA appropriations be removed so that the agency could be adequately prepared "to untangle the social, psychological, economic, political, technological and military complex of problems involved."

I reminded the Senate Appropriations Subcommittee in supporting the request for $15 million for ACDA that "these sums for defense, military aid and defense support cost each man, woman and child in the United States an average of $301 in taxes, yet these expenditures do not guarantee lasting peace."[26] A great deal of effort was put in that spring to give ACDA permanent status, including testimony by Elton Atwater. The FCNL viewed it as the indispensable agency in preparing for disarmament negotiations.

When the test ban treaty was up for consideration in the Congress, FCNL helped prepare Congressional speeches, appealed to their readers in August and September *Newsletters* and in the August 6 and 26 *Action Bulletins* for a flood of letters to Senators and put out a special fact sheet on the Nuclear Test Ban Treaty.

The August *Newsletter* listed 33 Senators who in the past had expressed reservations about such a treaty and who deserved special attention. Later, some of the shortcomings of the treaty were pointed out. The Administration failed to admit unequivocally the hazards of radiation — more government cover-up. The treaty permitted underground testing; it did not inhibit the use of nuclear weapons, nor slow the arms race in its most crucial area, the perfection of missile delivery systems. The treaty did not create even a rudimentary international inspection system. It made no use of such organizations as the International Court of Justice or the International Atomic Energy Agency.

Arthur Watson, president of William Penn College, testified before the Senate Foreign Relations Committee on August 27, in behalf of the FCNL, the Friends United Meeting and the Friends General Conference. "Most of us would agree," Watson commented, "that the Test Ban Treaty is only a little step, but it is an extremely important one. Its importance depends on the steps that may follow. . . . Let us hope that progress may be sure, safe, and swift."

Watson was invited to testify partly because he was an Iowa college president. It was hoped this testimony would favorably impress Senator Burke Hickenlooper of Iowa who was a key member of the Foreign Relations and Atomic Energy Committees.[27]

Among the opposition were the Liberty Lobby and Americans for National Security. By far the most effective opponent was nuclear physicist Dr. Edward Teller (father of the H-bomb) who actively testified and lobbied against the treaty. On September 24, 1963, after six weeks of hearings and debate, the Senate ratified the treaty 80 to 19, or 16 more than the required two-thirds majority for passage.

Senator Mansfield of Montana, the Senate Majority Leader, reminded his colleagues that: "We began in 1945 with the atomic bomb, with what we believed was. . . the ultimate gap. . . . Four years later the Russians began to close that gap. . . . In 1952 we opened what we believed was the decisive gap. . .with the hydrogen bomb. And. . .nine months later, that gap too was to close. . . . This furious and frantic race. . .has provided security to no nation."[28]

CIVIL DEFENSE: 1957-1964

The attitude of the FCNL toward the near hysterical propaganda campaign waged by a section of the Defense Department and by various private organizations to encourage the building of fallout shelters for alleged protection in a nuclear war was defined in policy statements issued in 1957 and in 1962.

While expressing sympathy with the natural desire to protect one's family, neighbors and self, the 1962 FCNL statement contended that "the only defense against nuclear attack is to abolish war itself. . . . With faith in God and in our fellow-men, we in the United States should use our time, energies and resources to build the conditions of lasting peace."[29]

The Department of Defense published a forty-six page pamphlet "Fallout Protection: What To Do about Nuclear Attack" which was reviewed in the *Washington Post* for January 1, 1962 by James R. Newman, member of the board of editors of the *Scientific American* and former Assistant Secretary of War. Newman wrote:

> . . .Nothing, I should think, more markedly exposes the irresponsibility, the indifference, and the duplicity of the Government's civil defense program than this pamphlet. There is no effective shelter program, there can be none. . . . It is a contemptible public relations hoax. It is designed to make you think you have a chance, when, in fact, you have none.

Eight scientists representing the Boston Area Faculty Group on Public Issues sent a letter to Congress on September 11, 1963, pointing out that the Office of Civil Defense put the total cost of a full-scale fallout shelter program at $5,820,000,000 or $40 a shelter space. The OCD proposed paying $25 per space and schools, hospitals, welfare institutions and the like would be expected to pay the rest of the cost. Of its effectiveness, the scientists revealed OCD estimates that even with 240,000,000 shelter spaces, a 2000 megaton attack would cost 60,000,000 American lives, a 5000 megaton attack 80,000,000 lives and a 7,500 megaton attack, 100,000,000 lives.[30] Such were the fantastic assumptions that fallout shelters would enable the United States to survive a nuclear war.

Frances Neely in particular, and Edward F. Snyder with what time he could spare from other duties, were the two staff members who, with other like-minded groups, tried to stem the tidal wave of pressure for shelter appropriations. For example, Stewart Pittman, head of the Office of Civil Defense, sent a list of sixty to seventy witnesses and organizations to the House Armed Services Committee that he hoped would be invited to testify for the civil defense program of shelters. One of them was Dean Francis Sayre of the Washington Cathedral. There were 108 witnesses altogether, a large percentage of which were rallied in behalf of the Office of Civil Defense. Contrast this with the prohibition put on the Arms Control and Disarmament Agency in 1963 barring them from using their own funds to promote their own legislation through Congress for arms control and disarmament.

On the same point of government-financed propaganda, Edward Snyder wrote to Senator Warren G. Magnuson, Chairman of the Independent Office Committee on October 23, 1963, saying:

> The request for $3.6 million for public information by the Office of Civil Defense is nearly twice the sum requested for the entire Department of State for its domestic public information program. The size of the OCD's request seems intended to help this particular government agency sell an unwilling public and a reluctant Congress on the need for an ineffective shelter system, a shelter system which couldn't prevent tens of millions of American citizens from being killed in a nuclear war. We appeal to your subcommittee to reject this effort. [31]

There was a greatly increased emphasis on civil defense by President Kennedy after he took office in 1961. Civil Defense functions were shifted to the Department of Defense and a fivefold increase in appropriations was voted in 1961. Total defense appropriations went up $6.4 billion that year, partly because of the increased tension with Cuba over the Bay of Pigs invasion and the Berlin Crisis.

It was reported that the President was considering a speech to the nation urging all households to construct a family fallout shelter and might send a civil defense pamphlet to sixty million heads of households. Edward Snyder and Marion Krebser expressed opposition to such a program in an October 24 interview with Arthur Schlesinger, Jr., Special Assistant to the President. The study by Edward Snyder, "Civil Defense: Shelters or Tombs?" was widely distributed.

In 1962 and 1963 the legislative battle over civil defense became intense, and efforts by FCNL through the *Newsletter, Action Bulletins,* special publications and Congressional interviews were multiplied. As one example, appointments were set up on Capitol Hill for a representative of 120 Southern California professors, and for some specialists who had been investigating the feasibility and cost of such a program. FCNL helped to distribute 2,700 copies of a twenty-seven-page report on "A National Shelter Program: Its Feasibility and Its Cost" prepared by nine experts from Amherst College and Columbia and Rutgers Universities. The full report was sent to members of the Executive Branch, Congressmen, governors, mayors, the press and college presidents. In cooperation with Congressman William Fitts Ryan each member of Congress was sent another critical analysis, "The Shelter-Centered Society."

A Roper poll, conducted for the Department of Defense, indicated a majority of Americans favoring the Administration's fallout shelter program. This was countered by a compilation of individual Congressmen's polls which showed that in forty out of forty-one instances a majority of their constituents *opposed* any shelter program.

Frances Neely, by phone and letter, rallied scientists and private organizations to testify against the shelter program, to write to members of Congress and to interview them in Washington.

Edward Bevilaqua, industrial chemist and member of the Scientists' Committee on Radiation Information, told a House Appropriations Subcommittee for the FCNL with regard to the proposed appropriations for a shelter program, "Abroad it could provide homes for one million families now shelterless. It could provide food for one million hungry mouths a year. It could be saving lives instead of being spent in a futile search for safety from disaster."[32]

Jesse A. Mock, editor of a weekly electric utility industrial magazine, in an item-by-item critical analysis of the proposed civil defense appropriations, pointed out to House and Senate

Appropriations Subcommittees that the President's fallout shelter program would not be able to protect the public from "fire and blast." It raised a question "of who shall enter and who shall be kept out. . . . The present request for some $695 million in new funds is more than triple the $207 million asked last year."[33]

As a result of the opposition expressed, the final appropriations for fiscal 1963 were only 17% of the President's request, or $130 million, which was still a huge sum. The shelter program was turned down temporarily, but the civil defense advocates were back in 1963 asking for authorization for a massive shelter program in schools and other public buildings.

FCNL presented statements by specialists in 1963 to four Congressional committees; three dealt with the shelter proposals, the other with the request for funds for all civil defense activities.

Johan W. Eliot of Ann Arbor, Michigan, assistant professor of maternal and child health in the University of Michigan School of Public Health, objected to the proposed shelter program from the standpoint of schools and hospitals. "Shelter space makes poor teaching space" and basement shelters would give poor protection from many natural disasters. Further, "present shelter plans involve serious health hazards."[34] Costs for real protection would be prohibitive. Eliot spoke at length about the immorality of the shelter idea. There was no proposed fallout protection for people in other lands. Who decides who stays outside when the door is closed in community shelters? Is it right to give federal support for schools underground but not above ground, he asked in view of the unwillingness of Congress to support wholesome school programs above ground? The proper business of our schools is to educate our children so that they can help create and preserve peace and freedom.

The associate editor of *Engineering News Record*, C.W. Griffin, Jr., based his testimony largely on a critical examination of the inadequacies of the government's cost estimate. "For a complete blast and fire shelter program for 120 million Americans, including land costs, food, medical supplies, bottled air supply, etc., Professor John Ullmann estimates a total cost of $250 to $300 billion."[35]

FCNL opposition to the shelter idea continued in 1964 when physicist William C. Davidon reminded the Appropriations Subcommittee that "It is becoming increasingly evident that the real conflicts that exist in the world cannot be settled with weapons."[36] Four civil defense bulletins, one each in January, March, June and September were put out.

In March 1964, a Senate Armed Services Subcommittee shelved

the shelter program but the Congress in 1964 appropriated $124 million for other civil defense activities. Even in calendar 1971, Congress voted 89.2 million dollars for civil defense activities which many considered largely boondoggle. A friend of mine defined civil defense as a frank admission on the part of the military that they cannot defend us by military means and that if the citizen is to survive he must dig his own rat holes and dig them now.

THE DISARMAMENT INFORMATION SERVICE: 1957-1963

The Disarmament Information Service was an informal luncheon meeting of representatives of about forty national nongovernmental organizations. It was a clearinghouse where information, ideas and action suggestions could be exchanged, without approving joint statements or binding any organizations to a given position. The DIS was initiated by the FCNL, which arranged the speakers and issued the invitations. An FCNL staff member usually chaired the sessions. Twenty-eight meetings were held between December 1957 and April 1963.

Among the speakers were Governor Harold E. Stassen and Ambassador James J. Wadsworth, both of whom served as Presidential Advisors on Disarmament; Philip Noel-Baker, MP, who was awarded the Nobel Peace Prize; Professors Seymour Melman and Emile Benoit of Columbia University, who were specialists on the economics of disarmament; S.R. Striganov, Counselor of the Soviet Embassy, who explained the Russian point of view; and nuclear physicist Hans Bethe. The outlook in Congress was reviewed by Senator Hubert H. Humphrey, Chairman of the Senate Subcommittee on Disarmament, and Congressman Chet Holifield, Chairman of the Joint Committee on Atomic Energy.

Attenders at these meetings were drawn from a wide range of civil groups including the National Council of Churches and several Protestant denominational agencies, the Catholic Association for International Peace, B'nai B'rith, the Jewish War Veterans, the National Jewish Welfare Board, the National Council of Jewish Women, the U.S. Chamber of Commerce, the AFL-CIO, the Farmers Union and American Farm Bureau Federation, Federation of American Scientists, the American Association of University Women, and the National Education Association.[37]

THE 1960 CAMPAIGN FOR DISARMAMENT

The 1960 Campaign for Disarmament was an intensive effort for nearly a year, sponsored by seven peace organizations including the FCNL. It was staffed by John Swomley, director on leave half-time from the Fellowship of Reconciliation, with Ruth Early as his assistant. Sanford Gottlieb of the Sane Nuclear Policy Committee served as coordinator.

The aim was to encourage political action in an election year toward a ten-point program for disarmament. The goals included a commitment by the United States to the achievement of total world disarmament under United Nations supervision and control, a nuclear test ban and a nonproliferation agreement, research and planning for every aspect of disarmament including orderly transition from defense to civilian work, and agreements for demilitarized zones in tension areas.

Testimony was given in person before the Republican and Democratic platform committees, and each member of these committees was written in advance. Every major presidential contender was written and asked regarding his position. After the conventions, evaluations of the records of Richard M. Nixon and John F. Kennedy were distributed across the country to disarmament rallies.

More than a hundred volunteers were recruited in various states to interview heads of organizations, to mobilize others to write letters and to hold disarmament meetings. A student car caravan under the direction of the Reverend Curtis Crawford visited forty-three cities in eleven states. Meetings were held indoors and outdoors, on campuses, at public squares and factory gates. When possible, local organizations were set up to carry on the cultivation of public opinion.

The cooperative campaign was terminated in part because John Swomley left to teach Christian ethics in St. Paul School of Theology in Kansas City, Missouri, and partly because finances were difficult to raise. Billions of shekels for arms, shoestrings for seeking disarmament.[38]

LETTER TO PRESIDENT KENNEDY: 1960

At the direction of the FCNL Annual Meeting, December 10, 1960, a ten-point letter was sent to President-elect John F. Kennedy commending him for his statement that "he will earnestly seek an over-all disarmament agreement of which limitations upon nuclear weapons tests, weapon grade fissionable material, biological and chemical warfare agents will be an essential and integral part." In addition to those aims outlined by the President, the letter urged him to specify that world disarmament under UN inspection and supervision be the basic goal of U.S. foreign policy and that general disarmament negotiations should be resumed. The President was urged to strengthen and expand the Disarmament Administration recently inaugurated by President Eisenhower. Disarmament efforts should be closely coordinated with political settlements. Opposition was expressed to further transfer of nuclear weapons to other countries.

The letter recommended (ten years ahead of President Nixon's initiative) that the People's Republic of China be invited to join the test ban talks and that ways be found to bring China into the community of nations. The United States should show by deeds as well as words that it is in earnest about disarmament by such moves as: setting up a pilot inspection station in the U.S. for monitoring nuclear tests: by earmarking at least one per cent of military appropriations for technical disarmament studies and pilot projects; cutting armament expenditures by ten per cent and using part of the savings for multilateral foreign aid; and by ending nuclear weapons production.[39]

PROPOSAL TO NAME A POLARIS SUBMARINE "WILLIAM PENN": 1962

When reports in the press revealed that consideration was being given in the Department of Defense to naming a Polaris submarine under construction the "William Penn," I wrote a vigorous letter on April 25, 1962, in behalf of twelve well-known Friends to Defense Secretary Robert S. McNamara opposing the idea. "To so name an instrument capable of killing millions of innocent men, women and children would completely misconstrue his life and teaching," asserted the letter. Recalling that William Penn was a man of deep religious conviction, I reminded Mr. McNamara that William Penn had written:

> But what sort of Christian must they be, I pray, that can hate in His name, who bids us love; and kill for His sake, that forbids killing, and commands love, even to enemies? O that we could see some men as eager to turn people to God, as they are to blow them up, and set them one against another. [40]

Those who joined in signing the letter included the chairman of the FCNL General Committee; the former chairman and executive secretary emeritus of the AFSC; the clerk and the general secretary and the chairman of the Board of Peace and Social Concerns of the Five Years Meeting of Friends; the clerks of North Carolina,

Philadelphia and Western Yearly Meetings, and the presidents of Haverford and William Penn Colleges.

When the Quaker delegation talked to President Kennedy he remarked that he had been receiving letters from Quakers objecting to naming a Polaris submarine "William Penn." With a wry smile, he assured them that this would not be done.[41]

FRIENDS WITNESS FOR WORLD ORDER: 1962

Nearly 1000 Friends joined in a Witness for World Order before the White House and the State Department, April 28-May 1, 1962, sponsored by eleven Quaker organizations including the FCNL. A delegation composed of Henry J. Cadbury, Edward F. Snyder, David Hartsough, Dorothy H. Hutchinson, Samuel R. Levering and George Willoughby appealed to President John F. Kennedy for more active leadership in developing world order which meant general and complete disarmament, peacefully enforced by a developed and strengthened United Nations as the way to achieve international justice and security.

The delegation commended the President for several actions he had taken, including new disarmament proposals at Geneva. He explained that up until that time the U.S. had not been able to conclude a test ban treaty with the Soviet Union because of disagreement over inspection.[42]

NONPROLIFERATION: 1958-1971

At the beginning of 1958 President Eisenhower asked Congress for authority to transfer atomic weapons information and materials to other nations. An attempt to report a bill without public hearings was opposed by Atomic Energy Committee member Chet Holifield who appealed to the FCNL and to me to actively oppose the President's request.

I spent a hectic time lining up opposition witnesses for the three days of public hearings which were finally scheduled. Charles C. Price, former Chairman of the Federation of American Scientists and of the United World Federalists, in testimony for the FCNL in the hearings, argued that the proposed legislation was contrary to previous disarmament proposals and United States positions and would run counter to serious consideration of international measures to regulate and control nuclear weapons. It would have an adverse effect not only on the Soviet Union, but on countries like Japan and India. Instead, it should be a major objective of American policy to avoid nuclear war.

As a result of pressure from FCNL and other organizations, which were unable to defeat the measure, Congress placed some restrictions on the bill which was passed. These included a proviso allowing Congress to disapprove any agreement within sixty days after its submission to Congress. Between mid-May and July 1959, the President submitted seven transfer agreements to Congress. FCNL alerted 3500 citizens to write their Congressmen. Other organizations were encouarged to testify in the two days of open hearings. Clarence E. Pickett denounced these transfer proposals as initiating a dangerous policy. The dangers of accidental or intentional war would increase and would be inconsistent with the efforts which were building up to end nuclear weapons tests. He called for a new kind of leadership and a new kind of thinking.

Several Congressmen, including William H. Meyer, George S. McGovern, Byron L. Johnson and Edith Green, introduced resolutions disapproving the transfer agreements. In the debate, Byron Johnson of Colorado quoted the arguments of the FCNL against the transfers and remarked that FCNL "has long and competently represented the members of the American Society of Friends. . .and has dealt long and favorably with members of Congress." These resolutions were bottled up by the promilitary Joint Atomic Energy Committee thus giving Congress no opportunity to vote on these measures and exercise their power to veto nuclear sharing agreements.[43]

Next came the Johnson Administration proposal for a multilateral nuclear force (MLF) which would include Germany, under strict U.S. control, ostensibly to prevent Germany from producing atomic weapons on her own. Herbert Graetz, New England businessman and Friend, volunteered several weeks of his time to augment other FCNL efforts to defeat this new weapons spread. A high official in the Defense Department told us that the MLF was a State Department idea and not a Defense Department recommendation and appealed to the FCNL to do all it could both at home and abroad to defeat the MLF. The year 1964 was a political convention and election year. In its proposed Platform Planks on International Affairs presented to the conventions, the FCNL declared: "We oppose the transfer of nuclear weapons to individual nations or otherwise." MLF was finally abandoned.

In November 1964, a nonproliferation agreement was discussed in interviews with Adrian Fisher and George Bunn, top officials of the Arms Control and Disarmament Agency, with key staff members of

Senators Frank Church and Joseph Clark, with Elmore Jackson, special assistant to the Secretary of State for International Organization Affairs, and with William Epstein, chief of Disarmament Affairs Group of the UN Secretariat. After three weeks with the Quaker United Nations Program, Edward Snyder wrote to Vice President Hubert Humphrey recommending that the President make a major speech before the UN calling upon all nations to sign a nonproliferation agreement and enclosed a draft of a proposed agreement.

FCNL staff and visitors discussed disarmament and nonproliferation in 1965 with approximately sixty Senators, Representatives and assistants. A background paper on nonproliferation and the MLF was produced and distributed, and 6400 copies of a nonproliferation speech by Senator Robert F. Kennedy were circulated.

By 1967, the disarmament debate shifted to the antiballistic missile (ABM), which was authorized by the Senate by a one-vote margin August 6, 1969, after one of the most hard fought legislative battles in disarmament history. Agitation for a Nonproliferation Treaty continued until it was approved by the Senate by an 83-15 vote March 13, 1969. I attended the signing ceremony by President Nixon and Ambassador Anatoly F. Dobrynin in the State Department on November 24, 1969.

ECONOMICS OF DISARMAMENT

When he was Secretary of Defense, Charles E. Wilson, testifying before the House Appropriations Subcommittee on the Department of Defense, January 20, 1959, lamented:

> I have said to a number of my friends that one of the serious things about this defense business is that so many Americans are getting a vested interest in it; properties, business, jobs, employment, votes, opportunities for promotion and advancement, bigger salaries for scientists, and all that. It is a troublesome business. [44]

In his final radio-TV message, Janaury 17, 1961, President Eisenhower warned the American people: "In the councils of government, we must guard against the acquisition of unwarranted influence, whether sought or unsought, by the military-industrial complex. The potential for the disastrous rise of misplaced power exists and will persist."

For two decades FCNL has worked hard on the economics of disarmament as well as the politics of disarmament. "Disarmament and Your Job" written by economist and FCNL Committee member, Emile Benoit, of Columbia University, and Ada Wardlaw, presented the thesis that with adequate planning by government, industry, labor and the public, cutbacks in defense spending and eventual disarmament could be achieved without a major depression or unemployment. One labor union bought over one thousand copies of the pamphlet, but they reportedly stayed on the office shelves because of internal opposition to discussing the subject with union members.

Another publication on "The Ascendency of the Military in American Life" went through several editions and was read into the *Congressional Record* by Senator Wayne Morse on May 22, 1952. In 1960 the thirty-two page pamphlet "The Big Hand in Your Pocket" was compiled, covering military expenditures, military aid, figures on the military establishment at home and scattered around the world, the labor force in defense industries, the impact of the military on the U.S. economy, military property and bases and the cost of veterans benefits. Galley proofs, before the pamphlet was even off the press, were taken to the speech-writing staffs of Senator John F. Kennedy and Vice President Nixon with the request that in their presidential campaigns they stress the necessity of trying to make progress toward substantial reduction of armament expenditures. The results were not earthshaking.

Criticism was frequently voiced about the "troublesome business" of arming the world. The United States is the largest arms merchant, accounting for half of the world's arms trade. By 1969 the United States was selling for cash or credit over $800 million worth of arms to third world countries. The adverse effect is shown by the fact that military spending in the developing countries has been growing twice as fast as the world total while economic standards of living have improved little in the last six years.

In fiscal 1973 the U.S. government-to-government arms sales totaled nearly $4 billion. This was almost double the sales two years previously of $2.07 billion. The sales for fiscal 1973 quadrupled the U.S. arms trade of $914 million in fiscal 1970.

Seven Quaker economists came together from Michigan to Connecticut for a whole day's session on May 31, 1956, with Grover Ensley and the staff of the Joint Congressional Committee on Economic Affairs. They reviewed a preliminary draft prepared by the Committee which dealt with the economics of disarmament. The discussion was partly in preparation for a major address which Grover Ensley was to make before eight hundred business executives who were to meet at Stanford University a few days later.[45]

Various testimonies were given over the years by Kenneth Boulding on different aspects of disarmament and employment. Because there was no adequate plan for solving all the questions in this area, Boulding urged the Senate Subcommittee on Disarmament on June 8, 1956, "that the full research resources of government be thrown into its construction."[46]

FCNL supported Senator McGovern's bills, year after year, for the establishment of a full-fledged government agency to deal with the economics of disarmament. While the Arms Control and Disarmament Agency made several studies and the Defense Department had some personnel concentrating on the problem of some areas where military bases were being closed, no adequate provisions have been made for the shifts in armament spending, let alone the more acute problems that will arise if and when far-reaching cutbacks are made in the direction of general disarmament. At a time in 1971 when strenuous efforts were being made by FCNL and other organizations to shift our national priorities and made real cuts in defense spending, a telephone call came from a Senator's office. The Senator's assistant said, "You people are dead right. But so long as the unemployment rate in our state is over six per cent, we can't vote with you."

Patricia Moles assembled a collection of statistics for each state including population figures, expenditures on schools, federal and state expenditures, defense spending and taxes. Her data enabled a citizen to better understand how government money affects the economy of each state. The FCNL has also printed lists of the one hundred largest defense contractors, with the number of retired military officers on the payroll of these contractors, the one hundred largest research grants beginning with the Massachusetts Institute of Technology, and the expenditures of the Atomic Energy Commission.

The interpenetration of business and industry was examined by Senator William Proxmire in March 1969, when he revealed that 2072 retired military officers of the rank of colonel or Navy captain and above were employed by the one hundred leading military contractors, which prosper on war preparations and which receive about three quarters of all prime war contracts. It is "a dangerous and shocking situation. It indicates the increasing influence of the

big contractors. . . . It is a real threat to the public interest,"
Proxmire declared.[47]

Almost a quarter of a century after World War II the United
States was maintaining in 1969, some 429 major and 2972 minor
overseas military bases, staffed by a million men, according to a
study completed by a team of thirty senior civilian and military
experts. These bases covered 4000 square miles in thirty foreign
countries as well as Hawaii and Alaska. In addition to the
servicemen, there were 500,000 dependents and 250,000 foreign
employees. The annual cost of keeping the bases functioning was
between four and five billion dollars.[48] In the United States the
acreage owned or controlled by the military is greater than the area
of the seven states of New Hampshire, Massachusetts, Rhode
Island, New Jersey, Delaware and Maryland combined.[49]

The waste, inefficiency and cost over-runs of the military are
almost incalculable. Government studies in 1959 disclosed that
twelve major weapons systems produced during the 1950's had
exceeded their original cost estimate by an average of 220 per cent.
Some swirled as high as 300 to 700 per cent above their originally
conceived prices.[50]

One example of the astronomical waste in Pentagon spending was
cited in an article by Bernard D. Nossiter in the *Washington Post*,
January 26, 1969. He summarized a forty-one page study made by a
key Government official. Nossiter wrote:

> The paper first examined thirteen major aircraft and missile programs,
> all with 'sophisticated' electronic systems built for the Air Force and the
> Navy, beginning in 1955, at a cost of 40 billion dollars. Of the thirteen,
> only four, costing 5 billion dollars could be relied upon to perform at
> more than seventy-five per cent of their specifications. Five others,
> costing 13 billion dollars, were rated as poor performers, breaking down
> twenty-five per cent more often than promised, or worse. Two more
> systems, costing 10 billion dollars, were dropped within three years,
> because of low "reliability." The last two, the B-70 bomber and the
> Skybolt missile, worked so badly they were canceled outright after an
> outlay of 2 billion dollars. . . . Some of the most inefficient firms doing
> business with the Pentagon earn the highest rewards.

Congressional logrolling by members of Congress for defense
contracts and installations in their districts is notorious. Lyndon B.
Johnson did well for Texas with defense and space contracts. For
several years the chairman of both the Armed Services Committees
were from Georgia, and that state received large contracts.
White-maned L. Mendel Rivers was more recently House Armed

Service Committee Chairman. Huge military installations dotted his district. Shortly before his death an air force organization put on a big luncheon for him at the Statler Hilton Hotel in Washington. He was quoted to the effect that he was glad he had one district to give to his country — "No, he was glad he had one country to give to his district!"

Some day our economy will not be based on manufacturing instruments of death and on the blood of our sons and others' sons. It will be a long, hard, bitterly fought road ahead to a civilian economy, for it is just about as hard to persuade the Americans to disarm as it is the Russians.

CHEMICAL AND BACTERIOLOGICAL WARFARE (CBW)

One 1968 incident that fired public interest in CBW was the Army denial, and later grudging admission, that lethal nerve gas had killed 6400 sheep near the CBW Dugway Proving Ground in Utah. This information was brought out in Congressional testimony which Representative Guy Vander Jagt of Michigan said confirmed "a pattern of deceit."

President Nixon, on November 25, 1969, proposed that the United States ratify the 1925 Geneva Protocol which prohibited the use of "asphyxiating, poisonous, or other gases, and of all analogous liquids, materials or devices." Although the United States signed the treaty, the Senate had never ratified it. This protocol has now been ratified by more than ninety countries. The Chemical Bacteriological Warfare (CBW) controversy over the last few years has been marked by secrecy, deceit, distortion and falsehoods — a story too long to trace here.

Edward Snyder expressed the distress of the FCNL in a letter to Henry Kissinger, December 18, 1970, and in a similar letter to one hundred and fifty members of Congress. He deplored the interpretation by the Defense Department that the protocol did not prohibit the use of biologically produced toxins, and, more importantly, of tear gas and defoliants, which had been so widely used in Vietnam. The previous day the United Nations General Assembly had voted 80 to 3 that it interpreted the Geneva Protocol to include tear gas and chemical defoliants. The United States was one of the three nations to vote against this resolution. The Federation of American Scientists termed the United States' position on the treaty "highly questionable legally, absurd politically, repugnant morally and foolish strategically." The public outcry in and out of Congress has stalled a Senate vote on ratifying the Geneva Protocol on the terms proposed by the Nixon Administration.

The impression has been given by President Nixon and the Defense Department that all bacteriological warfare activities have ceased, that biological weapons are being destroyed and that not much is being done in chemical warfare preparedness. With great fanfare it was announced that the facility at Fort Detrick, Maryland, would be converted into a cancer research center. Nation-wide attention was called to Fort Detrick in July 1959, by Lawrence Scott and his intrepid colleagues who picketed the facility for a long time and who later formed A Quaker Action Group (AQAG). The United States Army Medical Research Institute of Infectious Diseases (USAMRIID) is being expanded at Fort Detrick for defensive studies on biological research. Fort Detrick is the home base for the Army's Vegetation Control Division, which is responsible for herbicide research. Eventually the work will be shifted elsewhere.

Richard A. Fineberger wrote that the "United States Military still conducts a multimillion dollar biological research program." This country still has unspecified quantities of deadly microbes, facilities to produce large quantities and ways to deliver them.

The United States has not disavowed *chemical* warfare. It has disavowed only "first use" of it. This means that the Army is free to proceed with the development of gases and delivery systems. The U.S. acknowledges that it is doing this at budgetary levels little different from the spending that preceded Mr. Nixon's applause-winning announcement.[51]

Daniel S. Greenberg in an article published in the *Congressional Record* of October 11, 1972, reported that the total cost of procurement for chemical and biological systems was projected at $58.3 million for fiscal 1973. The over-all figures on CBW are hidden in the labyrinth of the Defense Department budget which tells nothing about expenditures for the Central Intelligence Agency.[52]

Regarding chemical warfare, Colonel Stanley D. Fair wrote in the periodical *Army* for April 1972, that "To the man in the street it must look like the U.S. Army is abandoning its chemical warfare capability. . . . Nothing could be farther from the truth, and it is time to set the record straight."[53]

The *Chemical and Engineering News* for January 22, 1973, (page 3) reported that the Chemical Corps, which dates back to 1918, would be merged with the Ordinance Corps. Some 1000 Chemical Corps officers (of whom about 39 per cent are professional chemists or chemical engineers) were transferred but "will continue to do chemical programs.''

In the full scale chemical warfare preparations which are currently going on, the emphasis now is on binary projectiles. Binary weapons are nerve gas delivery systems — usually artillery shells or rockets — in which the lethal agent is produced within the projectile by the mixing of two nontoxic materials after firing. This is partly a public relations device to reduce the widespread opposition to the storage of nerve gas containers which may leak and endanger people nearby.

After a detailed visit to Fort Detrick and the Edgewood Arsenal in 1972, Richard Novick wrote:

> New anti-plant agents are being developed that either inhibit plant growth or defoliate but 'do not kill' — more public relations to pacify the ecologists. . . . In particular, the U.S. has every intention of continuing the use of herbicides and 'harassing' agents in warfare in defiance of the Geneva Protocol, the United Nations, and general world opinion. . . .
> Now would be a good time to push for an international ban on further research and development of lethal chemicals; as well as U.S accession to the unmodified Geneva Protocol. [54]

The American Friends Service Committee's research unit, National Action/Research on the Military Industrial Complex, NARMIC, has provided a steady stream of invaluable military information on chemical-bacteriological warfare, as well as on the inhuman methods used in the Vietnam War such as antipersonnel bombs, napalm and indiscriminate bombing. It has also provided a flow of facts about the mistreatment of civilian prisoners and about the large continued military support of the South Vietnamese regime after U.S. combat troops have been withdrawn.

CHAPTER 13

Wars, Revolutions, and Interventions

Making war has been man's greatest industry, and participating in the struggle to abolish war has been the major task of the FCNL. Basically the eventual elimination of war rests upon four imperatives: effective *world organization,* drastic *world disarmament,* generous *world development* toward narrowing the gap between the richer and poorer nations, and far-reaching *world reconciliation* among nations, races and ideologies.

This chapter will deal specifically with measures directed against the Korean War, the Truman Doctrine and the North Atlantic Pact, and the U.S. military interventions in Lebanon, Cuba and Dominican Republic. The following chapter will be devoted to the Indochina War — the longest and most divisive war in American history.

THE SECOND WORLD WAR

The FCNL office was opened in November 1943, right in the middle of the Second World War. During the next two years, FCNL's work in relation to the war mainly concerned the rights of conscientious objectors to do constructive work at home and abroad, food for beleaguered Europe, and planning for peace, reconstruction and the establishment of the United Nations. We gave less support than I now think we should have to the efforts of Dorothy Hutchinson and Frederick J. Libby, Secretary of the National Council for the Prevention of War, in behalf of "Peace Now," which was aimed at shortening the war.

The Truman Doctrine:
Military Aid to Greece and Turkey, 1947

The Truman Doctrine was a watershed in postwar American foreign policy. The basic issue raised by the Truman Doctrine, as the FCNL and many other organizations saw it, was whether the United States should embark on a course of unilateral military aid to country after country *or* make an all-out effort to find some viable accommodation with the Soviet Union and undertake a monumental endeavor in seeking world disarmament.

The President, in proposing the Truman Doctrine in March 1947, asked Congress to appropriate $400 million for economic and military aid to Greece and Turkey. The British were pulling their troops out of this area, and it was argued that the U.S. should move into the "vacuum." A real problem of internal order and outside provocation existed in Greece but sending arms did not seem to us to be the proper answer.

In his address to Congress, Truman called for the U.S. to "help free peoples to maintain their free institutions and their national integrity against aggressive movements that seek to impose upon them totalitarian regimes." As in many other instances, the FCNL objected, not so much to the language of laudable goals, but to the context, the methods used to further those goals, and their far-reaching implications. The FCNL cautioned against beginning a policy of pouring arms into one country and then another and another, a policy which could lead the United States down the path of a catastrophic series of military interventions and wars. This policy, as we had feared, has characterized the period since 1947.

As an FCNL spokesman, Richard R. Wood told the Senate Foreign Relations Committee that he favored prompt and adequate relief. He proposed "that we protect the reputation of the United States by inviting the United Nations to set up at once a special commission to supervise the relief program." He recommended extending our relief program to other places where it was needed, such as Yugoslavia and the Ukraine. But as for military aid, "We need to get rid of the naive hope that we can deter any other important nation from policies we think we dislike by the threat of force, open or implied."[1]

Speaking for the American Veterans Committee, Charles G. Bolte opposed the shipment of American arms or military personnel to Greece or Turkey. "We cannot stop the spread of Communist ideology by bolstering a corrupt and reactionary regime, nor can we stop the Red Armies by giving $125 million worth of American arms to Greece. We believe the threat of Communism can only be defeated by a removal of those conditions of poverty which make Communism possible."[2]

In one of the most important testimonies ever presented for FCNL, Henry J. Cadbury, Biblical scholar and long-time leader in the Society of Friends, warned the House Foreign Affairs Committee against misusing the generous motive of relief. He asserted that to appeal to this motive and at the same time "to further enmity against others, to sugar-coat sheer military policy, is to prostitute the best sentiments of a world emerging with difficulty from the hatred and passion of war."[3] James M. Read noted in a letter to Clarence Pickett that Henry Cadbury's testimony "rocked the Committee in a way I've never seen them rocked before." Nevertheless, Congress voted to send military aid to Greece and Turkey as Truman had requested. The Senate voted approximately three to one in favor and the House approximately two to one in favor but these votes did not indicate the amount of real opposition and doubt in the minds of many members of Congress. Twenty-five years later Greece and Turkey are still repressive dictatorships, and only now is the ideological war between the Soviet Union and the United States beginning to abate. The Truman Doctrine by-passed the UN and was not unrelated to U.S. interests in Mideast oil. Instead of lessening the Cold War and halting the nuclear arms race, it was a stepping stone to the North Atlantic Pact and a vast build-up of regional military alliances.

The North Atlantic Pact: 1949

The *FCNL Washington Newsletter* for March 23, 1949, characterized the proposal for the North Atlantic Pact as one which "many people believe is the most far-reaching proposal in American foreign policy in recent years, possibly since the Monroe Doctrine was announced more than a hundred years ago." The Pact, eventually joined by fifteen countries including the United States, provides that "an armed attack against one or more of them in Europe or North America shall be considered an attack against them all" and obligates each one to undertake "individually and in concert with the other Parties, such action as it deems necessary, including the use of armed force, to restore and maintain the security of the North Atlantic area." The treaty provided for review in ten years, but set no time limit for its termination.

One of the major arguments for the treaty was that European economic recovery, which was heavily underwritten by the United

States, would not proceed successfully unless the nations of Europe were assured against the danger of aggression from the Soviet Union and her allies. The main purpose of the Pact, it was claimed, was to deter aggression. The Communists had taken control in Czechoslovakia in 1948 by a coup d'etat. It had not been possible to secure agreement with the Soviet Union on Berlin, on control of atomic energy, or on the organization of UN security forces. The Russians had boycotted most of the UN specialized agencies and had withdrawn from the World Health Organization. The Soviets had used the veto thirty times in the Security Council. The Pact would set a definite line beyond which Russia might not go. The advocates of the North Atlantic Treaty claimed that it was an essential measure for strengthening the United Nations because "the United Nations is not yet the perfected instrument of world security." The State Department argued that the Pact was really authorized by the Vandenberg Resolution adopted in 1948 by a Senate vote of 64-4. The resolution endorsed regional and other collective defense arrangements in accordance with the UN Charter.

Another point made by the defenders of the Pact, including Secretary of State Dean Acheson, was that it would not set a precedent for other regional military pacts. Many of us did not believe the State Department spokesman at that time. Very soon after came the SEATO (South East Asia Treaty Organization) Pact, which was frequently used by President Johnson as a legal justification for American intervention in Vietnam.

CENTO, the Central Treaty Organization, grew out of the Baghdad Pact of 1955 and was set up in Ankara, Turkey, in 1959. This treaty links the United States, Iran, Turkey and Pakistan in bilateral pacts for the purpose of collective security and resistance to aggression, direct or indirect.

At its annual meeting in January 1949, FCNL took a strong stand against the Pact. Its statement of legislative policy for that year opposed "attempts to form a North Atlantic Security Pact and other proposals for armed alliance in the guise of regional arrangements under the United Nations, because these, we believe, will further solidify the existing divisions in the world. . . ."

Barbara Grant helped me draft a tightly reasoned and heavily documented thirty-two page analysis[4] of the proposed treaty which was sent to most members of the Senate and circulated to key organizations and individuals. Recognizing the complexity of the world situation, the arguments advanced by the FCNL in this document called for a different course.

We argued that the world must choose whether it was going to put its faith in military force and arms or in the processes of reason, of reconciliation, of government, of law. Historically, military alliances had not succeeded in providing peace and security. Further, according to James P. Warburg in *Nation*, March 19, 1949, "the primary threat to the free nations of Europe at the present time is political — via Communist subversion or penetration — rather than military."

The treaty would overshadow and circumvent the UN in its procedures and expenditures, the sacrifices asked and the loyalty expected from its signatory nations. The signatories would become judges in their own cases, deciding the problem of aggression without any defined standards or procedures. They would be free to act without mediation and without the authorization of the Security Council. The signatories included three of the five members of the Security Council and all of the major colonial powers, representing more than fifty percent of the world's industrial capacity.

We further pointed out that world-wide security can be found only in a world-wide organization. Felix Morley commented as editor of *Human Events* that the projected treaty was clearly designed as a military alliance of some members of the United Nations against other members (the Soviet bloc) of the United Nations. Morley called the assertion that the UN Charter ever contemplated such a treaty an absurdity on the face of it.

The FCNL document in 1949 raised the question of whether the tendency of the Communists to incite or support revolutions in countries where political conditions were intolerable would invite intervention from signers of the Pact. French misrule of Indochina was cited as an instance. The policy of military intervention in behalf of the nations in the Pact could set a precedent for intervention elsewhere. The United States poured out billions of dollars of aid to help maintain the French position in Indochina, and this involvement led to the tragic U.S. intervention in Vietnam.

In regard to the economic implications of the treaty, Henry Cadbury had prophesied in his testimony that "the American people are asked to assume an unstated economic burden for an undetermined number of years in order to underwrite an economically unproductive arms race." The United States at that time was already spending one thousand dollars on its own armaments for every dollar that it spent on the UN. Under the North Atlantic Pact it was expected that the U.S. would spend at the outset about seventy times as much on arming Europe as we were spending on the United Nations. The cost would eventually soar to untold billions of dollars — money that should be spent on recovery from the war and on peaceful developments.

At the 1949 Cleveland Conference on the Churches and World Order, John Foster Dulles and Ambassador Charles Bohlen unveiled the main provisions of the Pact a few days before the definitive text was released to the press. The State Department was eager to get the approval of this representative church conference for the proposed treaty.

Several of us took a very active role at the conference in opposing such approval on the grounds that the churches should not endorse the arming of one section of the human race against another. The Pact would, in fact, endorse the arming of millions of Christians in the West against the millions of Christians in the Communist countries. We argued that, so soon after the enormous destruction of the Second World War, the leadership of the churches should be directed toward world-wide reconciliation and disarmament.

After the text of the Pact had been published, the FCNL called together representatives of fourteen national organizations to discuss their position on the Pact. Most of the individuals were against it, but many of the organizations they represented had taken no official position. People were urged to appear at hearings in opposition, or at least to ask questions about the Pact. Much space in the *Washington Newsletter* was devoted to an examination of the issues involved in the treaty. FCNL circulated nearly 30,000 copies of the text, so that people could read it for themselves. The American Friends Service Committee and FCNL prepared material for use in some twenty follow-up conferences to the important Cleveland conference. Ralpha Randall was employed for six weeks to augment FCNL's office work on the Pact.

Henry J. Cadbury marshalled the case against the treaty in testimony before the Senate Foreign Relations Committee and stirred up an extended discussion which occupied twenty-four pages of the printed record.[5] During this hearing, Cadbury was challenged as to the attitude of the members of the FCNL General Committee to the Pact, and he turned to me for an answer. I explained that our proposed statement of legislative policy had been circulated for consideration about three months before our last meeting. Very few committee members expressed dissent on this point in our proposed policy, although at that time the text of the treaty had not been released. Chairman Tom Connally wanted to know specifically how many of the FCNL General Committee had expressed support for the FCNL statement.

Since the correspondence on the shaping up of the policy

statement had been destroyed, I wrote a letter to the 120 members of the General Committee. Seventy-six replies were received in time for me to send the tabulation to the Foreign Relations Committee before the hearings went to the printer. Of the replies, 69 were against the North Atlantic Pact; 7 were in favor; 75 were opposed to the accompanying arms program; one, with some reservations, supported the arms program.

The North Atlantic Pact had been signed April 4, 1949, to become effective August 24. It was finally ratified by the Senate by a vote of 82 to 13 in July. In the three weeks of Senate debate preceding ratification, Senator Robert Taft observed that this treaty "means an armament race, and armament races in the past have led to war. The United Nations looks perhaps vainly to the reduction of armaments. The Atlantic Pact proposes to increase them."

Four days after Senate ratification of the Treaty, President Truman urged enactment of a foreign arms aid program to implement it. This became the Mutual Defense Assistance Act of 1949, which provided $1.3 billion in military aid to the twelve signatories and to Greece, Turkey, Iran, Korea and the Philippines.

NATO (North Atlantic Treaty Organization) was the agency set up to implement the Pact. NATO thus became the vehicle for carrying out the military implications of the treaty, for coordinating the stationing of troops in Europe and for justifying the vast build-up of U.S. military bases in Europe. In 1972 approximately 320,000 U.S. troops and their dependents remained in West Germany and more than 7,000 nuclear warheads were positioned in that country. In the twenty years following the organization of NATO, the United States has provided approximately $25 billion to its European partners, plus $10 billion under the Marshall Plan for European recovery,[6] plus an undisclosed net amount in direct and indirect costs of stationing U.S. troops in Europe.

IRON RULE IN CUBA UNDER BATISTA

Cuba in 1957 was under the iron rule of Batista. On May 6, Hiram Hilty and I questioned the U.S. Government, the United Nations and the Organization of American States about what they could do to challenge the growing repression in Cuba, which was deepening the possibilities of violent revolution. Hilty was on the faculty of Guilford College and had served in Cuba under the Mission Board of the Five Years Meeting of Friends.

The State Department official assigned to the Cuba desk reported that military and economic aid to Batista was being terminated. He expressed his concern over what might happen if a violent revolution occurred and was sensitive to the frequent charge that American foreign policy tended to support the repressive oligarchies and dictators in Latin America. Too often in the history of Latin America a revolution in the name of radical social change had overthrown one strong-arm government to replace it with another, he asserted.

The Washington representative of the U N did not see any feasible move which that organization could undertake at that time.

In response to our inquiry, Dr. Charles Fenwick, who was in the legal division of the Organization of American States, expressed pessimism whether the OAS could actually do anything. He read the various provisions for human rights and democratic procedures that were contained in the OAS agreements reached at Caracas. He commented on their very fine language and intent and the fact that the OAS had absolutely no machinery for carrying them out.

However, something could be done if there were a disposition to do it. If Secretary of State Dulles were to get up in an OAS meeting and say very firmly that there was a deep concern on the part of other states regarding the situation in Cuba, it could have a profound moral, if not legal, significance. The United States Government would have to be prepared to take some real abuse, because the Latin American countries were extremely sensitive to any seeming interference in their domestic affairs as a result of their unhappy experience over the last hundred years with the colossus of the North.

Quite informally and unofficially, Dr. Fenwick hinted that it would be very desirable for the American Friends Board of Missions to write a strong letter to the Organization of American States, to the United Nations, and to the U.S. State Department, voicing their views and concern. The formal replies would be couched in diplomatic language saying that little more could be done than what was already being done. But the registering of their views would have a much more important effect than any official reply would indicate.

Less than two years later Fidel Castro overthrew the Batista Government; while this brought many needed social reforms, many Cubans left because of the repressive policies of the Castro regime. The total number of persons registered at the Cuban Refugee Center in Miami, January 1, 1961, through May 18, 1973, was 451,827.[7]

CUBA: THE BAY OF PIGS INVASION, 1961

When the "Bay of Pigs" invasion of Cuba by Cuban exiles took place on April 17, 1961, Edward Snyder telephoned Robert Lyon, urging him to rush down from the Cambridge office of the American Friends Service Committee to participate with several of us in a series of interviews during the invasion with key officials in the White House, the State Department and the Congress.[8] Bob Lyon had just returned from his third visit to Cuba since Castro came into power. We did not know at that time that the Central Intelligence Agency had invested $45 million in aiding Cuban rebels to launch the invasion. Fidel Castro, the Cuban leader, was viewed by many in the State Department and in the United States as a menace who should be destroyed because of his sympathies with Communism.

Our first interview was held in the East Wing of the White House with Arthur Schlesinger, Jr., special assistant to President Kennedy. This meeting was arranged by Mary Blanshard of the Unitarian Fellowship of Social Justice, who was a personal friend of Schlesinger. The discussion centered on two major points: first, what initiative might be taken to stop the bloodshed; and, second, what long-range planning could be undertaken to bring about some kind of reconciliation between the two countries.

Although we had no inside military information, we did have the benefit of Bob Lyon's visits to Cuba. On the basis of his firsthand observations, we challenged the basic assumption of the Administration that once an anti-Castro military force landed in Cuba, the inhabitants would rise up en masse and overthrow Castro. The government had distributed arms widely, not the thing an insecure government does. Bob Lyon proposed that some third country — possibly Canada, Mexico, India, or even England — should be encouraged to introduce a resolution in the United Nations. Such a resolution might call for an immediate cease-fire, a program of mediation among Cubans themselves, and a UN-supervised free election in Cuba within a stated period of time.

We stressed that tacit approval of the use of violence in Cuba tended to undermine the U.S. commitment to mediation in Laos, the Congo and other areas of the world where serious conflict existed. In addition, the actions of our government were in violation of the Neutrality Act and the Charter of the Organization of American States. The Charter of the OAS reads: "No state or group of states has the right to intervene directly or indirectly, for any reason whatsoever, in the internal or external affairs of any other state."

That Schlesinger did not defend the invasion impressed me. Some time later it became evident that the Kennedy Administration considered the Bay of Pigs invasion as their greatest political mistake. President Kennedy had uncritically inherited and accepted the CIA proposal approved a year earlier by President Eisenhower to recruit, train, arm and ultimately launch an invading army of anti-Castro Cubans. President Kennedy accepted full political responsibility for the fiasco.

In none of our interviews on April 18 and 19 did we learn that any serious consideration had been given to what role the U.S. would take in the event that the counterrevolutionaries failed. By April 20, the invasion had collapsed, as Bob Lyon had predicted.

The day after talking with Schlesinger we were back in the White House, this time in the West Wing conferring with another Presidential assistant, Richard Goodwin. The conversation dealt not only with Cuba but also with the need for improving relations with Communist China.

Senators with whom we discussed the Cuban crisis included Long of Louisiana, Proxmire of Wisconsin, Sparkman of Alabama, Morse of Oregon, Metcalf of Montana, and Clark of Pennsylvania. A very thoughtful dialogue was held with Robert Estabrook, editor for the editorial page of the *Washington Post*.

Two really touchy interviews were held with a couple of officers in the Inter-American section of the State Department, probably because they were in between denying American involvement and getting ready to defend it. Involved was not only the still unrevealed degree of American complicity in the invasion, but also the explanation of American policy then being offered in the United Nations. Adlai Stevenson had at first denied American underwriting of the intervention, apparently because, even as U.S. Ambassador to the UN, he had not been fully informed. When the facts became known, he had to retract his previous words, in a way that made him look like a liar, a dupe or a fool. This embarrassing turn of events was an extremely unfortunate aspect of a wholly unsavory episode.

In some of our interviews, the action in Cuba was justified as an exception to the OAS Charter because the island was only ninety miles from the shores of the United States and was serving as a springboard for revolutionary agitation in Latin America. This period was one of many during the last three decades when self-righteousness and cant prevailed in official Washington.

Ed Duckles wrote from Mexico City that the United States was committing a drastic mistake, for our government's actions in Cuba were weakening democratic governments friendly to the United States. His plea was, "If only our leaders in the political parties in the United States could be made to realize that our present policies of recourse to violence and the use of economic blockades are playing directly into the hands of the Communists who are telling the people of Latin America that this is what they can expect from the United States."[9]

Prior to the invasion the FCNL had tried to warn of impending catastrophe. Early in 1961 we became concerned about the deterioration in U.S.-Cuban relations and tried to express this concern in a variety of ways. One of our first efforts was made after James Reston reported in the *New York Times* that there was a conflict within the Executive Branch as to how far the United States should go in supporting Cuban rebels. FCNL staff then began a crash campaign to encourage Congressional support for conciliation of the U.S.-Cuban dispute.

Two days before the invasion, Frances Neely, who had followed Cuban affairs closely over the last decade for the FCNL, wrote President Kennedy, raising many questions about our Cuban policy. She urged acceptance of offers of mediation in the quarrel between the Cuban and American governments, concluding her letter with the question: "Can Cuba's affiliation with the Communist block hurt us half as much as the United States will hurt itself if we use brute force, no matter how covert, to obtain political ends in a conflict with a nation of less than seven million population?"

Frances had prepared in early February a 26-page study entitled "Controversy over Cuba," analyzing what was happening there and warning against a tit-for-tat policy of antagonism. This study was distributed to about 5,000 persons. It called for direct negotiations with Cuban leaders in order to reach a mutually acceptable agreement on compensation to U.S. investors in Cuba; to seek ways of contributing to the developing of democratic institutions in Cuba and to help finance Cuba's program of social reform; and to review the status of the Guantanamo naval base.

After relations deteriorated to the Bay of Pigs invasion, Frances Neely and Edward Snyder sent out *Action Bulletins* on April 19 and 25, reviewing the crisis in Western hemisphere relations and calling for letters to President Kennedy and to members of Congress in opposition to the widespread sentiment in Washington for direct military intervention in Cuba.

In an attempt to reverse this ominous trend, Edward Snyder, Frances Neely and Stuart Innerst helped Representatives Frank Kowalski and Robert Kastenmeier draft a resolution proposing that the prisoners taken during the invasion be freed in exchange for nonmilitary equipment from the United States, including supplies for school lunches and milk for children. Unfortunately, this resolution did not receive favorable action in Congress. Finally, in December 1962, New York lawyer James B. Donovan was able to negotiate an agreement with the Castro Government, under which the United States ransomed 1,113 prisoners by a payment to the Cuban Government of $53 million in food and medicines plus $2.9 million in cash. In addition, Castro let between 3,500 and 4,500 relatives of freed prisoners leave Cuba.[10]

During the sixteen months after the invasion, relations with Cuba worsened. The House of Representatives on May 17, 1961, voted 404 to 2 to support collective sanctions by the Organization of American States against Cuba. By September Senator Smathers of Florida suggested that the United States liberate Cuba from the Castro influence unilaterally if necessary. Senators Kuchel and Bennett called for an end to all trade with the island. Cuba insisted that she was willing to negotiate all differences on a basis of equality, but the U.S. maintained that negotiations were unthinkable as long as Cuba retained ties with the Soviet Union.

In February 1962, the U.S. tightened its embargo on imports of sugar from Cuba to a prohibition of virtually all trade except food and medicines. One month later the U.S. sent a twenty-one member delegation to the Foreign Ministers Conference of the Organization of American States in Punta del Este to press for economic and diplomatic sanctions against Cuba if she refused to break her ties with the Communists within sixty days. The Foreign Ministers agreed to oust Cuba from the OAS because Cuba's "adherence to Marxism-Leninism is incompatible with the inter-American system."[11]

THE CUBAN MISSILE CRISIS: 1962

In the interval between the Bay of Pigs invasion and the Cuban missile crisis, the persistent efforts of the FCNL and others to bring about negotiations and reconciliation with Cuba had not succeeded. On October 22, President Kennedy revealed that surveillance photographs indicated that the Russians were setting up launching sites in Cuba for medium and intermediate range missiles and that they were sending jet bombers to the island capable of carrying nuclear weapons. Whereas the shorter range missiles could strike Washington, D.C., or the Panama Canal, the intermediate range missiles could threaten most of the major cities in the Western Hemisphere.

As late as four days before this speech, the Soviets had denied any build-up of offensive weapons in Cuba, contrary to what the photos revealed. Kennedy therefore accused the Soviets of having made deliberately false statements about their actions in Cuba and ordered a military "quarantine" of the island. All ships bound for Cuba would be halted and inspected, and those found to contain cargoes of offensive weapons would be turned back.

The United States had already begun to prepare for possible military action against Cuba. While denying that troop movements had any relation to the situation in Cuba, the Pentagon ordered that additional jet fighters and Marines be moved into southern Florida. On October 22, the President placed our armed forces across the world on alert and authorized the Secretary of Defense to call up 150,000 Reservists.

One hundred and eighty ships were deployed in the Caribbean. To lessen its vulnerability to attack by missiles, the Strategic Air Command was dispersed to civilian landing fields around the country. B-52 bombers were ordered into the air fully loaded with atomic weapons. As one bomber came down to land, another immediately took its place in the air. Secretary of Defense Robert McNamara characterized the days of the missile crisis as "a period of the most intense strain I have ever operated under." The U.S. was being girded for instant atomic warfare.[12]

The day after the President's speech, members of the Organization of American States met in an emergency session and adopted a resolution supporting United States' actions with respect to Cuba. The OAS further called for the immediate dismantling and withdrawal of all offensive weapons and recommended that member states take individual or collective actions to ensure that the Government of Cuba could not continue to receive from the Soviets military supplies which might threaten the peace and security of the hemisphere.

The U.S. had hoped for a similar resolution of support from the UN. But as accusations went round in the Security Council efforts were made to cool feelings on both sides and bring the parties to the conference table.

During the crisis week from October 22 to 28, there were almost daily communications between Kennedy and Khrushchev in an attempt to remove some of the heat from the situation and reach a solution. On October 26 a letter from Khrushchev arrived, proposing Soviet removal of offensive weapons from Cuba and an end to the introduction of further weapons in return for American termination of her blockade of Cuba and agreement not to invade the island. The next day a much more antagonistic letter arrived from the Soviet Union. This second letter seemed to deny the earlier one by promising Soviet removal of missiles from Cuba only if the United States removed similar missiles from Turkey near the Soviet border.

The Soviet letter of October 27 began what Robert Kennedy called "the most difficult twenty-four hours of the missile crisis." President Kennedy, not wanting to involve NATO in the crisis, was in a quandary. Convinced that military steps were the only ones the Soviets would understand, the Joint Chiefs of Staff recommended an air strike, followed by an invasion of Cuba. However, President Kennedy chose to respond to the more conciliatory of the two Khrushchev letters. In his reply, President Kennedy accepted the Russian proposal of removing offensive weapons from Cuba in return for assurances that the blockade would be lifted and that there would be no invasion of the island. The tensions of those seven days in Moscow and Washington eased when, on October 28, Khrushchev announced that dismantling had begun according to the terms which Kennedy had accepted in his reply.[13]

Edward Snyder and Frances Neely consider the Cuban missile crisis as the most intense and anguished period in the crisis-filled life of the FCNL. When President Kennedy announced his program of blockade and military threats, the Friends Committee focused its energies on keeping the dispute from escalating into a nuclear war. Wires were sent to the President and the Senate, urging restraint and adherence to U.S. treaty commitments to settle disputes by peaceful means, saying, "If the United States is worried about the possibility of Cuba becoming an offensive base, we should take this issue to the UN." Both before and after the President's speech, FCNL informed concerned Friends and various organizations across the country of the seriousness of the situation and urged them to wire the White House. FCNL staff encouraged Friends to call for negotiations and to protest any U.S. action which was not in conformity with the UN Charter.

An *Action Bulletin*, which was sent out on October 24 to 1,446 individuals across the country, made the following recommendation: "Negotiations are urged on both the U.S. and Soviet resolutions submitted to the UN. Neutral nations are taking initiatives to prevent fighting and bring the parties to the conference table. You can help by speaking out in your community against the President's perilous decision and by supporting a cooling-off period and negotiations at the UN."

Edward Snyder talked with Senators Hubert Humphrey and

Frank Church and arranged for representatives of several religious groups to meet with Seth Tillman of the Senate Foreign Relations Committee staff. Other discussions of the crisis were held with Congressional assistants.

The Washington office kept in close touch by telephone with the Quaker UN Program in New York City, while individuals met with representatives of several embassies in Washington.

FCNL teamed up with the Methodist Board of Peace and World Order for an emergency meeting on October 28 called by national church leaders to discuss the Cuba situation. Eighty-five prominent Americans later affixed their signatures to the following statement, which was drawn up at the meeting:

> ...War in the nuclear age can bring no victory to any nation. Courage in a time of crisis should be matched by courage in a time of opportunity. . . . As a free and peaceful nation why should we fear a reexamination of every crucial international question? The United Nations is a providential instrument for the consideration of every threatening problem — Cuba, Berlin, bases, disarmament, nuclear testing. . . . [14]

When the fear of immediate war subsided, the FCNL continued to encourage constructive solutions to the problem of U.S.-Cuban relations. The Committee opposed cutting Cuba out of the UN assistance program to diversify and improve agriculture, and it advocated a resumption of diplomatic relations and a restoration of trade. Partly because the Guantanamo Naval Base was considered by the U.S. as an outpost for the defense of the Panama Canal, the 1967 Statement of Legislative Policy urged "that strategic international areas such as the Panama Canal and the Suez Canal be ceded to the UN or put under UN guarantees to insure freedom of passage for all nations and the arbitration of all disputes over their management."

In retrospect, the Department of Defense in the spring of 1963 estimated "the out of pocket costs incurred by last fall's Cuban crisis. . .at about $184 million." President Kennedy had commented in February that the Communist threat to the hemisphere was not "primarily based on Cuba" but came from local action which "feeds on the hardships of the people there."

Ten years later, in 1973, the FCNL undertook an intensive effort to encourage the U.S. to resume normal diplomatic and trade relations with Cuba. Richard Post, a former U.S. Foreign Service officer working as Friend-in-Washington, conducted numerous interviews in Congress for the purpose of improving relations with Cuba and other Latin American countries.

THE MIDDLE EAST: 1969

The Middle East has been a tinder box for more than twenty-five years. Four wars have been fought there in that time, and still there is no stable peace.

Landrum Bolling, president of Earlham College, was invited by the FCNL to spend the month of March 1969 as Friend-in-Washington, exploring possibilities for a lasting political settlement in the Mideast. At that time, he conducted an intensive series of interviews with members of Congress, U.S. government representatives, UN officials, members of various embassies, and leaders of interested organizations. In one conversation in New York, Lord Caradon, British Ambassador to the United Nations, suggested to him that the Friends try to draw up some proposals for consideration. "The Americans have made some proposals, and so have the Russians," commented the Ambassador, "but there are really no propositions before the parties now which are the basis of serious negotiation. Why don't the Friends make a try?"

That weekend Landrum Bolling went back to Richmond, Indiana. He soon returned to Washington with the draft of a proposal which he discussed with U.S. officials and with Jews and Arabs. Since the FCNL concentrates mainly on legislation, the American Friends Service Committee took up this project and in late March organized a working party, which included Frances Neely from FCNL, to focus on a more comprehensive statement. Landrum Bolling spent much of the following year, often in company with Paul and Jean Johnson of the AFSC, shuttling back and forth between the Middle East and the United States, conferring with people in and out of government. After eighteen drafts the document was published by the AFSC under the title *Search for Peace in the Middle East*. Some 150,000 copies have been circulated, including a revised edition published by Fawcett.[15] The document has also been translated into three languages. It was anticipated that some of the ideas would not be acceptable to either many Jews or many Arabs. But this project was a serious attempt to weigh the various conflicting interests involved and to search for formulations which might help in achieving a solution to the Mideast conflict.

LEBANON: 1958

President Eisenhower, in an extraordinary move on Saturday,

January 5, 1957, addressed a Joint Session of Congress on the Middle East situation, even before he delivered his State of the Union message. He asked for blanket authority to employ the Armed Forces of the United States as he deemed "necessary to secure and protect the territorial integrity and political independence of any such nation or group of nations requesting such aid against overt armed aggression from any nation controlled by international Communism. . . ." There was no termination date in the resolution which was adopted to implement this grant of authority.

The FCNL strongly opposed such a sweeping delegation of powers. Even the President agreed that his proposal, which included transferring to the Middle East economic aid funds already appropriated, did little to meet the basic problems of the area. These unsolved questions included 900,000 Arab refugees, the conflict over the Suez Canal, the pressing need to develop water resources and the prolonged Arab-Israeli dispute. Even this far-reaching grant of authority under the Eisenhower doctrine was exceeded by the 1958 dispatch of troops to Lebanon.

A violent revolutionary outbreak occurred in Baghdad, Iraq, on July 14, 1958. Fearful of what might happen in nearby Lebanon, the President of Lebanon requested that some United States forces be stationed there. President Eisenhower dispatched 9,500 Marines, equipped with nuclear weapons, to that country, many of them landing within twenty-four hours.

Over the weekend Edward Snyder produced a six-page *Action Bulletin*, suggesting that readers write six letters, including ones to the President, their Congressman and Senators, UN Ambassador Henry Cabot Lodge and the editor of their local newspaper. He outlined a five-point program for governmental action. On Monday Jeanette Hadley typed the *Bulletin*. Tuesday and Wednesday, from 9 a.m. to 10 p.m., Alice Stout and an outside printer ran 14,000 sets through the multilith. Bill Hufford addressed envelopes and the stuffing was done as simultaneously as possible by other staff members and volunteers. Final copies were delivered to the post office Thursday afternoon. Additional printings were made soon after.

The *Bulletin* was mailed to key contacts by the Methodist Board of World Peace, the National Council of Churches, the Church of the Brethren, the American Friends Service Committee, and the Five Years Meeting of Friends. Representatives of nongovernmental organizations were called together at the headquarters of the American Association of University Women to review the situation and to discuss possible strategy.

In a constructive statement to the UN General Assembly, August 13, President Eisenhower urged the UN to adopt three of the measures which FCNL and others had been advocating for the Middle East — creation of a UN Police Force, economic development and control of the arms traffic in the area.

As troops were landing in Lebanon on July 15, 1958, Congressman Henry Reuss of Wisconsin had risen in the House of Representatives and declared that "by intervening, we risk not only World War III, but also the moral revulsion of the uncommitted." He criticized President Eisenhower for intervening without consulting Congress and without debate. Speaker Sam Rayburn cut off criticism, refusing to let him proceed and saying that "in times like these we had better allow matters to develop rather than making remarks about them."

Interestingly enough, the Speaker's remarks were expunged from the printed *Congressional Record.* But the story went out over TV and radio that the Congressman had not been allowed to voice criticism of this military move in detail. People wrote in from all over the country. When three of us called upon the Congressman to commend him for exercising his right as a citizen to speak out on what he believed was a dangerous course, he thanked us and asked if we would like to see his mail.

An Air Force colonel who had served in the Middle East wrote from California that from his point of view such a move was the last thing the U.S. should do if it wanted to retain the respect of that part of the world. A missionary who had lived many years in that area wrote in a similar vein. One of his staff said to me, "Do you know what impressed the Congressman most?" He picked up a postcard on which there were words printed in block letters, "God Bless You." One need not write a volume to impress a member of Congress. William Wrigley, Jr., who built the Wrigley Tower in Chicago from the profits of chewing gum, had as his motto, "Tell them quick and tell them often."

On the following day Congressman Emanuel Cellar of New York asked for consent to make a one-minute speech. Speaker Rayburn told him, "Not if it is controversial. The chair is not going to recognize members to talk about foreign affairs in this critical situation." Upon learning that Mr. Cellar desired to congratulate the President, he was allowed to continue.[16]

U.S. troops in Lebanon were finally withdrawn in October, after having been stationed there for three months.

DOMINICAN REPUBLIC: 1965

To believe that the pressures for reform in Latin America are created by Communist activities is childish. The turbulence that pervades the politics of most of the Latin American countries stems from the prevalence of ancient and rigid social conditions and institutions inimical to economic development and social change. As long as a handful of men own almost all the land, and a few foreign corporations control the mineral wealth, the public utilities and plantations, Latin America will be torn by violence and instability. The Communists are not responsible for these conditions; they only exploit them to their own advantage.

— Edmundo Flores, "Latin America-
Alliance for Reaction," *The Nation*
200, No. 25, June 21, 1965, p. 662.

In another crisis of conscience and commitment President Lyndon Johnson on April 28, 1965, sent into the Dominican Republic the first contingent of an eventual 23,000 American troops to protect 1,300 American lives and to block a rebellion. Dominican rebels had tried to reinstall the democratically-elected Juan Bosch, who had been driven from the Presidency by a military coup in 1963. It was alleged that the rebellion was led by Communists, who were trying to take over the Dominican Republic as they had assumed power in Cuba. A social revolution anywhere in Latin America is likely to involve a certain number of Communists.

This intervention flatly violated the Charter of the Organization of American States. As already stated in this chapter regarding the Bay of Pigs invasion in Cuba, article 15 of the Charter denies the right of any state or group of states "to intervene, directly or indirectly for any reason whatsoever, in the internal or external affairs of any other State." Article 17 forbids "military occupation. . .on any ground whatever."

Trujillo had ruled the Dominican Republic tyrannically for thirty-one years until his assassination in 1961. During these many years of rule he had received considerable U.S. support. At the time of the intervention General Elias Wessin y Wessin was head of the military junta. Concerning the General, *The Nation* editorialized, "The fact that he was an outstanding practitioner of murder, both personal and wholesale, did not render him odious" to the United States.[17]

Samuel Shapiro, professor of history at Notre Dame University, declared in the next issue of *The Nation* that Juan Bosch "is no Communist, and never has been accused of being one by anybody to the left of the John Birch Society." A poet, professor, historian and novelist, Bosch became President in 1962, by a 2-to-1 margin, in an apparently honest election and had enjoyed American support during the eight months of his regime before he was deposed.

The sending of American troops was criticized by many Latin countries, such as Peru, Colombia, Chile, Venezuela, Uruguay, Ecuador, Brazil, Mexico and Costa Rica as a violation of the OAS Charter. The next *FCNL Newsletter* after the intervention reviewed the developments and urged its readers to wire the President and their Senators asking them to stem the U.S. trend toward unilateral military action both in the Dominican Republic and in Vietnam.

The *Newsletter* quoted Senator Joseph Clark of Pennsylvania who told his colleagues on May 14:

> . . . .there is a very grave question as to whether there is now or ever was a genuine threat of a Communist coup. . .In my opinion, for every Communist. . .we rout out or kill. . .we make 100 and perhaps 1000 other Communists by the ruthless methods of our intervention. . .in violation of our treaty commitments. I believe we ought to look pretty carefully. . .to the charge. . .that the real forces behind the counter-revolution. . .are economic interests, American and Dominican alike. . .which are concerned lest a liberal government come into office with power to enforce a badly and long-needed land reform, to see that adequate taxes are collected from the very rich. . .and that in due course we can have a Government which is not controlled by a military junta. . . . [18]

FCNL encouraged intensive Congressional discussion of the implication of this illegal, unilateral intervention. On July 13, approximately sixty representatives of nongovernmental organizations were called together for an in-depth discussion of the Dominican crisis. The speakers were Don Kurzman, *Washington Post* reporter in Santo Domingo during the crisis, and Gonzalo Facio, Costa Rican Ambassador to the United States and to the OAS.

Proctor Lippincott, who did his two-years' alternative service with the Friends Committee and who worked with me during much of that time, took a special interest in Latin American affairs. He joined a group who went to the Dominican Republic to observe the elections in 1966. These observers went under the auspices of the Committee for Free Elections in the Dominican Republic — a committee of distinguished American citizens concerned about honest election and the restoration of more democracy in the Dominican Republic.

THE KOREAN WAR: 1950-1953

On Sunday morning, June 25, 1950, the North Korean army crossed the 38th parallel into South Korea.[19]

At the end of World War II, an agreement had been reached between the Pentagon and the U.S.S.R. that the Russians would supervise the demobilization and repatriation of Japanese soldiers north of the 38th parallel in Korea while the U.S. would do the same south of that line. Subsequently, the Russians gave substantial aid to the area north of the parallel, while the United States maintained troops in the south and helped in that area's postwar reconstruction. In time, what was envisaged as a temporary demarcation line hardened into a rigid political division and threats began to be issued by each side to unify Korea by force. On that fateful morning when the North Korean army drove across the border toward the South Korean capital of Seoul, the threat materialized.

On June 26, the morning after the invasion was launched, I telephoned the American Friends Service Committee in Philadelphia, the American Association for the United Nations and the National Council of Churches in New York City. I asked them whether they, singly or in concert, would urge President Truman to appeal for a cease-fire and for efforts at mediation and request him not to commit American military forces to Korea at that juncture. Unfortunately, these organizations did not feel free to act in this way at that time. I did not know until weeks later when the UN documents were published that the recommendations of the UN Commission in Korea were quite similar to what I had proposed.

The next day, as I recall, the Point IV Information Committee, composed of representatives of nongovernmental organizations concerned with economic aid and technical assistance, had a luncheon at which the American Ambassador to Nicaragua spoke. When the meeting was over, I shared his taxi back to the State Department. I asked him, "Can we get the President to hold out for a cease-fire and try to get this war stopped now?" The Ambassador replied, "Sorry, son, the President committed American military forces at eleven o'clock this morning."

The biennial meeting at Cape May of the Friends General Conference, which brought together hundreds of Friends for worship and discussion, took place during that week. Friends there encouraged the FCNL to continue seeking an end to the war. Our efforts turned to exploring possible ways of mediation. We discussed this problem with a number of Senators, including Senators

Hendrickson of New Jersey, Morse of Oregon and Humphrey of Minnesota. (See the chapter on "Memorable Interviews" for the discussion with Senator Humphrey.)

The July 1950 issue of the *FCNL Washington Newsletter* was entirely devoted to the Korean conflict. It reviewed the efforts for mediation up until late July and discussed some basic factors in a solution. Enclosed with the *Newsletter* was a background report on Korea written by Stewart Meacham. For ten months in 1947 Meacham had been a labor advisor to Lieutenant General John R. Hodge, who at that time was in command of the U.S. occupation forces in South Korea. Some years later Stewart Meachem served as head of the peace education program of the American Friends Service Committee. His background report stated that the regime of Syngman Rhee had been "marked by an intensification of the police state character of the South Korean government" and cited some of the repressive measures which had been carried out in South Korea. This article drew a bitter attack on the FCNL from an official spokesman and apologist for Syngman Rhee, but the essential facts were not controverted.

In many respects August 7 and 8, 1950, were two of the most crowded and significant days which I spent during my first decade in Washington. The FCNL helped bring the outstanding Christian leader, Dr. E. Stanley Jones, to Washington for two days of conversations on the Korean question and on some of the broader aspects of East-West relationships. Annalee Stewart, who had arranged many of the appointments, and I accompanied him on most of his talks with some thirty people in Congress and in the State Department.

For forty-three years Dr. Jones had spent much of his time in India. In May, he had talked with his long-time friend, Prime Minister Nehru, asking him whether he might be able to use his good offices in resolving some of the difficulties between East and West. Jones was convinced of Nehru's sincerity and of his general sympathy with democracy. During the summer of 1950, Nehru suggested that efforts be made to end the war in Korea by setting up a commission composed of the representatives of nonpermanent nations on the UN Security Council. This commission would be empowered to receive and make proposals to end the Korean conflict.

In Congress there was a good deal of hostility toward India because India had taken an independent line in the UN and did not always vote with the United States in spite of large-scale American aid. Nevertheless, as Dr. Jones tried to build understanding between the United States and Asia, he was listened to in Washington with respect and often with real eagerness because of his long and intimate experience in India.

Senator H. Alexander Smith of New Jersey welcomed Stanley Jones very warmly and asked his opinion of an idea he had. The United States, according to the Senator, should conduct a broad peace offensive in Korea before the Soviet Union did because of the likelihood that very soon the Soviets might make a peace offer concerning Korea which the U.S. could not accept. If the Russians made an offer that the U.S. rejected, the U.S. would appear to be rejecting peace and behaving like a warmonger. As soon as the interview was over, the Senator planned to consult with John Foster Dulles about whether the U.S. could initiate a real peace offensive. When Dr. Jones advocated the recognition of Communist China as one step toward peace in the Far East, the Senator remarked that, while he could not accept the idea yet, he was more ready to discuss it than he had been two months earlier. As I remember, two months before he had shaken his fist in his visitor's face and asserted, "You are as wrong as you can be, Dr. Jones."

Senator Brien McMahon of Connecticut was very responsive. He believed that if the State Department had taken a real initiative for a major change in policy toward the Soviet Union, as he had urged in February, the present trouble in Korea might have been headed off, although Assistant Secretary of State Hickerson was still not willing to grant such a possibility. (See the chapter on "Memorable Interviews" for a report on McMahon's later reflections.) According to the Senator, Stalin could not have bought for a billion dollars the damage that Senator Joe McCarthy had done to our democratic institutions in the United States through his smear tactics against many of the liberals of that period. McMahon indicated that he was giving serious consideration to a further presentation of his views on peace and disarmament but had not yet decided if, when, or how. E. Stanley Jones urged the Senator very strongly to stand by his convictions and speak out. Jones believed that men like McMahon must give us the leadership we need. He believed that the laws of the universe were on our side if the right thing was done.

Senator Frank Graham of North Carolina stressed that the United Nations, with the help of the United States and other countries, must take vigorous and effective action against aggression or there would be no United Nations. Graham reviewed the UN experience in mediating in Indonesia and gave a vivid firsthand account of some of his discussions with the Dutch. One of Graham's hardest problems was to get the Dutch to agree to the proposition which finally broke the deadlock.

The most outspoken of the Senators was Hickenlooper of Iowa. In the discussion over Korea, he countered Dr. Jones's attempts to bring an understanding of the East into the conversation. The United States had been generous beyond any nation in history, contended Senator Hickenlooper; why should American citizens keep criticizing our foreign policy? We had given billions of dollars in economic aid through the Marshall Plan and had given military aid to many countries. There would be no peace until the Soviet Union gave up their program of world domination, which is a tenet of Communism. None of us wanted war, none of us looked with anything but regret upon the destruction in Korea, but appeasement had never paid and the Soviet Union must be stopped.

INTERVIEW WITH PRESIDENT TRUMAN

Senator Hill of Alabama thought it would be useful for Dr. Jones to talk with President Truman and agreed to join with other Senators to open the way. Through his initiative and that of Senator Graham, Dr. Jones did have a very forthright meeting with the President on September 1, 1950.

The interview was a ringing appeal to the President to accept the good offices of Nehru in seeking a settlement of the Korean conflict and for the President to go to the opening session of the UN Assembly and make a bold and dramatic proposal for peace based on India's suggestion. The President was very much opposed to Nehru's earlier recommendation that bringing Communist China into the UN be a part of the settlement, a position which Nehru later modified. Some excerpts from the notes on the interview by Dr. Jones follow:

> . . .When I went in the President greeted me by saying: "Senator Graham gave you a tremendous buildup. If you are half as good as he says you are, then you are a wonder." I said to him that I had come to try to interpret the situation from the standpoint of the East. . . . Then I said: "Nehru, whom I have known across the years is sincere, honest and important. When he speaks the awakening East speaks through him, for they look on him as their spokesman. . . . If you win Nehru, you win the hundreds of millions of the East, if you lose him you lose the East. Therefore when he made the proposal of offering his good offices to help in a peaceful settlement of the Korean conflict that was important."
>
> Nehru has clarified his position in a speech before the Indian Parliament on August 3rd in which he said: "India's policy on Korea is based on

three main considerations. Firstly, that an act of aggression had been committed by North Korea over South Korea. This aggression is wrong and has to be condemned, and it must be resisted. Secondly, for the future insofar as it is possible, war should not spread beyond Korea. No other question should be tied up with the Korean trouble and means must be explored for ending the war. Thirdly, the future of Korea must be decided, naturally, by the Koreans themselves — in just what form or shape I cannot say."

The President said at once: "I can accept that." I then called his attention to the fact that "Here in this statement Nehru had taken out the suggestion about bringing Communist China into the United Nations in order to make a better atmosphere in which peace might more easily be found."

"Since then," I said, "Nehru has changed his suggestion from offering his personal good offices to try to find peace to the suggestion that 'the little Security Council,' made up of six nonpermanent members should work out a basis of peace for the settlement of the Korean war and present it to the big Security Council. This puts Nehru's proposals for peace within the framework of UN instead of basing it on one man outside the UN."

"Now, how would it do, Mr. President, for you to go personally to the opening session of the UN Assembly and make a bold and dramatic proposal for peace based on India's suggestion about the little Security Council."

"If you did this, you would kill three birds with one stone: (1) You would prove that this country believes in democracy in that it is willing to be guided, in an important matter, by the smaller nations. (2) You would prove to the East that this country is not there for imperialistic purposes.

They are not sure why we are in the East. They saw Britain come to trade and stay to rule. Have we come with apparently philanthropic purposes only to stay to dominate? They are not sure, for colonialism has bitten deep into the consciousness of the East. If we would accept this proposal of India it would show that we are willing to be guided by the East in important matters concerning the East. This would do more to dispel questions of our intentions than all our propaganda directed to the East. (3) It would give us a chance to settle the Korean war by negotiations without its spreading to a world war. We should pledge ourselves beforehand to accept the recommendations of the little Security Council."

The President's comment was: "I will not bind this country beforehand to accept recommendations which may include the bringing of Communist China into the United Nations as a part of the settlement." My reply was: "But, Mr. President, couldn't you hedge your acceptance about with some such proviso as this: 'Provided the little Security Council in its recommendations would confine itself to Korea itself and not bring in extraneous matters such as the bringing of Communist China into the United Nations, a matter which must be settled on its own merits'?" To this he made no reply, but his attitude gave half-assent. . . .

He then went on to tell the awful things the Russians had done; in doing so, he cited the fact that a German bishop had sat in the very chair I was seated in and with tears in his eyes told how the Russians had taken a hundred thousand children and shipped them to Russian territory for the purposes of making Communists out of them. I replied: "Mr. President, I'm not afraid of the badnesses of the Communists so much as I am of their goodnesses, for it is the good things that make it float. The more tyrannical and inhuman they become, the quicker they fall; for the people will stand just so much, then they begin to rise and revolt." To which the President replied: "I hope so, but I'm afraid they won't do it within a generation. . . ." I then added: "To the people's possible revolt we must add the fact that this is a moral universe and individuals and nations don't break the laws of the moral universe written into the constitution of things — they break themselves upon these laws. Whoever has the first or intermediate word, the moral universe is going to have the last word." "I believe that," said the President.

I reminded the President that he had been elected by the common people and that therefore in this crisis he should be the voice of the common people. The common people everywhere, on both sides of the curtain, want peace. They don't want war. "You must voice that cry for peace if you are to fulfill your destiny." He replied: "I am trying earnestly for peace." "You must try harder and more dramatically," I suggested.

"For," I continued, "to get into a third world war will not settle the issue of Communism. You might defeat Russia and not defeat Communism. Nobody would win the war even though one side might crawl out as the survivor. Conditions of despair and poverty and ruin would be created in which Communism would spread even among us. For Communism spreads out of postwar ruin and despair. Our policy should be twofold — first, a short-range policy of settling the Korean conflict before it develops into a world war; second, a long-range policy of creating a world order, a world government, in which Russia under collective security would be free to carry out her way of life within Russia. America would be free to carry out her way of life under collective security within America. All other nations the same." He agreed.

Then I added, "Mr. President, we are organizing a Seven Day Continuous Vigil of Prayer throughout the twenty-four hours in shifts of an hour, praying for peace and especially for you as you make these decisions. This will be held possibly in the Epiphany Episcopal Church in downtown Washington beginning the day the UN Assembly will open September 19." He was very interested and expressed his gratitude. He thanked me for coming.

As I was leaving I said: "The last time I was in this room, Mr. President, it was three days before Pearl Harbor and I was on the same mission — to try to find a way to peace." The President replied: "At that time I was in Missouri." [20]

Instead of the proposed seven-day vigil, the Washington

Federation of Churches arranged for 14 churches to be open for prayer and meditation on the day the General Assembly opened, September 19.

In these talks with Dr. Jones, Senator Tom Connally, Chairman of the Senate Foreign Relations Committee, and Chairman John Kee of the House Foreign Affairs Committee both showed their advanced age. Their loss of vigor seemed to us a tragic limitation to the dynamic and enlightened vision needed from both committees for the conduct of our foreign relations.

Representative Kee, however, had suggested that we arrange with Congressman Mike Mansfield, Chairman of the Far East Subcommittee, for Dr. Jones to speak to the members of the Subcommittee the next morning. When Dr. Jones concluded his presentation, Chairman Mansfield spoke very highly of his great service as a churchman and missionary and thanked him for his interpretation of India and the Far East in which Mansfield himself was so much interested. One of the men present was Thomas E. Morgan, who later became Chairman of the House Foreign Affairs Committee. Mansfield has served as Senate Majority leader since 1961.

The most skeptical person interviewed was David Lawrence, editor of *U.S. News and World Report.* He thought Secretary of State Acheson, whom he knew very well personally, ought to be replaced. The world must deal with aggression firmly and vigorously without compromise. He was more critical of the Russians than anyone else with whom we talked and less responsive to the idea of offering a peace initiative before the Russians and their North Korean puppets had been taught a lesson. He had great qualms about Nehru and India because of their support of the Soviet Union on procedural questions in the United Nations. Nor was he convinced of either the reliability or the motives of the Indians.

Another lively discussion was held with George C. McGhee, the Assistant Secretary of State for Near East, South Asian and African Affairs, and with three other State Department staff officers. When Dr. Jones expressed his regret that Nehru's proposals for mediation had not received the attention they deserved, Secretary McGhee vigorously denied that the U.S. Government had treated Mr. Nehru and the Indian proposals cavalierly or without full, frank and sympathetic consideration. In the Assistant Secretary's view, the proposals of Nehru were not for mediation nor could they form the basis of mediation. Mr. Nehru had dragged recognition of Communist China into these proposals and that issue was not related to the Korean crisis. The U.S. was not by-passing Nehru; the State Department was in constant touch with him and wanted to use India's services if they could. But the Secretary wanted to make quite clear to us that U.S. policy had been right in the past and there was every reason to believe that our policy was right at that time. The U.S. was willing to consider all peace efforts, but the United Nations must be upheld in its action against aggression. He expressed appreciation to his visitors for the spirit which had motivated our visit and assured us that the State Department was always ready and willing to listen.

A short time following the conversations just reviewed and after the Chinese had crossed the Yalu River to intervene in behalf of the North Koreans, E. Stanley Jones and I called on Dean Rusk, at that time Assistant Secretary of State for Far Eastern Affairs. We referred to the Indian suggestion that representatives of the nations on the UN Security Council might be named to a commission to receive or make recommendations for a Korean settlement. Let the U.S., we suggested, name the representatives for such a commission if the Indian proposal was not satisfactory. The important thing, we insisted, was that third party judgment should be used when two countries in conflict could not settle their differences. This was the time to establish the principle of third party judgment. To go on with the Korean War was to make the United Nations a belligerent and not a judge or a peacemaker. Continuation of the war would increasingly destroy the country we were ostensibly trying to defend. But Dean Rusk did not think the principle could be applied then and turned the idea down.

These sketchy reports of some interviews early in the three-year Korean War will, I hope, give a little insight into the psychology of that time — a sudden plunge into war under the UN flag in the midst of a protracted and intense Cold War between the U.S. and the Soviet Union. The Cold War included the diplomatic and economic isolation of Communist China by our government. McCarthyism and virulent anticommunism dominated the scene at home.

A "new approach" to settling the Korean conflict was made in September 1952 by Senator Ralph E. Flanders of Vermont. He proposed establishing a neutral zone in northwest Korea; uniting the industrial north and the agricultural south to form a self-contained and high level economy; rebuilding destroyed factories, highways, railways and homes under UN supervision (the U.S. alone was spending $6 billion each year on the war); and, after a period of reconstruction, holding a UN-supervised free election in Korea.

There followed an example of lobbying in reverse. Some time afterwards, the Senator called me in and gave me quite a dressing down because he felt that the FCNL had not given him sufficient support for his proposal. That was the year of our all-out but successful effort to defeat UMT and of our involvement in various other issues. Leaving aside the question of whether the Senator's proposals were as well thought out as they could have been, I acknowledged that the criticism was well deserved.

All the efforts for mediation were fruitless, and the Korean War went on until an armistice finally halted the slaughter three years after it had begun. More than 5,700,000 Americans served in our Armed Forces in Korea, and conscription was extended to help fight the war. American casualties included 33,629 battle deaths, 20,617 other deaths and 103,284 wounded. But the basic problems between North and South Korea were never settled.

I have visited South Korea twice since the Korean War and can testify to the devastating spiritual and physical cost of that war, the repressive nature of the Park government in South Korea, the continued fear of invasion from North Korea, and the staggering problems still facing South Korea. For twenty years the 38th parallel has been perhaps the most hermetically sealed border in the world with virtually no exchange of mail or visits between separated families. As this is being written, protracted talks between the North and South Korean Red Cross societies and secret negotiations between officials of the two governments have resulted in an agreement to work toward peaceful reunification and to install a hot line for communication between the two capitals, and to work toward possible reunion of families.

In the tortuous and uphill struggle to build an effective world government and a genuine international police system, the intervention in Korea marked a moral advance in *purpose* — international responsibility and action by the United Nations to overcome aggression. But in *method* it was the age-old means of war and indiscriminate destruction.

Stopping a war after it has started is much like trying to stop a flood at full tide, which can only be stopped by measures like reclamation, reforestation, reservoirs, and other means of curtailing a flood before it develops full force.

The lesson of the Korean War is that every effort should be made to prevent another UN-sponsored war. In early 1973 the U.S. was still trying to extricate itself from the longest and most divisive war in U.S. history — the Vietnam War — which is the subject of the next two chapters.

CHAPTER 14

Vietnam: 1954-1968

DeGaulle's Warning to President Kennedy, June 1961

You will find that intervention in this area will be an endless entanglement. Once a nation has been aroused no foreign power, however strong, can impose its will upon it. You will discover this for yourselves. For even if you find local leaders who in their own interests are prepared to obey you, the people will not agree to it, and indeed do not want you. The ideology which you invoke will make no difference. Indeed, in the eyes of the masses it will become identified with your will to power. That is why the more you become involved out there against Communism, the more the Communists will appear as the champions of national independence and the more support they will receive, if only from despair.

We French have had experience of it. You Americans wanted to take our place in Indochina. Now you want to take over where we left off and revive a war which we brought to an end. I predict that you will sink step by step into a bottomless military and political quagmire, however much you spend in men and money. What you, we and others ought to do for unhappy Asia is not to take over the running of these States ourselves but to provide them with the means to escape from the misery and humiliation which, there as elsewhere, are the causes of totalitarian regimes. I tell you this in the name of the West.

> — "DeGaulle's Warning to Kennedy:
> An 'Endless Entanglement' in Vietnam,"
> the *New York Times*, March 15, 1972,
> excerpts from final volume of
> Charles DeGaulle, *Memoirs of Hope, Renewal and Endeavor.*

Surely, of all the lessons to be learned from the study of history, one of the most important must be, how governments, by carefully collecting military and diplomatic intelligence, submitting them to intricate analysis by trained specialists and then turning over the results for judgment to responsible politicians and statesmen, do in the end come to make all those damn-fool decisions. . . . Presidents Kennedy and Johnson decided the United States could get into a war in Asia without deciding just how to get out. . . .

> — A.M. Rosenthal in the Book Review
> Section of the *New York Times*, page 3,
> June 3, 1973.

Based on false assumptions and fought for unattainable goals, the Vietnam War has been the most divisive episode in our history since the War Between the States in 1861. To justify the war, successive administrations — as revealed in the Pentagon Papers and scores of books — deluded themselves, withheld vital information and deceived the people.

My words cannot portray the unmitigated tragedy of the deaths of countless soldiers on all sides of the war, the suffering of the women and children who were the victims of indiscriminate bombings, the destruction of cities and villages, of crops and forests, or the loss of faith in their government by millions of American citizens.[1]

This has been a war of indescribable barbarity, waged with inhuman weapons including napalm and antipersonnel bombs — weapons which are totally unconscious of the suffering they have caused. Some of the disastrous effects of this war to date are summarized at the end of the next chapter.

"Step by Step Into a Bottomless Quagmire"

President Eisenhower made the first U.S. commitment to South Vietnam with his letter of support on October 1, 1954, to Ngo Dinh Diem, according to Rowland Evans and Robert Novak in their book, *Lyndon B. Johnson: The Exercise of Power* (New York: American Library, Inc., 1966, pp. 530-31). Eisenhower and Dulles initiated the practice of military intervention when they introduced 800 "advisors" into Vietnam and assigned to that country the Michigan State University "training" group in counterinsurgency. President Kennedy escalated the involvement by increasing the "advisors" to 16,000 and by expanding military aid and support.

During the presidential campaign in 1964, President Johnson repeatedly asserted that he would not expand the war. In his message to Congress on August 5, asking for the blanket grant of authority in the Gulf of Tonkin Resolution, the President said:

> "As I have repeatedly made clear, the U.S. intends no rashness, and seeks no wider war."

In the heat of the campaign against Senator Barry Goldwater, whose ideas he denounced but embraced when he was reelected, President Johnson said in Akron, Ohio, on October 2, 1964:

> ". . . . we are not about to send American boys nine or ten thousand miles away from home to do what Asian boys ought to do for themselves."

Nevertheless, under President Johnson, the number of American troops in South Vietnam reached 565,000 and relentless bombing, with some pauses, was launched against North Vietnam.

President Nixon was quoted during the 1968 campaign that he had a plan to end the war, but on April 30, 1970, came the U.S. invasion ("incursion" was the polite term used by the administration) of Cambodia, which aroused a storm of protests and demonstrations. One critic described this method of "winding down the war" as "bombing four countries and invading two in order to withdraw from one."

During the first four and one-half years of the Nixon Administration, most of the American ground troops were withdrawn from South Vietnam, but there still remain a sizable number of military advisors to the South Vietnamese Army and Air Force and thousands of Air Force personnel in Thailand, Guam and Okinawa. Two peace agreements worked out through prolonged negotiations with North Vietnam have reduced the fighting. But rockets from the NLF and indiscriminate use of artillery by ARVN troops continue to take a heavy toll of civilian casualties, while hundreds of undetonated mines lie in wait for children at play or farmers on their way to the fields.

An all too servile Congress has abdicated its responsibility to oversee and check Presidential power. Congress voted overwhelmingly to grant two blank checks for using Presidential military authority without further Congressional approval. These actions were the Formosa Resolution of 1955 and the Gulf of Tonkin Resolution nine years later. In spite of growing opposition in the country and in Congress, appropriations for the war were voted year after year until June 1973 when both Houses voted to end funds for the bombing of Cambodia as a rider to an appropriations bill. This was vetoed by President Nixon. Finally, a compromise was accepted to end the bombing by August 15, 1973. Not until 1972 was there a clear-cut vote on the war in the House of Representatives.

In condemning American intervention in what was essentially an internal revolution against a repressive and despotic regime in South Vietnam under Bao Dai, Diem and Thieu, the FCNL also condemns the violence of the Vietcong, the assassination of the village chiefs, the terror by day and night, and the action by North Vietnam which forced some 800,000 people to flee to South Vietnam.

John F. Kennedy, in his address to Latin American diplomats at the White House on March 9, 1962, said: "If we make peaceful revolution impossible, we make violent revolution inevitable." As American citizens, we are constantly haunted and challenged by the problem of how to achieve peaceful change in our own and other countries and how to end U.S. support for unjust and dictatorial regimes in country after country.

The Friends Committee shares the concern for the announced U.S. goals of freedom for small nations and of respect for treaties and commitments. The FCNL also has been apprehensive about possible Communist territorial expansion and subversion in Europe and Asia. We do, however, believe that these objectives of peace, justice and freedom have to be pursued and achieved by means other than war.

Rise of the Vietminh: 1941-1953

During the Second World War the Japanese troops who had come into Indochina cooperated with the Vichy French collaborationist government to control the area. Attempts were made to quell local opposition from the Vietnamese secret societies. The largest of these societies, the Vietminh, was made up mostly of North Vietnamese nationalists headed by Ho Chi Minh. It was these Vietminh who formed the core of the Vietcong, a term used by the Saigon government for any opposition, including the National Liberation Front (NLF) later founded by South Vietnamese nationalists and intellectuals.

The Vietminh ultimately defeated the French in May 1954, and since then they have joined with the NLF in warring against the American-backed South Vietnamese regime. Ho Chi Minh turned to the United States for sympathy in his war against the French. Instead of encouragement from the United States, he met with disdain. One can only speculate how different the course of history might have been if the United States had collaborated with the Vietminh in their struggle for independence, instead of trying to prop up a disintegrating French colonial system. The American Government had decided to help the French long before, beginning in 1945 when they sold the French $160 million worth of material. By the end of the nine-year period the U.S. was paying eighty per cent of the cost of the war to the French and had invested more than $2 billion in U.S. aid!

"Is the United States moving toward a shooting war in Southeast Asia?" headlined the *FCNL Washington Newsletter*, April 15, 1954. Secretary of State John Foster Dulles and Admiral Arthur W. Radford, Chairman of the Joint Chiefs of Staff, supported by Vice President Richard Nixon, proposed a one-shot air strike at Dien Bien Phu in behalf of the French with the help of the American Navy carriers and Air Force planes based in the Philippines.

In an off-the-record speech on April 16, 1954, Vice President Nixon was reported to have said that if the French withdrew, Indochina would become Communist dominated within a month. "The United States, as leader of the Free World, cannot afford further retreat in Asia. It is hoped the United States will not have to send troops there, but if this government cannot avoid it, the Administration must face up to the situation and dispatch troops."[2] This intervention proposal was turned down by President Eisenhower when he was faced with determined opposition by Army Chief of Staff General Matthew B. Ridgway, by some influential members of Congress, and by especially strong British resistance to the idea.

Fred Burdick, editor of a personal newssheet entitled *Capitol Gist*, took a poll of more than a hundred members of Congress in February 1954. To the question "Do you favor sending U.S. armed forces to intervene in the Indochina war?" 1% answered "Yes," 86% answered "No" and 13% were undecided. To the second question "Do you favor the United Nations making every effort to arrange a cease-fire in Indochina?" 66% were in favor, 11% were against and a larger number, 23%, were undecided. When Fred Burdick interviewed the late Everett M. Dirksen, soon to be Senate Minority Leader, the Senator commented, "They will never send American troops to Indochina if they depend on a vote here." Senator Wayne Morse of Oregon believed that "the Administration is leading us into an all-out war in Asia. The UN should use all its sanctions available to get a cease-fire and armistice."

THE GENEVA CONFERENCE: 1954

The French defeat at Dien Bien Phu brought the First Indochina

War to an end. The Geneva Conference, convened several weeks before the shattering French defeat at Dien Bien Phu in May, was an attempt at a permanent settlement of the Indochina crisis. Much of what was achieved at Geneva was later made void by the U.S. actions in foreign policy, including the SEATO Pact, which was designed by Dulles as an alternative to the Geneva accords, which he had ignored, and as a bulwark against Communist expansion. The SEATO Pact has been used by successive administrations as a justification for American intervention, although there is no evidence that South Vietnam has ever made a request for SEATO assistance.

The Geneva Conference drew up detailed arrangements for a cease-fire between France and the Vietminh and provisions for elections by July 1956. The U.S. and the Saigon regime refused to sign the Geneva accords. They did not insist that elections be held, even though Undersecretary of State Bedell Smith had said at the Geneva Conference that the U.S. position was that "We shall continue to seek unity through free elections."[3] One reason for Saigon's refusal, with U.S. support, to hold elections was the fear that Ho Chi Minh would win and unify Vietnam under his leadership. In understanding what followed in Vietnam, it is important to remember that the Armistice Agreement was a military truce between the Vietminh and the French Military Command, using the 17th parallel as a temporary position for withdrawal and regroupment of troops in the North and South. The Geneva text says: "The military demarcation line is provisional, and should not in any way be interpreted as constituting a political or territorial boundary."[4]

While some infiltration from the North had been going on for years, according to reports, Northern troop movements into the South did not begin until 1964.[5] Despite the fact that the United States did recognize Vietnam as a single nation (at this time), it violated the Geneva Agreements by surreptitiously supplying South Vietnam with immense amounts of U.S. arms, military personnel, and war material to support Diem.

The establishment of the Southeast Asia Treaty Organization (SEATO) and spiraling U.S. military aid to the puppet regime in South Vietnam seriously undermined the Geneva accords. The SEATO Treaty has often been used as a justification for U.S. intervention in Vietnam. Arthur Larsen, director of the Duke University's Rule of Law Research Center, has noted: "The true fact is that the United States has had no obligation to South Vietnam or anyone else under the SEATO Treaty to use its own armed forces in the defense of South Vietnam."[6]

Some FCNL Actions: 1954

The April 1954 *Washington Newsletter* not only warned against getting involved in a shooting war but called for a general settlement in Asia which would include shifting the emphasis of the conflict from a military basis to a political and economic one. It was time to resume trade with Communist bloc nations and to seek self-government or independence for colonial people.

In May, *Newsletter* readers were urged to continue writing to President Eisenhower, Secretary Dulles, Congress and daily papers opposing the dispatch of any U.S. troops to Indochina and pressing for a settlement and cease-fire at Geneva or at the United Nations. Renewed efforts for international disarmament should be made, while the United States should undertake a wholehearted and sacrificial program to build up the well-being of the people of Southeast Asia.

Lewis Hoskins, executive secretary of the American Friends Service Committee, stopped off in Washington after having spent two weeks at the Geneva Conference. He reiterated to a number of Senators some of the FCNL proposals which, it was hoped, could be achieved at Geneva. During the mid-Eisenhower years of 1954-55, FCNL crusaded against the growing military commitment to Vietnam and urged the United States to make common cause with the downtrodden, the hungry and the suffering peoples of the world through increased economic aid and technical assistance.[7]

The Formosa Resolution: 1955

The Formosa Resolution, a flagrant blank-check grant of authority, was jammed through Congress in five days in January 1955 at the insistence of Secretary Dulles and President Eisenhower, because it was feared that Mainland China might seize the Pescadores or even attack Formosa (Taiwan). The resolution was adopted with little discussion and startling speed. The House Foreign Affairs Committee approved the resolution after five hours of hearings and the House adopted it by a vote of 410-3. After three days of spirited and sometimes stormy debate, only three Senators voted against the measure: Morse, Lehman and Langer. Senator Morse declared, "No man in public office, however worthy he may be, deserves such a pre-dated vote of confidence."[8] The Formosa

Resolution set a precedent for the Gulf of Tonkin Resolution in 1964, which President Johnson often used as an authorization for his deepening military involvement in Vietnam.

A few minutes after he signed the resolution on the morning of January 29, the President left to play golf in Georgia and Mr. Dulles went to the Bahamas for a week of fishing.

NONCOMBAT INVOLVEMENT: 1956-1961

The period between 1956 and 1961, during the later Eisenhower years, was the time when the FCNL was primarily concerned with the struggle between Mainland China and Taiwan and with the growing problems in Laos. This was the period during which the U.S. Government began its long and weary rounds of self-deception and deception of the American people. These were the years of deepening military involvement short of major action on the battlefield. Even though much has been revealed in the Pentagon Papers and the voluminous press reports, I doubt very much that the American people yet know, in any detail, the story of CIA subsidies and activities in Laos, Cambodia and Vietnam during the last 20 years.

J. Stuart Innerst, while serving as FCNL Friend-in-Washington in 1960-61, prepared a document entitled "Light on Laos." Since both the Soviet Union and the United States were sending military supplies in violation of the Geneva Treaty, this little country had become a battleground of contending forces in the East-West conflict. Innerst recommended the reactivation of the International Commission for Supervision and Control of Laos and called upon all nations to respect the provisions of the Geneva Treaty for the neutralization of Laos. He proposed that any technical aid given to Laos be channeled through an agency of the United Nations to insure that it would be used for economic and social development and not for subversion.

AGAINST INCREASING MILITARY INTERVENTION: 1962-1963

John F. Kennedy became President in January 1961. He inherited the assignment of 800 "advisors" and the Michigan State University "training group" in South Vietnam. While not accepting Defense Secretary McNamara's recommendation for a full-scale shipment of troops supposedly sufficient to achieve military victory, Kennedy nevertheless did commit 16,000 American soldiers as "advisors" to the ARVN, the Army of the Republic of Vietnam. This was the crucial escalation, in my opinion, which established the fateful policy of U.S. military commitment to South Vietnam. During his term as President, Kennedy increased military aid to the Diem government, reinforced the South Vietnam Air Force, and endorsed a CIA sabotage program in Laos and in North and South Vietnam.

James Reston wrote in the *New York Times*, February 14, 1962, that "the United States is now involved in an undeclared war in South Vietnam," and a few days later, Homer Bigart expressed in the *New York Times* his belief that the United States seemed inextricably committed to a long inconclusive war. On January 31, 1963, Defense Secretary McNamara expressed the fatal euphoria of one top government official: "The war in Vietnam is going well and will succeed." On the same day, Admiral Felt confidently predicted victory for Saigon within three years.

The FCNL and a few members of Congress like Senator Mike Mansfield and Representative Robert W. Kastenmeier tried to counter this unjustified governmental optimism and to call attention to the build-up of troops in Vietnam and Thailand. Few Americans responded to the plea of the FCNL and others to register complaints about the torture of prisoners by South Vietnamese soldiers while American advisors looked on.

"Is the United States backing into a possible long-term war in Vietnam without the specific Congressional authorization required by the Constitution?" pointedly asked the editors of the FCNL *Washington Newsletter* in March 1962. "Can Communism be checked in Vietnam by U.S. support for an unpopular regime?"

To better publicize U.S. involvement in Vietnam, FCNL circulated many copies of Senator Mike Mansfield's speech at the Michigan State University commencement in which he described our government's policy in Southeast Asia as "at best, a mark-time course of years and decades of immense cost. . .and at worst. . .a collision course."[9] At an informal dinner arranged by FCNL and others, at the Congressional Hotel one block from the Capitol on May 23, 1962, Professor Hans Morgenthau of the University of Chicago gave a vigorous warning about the trend of U.S. policy. The dinner was attended by seven Representatives, ten Senatorial or Congressional assistants and fourteen leaders of nongovernmental organizations. Morganthau has been an outspoken critic of the war for more than ten years.

As one effort to stem the trend toward U.S. involvement, the Vietnam Information Committee was launched by the Unitarian Fellowship for Social Justice, the Women's International League for

Peace and Freedom, and the FCNL at a luncheon on October 3, 1963. U.S. military and political policies in Vietnam were discussed by Dr. Ngo Ton Dat, former First Secretary, Embassy of South Vietnam, and Dr. Erich Wulff, a German psychiatrist who was an eyewitness of the May 8 demonstration in Hue, when the Buddhists were celebrating the birthday of Buddha and protesting the persecution by the Diem government. This meeting, attended by eighty representatives of national organizations and senatorial offices, was the forerunner of many later luncheon meetings to review developments in Indochina and discuss antiwar strategy.

During the year, a delegation of representatives of nongovernmental organizations, including Frances Neely and me from FCNL, conferred with Senate Foreign Relations Committee member Frank Church. At the peak of the impasse with Diem, the Senator and 31 others introduced a resolution calling for an end to all aid to South Vietnam until their government made a "determined" effort to regain popular support. Although S.R. 196 passed the Foreign Relations Committee in a much watered-down version, it was not acted upon by the Senate. However, it was one of the real beginnings of opposition to the war.

GULF OF TONKIN INCIDENT AND LYNDON B. JOHNSON PROMISES: 1964

The Gulf of Tonkin episode exploded on August 2, 1964, and all the facts are still not clear. The *U.S. Destroyer Maddox* allegedly was attacked off the coast of North Vietnam in the Gulf of Tonkin by three North Vietnamese PT boats with torpedoes and gunfire and again on August 4. It was claimed by some of the skeptics that these incidents were not unprovoked because they occurred after units of the South Vietnamese navy had acted without the knowledge of the U.S. Navy in raiding the island of Hon He, about ten miles off the coast of North Vietnam. The response of the U.S. Navy was quick and decisive in launching a counter-offensive against North Vietnam. Daniel Ellsberg, a former Defense Department official who released the Pentagon Papers, has characterized as "lies" some of the Defense Department statements on the Gulf of Tonkin incident which he helped formulate.

Both Houses passed what is usually called the "Gulf of Tonkin Resolution" only three days after the President requested it. This Act stated that the Congress approves that the President "take all necessary measures to repel any armed attack against the forces of the United States and to prevent further aggression. . . ."[10]

The overwhelming favorable vote (502-2) for the Resolution, which many Congressmen later regretted and which was later repealed, had only two brave dissenters, Senators Morse and Gruening. The actual vote, however, did not reflect the true anxiety of many members of Congress.

The Tonkin Gulf Resolution was a sad symbol of the abdication of Congressional power. President Johnson willingly accepted the grant of authority and interpreted the Resolution as carte blanche to send all necessary troops to Vietnam. (Troop levels rose from 23,300 in 1964 to 184,300 in 1965, to 385,300 in 1966, to 485,000 in 1967, before peaking at about 550,000 in 1968.[11]) More seriously, Congress, by its action, had closed the door on possible substantive negotiations and peaceful solutions in conjunction with the UN. President Johnson, by repudiating his campaign promises not to widen the war or send American troops to fight in Asia, greatly widened the credibility gap.

FCNL rightly viewed this Tonkin Gulf situation with foreboding. During August 5 and 6, the office telephoned key contacts in thirty-six states, urging them to rally telegrams to the President and Senators. It was suggested that such wires might call upon our government to adopt UN Secretary General U Thant's recommendation to reconvene the Geneva Conference in order to involve the UN in policing any agreement that might result from the Conference. Frances Neely reinforced these suggestions by producing FCNL's first major analysis of Vietnam, entitled "What Really Happened in the Gulf of Tonkin." Her skepticism about the reports first released and her prophetic insights were amply borne out by the revelations over the next decade. The paper was widely circulated to Congressional offices, the press and FCNL contacts. It proved a valuable source of information and quotes on the situation in Vietnam.[12]

At the same time, FCNL tried to discuss Vietnam events with governmental officials. Several organizational representatives called together by the Council for a Livable World had lunch on August 5 with Arthur Barber, Assistant Secretary of Defense for International Security and Disarmament. In his view, which later developments proved wrong, the American action in the Gulf of Tonkin was only a measured response which would not expand into another Korean War.

A few days before the Gulf of Tonkin incident, I had posed a series of questions to Senator George Aiken of Vermont, ranking Republican on the Senate Foreign Relations Committee. I asked him about the implications of a continued war in Vietnam and what that might mean in American involvement. The Senator replied with a smile that if he knew the answer, he would immediately convey his insight to the White House. His criticism of the war had not made much of an impact on the country, but his remarks were heard by the Administration. The Senator was troubled about the civilian situation in South Vietnam, and he suspected that the Administration and the Defense Department were not providing all the facts for the American people.

Although Senator Aiken was unhappy about American entanglement in Vietnam, he hesitated to speak out forthrightly because he had no clear answers at that time nor did he see the right road ahead. He was also reluctant to put himself in such an outspoken position as that of Democrat Wayne Morse. Aiken hesitated to play the role of opposition leader. Here, then, was a vivid example of the crisis in senatorial leadership regarding Vietnam — a man troubled by the drift into barbarous war yet unwilling or unable to do his utmost to halt the juggernaut of military and moral destruction. Years later, Senator Aiken spoke out more decisively. With a wry smile he kept saying: "Let's declare we have won the war, and get out!"

Throughout the year, FCNL brought speakers and Vietnam experts to Capitol Hill to speak to Congressmen and concerned citizens. On March 11, the Vietnam Information Committee, launched in part the previous year by FCNL, had listened to the leading Vietnam expert, Bernard B. Fall, analyze the course of events there. He pictured the U.S. policy as having been riddled with errors, delusions and lies. The body count of enemy dead was an illusion, as were almost all war statistics. The situation in the villages of South Vietnam had been deteriorating since 1957 when Diem finally destroyed the village hierarchy, but the U.S. Government refused to recognize the seriousness of the situation. He discounted the effectiveness of any bombing of North Vietnam, a tactic which the U.S. tried, nonetheless, the following years. In Dr. Fall's opinion, there would have to be negotiation and settlement sooner or later, unless the Johnson Administration wished to leave the Vietnamese war in the shadowland between unattainable victory and unacceptable surrender. Dr. Fall's speech precipitated an FCNL "Write to the President" drive, in cooperation with other peace organizations. Even before the Gulf of Tonkin incident, FCNL had urged its friends and contacts to implore the President to avert the looming crisis in Vietnam.

Open U.S. Military Action Begins, Opposition to the War Mounts: 1965

The year 1965 marked the beginning of a concerted drive against the Vietnam War by FCNL, Congressional doves and the general public. Since the assassination of Diem in 1963, South Vietnam had had one civilian or military government after another. It was not until June 1965, that the Ky-Thieu regime took over. In the meantime, Vietcong strength had grown, and those Vietnamese in power were increasingly unwilling to seek a negotiated peace or to communicate with the National Liberation Front.

The North Vietnamese air attack on an American base at Pleiku in early February 1965 was immediately followed by the initiation of American bombing raids on North Vietnam, three weeks after Inauguration, three months after L.B. Johnson's election on peace pledges. Despite several pauses, the bombing continued until after Christmas 1972. Because North Vietnam did not immediately collapse, more American troops were sent in, precipitating large-scale North Vietnamese troop infiltration into the South. In spite of continued Buddhist persecution by the Saigon government, dramatized by a number of burning suicides, the U.S. Government steadfastly maintained its support of the South Vietnamese regime, almost to the exclusion of efforts for peace. The President totally rejected many peace feelers sent out by U Thant. Until his April 7 Johns Hopkins speech, President Johnson's position was completely intransigent. Eisenhower and Kennedy when committing troops usually talked about negotiating as well as fighting. But until the Johns Hopkins speech, Johnson did not even offer the negotiating track — even an unrealistic offer.

In the April 7 speech the President did offer to enter into "unconditional discussions" with any of the "governments concerned" and promised a postwar reconstruction fund of one billion dollars subject to Congressional approval.

Two days after the President increased troop strength from 75,000 to 125,000 in July, he called for a UN settlement of the war, but the U.S. Government never formally referred the question of the Vietnam War to the UN for working out a settlement. The U.S. continued to refuse to negotiate with the National Liberation Front.

In his January 15 speech, Senator George McGovern opposed extending the war to the North and expressed his disapproval of the air strikes in Laos. He proposed a five-point program for negotiation and a political settlement and called expanding military involvement "an act of folly." Senators Gruening and Church spoke in very much the same vein following Senator McGovern's remarks.

Intensified efforts were made to encourage members of Congress to speak out more courageously. The number of interviews increased dramatically in 1965, partially inspired by the joint AFSC-FCNL spring visitation program initiated in 1965. Calls on members of Congress in their Washington offices numbered more than 600, supplemented by the increasing number of constituents who arranged interviews with the Congressmen in their home districts. More than seventy Friends from Philadelphia and New Jersey responded to a Philadelphia Yearly Meeting appeal in mid-April by visiting Senators, and State Department and Pentagon officials in Washington.

Many Friends were among the more than 500 people from twenty-eight states and twenty other religious groups at the interfaith vigil before the Pentagon May 11-12, 1965. Following a three and one-half mile walk through the city to the Pentagon, vigilers stood along three sides of the huge building, witnessing to their concern over the escalation of the war and registering the hope that the United States would continue to press for a settlement through unconditional discussions. C. Edward Behre of the FCNL Administrative Committee was coordinator for the vigil and Frances Neely and Edward Snyder served on the vigil executive committee.

Edward Snyder also coordinated a three-day interfaith legislative effort, which included sixty Christian and Jewish leaders from thirteen states and fourteen religious groups. They not only visited the offices of many Congressmen, but also spoke with Vice President Humphrey.

In 1965, Edward Snyder was in delegations carrying FCNL's antiwar views directly to top Administration officials, including Defense Secretary McNamara, Secretary of State Rusk, and Vice President Hubert H. Humphrey. Twice in 1965 FCNL spokesmen visited Chester Cooper, aide to Presidential Assistant McGeorge Bundy. At the first visit in February, petitions which contained more than two thousand signatures gathered by the AFSC and the FCNL were presented to him.

A second delegation on June 4 brought 1100 more signatures from 17 states and the District of Columbia to Chester Cooper. Participating in that interview were FCNL staff members Edward Snyder, Charles Harker and Frances Neely, and Friend-in-Washington, Matt Thomson. The visitors advanced the following points: (1) the United States has been undermining international institutions and the development of international law by its unilateral action in South Vietnam and the Dominican Republic; (2) the bombing of North Vietnam and the suffering of the Vietnamese people must be brought to an end; (3) not only must U.S.-China policy be changed, but the American people also are more ready for these kinds of changes than the Administration realizes.

Cooper criticized the role of nongovernmental groups for berating the Administration without sending similar telegrams to the Vietcong and the North Vietnamese. He did not think it would make the slightest difference whether Communist China were in the UN or not. Cooper stressed that the South Vietnamese had chosen freedom and asked if it were moral to desert them now. He reiterated that the United States was anxious to negotiate, as evidenced by the bombing pause, but no encouragement had been received from the other side.

According to Chester Cooper, about five per cent of Vietnam information was confidential. As a result, Administration actions based on this information seemed incomprehensible to some citizens. Throughout the interview, Cooper kept trying to assure the delegation that he was for the same goals they supported. It was just that many of the things which they advocated had been considered and rejected on the basis of the five per cent of secret information.

Luncheon meetings were particularly important during the year. Representatives of national organizations were called together for luncheons at different times to meet with Tran Van Dinh, former Acting Ambassador to the United States from South Vietnam; Phillippe Devillers, French authority on Vietnam, journalist and head of the political science department at the University of Paris; Stephen Cary, associate secretary of AFSC, recently returned from three months in Vietnam; and a delegation of Japanese Christians. These Japanese spent two weeks in this country in late July calling for an end to the bombing and fighting and for recognition of, and negotiation with, the Vietcong. I also set up interviews between members of Congress and Administration officials and these visiting speakers.

FCNL staff members participated in other movements in the country. As a representative of Philadelphia Yearly Meeting, I helped formulate a strong statement on Vietnam at the National Council of Churches Sixth World Order Study Conference in St. Louis, October 20-23. After prolonged consideration, an important statement was adopted by the General Board of the National Council of Churches assembled in Madison, Wisconsin, in December.

Besides the emphasis on Vietnam in the monthly *Washington Newsletter*, the FCNL printed and circulated twenty-five studies, documents and reprints as its part of the pressure on Congress. In the early months of the year, nearly a thousand *Newsletter* readers returned cards indicating that they had written letters to Congress, to the President and to newspaper editors urging negotiations on Vietnam.

The Friends Committee continued its appeals by correspondence directly to Administration officials. My March 19 letter to Vice President Humphrey expressed our distress over the way things had developed in Vietnam:

> Neither negotiations nor a cease-fire nor a settlement is in any sense easy, but we must press tirelessly for them. The United States says it will not negotiate when it is losing, but does that mean that we will continue the war until the Communists are losing, and expect them to be more Christian than we are? [13]

The President's call for unconditional negotiations brought a commendatory letter from Ed Snyder, who also pled for an immediate end to the bombing of North Vietnam.

AFSC VISITATIONS: 1965-1972

For six years beginning in 1965, the Peace Education Division of the American Friends Service Committee, under the direction of Stewart Meacham, cooperated with the FCNL in bringing key men and women from AFSC's eleven regions for intensive interviewing of Congressmen on the Indochina War. (The 1971 and 1972 visitations concentrated on opposing the draft.)

These annual springtime visitations, each lasting more than a week, reached nearly one-half of the offices of the members of Congress. Between 140 and 165 of these visits were with Senators and Representatives in person, and the balance were with their legislative or administrative assistants. To facilitate interviews, visitors were introduced by letters from constituents of the Congressmen. Each year several strategic interviews were held with officials of the Administration.

It is almost impossible to reduce this effort to a precise statistical summary, but some trends were noticeable through 1968, the last year tabulated. Those members of Congress interviewed — not necessarily the same ones each year — who were strongly critical of the war increased from fifteen in 1965 to fifty-one in 1968, while those who were critical in some way doubled from 27 to 50. Those

who strongly supported the Administration dwindled from 94 in
1965 to about 40 in 1968.

Not only was the impact on Congress considerable, but each
person could also utilize his Washington experiences in his home area
to educate fellow constituents. This follow-up was considered as
important as the visitations themselves.

In one of the 1965 special interviews, the AFSC and FCNL
expressed concern to Secretary of State Rusk that the government
and the American people seemed to be increasingly immune to the
vast human cost of the war.

Those who did the interviewing found a growing disillusionment
with the course of the war, but many Congressmen were still
unwilling to oppose the President because of what their constituents
might think. The fear of Communism remained the basis of most
support for the war. There was a widespread feeling that information
was being withheld from Congress. But Congressmen remained
hesitant to vote against appropriations because they also feared loss
of federal funds for their districts and a constituent reaction to
"letting the boys down." Nevertheless, visitation participants were
encouraged by the reception they received from the Congressmen,
and the success of the visitations led to two new Congressional
interview programs in 1966.

WEDNESDAYS IN WASHINGTON AND CHALLENGE TO THE CONSCIENCE OF AMERICA: 1966

In South Vietnam, 1966 was marked by widespread and prolonged
Buddhist protests and demonstrations against the Ky government,
particularly in Saigon, Danang and Hue. There were ten Buddhist
suicides by fire — immolation — between May 29 and June 17. U.S.
Ambassador Lodge lauded Saigon's suppression of the Buddhist
rebellion as a "solid political victory."

Anticipated major escalation of the war in February was
temporarily halted by fierce opposition in Congress. (FCNL had pled
with Congressional members through a forceful letter asking for full
Congressional debate on the $12.7 billion military request. Reprints
of pictures showing the suffering of Vietnamese peasants were
enclosed with the letter.) The Senate Foreign Relations Committee
did open hearings on February 4 for proponents and opponents of the
war, but full House debate was still five years away.

Throughout the year, five *FCNL Action Bulletins* (January,
February, June, October and December) urged constant

correspondence to halt the trend of the war. Apparently Congressional mail had been very uneven, ranging from 100-1 against escalation (Senator Mansfield) to ninety-nine percent in favor (to a proescalation Senator). Yet other members of Congress who should have taken stronger positions reported very light mail.

By midsummer, perhaps because more and more energy was diverted to demonstrations, letters to Congress had dropped off drastically. In response, FCNL altered the tack of its correspondence to a campaign against the cost of the war in human terms. The atrocities were outrageous, civilian losses absolutely staggering. The U.S. had spent 10,000 times as much to kill one enemy soldier as it gave to South Vietnam for the accidental loss of one civilian. Yet civilian deaths were tenfold the estimated number of enemy soldiers killed.[14]

Special funds amounting to $15,000 earmarked by the Administrative Committee for work against the Vietnam War enabled the FCNL to expand its activities and to begin two new programs in 1966: "Wednesdays in Washington" and "Vietnam: Challenge to the Conscience of America." The "Wednesdays in Washington" program, which began as the project of several Friends organizations and grew into a cooperative effort of ten religious groups, brought more than 250 people from thirty-six states to Washington between the end of March and late June to share with Congress their concern for ending the war. Participants made nearly 500 visits to Congressional offices. Attendance at the Tuesday evening briefing session tripled during the program.

Fourteen Catholic, Protestant and Jewish groups[15] joined FCNL in either sponsoring or endorsing an after-election program, "Vietnam: Challenge to the Conscience of America," which called upon members of the religious community to visit their Congressmen at home during December and early January. This was to be followed up by interviews with Congressmen in Washington during February and community action at home in March, April and May 1967. One emphasis of the "Challenge" was to cut back on supplemental and regular funds for the war. FCNL mailed flyers describing this program to its mailing list in December and took major responsibility for coordinating and staffing the project. David Hartsough helped develop a list of key contact people around the country. (After having completed his master's degree at Columbia University, Dave had rejoined the staff to devote full time to Vietnam issues.)

FURTHER FCNL ACTIVITIES: 1966

FCNL expanded its antiwar activities with other groups. As a member of the planning committee of the Interreligious Committee on World Peace, I was a section leader at the Committee's Washington conclave in 1966. This meeting, which brought together Catholic, Protestant and Jewish leaders, was a prelude to the World Interreligious Conference, which included Hindus, Buddhists and Moslems, in Kyoto in 1970. The meeting marked the beginning of concerted cooperation among the three major American religious groups in the field of peace. The 450 attenders supported the proposals of Senators Gore and Clark for a cease-fire and for free and open elections in South Vietnam.

FCNL also worked closely with the AFSC. Throughout the year, but particularly at the time of the February Vigil for Peace, more than one hundred Friends from nearly thirty states aided FCNL in distributing in person the very important AFSC working paper, *Peace in Vietnam.* This paper formed the basis of much of FCNL's lobbying effort before it adopted its own statement late in 1966. There was also cooperation in showing the film, "The Time of the Locust," to Congress, nongovernmental organizations and the press. This film vividly portrayed the brutality and cruelty of the war.

The February Vigil for Peace, which was a cooperative effort of the Friends Coordinating Committee on Peace and the FCNL, attracted about 500 Friends from around the country and Canada. FCNL served on the planning committee for the four-day conference and vigil, with special responsibility for the legislative activities on the last day.

Staff members of FCNL contributed their efforts to publicizing and distributing "The Politics of Escalation," a citizen White Paper prepared by scholars from Berkeley and St. Louis. Vance Hartke of Indiana summarized the study on the Senate floor in a speech which was also distributed to the FCNL mailing list.

One of the major projects of American and Canadian Friends during 1966 was an attempt to open the way for the shipment of relief supplies to all factions in Vietnam. Beginning in July, FCNL cooperated with representatives of Baltimore and New York Yearly Meetings in their endeavors to end the prohibition against sending relief and medical supplies to suffering civilians, particularly those in North Vietnam. New York Yearly Meeting called upon:

Friends to express their faith in new, creative and even dangerous

.. ays. For the Kingdom of God will not come if our faith is weak and our voice is timid. Our light must shine forth with unmistakable clarity to divert a frightened world from the path of chaos.   [16]

Late in June, FCNL provided headquarters for approximately 130 Friends from the biennial Cape May Friends General Conference. They had come to Washington to bring their protest of the bombing of Hanoi and Haiphong oil refineries to Congress and the President. While some Friends stood in silent vigil before the White House, others discussed this disheartening development with their Congressmen and a third group waited in the Senate gallery to hear the debate on the issue and to discourage Congress from going home for the July 4 recess. Those in the gallery were arrested for refusing to leave.

William Penn House, located near the Capitol and the FCNL office, opened in September under the direction of Robert and Sally Cory. It quickly became the focal point for nearly a hundred meetings a year, many of them in cooperation with the FCNL. Luncheons were held for Congressional staff on a variety of questions but often centering on Vietnam. Seminar programs were arranged for Quaker pastors and other leaders, high school and college students, and for the United Society of Friends Women. The House served also as a meeting place for many strategy sessions of nongovernmental organizations with headquarters in Washington.

VISITORS TO WASHINGTON: 1966

FCNL served as liaison between Congress and many illustrious visitors to Washington. Included among the visitors for whom meetings or interviews were arranged were Makota Oda, novelist and chairman of the Japan Peace in Vietnam Committee; Kenkichi Konishi, foreign correspondent for the *Mainichi* newspaper in Japan; Jean Lacouture of *Le Monde*, Paris; and Stanley Andrews, former administrator of the Point Four technical assistance program, who, upon return from visiting among the people of Vietnam, discussed the evolution of U.S. policy in Vietnam and its weaknesses.

Dr. Nguyen Thi Hue, American-educated assistant professor at the Vietnamese Institute of Administration, in speaking to Congressmen, discounted the threat of a blood bath after the war, declaring that there had been a continual blood bath during the war. She emphasized the need to set up a stable civilian government in South Vietnam. She had recently withdrawn from membership in the Provisional Committee To Draft the Election Laws in Vietnam because of irregularities.

Twice in September the staff arranged Congressional and Administration appointments for Russell Johnson, program director of the New England office of the AFSC, to relate his observations as a member of the "Americans Want To Know" mission to survey the Cambodian border.

In a separate action, William Hanson, attorney and co-chairman of the Seattle, Washington, Committee To End Violence in Vietnam, presented petitions calling for peace in Vietnam to Administration officials and members of Congress.

A particularly important visitor to Washington was influential British Statesman Philip Noel-Baker. In addressing the Disarmament Information Service luncheon, the 1959 Nobel Peace Prize winner spoke not only on disarmament but also on the British view of the war. FCNL distributed copies of his House of Commons address of February 8, 1966, when he had called for an end to the bombing of North Vietnam, for neutralization of North and South, and for mutual armament reduction. He had told the House of Commons:

> It is sheer illusion to believe that Communist ideas can be destroyed by guns and bombs. As the Prime Minister said today, war creates the misery and chaos on which Communism breeds.
>
> Let us end the war and then let us work with Russia and perhaps with China to free the Asian people from their ancient enemies of serfdom, usury, ignorance and disease. [17]

On September 11, 1966, FCNL issued a policy statement on Vietnam for study and comment. It said in part:

> We recognize the expressed concern of our government for the independence and freedom of small countries and the right of the inhabitants of South Vietnam to have a voice in their own government and to be free from terror. Nevertheless, we believe that the method of answering terror with napalm bombing and widespread military violence is not the method calculated to achieve those ends. . . . we see the need to bring the fighting and killing to an end immediately and to reach a compromise settlement as rapidly as possible. [18]

The statement accused the U.S. Government of not meeting the minimum conditions for negotiations proposed by UN Secretary General U Thant.

The statement then spelled out six measures through which the Committee believed a solution could be found: negotiations in good faith, peaceful deeds as well as words, disassociation from military action by other nations, self-determination through participation by all groups in South Vietnam in free elections, massive economic assistance in rebuilding, and accommodation with China.

THE ELECTIONS AS A TOOL FOR PEACE: 1966

As a nonpartisan organization, the FCNL does not officially endorse or oppose candidates for public office. It does devote one newsletter each year to voting records of incumbent members of Congress on selected issues. During the summer and fall of 1966, FCNL put major effort on foreign policy issues during the November Congressional election campaign. The FCNL kept revising and publishing a list, without official endorsement, of peace candidates and sending them materials on Vietnam, military spending and other issues in foreign relations. During October, a mailing with various documents on Vietnam was sent to approximately 1100 candidates for Congress.

Three members of the FCNL General Committee ran for seats in Congress in opposition to the President's Vietnam policy. Sheldon Clark, Ohio, and William Martin, Maryland, campaigned for seats in the House and Herbert Hoover, Iowa, campaigned for the Senate. None of the three won election.

BRINGING THE WAR HOME TO CONGRESS: 1967

FCNL began 1967 by calling for the fulfillment of three points in its January *Washington Newsletter*. Congress should: (1) construct a better climate for negotiations along the lines suggested by U Thant; (2) oppose further escalation by rejecting further money bills; (3) attempt to assure more concern and better treatment of the Vietnamese people by calling for an end to napalm, antipersonnel bombs, defoliants, etc., and by reviewing the terms of the 1949 Geneva Convention dealing with prisoners of war and the protection of civilians. In addition, if the door were opened to China at the UN, it was felt that peace negotiations would be more likely to succeed, especially if the negotiations were held under the auspices of the UN.

At various times during 1967, some twenty recent visitors to North or South Vietnam, Laos or Cambodia vividly portrayed to Congress and officials in executive agencies, during FCNL-scheduled interviews, the disastrous effects of the war on those countries.

An intensive schedule was set up for long-time Vietnamese diplomat, Tran Van Dinh, who was then in Washington, serving as a journalist and representative of the Vietnamese Buddhists. He dwelt on what U.S. Senators could do to facilitate genuinely free elections which could lead to a civilian government and a negotiated peace.

Don Luce was viewed by the State Department as their ablest and sharpest critic. For nine years he had been in Vietnam as director of the International Voluntary Service program and had finally resigned in protest against the U.S. military operations. At one lunch meeting, arranged by FCNL, fourteen Senators stayed for more than an hour listening attentively; another time thirty-five Senatorial assistants met with him. One Senator talked with Luce for four hours. A meeting on the House side brought out thirty-five Representatives. Among the Administration officials with whom he conferred were Ambassador-at-Large W. Averell Harriman and William Bundy, Assistant Secretary of State for East Asian and Pacific Affairs. Luce aroused nation-wide publicity when he later led some Congressmen to the infamous South Vietnamese "tiger cages" where political prisoners were incarcerated under terrible conditions.

The former deputy director of IVS, Gene Stoltzfus, who resigned with Don Luce, had long discussions with Senator Eugene McCarthy's staff when they were helping the Senator formulate his position as a potential Presidential peace candidate.

Riri Kakayama, leading Buddhist monk from Japan, spent the last two weeks in September telling Congressmen about Buddhist concerns for peace and his plan to mobilize all the world religions to move both sides to stop hostilities in Vietnam.

Dr. David Wurfel from the University of Missouri was an observer of the South Vietnamese elections for the Methodist Division of World Peace, SANE, the Unitarian Universalists, and the FCNL from August 14 to September 10, 1967. An official delegation sent by the U.S. Government had issued a whitewash of the elections based on a brief and cursory visit. But Wurfel dug out the facts, and his damaging findings, widely circulated in U.S. official and Congressional circles, were the subject of a well-attended press conference. His report, which was reprinted by FCNL, stated that "The exclusion of the candidacies of General Duong Van Minh and Dr. Au Trong Thanh denied the people of South Vietnam true freedom of choice. . . . The relative freedom of the campaign was badly marred by the closing of three newspapers. . . . Fraud on election day was extensive." The Vietnamese generally viewed the election as illegal since they considered the results of the election predetermined by U.S. backing for Generals Thieu and Ky.

Four AFSC staff members — Bronson Clark, Paul Johnson, David Stickney and Stewart Meacham, who had had firsthand experience in North or South Vietnam or Cambodia — shared their insights with key members of Congress. The FCNL helped recruit witnesses for hearings on refugees and civilian casualties in South Vietnam before the Subcommittee headed by Senator Edward Kennedy.

At the close of the Fourth Friends World Conference in Guilford, North Carolina, I was one of six international delegates, including the Conference chairman, Lewis E. Waddilove of Great Britain, and Senator Lawrence Williamson of Australia, who expressed Friends deep apprehension about the war to Hayward Isham, Acting Director of the Vietnam Task Force in the State Department.

With FCNL assistance, five members of the crew of the Phoenix mercy ship, Betty Boardman, Carl Zietlow, Phil Drath, Ivan Massar and Horace Champney, expressed their anguish over the suffering of the Vietnamese people to about sixty members of Congress or their staff. These included Senators Robert Kennedy, Mark Hatfield and Frank Church, current outspoken critics, and Senator Edward Brooke, a later critic of the U.S. war policy.

Because the U.S. bombing of North Vietnam had been causing so many casualties and hardships, the Quaker Action Group had outfitted the Phoenix with medical supplies for at least a symbolic gesture of compassion for these victims. The U.S. fleet would not allow the Phoenix to land in Haiphong. On November 20, the FCNL sent telegrams to the State Department and the Vietnamese Ambassador, asking that the Phoenix crew be allowed to dock at Danang to deliver medical supplies to the South Vietnamese Red Cross and the Buddhists who had suffered so much persecution because of their opposition to the Saigon government. Instead, at Danang harbor, South Vietnamese government men met the ship and asked that the supplies be given them for delivery.

The story of Quaker opposition to the Pool Bill, which would have forbidden relief to the victims of American bombing in North Vietnam, is recounted in the chapter on civil liberties. Fortunately the bill never reached the House floor for a vote.

President Johnson's request for a 10% surtax, considered mainly as extra financing for the war, was the focus of a second campaign by the FCNL. In late August, five staff members spent several days on the phone compiling Congressional views on the proposed surtax. This tally was sent to FCNL district contacts with the appeal to start a flood of letters regardless of their Congressman's current attitude. Other groups found the survey very helpful in their lobby effort. For visitors to Washington, a nine-page evaluation of the surtax formed the basis of discussion with about a third of the Congressional offices, with special emphasis on the House and Senate Finance Committees. Eventually the surtax was passed in a changed form, but there were a large number of "Nays."

A twenty-two page brief spelling out FCNL's objection to military appropriations for escalating the war was inserted in the *Congressional Record* by Senator Morse, who indicated that he was in agreement with much of the content and aim of the document.

Warren Griffiths of Wilmington College, who twice served a year on the FCNL staff, uncovered the fact that seventeen out of the twenty-one Congressmen who voted against the $12 billion appropriation, or for the Brown amendment directed toward the same objective, had been in contact with the FCNL.

A fourth legislative effort which took FCNL staff to more than fifty Senatorial offices was to strengthen the so-called "Mansfield resolution," encouraging the President to take the conflict to the UN to be settled along the principles of the Geneva accords. FCNL asked Senators to call for a halt in the bombing and to announce a willingness to negotiate directly with the NLF.

Joint efforts with other groups included the continuation of the "Vietnam Challenge" program begun in 1966, participation in the organization of the National Citizens Campaign for "Negotiation Now" and laying the groundwork for the "Vietnam Summer" program.

Negotiation Now called upon U Thant, the U.S., North Vietnam and the NLF to initiate negotiations. I was in the delegation from the Citizens Campaign which conferred at the close of their National Assembly in Washington with Undersecretary of State Nicholas de B. Katzenbach. The delegation stressed the need for prompt negotiations in the Vietnam conflict, including direct talks with the NLF with whom the U.S. up to that time had refused to deal, and an end to the bombing of North Vietnam.

Three strong and influential voices were added to the protagonists for peace in Vietnam when the Business Executive Move for Peace in Vietnam (BEM) and the two Kentucky Republican Senators joined the ranks. Baltimore Friend Henry E. Niles, president of the Baltimore Life Insurance Company, took the initiative in launching the BEM and has served as its national chairman since. This is the first time in my memory that businessmen as such have banded together to work as a force for peace. The BEM embarked on its crusade in September with an open letter to the President urging cessation of the bombing, de-escalation of military activity and negotiation with all parties then fighting. At one of the first meetings of BEM, Senator Thurston B. Morton expressed his detailed criticism of the war. Senator John Sherman Cooper, former Ambassador in India, became a recognized critic as co-sponsor of the 1970 Cooper-Church Amendment.

Despite the President's conciliatory speech in March 1968, the BEM picked up momentum in its strong pressure on Congress to make peace in Vietnam. Through FCNL, BEM secured special appointments with people such as Senator Dirksen and Congressman Gerald Ford. In the following years, FCNL continued to cooperate with BEM and was encouraged by its work.

FCNL played a similar role in arranging Congressional interviews for the Clergy and Laymen Concerned About Vietnam (CALCAV) yearly mobilizations in Washington. CALCAV, based in New York, had been founded in early 1966 to coordinate local activities of the three major religious groups for nation-wide impact. Attenders of the CALCAV annual visits to Washington usually numbered in the thousands, and by sheer numbers they were better able to reach sympathetic Congressmen and Administration or Pentagon supporters. Frances Neely and David Hartsough, two very knowledgeable and experienced members of FCNL, served as discussion leaders in the 1969 CALCAV mobilization.

The FCNL published 50,000 copies of "Vietnam: The Hard Questions" as part of the arsenal of material distributed by Vietnam summer volunteers who put on a massive cooperative national campaign to reach new people and new communities in order to arouse the conscience of the nation. Altogether 76 publications relating to the war were printed or distributed by the FCNL during the year.[19]

Although mammoth efforts of the antiwar forces successfully mobilized a larger number of war critics than ever before in Congress and around the country, this crusade did not succeed in reaching the goal of ending the war through Congressional action or Presidential decision in 1967.

BLOODLETTING CONTINUES: 1968

Two tragic assassinations rocked the country in 1968. With the death of Dr. Martin Luther King the United States lost its leading apostle of nonviolence. The murder of Senator Robert F. Kennedy removed a major contender for the Presidency.

One of the outstanding events in 18 years' striving against the Vietnam War was David Schoenbrun's February 6 visit, scheduled by David Hartsough. David Schoenbrun, a former CBS correspondent who had covered the 1954 Geneva Conference, had been a frequent visitor to North and South Vietnam, and he knew Ho Chi Minh personally. As a Paris correspondent for fifteen years, he was the only American to witness the French defeat at Dien Bien Phu. Correspondent Schoenbrun was a particularly effective speaker because of his firsthand experience and because of the respect he had earned as a skillful reporter.

Mr. Schoenbrun met first with thirty-two Congressional assistants sponsored by Congressmen Ben Rosenthal. He reviewed how the U.S. had become involved, the significance of recent events in Vietnam and ways in which the U.S. might extricate itself. He then confronted quite a mixture of doves and hawks among the eleven Senators and forty Senatorial assistants for a second round of discussion. Senators Hatfield and McGovern sponsored this assemblage as well as Schoenbrun's film talk, "How We Got In, How We Can Get Out," six weeks later for 170 lawmakers. The third meeting was a stormy session with nearly sixty Representatives (many supporters of the war) who had been invited by Congressmen Don Fraser and Fred Schwengel.

The proposals advanced by David Schoenbrun were along the following lines: stop bombing and start talking with the North Vietnamese and the National Liberation Front; stop the search and destroy missions in South Vietnam; try to get the Soviet Union and Britain to reconvene another Geneva Conference; and try to arrange a cease-fire. During a two-year cease-fire, the U.S. could withdraw its troops, work for a settlement, help prepare for internationally supervised elections and begin rebuilding the country.

FCNL human relations secretary, Edward T. Anderson, appealed to the Republican Convention platform committee in Miami to adopt a plank calling for an end to the war. Stephen L. Angell, Jr., FCNL chairman, made a similar appeal to the Democratic platform committee in Chicago.

Vice President Humphrey was very difficult to convince. For much of his term, he had been an evangelistic supporter of the war, and as a result FCNL tried three times to encourage him to take a more decisive stand against his President's policy. I wrote him on June 18 calling upon the U.S. to initiate an immediate cease-fire, to stop the bombing and to make a statement that the NLF should be a party to the negotiations. The Vice President, in his reply, urged patience. On July 2, two of us had a follow-up conference with his special assistant, William Welsh, to reiterate these points. Then on

September 27, as the Presidential campaign was in full swing between Nixon and Humphrey, Annalee Stewart, David Hartsough and I had the privilege of reviewing with Welsh a draft of the Vice President's forthcoming speech on foreign policy and we again urged a stronger break with President Johnson on Vietnam policy. Apparently the Vice President did make some modifications before the speech was given a few days later in Salt Lake City, but one still wonders whether Humphrey might have won the election had he taken a more forthright stand against the war even that late in the campaign.

In the late 1960's, FCNL added the responsibility of briefing Congressmen as they began to travel more to Southeast Asia. These Congressional trips, with the benefits of previous FCNL briefings, were preferable to Administration-led tours. Congressmen seemed to be most appreciative of the valuable service supplied by FCNL.

The main speakers in Washington were AFSC personnel. Upon his return from a month's tour of Laos and Cambodia, Bronson Clark was back in Washington for fifty Congressional appointments. John Sullivan, executive secretary of the AFSC Pacific Northwest Region, made many visits to the Hill, as did Dr. Marjorie Nelson. An AFSC doctor in Vietnam, Marjorie Nelson had been captured during the Tet offensive but was later released. She was particularly well-qualified to speak on the inhuman side of the war. Her testimony rated a *New York Times* front-page story. Carl Zietlow, a Phoenix crew member, returned to Capitol Hill, after nine months in Cambodia, to suggest a possible meeting between Congressmen and some North Vietnamese political leaders which unfortunately was never realized.

Russell Johnson met with the senior staff of Presidential candidates Robert Kennedy, Eugene McCarthy and Richard Nixon. During his six weeks in Vietnam, Thailand and Cambodia, he had talked to representatives of North Vietnam, the NLF and other nationalist leaders on both sides of the conflict. He also spoke to a bipartisan group of Congressmen on the possible ingredients of a political settlement as viewed by the Vietnamese.

Certainly these visitors and others had observed a considerable shift in Congressional feelings in 1968 from the previous years. Although a rough estimate by one of the members of the AFSC visitation team divided the hawk, dove and uncommitted sentiment about evenly, antiwar campaigners seemed to be more vocal without being able to muster the votes. Public opinion by October had risen to fifty-four percent against having gone into Vietnam.[19]

As in the previous year, FCNL participated in the activities of two of the most important antiwar movements at the time. Both CALCAV and BEM held conferences in the spring which brought in people from around the nation to confer and lobby. In preparation for the New Hampshire Presidential Primary, CALCAV printed a very important advertisement called"Who's Right? Who's Wrong? — on Vietnam." It was a summary of the status of the war to date, with quotes from important people in every field of American life. Its refutation of the war was very strong.

It was quite a busy spring after President Johnson's March 31st speech announcing a halt to the bombing and the initiation of peace talks. FCNL issued 10,500 copies of an *Action Bulletin* in April urging that immediate action be taken for the duration of the pause. It was time to acknowledge the deteriorating situation in Vietnam and to strive for viable alternatives, no matter who was President.

CHAPTER 15

The Later Years of Vietnam: 1969-1973

A PLAN TO END THE WAR? 1969

Salamanca, N.Y. [AP] — When Keith K. Franklin, 19, left for duty as an Army medic in Vietnam, he gave his parents a sealed envelope and told them to open it only if he were killed.

Franklin was killed last Tuesday in Cambodia. In the envelope was a letter saying, "The war that has taken my life. . .is immoral, unlawful and an atrocity."

Richard Nixon had indicated during the 1968 campaign, according to press reports, that he had a plan to end the Vietnam War. President Nixon's first year in office witnessed more resolutions in Congress aimed at terminating the war than previously. Expanded peace talks resumed in Paris, and there were more protests and demonstrations than ever before. Nevertheless, intensified public pressure brought little significant change in Administration policy toward the war. The war as an issue began to be defused with the reduction of troops, and the transfer of more of the fighting to the South Vietnamese or "Vietnamization," but in reality, only the character of the war was changed. After ten weeks of haggling, the new Paris Peace Talks convened around a thirteen-foot circular table. The President reduced the U.S. troop strength, in excess of half a million men, by more than 60,000. Senators like George McGovern characterized Vietnamization as "basically an effort to tranquillize the conscience of the American people while our government wages a cruel and needless war by proxy."[1]

As Congressional criticism spread to many phases of the conduct of the war, the State Department searched in vain for any formal request from South Vietnam for U.S. intervention with combat troops. No such request was produced.

On March 25, 1969, Representative Paul Findley of Illinois inserted in the *Congressional Record* a list of 31,379 names of Americans who had died fighting in Vietnam. He did this to call "to the attention of the Administration and the American people. . .as no other arrangement of words can possibly do, the true dimension of the war."[2]

Later in the year, A Quaker Action Group, (AQAG), assembled on the steps of the Capitol over a period of weeks and read the names. FCNL staff members George Bliss and David Hartsough were among those arrested in 1969 and taken to D.C. jails. Finally a federal court overruled the indictments as a violation of civil and political rights and the cases were dropped. Even some Congressmen had joined them in their vigil to uphold their right to assemble peacefully and petition their government.

Also during the summer, AQAG and AFSC launched a special three-month's project in Washington with a meeting for worship in front of the White House on July 7. Cecil and Pauline Hinshaw and Holmes Brown were in charge of this summer enterprise aimed at serving the great number of people coming to visit Congress and meeting the desire for accurate information and suggestions for action by the AFSC constituency. In one of the five bulletins they issued, Cecil Hinshaw and Margaret Snyder excerpted the book *The Betrayal* by Col. William R. Corson, (New York, Norton, 1968.) From firsthand experience, Col. Corson vividly portrayed the corruption, coercion and physical torture by the South Vietnamese government, the brutal effects of the escalating war on the civilians and the failure of the Americans to "win the hearts and minds of the (Vietnamese) people."

APPEALS TO RICHARD NIXON AND HENRY KISSINGER

The FCNL continued to reach out directly to the Administration. During the campaign in the fall of 1968, a request had been made for an interview with Richard Nixon on behalf of the Friends United Meeting, the Friends General Conference, the Friends World Committee, the American Friends Service Committee, and the Friends Committee on National Legislation. It was hoped that such a meeting might be possible before the election, or, if not, at some time following the election. To the disappointment of these Friends agencies, no such interview was ever granted.

On March 17, 1969, Stephen L. Angell Jr., chairman of the FCNL General Committee, Samuel R. Levering, chairman of the Executive Council, and I, as secretary emeritus, sent a letter to President Nixon. It discussed our most troublesome topics: Vietnam, disarmament, the antiballistic missile (ABM), and China. The Administrative Committee approved my follow-up letter after the first message had been answered by a major-general who mentioned only ABM.

Next, both AFSC and FCNL tried to confer with the President's chief advisor on foreign affairs, Henry A. Kissinger. George Sawyer, an FCNL Executive Council member from Indiana, was one of the White House visitors. At the first visit, Mr. Kissinger asked for more time to demonstrate the Administration's intentions to curtail the war. While the discussions were pointed and frank, after three visits the AFSC delegation saw no significant change in policy as a result, and the visitors were "astonished at the absolute rigidity of the Administration."[3] David Hartsough made a parallel effort for FCNL in five lengthy talks with Dean Moor, assistant to Henry Kissinger, but his results were much the same.

QUAKER OPPOSITION TO THE WAR INCREASES

On July 16, Charles Harker and I accompanied Joe Elder, an AFSC Board member, on a visit to former U.S. negotiator in Paris, W. Averell Harriman. Elder shared impressions gleaned from his many conversations with officials in North Vietnam. He had made two trips to Hanoi to deliver open-heart surgical equipment for the AFSC. Joe Elder also talked with Henry Kissinger, foreign policy advisor to President Nixon.

In the spring, FCNL had taken part in two very important committees formed in Washington. The first, A New Coalition on National Priorities and Military Policy, had its inception at a press conference. One of its initial actions was to stage a conference in late February. That conference, at which Senator McGovern was a leading speaker, drew nearly three hundred people from thirty-three states. Frances Neely, FCNL's military expert, served as vice chairman of this inter-organizational committee dedicated to reducing the military budget and transferring the funds to pressing domestic needs.

In another committee involving the FCNL, the Fellowship of Reconciliation took the initiative in assembling an interfaith committee, of which I was a member, to plan for a delegation to visit

Vietnam in May and June, 1969. The eight-member delegation chosen by the Hoa Binh Ad Hoc Committee included one Congressman, John Conyers, Jr., of Detroit, and Robert Drinan, Dean of the Boston College Law School, who later was elected to Congress in 1970, and Retired Rear Admiral Arnold E. True, a Friend from California. This delegation reported back at a press conference in the House Office Building on its distressing findings of very limited political and religious freedom in South Vietnam. As Congressmen spoke on the House floor and around the country, their speeches were given wide publicity.

Leonard Tinker and Ken Kirkpatrick, AFSC Peace Education Secretaries, returned in May (1969) from their observations at the Paris Peace talks. While there, they had the opportunity of conferring with spokesmen not only for the United States, but also for the Saigon regime, the National Liberation Front, and the North Vietnamese. Forty Congressmen gathered at a luncheon, arranged by FCNL, to listen to their firsthand report on the talks. Senator Vance Hartke sponsored a similar occasion for some of his Senate colleagues, and a William Penn House luncheon with the two returnees was arranged for Congressional Assistants. Even key officials in the White House and State Department were able to hear from these men.

WASHINGTON BECOMES CENTER FOR ANTIWAR DEMONSTRATIONS

Washington in 1969 was the site of many demonstrations, including an AFSC-sponsored one in May and two national ones in the fall. The May 5 public witness, which attracted about fourteen hundred Friends including most of the members of the AFSC Board of Directors, concluded with a meeting for worship on the White House sidewalk.

The FCNL does not make a practice of sponsoring demonstrations except when they are under Quaker auspices and subject to strict discipline, but the Committee does its best to serve those who come to Washington with legislative briefings and suggestions for making their voices heard in Congress. Thus FCNL was quite busy in the fall during the Moratorium and Mobilization, which added to an already busy schedule.

An estimated million Americans participated in antiwar demonstrations, protest rallies, and peace vigils across the country on "Vietnam Moratorium" day, October 15. FCNL staff spoke at school assemblies and other meetings in connection with these observances. Edward Snyder was scheduled to speak to the

Sandy Spring Friends School during the Moratorium on the same program with Clark Clifford, at one time Assistant Secretary of Defense. This coincidence led to a lively correspondence in which Edward urged him to take a much stronger antiwar stand. Clifford did later become an outspoken critic of the war.

FCNL regional offices also urged their constituents to halt business as usual for a day. Some eighty Congressmen announced their support, with fifty active participants in the Moratorium as an example of a "peaceful demonstration for peace." Probably as many members of Congress, however, objected to the demonstration as a gesture of support for Hanoi. Vice President Agnew characterized the protesters as an "effete corps of impudent snobs."

A month later, under the direction of the more militant New Mobilization Committee To End the War in Vietnam (New Mobe), an estimated two hundred fifty thousand flocked to Washington for the mobilization characterized as the biggest demonstration in the nation's capital in American history. It was preceded with a "March against Death" from the Pentagon to the foot of the Capitol. As each marcher passed the White House, he or she called out the name of one American war dead. There was much less Congressional support for the Mobilization than there had been for the Moratorium a month before, but the New Mobe continued to plan for more protests.

CONGRESS FAILS TO PASS ANTIWAR LEGISLATION

Both Houses were busy with various antiwar and prowar proposals. In a Legislative Information Bulletin issued October 22, FCNL highlighted three resolutions for commendation.

One was a "withdraw now" resolution, and another set a December 1, 1970, deadline for ending military and financial assistance in Vietnam.

David Hartsough was not only active in getting some of these resolutions drawn up and sponsored, but he was also a moving spirit in initiating what was intended to be the first full-dress debate in the House, scheduled to last all night, on the eve of the nation-wide October 15 Moratorium. At the height of the debate, and after a series of speeches very critical of Administration policy, Administration supporters adjourned the House with one of those razor-thin majorities, 112-110.

A month and a half later, the House passed an Administration-endorsed resolution, by a vote of 333-55. It backed the President's plan to negotiate a "just peace" in Vietnam. It was adopted under a closed rule which prevented any clarifying amendment to be offered by a House member who did not want to give endorsement to all of the Administration war policies. The FCNL opposed this measure as a rubber-stamp approval for Nixon to continue the war. The proponents of the war seemed to believe that the best way to handle the Vietnam issue was to go right ahead with the war, but not to reveal too much, or discuss it in full.

The year 1969 marked Edward Snyder's return to Washington after a two-year sabbatical with the AFSC. He had been based in Singapore where he served as Quaker International Affairs Representative in Southeast Asia and director of seminars for diplomats. He found many of the Congressmen with whom he talked more responsive and more troubled than they had been two years earlier. His work had taken him to South Vietnam frequently and to Cambodia fourteen times. Snyder also had numerous discussions with the North Vietnamese and the National Liberation Front (NLF) officials concerning medical supplies and the release of Quaker doctor, Marjorie Nelson, who was captured by the NLF and released unharmed some two months later. Yet despite the persistent efforts of people like Ed Snyder and many whose interviews have been omitted for lack of space, with the exception of troop withdrawals, prospects for peace in Vietnam remained bleak. As Congress grew more responsive, the Administration grew less so. A peaceful solution of the conflict was indeed not apparent.

THE INVASION OF CAMBODIA: 1970

The invasion of Cambodia, April 30, 1970, aimed at clearing out the sanctuaries, used by the North Vietnamese for raids on the South, sparked intense criticism in the country and a determined effort on the part of Senate liberals to end the war. The United States continued to avoid dealing with the two "nonnegotiable" demands of the North Vietnamese for a definite commitment to a schedule for withdrawal of American forces and for a transitional coalition regime to rule in Saigon until such time as a permanent government could be constituted. "I would rather be a one-term President," countered Mr. Nixon in response to criticism from Senator Aiken, "and do what I believe is right, than be a two-term President at the cost of seeing American become a second-rate power and to see this nation accept the first defeat in its proud 190-year history."[4]

The Cambodian invasion, without prior consultation with Congress, ushered in the busiest telephone week in FCNL history. The four trunk lines were busy all day long with incoming calls from Maine to Seattle. Calls came especially from college and university students, expressing their alarm and indignation and asking what they could do to oppose the unprecedented military move.

Tens of thousands of students and others came to Washington to lobby, and FCNL briefed many of them. A team from Haverford College worked out plans in the FCNL office to bring the entire plant from Haverford including the president, the faculty and janitorial staff for a day of seminars, interviews and speeches by members of both Houses of Congress. The first ten days in May were probably the largest spontaneous lobbying effort in our nation's history. Those anxious days culminated in a huge demonstration May 9 called by the New Mobilization on the ellipse just south of the White House.

The report of the President's Commission on Campus Unrest published September 26, estimated that in the spring of 1970 "nearly one third of approximately 2500 colleges and universities had experienced some kind of protest activity" over the combined issues of the Cambodian invasion and the deaths and injuries at Kent State University and Jackson State College at the hands of officials entrusted to keep peace. Some 448 colleges and universities were still closed or affected by strikes by May 10th.[5]

Soon after the invasion, Edward Snyder made a lightning trip to Cambodia, his fifteenth visit to that country. On his return he wrote in the June 1970 *Newsletter* that "in Cambodia everyone has lost and no one has won. . . . In Saigon I found a sense of hopelessness and helplessness. A year ago there was hope of peace. Now the war seems interminable." This visit sparked considerable interest in Congress. A luncheon, arranged by Senator McGovern to discuss his impressions, was attended by Senators Edward Kennedy, Hughes, Montoya, Eagleton, Moss and Stephen Young. Four House members were hosts at a luncheon for fifteen Representatives and Ed Snyder.

Ed Snyder had at least five occasions to brief members of Congress or their staffs before their visits to Indochina. He suggested persons to see who would give a better balanced picture of the entire situation. Among Snyder's many reporting trips during the year was a tour of the Far West including Portland, Corvallis, Eugene and San Francisco.

THE COOPER-CHURCH AND MCGOVERN-HATFIELD RESOLUTIONS:
1970

One result of the Cambodian invasion was a flurry of amendments in Congress against the war. Two very important measures were introduced in the Senate which FCNL actively helped to draft. One of these, sponsored by Senators Frank Church and John Sherman Cooper of Kentucky, was passed by the Senate. The vote came on June 30 after thirty-four days of debate and two hundred eighty-eight speeches. The tally was fifty-eight to thirty-seven for an amendment which barred the President from spending any funds, without Congressional consent, after July 1, to retain U.S. forces in Cambodia. Action on the measure had been delayed by Administration supporters until the last departure of American troops from Cambodia, leaving the amendment largely symbolic.

Although the actual effect of the bill was slight, it did represent the first limitation ever voted on the President's powers as Commander-in-Chief during a war situation (even though the war had not been officially declared.) Its advocates argued that the bill would at least prevent future Cambodias. A final amended version cleared the House in December and was overwhelmingly passed by the Senate.

The McGovern-Hatfield End-the-War amendment (to the $19.2 billion military procurement bill) would have prohibited funds for use in Vietnam after December 31, 1970, except for the purpose of withdrawal. FCNL, McGovern and Hatfield and other co-sponsors including Senators Alan Cranston, Harold Hughes and Charles Goodell, worked hard for the passage of the bill, but on September 1, thirty-nine votes and one pair were recorded for the measure and fifty-five votes against. If nine senators had switched their votes to "yea," the bill would have passed. One hundred House members introduced similar legislation (H. Res. 1000), but no vote was taken in the House because of the Senate defeat.

On their way to the press conference after the vote, both Senators Hatfield and McGovern shook hands with me and thanked the FCNL for its very active support of their efforts. David Hartsough had worked very closely for weeks with staff members of the chief sponsors of these two bills in drafting the language and in soliciting support particularly among Republicans in both Houses.

In November 1970 only three opposition witnesses testified before the House Foreign Affairs Committee and none before the Senate Committee on the Administration's request for an additional half billion dollars in military and economic aid, earmarked primarily for Cambodia. Edward Snyder gave FCNL's statement in a personal appearance December 2 before the House Foreign Affairs Committee against military aid to Cambodia, drawing heavily on his visit to

Cambodia earlier in the year for AFSC just after U.S. troops entered Cambodia. He also argued against the Nixon Doctrine of sending military supplies to other nations. This FCNL document was the only opposition statement included in the printed Senate hearings and was placed in the *Congressional Record* by Senator McGovern on December 16.

One of the notable volunteer efforts was made by Chaplain Morrison, then associate professor of history at Waterloo Lutheran University in Ontario, Canada. He spent July and August gathering witnesses and encouraging House hearings on the brutal treatment by the Saigon regime of prisoners at Con Son and elsewhere. He also spent a great deal of time on the McGovern-Hatfield amendment.

One of the major Vietnam issues during the election was the release of prisoners of war. Certainly none has been more politically exploited. FCNL worked hard to provide a clear understanding of the whole issue and a letter to Senator Church found its way into the June 2 *Congressional Record*. Edward Snyder's letter concluded: "If we are truly concerned for the welfare of prisoners of war in Vietnam, Cambodia and Laos, it seems to me the best way to secure their release is in the context of a general agreement to end the war in Indochina."[6]

FCNL Works To Curtail Military Spending and To Free Political Prisoners

While FCNL opposition to the war in Indochina continued unabated in the late 60's and early 70's, Frances Neely concentrated on increasing FCNL attention and expertise on the maze of Pentagon spending proposals. FCNL legislative efforts under her able guidance focused more and more on whittling down money bills for military appropriations in general. Special attention was given to cutting military manpower and related costs. Manpower cuts, especially overseas troops, have large foreign policy implications. Manpower cuts also reduce military spending markedly since total manpower costs now account for more than half of all Pentagon spending. Cuts in manpower also reduce the need for the draft. The January 1970 *Newsletter* reported that some 50% of the Senate and 32% of the House voted for cuts in military spending in 1969. The final appropriation of $70 billion for the Department of Defense of the fiscal year ending June 30, 1970, was $5 billion less than the Administration had requested.

In the brief 1970 year-end FCNL annual report, Frances Neely and the staff associated with her in the struggle to reduce military spending had sixty-five entries describing a wide range of activities in which they had engaged during the year.

Just one of the many documents circulated in Congress was a two-page FCNL "Appeal to Reason for Major Cuts in Military Spending." This June appeal urged House members to reduce the U.S. troop level in Europe and Asia, to eliminate funds for the ABM, MIRV, and the B-1 bomber, and to make at least a 5-10% cut in the appropriation bill.

When it became known that the Department of Defense Appropriations Bill would be considered by the House on October 8, a letter was distributed on October 6 to two hundred-fifty Representatives urging them to be on the floor and to vote for the ceiling and troop withdrawal amendments which would be offered to the main bill. One of the handicaps to the passage of liberal legislation is a set of parliamentary tactics sometimes used to defeat such measures. The amendment to cut back defense spending to $65 billion and the amendment to withdraw 50,000 troops from Europe were defeated by *unrecorded voice votes* between 7 and 7:15 p.m. when less than 100 of 435 Representatives were present.[7] Therefore there was no record available to the public on who voted or how on the specific issues. Before the House changed its rules this tactic was particularly common on controversial issues, as it allowed a member to escape being answerable for his vote.

On May 6, Frederick Alan Koomanoff, a research engineer and systems analyst, told the House Appropriations Defense Subcommittee that more than $1 trillion had been spent by the military since 1940, which had brought us neither peace nor security. He pointed out that the Appropriations Committee had not seriously considered the necessity of reordering our national priorities. It was instead proposing to spend seven hundred fifty times as much for defense as they had appropriated to "find an answer to the unresolved and suicidal arms race through the efforts of the Arms Control and Disarmament Agency. . . . It is three times as much as the federal government appropriated last year for all federal expenditures on welfare, housing, education, and health."[8]

Throughout this period Frances Neely played a key role in helping to create and sustain the Coalition on National Priorities and Military Policy, a group of peace, religious, labor, and other organizations, which was dedicated to the reduction of military spending, the conversion of American industry to peacetime production, and the spending of funds on domestic rather than military projects.

1971

THE PEOPLE'S REPUBLIC OF CHINA SEATED IN THE UN
END THE WAR RESOLUTIONS DEFEATED,
BUT HOUSE OPPOSITION MOUNTS

As late as December 10, 1970, President Nixon had said: "We have no plans to change our policy with regard to the admission of Red China into the United Nations at this time."

Six months later, the situation had changed dramatically. The President announced that following secret communications and contacts he had arranged to visit China. Edward Snyder wrote President Nixon on July 16: "Your announcement last night of your forthcoming visit to China was wonderful news. We are grateful that you have taken this initiative, and we pray that your journey will be successful in beginning a new era of constructive United States-Chinese relations."[9]

The Peoples Republic of China was seated in the United Nations after twenty-two years of American opposition. Taiwan lost its seat in the General Assembly and on the Security Council.

For more than two decades, the FCNL had advocated the seating of the People's Head Republic of China without any naive illusion that improved relations would be easy with a Communist government after more than twenty years of bitter isolation and rejection. However, relations have greatly improved, exchange of diplomatic missions just short of full diplomatic recognition have taken place, and visits of Americans to Mainland China have multiplied. A visiting troupe of Chinese acrobats has thrilled American audiences and television viewers.

MANY AMERICAN TROOPS WITHDRAWN

American troop strength was down to 180,000 by December 1, from 337,000 at the end of 1970. American casualties were decreased but not eliminated. However, U.S. planes continued to rain down death and destruction at an unrelenting pace on North and South Vietnam and Laos. The numbers of U.S. Prisoners of War and Missing in Action were increasing because of the devastating air war. By the beginning of 1971, more than 82% of the prisoners were pilots or air crew members.

This was also the year of the revelations about the My Lai

massacre which had taken place in March 1968 and which had been a subject of denials and cover-ups which stunned many Americans. Estimates of the total number massacred at My Lai ranged from one hundred to six hundred.[10] First Lieutenant William L. Calley, Jr., 27, was given a life sentence for his part in the slaying. His sentence was commuted to twenty years by President Nixon, which makes him eligible for parole after ten years. Calley's superior officer, Captain Ernest L. Medina, was acquitted of any responsibility for the massacre. Of the twenty-five officers and men charged, one was convicted, four were acquitted, and the charges against the remainder were dismissed.

Many of the American people seemed oblivious to much of what was going on in the war, as the Administration refused to disclose pertinent facts and the exact cost of the war, which was being paid for by the American taxpayers.

Although Congressional opposition to the war continued to mount, particularly in the House, not one of the legislative proposals for ending the war was able to muster enough votes to clear both Houses. The only antiwar measure enacted was the repeal of the Gulf of Tonkin Resolution in January because "recent legislation and Executive statements make the 1964 legislation unnecessary for the prosecution of U.S. foreign policy."[11] One might add "unnecessary for the continued prosecution of the war."

The Cooper-Church amendment to the foreign aid bill, which would have prohibited funds for the war except as needed for withdrawal, was subjected to such heavy Administration lobbying that it failed by the close margin 44-48. This vote, however, precipitated a closer look at the foreign aid bill which revealed some one billion dollars for military and supporting assistance to Southeast Asia. The bill was soundly defeated 27-41 the day after the Cooper-Church setback.

The only measure to make some real headway in Congress was a Mansfield amendment in several forms. Although it was not as strong as the Nedzi-Whalen cut-funds amendment, which garnered 158 votes (the highest opposition to date), the Mansfield amendment was passed twice by the Senate. It was defeated by the House 193-215 (largest number of critics for 1971), but was restored to the military procurement bill by a joint conference committee. The President did sign it, while maintaining that he did not intend to be bound by it. In essence, it was a declaration of U.S. policy to terminate at the earliest possible date all military operations in Indochina subject to the release of all American POWs.

It is interesting to note the increase in war opposition, especially in the House from 158 in June to 193 in October 1971. A Gallup poll released in May, indicated that 61% of those interviewed across the country felt that it had been a mistake to send troops to Vietnam.[12]

FCNL efforts were directed at encouraging and supporting the volume of legislation aimed at ending the war. Concurrently, FCNL waged an unsuccessful drive to end the draft and to prevent draftees from going to Vietnam. Because of the staggering amount of legislation and some of the confusing voting, FCNL constantly distributed resumes of Congressional attitudes, votes and the names of members of Congress to be pressed a bit harder.

The Friends Committee was especially active in the organization and programming of "Set the Date Now." This was a coalition of twenty-three religious and other groups asking for withdrawal by December 31, 1971. Edward Snyder was on the steering committee and took considerable responsibility in developing legislative strategy. He arranged speakers and briefings at the June 7 convocation and helped formulate the legislative policy which emerged from the October 7-8 strategy meeting.

The Lawyers Committee To End the War also drew on his services in formulating their legislative activities.

AFSC and FCNL both worked on the problem of the POWs and MIAs (Missing in Action). Edward Snyder worked closely with the POW wives who were determined not to let the issue become a political wedge for the Administration. Stewart Meacham of the AFSC gave testimony for the Committee of Liaison to the House Foreign Affairs Committee on March 21 regarding American POWs held in North Vietnam. Although not directly related to the POW issue, an American pacifist trip to Paris undoubtedly brought the issue into the open. The trip, sponsored by AFSC, the Fellowship of Reconciliation, and Clergy and Laymen Concerned, brought 171 Americans from 41 states to confer with members of all four delegations at the Peace talks. Later these pacifists were some of the many Washington visitors who conferred with Congressmen.

Jon Newkirk, who succeeded David Hartsough in September 1970 as the FCNL Vietnam staff member, was responsible for various luncheons and visits in Washington. He arranged a luncheon at William Penn House for Nguyen Thang Canh, Asia Secretary for the World Council of Churches, on January 13. Jon Newkirk was also instrumental in bringing to Washington more than forty-five persons who had spent from two to five years in Vietnam or Laos in civilian jobs, for interviews with governmental officials.

On the Hill it was a busy time, but he still managed to assist Hugh Manke, director of International Voluntary Services in Vietnam, in preparing strong and persuasive testimony for the Senate Subcommittee on Refugees, chaired by Senator Kennedy in April.

Beth Burbank, a research intern, gathered information for various background legislative memos and helped circulate to Congressional offices in December, material on the automated war prepared by AFSC-NARMIC (National Action Research on the Military-Industrial Complex). She was instrumental in setting up a briefing in the Senate Office Building on the effects of antipersonnel bombs and other weapons which are so crippling to civilians as well as soldiers. Thereafter, AFSC took over the showing of the program all over the country. Indeed, the growing air war has become the most fearful aspect of the "wound down" war. Many of the devices now used in Vietnam are or will be used in domestic police work in the near future.

One of Jon Newkirk's projects in 1970 had been cooperating on a questionnaire for returned Vietnam volunteers and others dealing with the economy and postwar needs of Vietnam. In handling the question of U.S. assistance to Vietnam, one person expressed a feeling that many antiwar crusaders have experienced for years:

> I'm sure you have heard about the elephant who was taking a stroll through the woods one afternoon, when suddenly he became aware of the fact that he had just stepped on a mother partridge. Around his feet, he saw the little covey of orphans scampering tragically. But moved in his heart, the elephant looked down on the little partridges and with tears in his eyes he said, 'Ah, but I too have maternal instincts.' Whereupon he sat upon them. [13]

1972
Senate Votes To End Vietnam Funds

In the year 1972 the Senate finally mustered a majority to cut off funds for the Indochina War under certain conditions. But the House did not, and the war continued. The bombing of North Vietnam was greatly intensified in December. Ten legislative memos and one Action Bulletin were prepared and distributed during the year to interested persons including Congress, among nongovernmental organization colleagues, the press and the public.

Legislative goals included both a fund cut-off, and a statement of policy calling for an end to the war. Neither proposition received a majority in both Houses in 1971 nor in 1972. In July antiwar Senators were able for the first time to maintain a slim but solid majority of 49-47 to cut off all funds for the war. But most House Republicans joined by Speaker Carl Albert of Oklahoma and Majority Leader Hale Boggs of Louisiana and some Democrats teamed up to continue funding the war as President Nixon had requested.

An Emergency Convocation To End the War was held May 10-11, 1972, just after the blockading and mining of North Vietnam and the vastly increased air war began. Some ten members of Congress spoke at this convocation. Edward Snyder devoted considerable time to this event as "issue manager" for the Washington Inter-Religious Staff Council and as an active member of the initiating organization, "Set the Date Now." Among the nonreligious sponsoring organizations were Americans for Democratic Action, National Education Association, Business Executives Move for Peace in Vietnam (BEM), National Student Lobby, and the American Federation of State, County and Municipal Employees.

Testimony was given before the Senate Foreign Relations Committee on two subjects especially involving the war. On April 5 Louis Kubicka drew on his four year's experience in Vietnam to point out the deficiencies in S. 2497 to establish a Vietnam Children's Care Agency. He stressed that ending the war, and not just American involvement in the war coupled with some aid, was the primary requirement for helping the children. Clarence H. Yarrow criticized the United States for greatly accelerating the air war at the same time that it was removing ground troops and the Nixon doctrine of expecting our client states to do the fighting for us instead of an all-out determination to end the war.

Orders broke all records for the August-September 1972 number of the *FCNL Washington Newsletter* analyzing the positions on key issues of Presidential candidates Richard M. Nixon and George McGovern, and Vice Presidential candidates Spiro T. Agnew and Robert Sargent Shriver. More than 100,000 copies were printed and distributed with many commendations for its objectivity and usefulness.

In spite of intensive negotiations and the withdrawal of a large proportion of American ground troops, at year's end the Vietnam War continued its devastating course.

1973

AMERICAN COMBAT ROLE ENDS
BUT HEAVY MILITARY INVOLVEMENT CONTINUES

Although the Nixon Administration kept insisting that the "war was winding down," it was not until August 15, 1973, that bombing in Cambodia was halted by a compromise between the President and Congress on ending the U.S. combat role in Southeast Asia. But massive American military involvement persists in the continuing civil war. Congress in December voted $900 million in military aid to South Vietnam, but nothing for the reconstruction of heavily bombed North Vietnam, as had been promised by President Johnson.

At the end of 1973, the American government was continuing to support the South Vietnamese government in its opposition to fulfilling the Paris agreements earlier in the year designed to work out an accommodation with the Provisional Revolutionary Government. Because of the continuing civil war it is estimated that more than 50,000 South Vietnamese were killed in 1973, or as many as the United States lost during the entire war.

The U.S. has been paying 80 per cent of the cost of the Saigon government, providing huge military supplies and hundreds and hundreds of advisors for the military operations of the South Vietnamese army and air force. South Vietnam now has the fourth largest military establishment in the world. It was reported by a returned AFSC worker in Da Nang that one Texas firm employed 1500 American civilians to operate one of the large air bases. In September 582,000 barrels of oil were shipped to South Vietnam.

The Thieu government regards any opposition to the war, or any neutral attitude as being pro-Communist, illegal and subject to criminal penalties. The American AID budget included payment for the maintenance of 552 prisons in South Vietnam. Estimates of political prisoners run between 80,000 and 200,000. These prisoners are oftentimes subject to torture, and many without ever being brought to trial.[14]

Edward F. Snyder has provided the following brief summary of FCNL efforts to stop the continuing war in 1973 — 1973 was the culmination of nine years of intensive anti-Indochina war activity by FCNL.

The year opened with citizen outrage at the devastating U.S. Christmas-time bombing of North Vietnam. This public outrage was focused on the newly arriving 93rd Congress through the Religious Convocation and Congressional Visitation for Peace, co-sponsored by AFSC and Clergy and Laity Concerned on January 3 and 4. FCNL played a leading role in identifying legislative strategy and organizing Congressional visits. This was one of the largest and most effective antiwar lobbies ever to come to Washington. I believe the clear message to the Administration of a potential bombing cut-off by Congress was a major stimulus to the Administration to compromise its aims and sign the Vietnam cease-fire agreement January 27. FCNL also helped organize and provide legislative information at a cold, windy spot near the Washington Monument to the huge crowd that turned out for the Counter Inaugural on January 20.

The Coalition To Stop Funding the War, made up of major religious and peace organizations and some labor, education, and other groups, was formed in early January and remained active throughout the year. Snyder was co-chairman of the Coalition with Dudley Ward of the United Methodist Church, and involvement with it took considerable time.

During the quiet period when U.S. direct military action was ending and POW's were being returned, we attempted through legislative memoranda and testimony by George Kahin of Cornell University to build support for the Case-Church proposal against U.S. military reinvolvement in Indochina.

In late April we helped identify the Administration strategy of obtaining Congressional approval of Cambodian bombing through the obscure device of authorizing transfer authority in the Second Supplemental Appropriations bill. There were numerous contacts with Reps. Addabbo and Giaimo and offices of Speaker Albert and Majority Leader O'Neill, and intense activity in advance of the May 10 House vote and throughout June, leading up to the decisive votes during the last week of June which resulted in a complete bombing halt as of August 15.

As direct U.S. military action ended, attention shifted to indirect U.S. involvement in Indochina, and also to related efforts to end all U.S. military aid abroad. John Plank of the University of Connecticut testified for FCNL on May 4 against foreign military aid in general before the Senate Foreign Relations Committee.

Special attention was given to ending U.S. aid for the repressive police and prison system in South Vietnam. John Champlin, M.D., testified on this and related U.S. aid issues on June 11 before the House Foreign Affairs Committee. We worked on these subjects and were glad to see several proposals accepted and language included in reports. (End of Snyder report.)

The FCNL first warned in 1954 against U.S. military involvement in Vietnam. How long will it be before peace is really established, effective political cooperation between North and South Vietnam is restored, and war-ravaged Vietnam can be rebuilt? How long will the

FCNL have to keep working for these goals and for the end of U.S. support of the repressive, dictatorial Thieu regime?

On February 29, 1969, Roger Marshall wrote a letter home from Vietnam in which he said: "It would be clearly impossible to describe clearly what I saw inside. It would be like looking through a hole into Hell. . . . When Vietnam is entered into the annals of history, it will be a deep adherent scar on the record of the children of God."[15]

The Cost of War in Indochina

Cold statistics can only hint at the total human tragedy of the war in Indochina. The following figures were supplied by the Department of Defense, May 15, 1973, before the bombing of Cambodia and Laos had been stopped. The figures on refugees are from the Kennedy Senate Subcommittee on Refugees.

I. U.S. military *hostile deaths* in S.E. Asia
1/1/61 - 5/5/73   46,002
U.S. military *nonhostile deaths* in S.E. Asia
1/1/61 - 12/12/72 - air, truck accidents, disease   9,830
U.S. military wounded in S.E. Asia
1/1/61 - 5/5/73
    hospitalized   153,312
    nonhospitalized 150,341
        Total   303,653

II. South Vietnamese military *hostile deaths* - 1/1/60 - 12/12/72   195,137
South Vietnamese *wounded* - same period (no nonhostile death count available)   494,931

III. "Enemy" military deaths - 1/1/60 - 12/12/72   927,168

IV. Financial Cost of the War to U.S. -
Full budgeted costs, FY 1965 - FY 1973 (est)* $137.428 billion

*Economists figure that the total long term cost of the war on account of pensions, interest on the national debt, and other continuing expenditures will reach two or three times the figure through June 1973.

The authors of the Cornell University *Air War in Indochina*, (Revised Edition; Beacon Press, 1971, p. 108) say: "In round figures, the aggregate incremental *direct* economic cost of the Indochina war to the United States, through the six fiscal years to mid-1971, has been around $200 billion — about double the budgetary incremental costs. This figure does not include unmeasured economic costs, or any non-American costs."

V.   Allied bomb tonnage - 1/1/66 - 3/30/73   7,288,965 tons
     (Postceasefire by country, from
     1/27/73 - 4/30/73   Cambodia   82,837
                                 Laos   63,082

VI. Loss of U.S. planes and helicopters,
     over North Vietnam, South Vietnam,
     and Laos
       U.S. *airplanes downed*, 1/1/61 -
       1/27/73   hostile   1,648
                                 nonhostile   2,049
       U.S. *helicopters   downed*, 1/1/61 -
       1/27/73   hostile   2,282
                                 nonhostile   2,583

VII. Civilian Casualties, Refugees, Dis-
     placed Persons
     Cambodia: Displaced persons and
     refugees as of April 1973 (this is
     nearly half the total population of 6.5
     million)   2,957,000
     South Vietnam: Registered refugees,
     1965 to May 16, 1973   5,981,600
     Refugees and other war victims 1965
     to February 1973 (over half South
     Vietnam's population)   10,105,400

VIII. Mixed blood GI Children in Vietnam
     (est.)   16   25,000   [16]

CHAPTER 16

Some Memorable Interviews

DWIGHT D. EISENHOWER

During the height of the political campaign after the national political conventions in 1952, I proposed interviewing the two candidates on the question of peace and disarmament. Seven of us representing church, peace and veterans organizations met with General Eisenhower at the Hotel Commodore in New York City on September 30.[1] A similar delegation conferred with Governor Adlai Stevenson in Springfield on October 20.

Mr. Eisenhower greeted us warmly and referred to his interview the day before with a bishop whom he had mistakenly pictured as somebody else. This informal reference to the awesome task of keeping all the church people straight broke the ice.

The delegation asked me to make the initial statement. I summarized the main points on the memorandum we handed to him by saying that our bipartisan delegation wanted to concentrate in this interview on the issue of general disarmament. The General had earlier asserted that disarmament was "essential to a stable, enduring peace." We asked him to emphasize this conviction in his campaign and, if elected, to push negotiations for a just and practical plan for world disarmament. We urged that American leadership on this question should be prophetic, continuous and emphatic.

The memorandum was signed by the executive secretaries of the appropriate boards or councils of the American Baptist Convention, the Methodist Church, the Presbyterian Church in the U.S.A., the Disciples of Christ and the Friends Committee on National Legislation. Other signatories included the National Chairman of the American Veterans Committee, the Legislative Secretary of the

Women's International League for Peace and Freedom, the Chairman of the People's Mandate Committee, and John Inman, as an individual. (Inman was a staff member of the Church Peace Union.)

After this presentation, Mr. Eisenhower replied that the disarmament issue was like the question of the chicken and the egg — which comes first? The world needed faith and confidence before it could disarm. Ever since the 1930's the General had been in favor of disarmament. He commented, "You don't have to convince me of its necessity. I stressed it in the Silver Lecture at Columbia University in 1950." There was one minimum essential, according to the General, and that was honest and thoroughgoing inspection, which the Russians had not yet agreed upon.

We replied that the delegation was united on the need for thorough-going inspection. Charles F. Boss, Jr., executive secretary of the Board of World Peace of the Methodist Church, asked, "Don't you think it is time that America must seize the initiative and capture the imagination of the world?"

General Eisenhower reaffirmed that there could be no long-range peace without disarmament. The idea ought to be nailed to the masthead; it ought to be repeated every day; churches ought to develop public opinion for it and teach it in their schools; social and cultural organizations ought to be educated for it.

Charles Boss then remarked that a representative of the National Council of Churches had hoped to join the delegation but was out of town. He had asked Boss to present to Mr. Eisenhower the statement adopted by the National Council the previous week which said in part that God is interested in politics because he is interested in his children. The General laughed heartily as he reached for the statement.

Mr. Eisenhower repeated his insistence on inspection and pointed out that we were such a strong nation, if we did not have any arms at all, we would still be a potential threat in the minds of others because of our productive capacity, which tends to create a certain amount of fear in others. He would be in favor of taking every atom bomb we had and throwing each one away if there were an honest system of inspection. In the United States, newspapers told nearly everything and such publicity is one of the prices we pay for the democratic process. All the information published in the American press is accessible to people behind the Iron Curtain.

We returned to the necessity of disarmament if the world is to achieve economic solvency and to the storm warnings just issued by the Economic Commission for Europe. We reminded him that the United Nations Economic Survey of Europe for 1951 had estimated that the defense outlays in the leading industrial countries of Europe, the Soviet Union and the United States were about equivalent to the total national income of all the underdeveloped countries. In other words, the major nations of the world were spending more for arms than half the human race received in total income.

Annalee Stewart referred to her recent trip to Europe where people were interested to know that American voices in support of disarmament were raised on a bipartisan basis, such as by Senators Flanders and McMahon, and that this had raised hopes in both Europe and Asia. If Eisenhower would speak out as they had done, she was certain it would bring a real response.

Mabel Vernon stated that she had been impressed by what the General had already said about peace. She was concerned that he had not spoken much about disarmament and asked whether he would talk about it every day? He smiled and affirmed that when one makes speeches it is easy to leave out points one intends to make.

After the interview, we visited further with Senator Frank Carlson of Kansas, who traveled with Presidential candidate Eisenhower every day from the time of his nomination to his election. The Senator assured us we were free to refer to this interview because the General always said what he honestly believed.

In retrospect, General Eisenhower was probably the one man in the United States in the period after World War II who could best have led this nation in pressing for a drastic program of general disarmament — one of the imperatives of peace. So far as I saw the press reports, he did not talk about this issue in the campaign. The President did mention disarmament in his inaugural address, when, after stressing that the first task of statesmanship is "to develop the strength that will deter the forces of aggression and promote the conditions of peace," he went on to say:

> In the light of this principle, we stand ready to engage with any and all others in joint efforts to remove the causes of mutual fear and distrust among nations, and so to make possible drastic reduction of armaments. [2]

He later spoke out on "atoms-for-peace," but that was a program for the international peaceful development of atomic energy and did not insist on atomic disarmament. The President did appoint former Governor Harold E. Stassen as his special disarmament advisor with

Cabinet rank from 1955 to 1958 but Eisenhower did not push for general disarmament with the vigor I thought he should have. His strongest words were reserved for eight years later, when in perhaps his last speech before turning over the Presidency to John F. Kennedy, he stated on January 17, 1961:

> This conjunction of an immense military establishment and large arms industry is new in the American experience. The total influence — economic, political, even spiritual — is felt in every city, every State house, every office of the Federal Government. . . . In the councils of government, we must guard against the acquisition of unwarranted influence, whether sought or unsought, by the military-industrial complex. . . . Disarmament, with mutual honor and confidence, is a continuing imperative. Together we must learn how to compose differences, not with arms, but with intellect and decent purpose. Because this need is so sharp and apparent I confess that I lay down my official responsibilities in this field with a definite sense of disappointment. . . . [3]

An earlier and eloquent speech on the cost of armaments was made by President Eisenhower on April 16, 1953, when he declared:

> Every gun that is made, every warship launched, every rocket fired signifies, in the final sense, a theft from those who hunger and are not fed, those who are cold and not clothed. This world in arms is not spending money alone. . . . It is spending the sweat of its laborers, the genius of its scientists, the hopes of its children. [4]

President Eisenhower was scheduled to visit Japan on June 19, 1960, to celebrate the 100th anniversary of Japanese-American relations. After the arrangements for his visit had been made, a group of Japanese Christians wrote me a letter urging the President not to come to Japan because under the circumstances his visit would be greatly misunderstood and the President might become the object of violent demonstrations.

Eisenhower's visit was to coincide with the Japanese ratification of the U.S.-Japanese Security Treaty. A great number of people from various levels of society participated in demonstrations against the treaty. Opposition was directed largely against the military provisions for retaining numerous U.S. bases and a large number of U.S. troops in Japan and Okinawa. Esther Rhoads, a Friend who had spent more than thirty years in Japan, and I appeared before the Senate Foreign Relations Committee on June 7 in opposition to the treaty. As the only opposition witnesses, we attempted to picture how the Japanese felt. In my testimony I explained, "Fifteen years after the war, they are apprehensive about another decade or an indefinite stationing of American troops in Japan with all the incidents and influence attendant upon foreign troops on their soil."

The growing protests in Japan were aimed not only at American militarism but also against the haughty and antidemocratic regime of Prime Minister Kishi. If the President were to arrive in Japan as scheduled, it would be interpreted as intervention in an election campaign on the side of the very unpopular Mr. Kishi and might subject the President to any kind of indignity.

As an American citizen I did not want to see the President embarrassed or humiliated by unseen and unfortunate circumstances and as a friend of Japan I did not want the President's prestige, even unconsciously, put behind the autocratic and militaristic Prime Minister; therefore, I made three moves. I got in touch with Vice President Nixon's office and told one of his staff members about the letter. Since Senator Carlson had been so close to President Eisenhower, I relayed the information to him with a suggestion that the President change his projected schedule and postpone his visit to Japan. I sent a copy of the letter on June 11 to the President and went to the White House to talk with Frederick Fox of the President's staff about the problem.

The reply which I received was that the President had already started on his trip to other countries and it was too late for him to change his plans. At the last minute, however, the Japanese Government withdrew the invitation, and President Eisenhower's visit to Japan was cancelled.[5]

GOVERNOR ADLAI E. STEVENSON

The parallel interview with Democratic Presidential candidate Adlai Stevenson took place in Springfield, Illinois, on October 20, 1952,[6] just a few days before his defeat at the polls. John H. Ferguson, professor of government at Penn State University, represented the FCNL. Other members of the delegation were Charles F. Boss, Jr., Harold A. Bosley, Elsie Picon, Mabel Vernon and Mrs. Milton Epstein. Representatives of the National Council for the Prevention of War, the National Council of Jewish Women and the Post War World Council added their signatures to those who had signed the Eisenhower memorandum.

Quoting Stevenson's comment that the "arms race must end

before it ends us," the visitors spoke of the social cost of the arms race, the slow progress of disarmament negotiations, and their hope that the Governor would continue to give unwavering support to the United Nations and its objectives. They noted that representatives of nongovernmental organizations had been told at numerous State Department briefings that military strength would facilitate negotiations and agreements with the Soviet Union; yet no agreements were in sight. On the slightly encouraging side, where the State Department formerly had one man and a half working on disarmament plans, it now had a contingent of six or seven and a panel of consultants composed of several distinguished scientists to review plans and proposals for world disarmament.

Mabel Vernon commented that she had read addresses made by Governor Stevenson before his nomination and had found in several of them the assertion that we must end the arms race before it ends us and that we must pursue disarmament with all the intensity and purposefulness with which we build armaments. In the speeches she had read since his nomination, and she had followed them carefully, she had seen only two references to disarmament, one in the San Francisco address on foreign policy and one in the address on atomic energy at Hartford.

Governor Stevenson listened attentively. He supported the UN and, indeed, had helped with its formation. He had written the speeches given by the President and the Secretary of State at the First General Assembly. Stevenson was for disarmament and had often stated this during the campaign; the problem is not the goal but the means of achieving it. Disarmament must follow, rather than precede, political settlements and restoration of confidence.

But, maintained the Governor, it takes the cooperation of the Soviets to achieve disarmament and relax tensions. After the war we "disarmed utterly." We tried negotiation from weakness. It failed. Soviet tactics forced us to build strength for the purpose of achieving peace. This policy of strength had been succeeding, according to Stevenson, and should lead to successful negotiations with the Soviets.

However, the Governor admitted, it was difficult to stop the arms race once it had started. Perhaps the proper stopping point had been reached. The American people find it difficult to "conciliate and compromise." Too often when the Governor suggested negotiation and conciliation, he was greeted with the accusation of being an appeaser. He did say that before he was Governor of Illinois he spent some time urging the World Federalists to study and emphasize the importance of disarmament.

The Governor remained cordial, forthright and frank throughout the interview. He listened carefully and appeared to be eager to understand the point of view of his visitors, although he gave little indication of how far he would comply with their requests. Early in the discussion he was given a copy of the American Friends Service Committee pamphlet on disarmament. Leafing through it, he said, "this looks as if it would be helpful." A dozen copies were left with him for distribution to his staff.

Perhaps what surprised and concerned the delegation most was the Governor's foursquare support of the Truman-Acheson foreign policy of unilateral military intervention and negotiation from strength. Some of the group thought that his remarks to the effect that the U.S. had disarmed after the war were naive and inadequate, since for a time the U.S. had had a monopoly of atom bombs and a sizable fleet in reserve. Thus, his easy assumption that we could succeed and were succeeding in our relations with the Soviet Union seemed untenable.

The Governor's attitude gave Mabel Vernon the impression that if elected he would try with "intensity and purposefulness" to find the means of ending the arms race. Charles Boss agreed, for he wrote to me after the interview:

> For myself, I came away convinced that the intellectual insight and comprehension of Governor Stevenson were far superior to that of General Eisenhower. I think Governor Stevenson not only fully understood the United Nations background, the need for and conditions of disarmament, but believed that it is the obligation of the United States, with other powers, to seek at the earliest time, conditions to make possible the disarmament of the world. . . . I think that he has a more flexible attitude and himself stated that the problem is to create the conditions which make negotiation possible. [7]

STEVENSON ON ENDING NUCLEAR BOMB TESTS

Often lobbying has to be done catch as catch can on the fly. That was the case when I went to see Adlai Stevenson at the Wardman Park Hotel in Washington. He had been one of the first political leaders to call for the ending of H-bomb tests.

On April 21, 1956, three days before my visit, Governor Stevenson had addressed the American Society of Newspaper Editors, expressing his belief that: ". . . .we should give prompt and earnest consideration to stopping further tests of the hydrogen bomb, as

Commissioner Murray of the Atomic Energy Commission recently proposed. As a layman, I questioned the sense in multiplying and enlarging weapons of a destructive power already almost incomprehensible. Of course, I would call upon other nations to follow our lead."[8] President Eisenhower and Vice President Nixon at that time were favoring the continuance of tests.

At the time of my visit, Stevenson was involved in a prolonged discussion with some other leaders of the Democratic party, and I had to wait for two or three hours. When the Governor emerged, I walked into the elevator with him and rode down the four floors to the lobby, while I expressed our appreciation for his outspoken appeal to end the testing of atom bombs.

The Governor replied that he was grateful to hear those words from a Friend, because he had been receiving a lot of criticism for having made such a proposal. Then he dashed for the airport to take a plane to New York. Two of us gathered up some material on bomb testing and disarmament, including an excellent statement by the Democratic Council in California against bomb testing. We jumped into a taxi, rushed to the airport and stationed ourselves at the exit door through which Stevenson would go to catch his plane. As he whisked by us we gave him the material, for which he thanked us, and expressed our hope that he would have an opportunity to read it enroute to New York. Nine years later in 1963 a limited test-ban treaty was finally ratified.

HUMPHREY, NIXON AND KENNEDY

Responding to an FCNL suggestion, the Washington representatives of the Protestant denominations scheduled visits to four Presidential hopefuls for April 21, 1960, well before the political conventions.[9] Senator Symington of Missouri cancelled his appointment at the last moment. All the interviews took place on the same day. It was a day to be remembered because, among the other three — Hubert H. Humphrey, Richard M. Nixon and John F. Kennedy — two were to be elected President and one was to become Vice President.

Each candidate was invited to discuss the three areas of foreign policy which the churches were emphasizing that year. The subjects were foreign economic aid, disarmament and how to improve East-West relations with particular reference to political settlements. Fourteen of us, representing various denominations and the National Council of Churches, participated in the interviews, each of which lasted nearly an hour.

Our first interview was with Senator Humphrey. When he arrived and began to speak to us, he showered us with a great variety of imaginative and pertinent ideas. On disarmament he appeared much more emotionally involved than the other two candidates, who handled that question with detachment.

Mr. Humphrey raised the question of what he should do with reference to the West Virginia primary campaign, in which he and Senator Kennedy were then engaged. Senator Humphrey had been receiving vicious hate mail, such as he had never received before, based on the assumption that his opposition to Mr. Kennedy was rooted in religious bigotry. Humphrey indicated that he was discouraged and wondered whether he should withdraw from the primary race.

Richard Nixon, then Vice President, disclosed that the Eisenhower Administration had some undertakings on disarmament which he was not at liberty to reveal at that time but which he hoped would move us forward. His views were more stereotyped, unimaginative and detached than those of the other two. In regard to economic aid, he emphasized that a successful program depends not only upon administrative initiative but also upon legislative responsibility. Not once in eight years, he pointed out, had Congress appropriated all the funds which the President had requested.

Senator Kennedy gave a careful, urbane, astute review of his ideas on these three subjects. He did not put much thrust into his discussion on disarmament. His listeners knew that he had never attended a session of the Senate Disarmament Subcommittee, of which he was a member, and of which Senator Humphrey was chairman.

The question of a Catholic running for the Presidency had stirred up a lot of controversy in the country. In this particular interview, the delegation had decided not to raise this issue, becuase we were concentrating on the area of foreign policy and because we had not been authorized by our denominations to make official representations of this subject. But when Senator Kennedy had finished his comments on foreign policy, he brought up the subject. Just prior to our interview he had spoken at a luncheon of the American Society of Newspaper Editors, and he passed out copies of his address. He told us:

> I have been a member of the House of Representatives for six years and am now a Senator. I am a practicing Catholic, but I am my own man politically. In public office I have never taken my orders from the priesthood, the hierarchy or the Vatican.

The interviews would have been more satisfactory had we arranged for a real dialogue instead of mainly listening to the candidates' exposition of their views. There was not much opportunity for church representatives to speak at length, but in general the views of the religious community on these questions were well known. Some of us followed up this series with further conversations and presentation of a variety of material to the speech writers and staff members of the candidates.

Our interviews had been held in a friendly setting in the respective offices of the candidates in the Senate Office Building. We had been privileged in a single day to hear the views on three important questions of three men who have been pitted against each other politically and who have since played such a large part in American politics.

We did not anticipate at that time that these three men would play such an important role in deepening our involvement in Vietnam. President Kennedy multiplied the number of military advisors and set the course of military intervention. Vice President Humphrey supported with evangelistic fervor President Johnson's escalation of the war and the bombing of North Vietnam. Humphrey began to reverse his position too late to retrieve his political fortune or to defeat Nixon in the election of 1968. President Nixon "wound down" the war by widespread attacks on Cambodia and Laos and by ordering the resumption of heavy and continuous bombing of North Vietnam, the mining of the ports of Haiphong and other coastal cities, and the bombing of Cambodia in the summer of 1973 until August 15th when the funds were cut off by Congressional action.

RICHARD M. NIXON

On the controversy over what should be done about the royalties from offshore oil in the oceans adjacent to Louisiana, Texas and California, the FCNL took the position that one of our greatest natural assets should go to our greatest human asset, our children.

Mrs. Lorraine Shevlin, now the wife of former Senator John Sherman Cooper of Kentucky, volunteered to do some lobbying for the FCNL, and I accompanied her on a number of interviews. She knew almost everybody in official Washington. Her brother had been Nixon's finance manager in the Vice Presidential campaign. Mrs. Shevlin set up an appointment for us with Vice President Nixon in his office in the Capitol to talk about oil for education.

The interview took place on the day when the Vice President was announcing a round-the-world tour. While a string of newspaper correspondents came to see him, we cooled our heels for an hour and a half in the Senate lobby. After we had been ushered in to the Vice President's office, we asked him what the attitude of President Eisenhower was on the question of oil for education and expressed our hope that the President would support the proposal to allocate these royalties to the federal government for education and not to the states for general revenues. Nixon replied he really did not know the President's position on that particular question but that he would try to find out. In our discussion on the need for more money for education, I reminded him that twice he had cast the deciding vote against federal aid to education — once in the Education and Labor Committee and once on the House Floor.

We never did learn what the President's position was. None of the bills introduced over the years earmarking offshore revenues for aid to education ever passed Congress.

Mrs. Shevlin and I were interested in the intrinsic merits of the social use of our natural resources. But oil for education turned out to have political implications in the next election. It was a close election for the control of the Senate. As I recall, it took some days before the contests in New Jersey and Oregon were decided. Liberal Republican Senator Clifford Case of New Jersey won. Senator Guy Cordon of Oregon, a conservative who had based his campaign in part on allocating oil revenues to the states on the basis of states rights, lost his bid for reelection. This was, of course, not the only issue involved, but it played a part in his defeat. His failure to be reelected meant that the Republicans lost their majority in the Senate, lost all their committee chairmanships, and now sixteen years later are still the minority party in the Senate, as they are also in the House of Representatives.

SENATOR HUBERT H. HUMPHREY

Staff members of the FCNL had many interviews over the years with Senator Humphrey or with his aides on questions of food for peace, disarmament and civil rights — three of the issues on which he exerted strong leadership. One of my earliest dialogues with the Senator took place in the summer of 1950 on the question of ending the Korean War.

It was late in the afternoon when I saw him. My plea was that every effort ought to be exerted to end the war immediately in spite of the obvious difficulties. Military action by the United States under the aegis of the United Nations was destroying the country that ostensibly we were trying to defend. War, even in the name of collective security and of the obligations of the Charter, was still war and was undermining the UN.

The Senator argued that you could not negotiate with an aggressor, that you couldn't negotiate when you were losing, that you could not negotiate now. The debate was a very lively one, for the Senator is no easy protagonist. Finally the two of us called it a draw, for neither could convince the other.

Then Mr. Humphrey picked up an editorial from a Minnesota newspaper and read it to me. The editor had attacked him bitterly, not for one of his weaknesses, but for one of his virtues — his strong support of civil rights for Blacks and other minorities. "I get this kind of attack not from one paper but from many papers, and not once in a while but a lot of the time. Raymond, I have been asking myself whether it is worthwhile to stay in politics." I encouarged him to stay in politics because of the importance of his leadership in the struggle to achieve racial justice, to overcome world hunger and to end the arms race.

SENATOR BRIEN McMAHON

In the spring of 1952 Senator Brien McMahon of Connecticut reviewed for Annalee Stewart and me the events of early February 1950. We had been in frequent touch with him since the end of World War II because he led the efforts for the civilian control of atomic energy and was an outspoken champion for disarmament. We knew that the Senator was not well, but we did not anticipate that he would die in July of 1952, three or four months after our interview.

When President Truman announced that he had ordered the Atomic Energy Commission to proceed with the development of the hydrogen bomb, the Senator decided that he must deliver a speech on the nuclear arms race, on which he had reflected for many months. In his remarks on the Senate floor on February 2, 1950, he supported the President's decision as necessary. But he emphasized "moving heaven and earth to stop the armaments race, to establish atomic peace, and to make possible atomic created abundance among all men."

At that time, the United States was spending about $15 billion a year on armaments. McMahon proposed taking two-thirds of this amount every year for a five-year period and spreading it over three programs: President Truman's Point IV proposal for technical assistance to underdeveloped countries, development of atomic energy everywhere for peace, and general economic aid and help to all countries, including Russia. This speech reverberated around the world and received more attention abroad than at home. The FCNL distributed thousands of copies of his speech, as well as of the even more far-reaching appeal four days later in the Senate by Senator Millard Tydings, Chairman of the Senate Armed Services Committee, who proposed disarmament down to rifles. Senator McMahon knew more aobut the threat of atomic warfare than any of the other ninety-five Senators, because he was chairman of the Joint Committee on Atomic Energy and a member of the Senate Foreign Relations Committee.

Senator McMahon's plaintive comment to us was that, if the President and the Secretary of State had seized upon the initiative of these two leading Democratic Senators and had launched a vigorous drive for conversations and eventual agreement with the Russians on political settlements and disarmament, the Korean War might have been prevented. Had there been in 1950 a really earnest search for mutual understanding between the United States and the Soviet Union, the Russians would have refrained from backing the North Koreans in their attack on South Korea on June 25. Conjecture does not lead to absolute certainty, but the Senator felt that the odds were high that the war might have been averted.

It is hard to resist an even bolder speculation. Had Senator McMahon's proposal for large-scale technical assistance to developing nations and improved relations with the Communist states been heeded, our country's standing in Asia and Latin America might rest today in a series of peaceful alliances with popular governments rather than a series of military alliances with repressive regimes. Indeed, even the tragedy of American military involvement in Vietnam might have been avoided.

But what happened? The Senator's hopes for Administration support were shattered. In his next press conference President Truman threw cold water on the idea and very soon afterwards Secretary of State Dean Acheson made his famous speech emphasizing his theory that the only way to peace was "negotiating from strength."

So this call by two influential senators for the United States to take steps to melt the Cold War and to make efforts toward halting an arms race in nuclear weapons was rejected by the Administration to the detriment of what Senator McMahon believed was the true interest of the United States.

There are two lessons which one might learn from this interview.

First, there are forks in the road from time to time in foreign policy, and if the wrong one is taken, it may lead to disaster. The second lesson is that there is no substitute under our form of government for strong leadership and initiative by the President and the Secretary of State in developing and carrying out a constructive foreign policy of peace and international cooperation.

JOINT CONGRESSIONAL ECONOMIC STAFF

How to shift from an economy heavily based on military spending to reliance upon civilian expenditures has been a continued concern of FCNL. Arrangements were made for a day-long session of Quaker economists with the staff of the Joint Congressional Committee on Economic Affairs on May 31, 1956. Included were Professors Raymond Whittelsey of the Wharton School of Business, University of Pennsylvania, Paul Nelson of Denison College, Howard Teaf of Haverford College, Kenneth Boulding of the University of Michigan, Francis D. Tyson of the University of Pittsburgh, and Stacey Widdicombe with the Ford Foundation. The Congressional staff, headed by Grover Ensley, had prepared a rough preliminary draft dealing with the economic aspects of disarmament, which formed a basis for discussion. Grover Ensley was also preparing a speech on the problems of conversion to be made in June at Stanford University before 800 business executives.

The group had the opportunity to lunch with Senator Paul Douglas, one of the two economists in Congress at that time, and Representative Richard Bolling of Missouri, both of whom were members of the Joint Congressional Committee.

The purpose of the interview was to encourage the Joint Committee to take a stronger lead in educating the Congress on the beneficial economic results of switching from military to civilian spending and to demonstrate that the problems, such as unemployment, which were created by cutbacks, could be solved. In the lively discussion during the day reference was made to the impossibility up to that time of passing appropriations for federal aid to education because of the parochial school issue, as compared to the relative ease with which money was voted by Congress for building highways. Referring to the difficulty of getting subsidies for building classrooms for our children and the contrasting ease with which huge sums were appropriated to put concrete pavement under our Chevrolets and Cadillacs, Kenneth Boulding wisecracked, "Isn't it interesting that concrete has neither race, creed nor color?"

John Bell Williams

After the devastation of the Second World War when humanitarian legislation was urgently needed to minister to the plight of war victims in other countries, Betty Jacob came to Washington for some intensive lobbying in behalf of more generous economic aid and the United Nations Children's Fund. When we called on Representative John Bell Williams of Mississippi, his response was that he found nothing in the U.S. Constitution to warrant appropriating one dime for helping anybody outside the United States. Gifts to private charity or programs like those of the American Friends Service Committee were all right, but no government money should be appropriated for needy non-Americans.

One of his arms was missing at the elbow from an injury in the war, so I appealed to him as a veteran. What had he fought the war for, if not for a better world afterwards? I appealed to him as an American — as a citizen of a country which ought to be concerned with the welfare of the world and should be generous and compassionate. I appealed to him as a Christian, who ought to be thinking about the world as one human family. I appealed to him as a Baptist, who should treat men as brothers. None of my arguments seemed to touch him.

In lobbying as in many other endeavors one does not win them all, and once in awhile one comes up against a human stone wall. Some years afterward John Bell Williams was elected Governor of Mississippi.

Colonel Frank A. Partridge

At the suggestion of General Shedd, Deputy Chief of the Army, Colonel Frank A. Partridge met on September 13, 1940,[10] with three of us on problems which the Army would meet in dealing with conscientious objectors under the conscription act which was in the final stages of consideration in Congress. The delegation consisted of Thomas A. Foulke, chairman of the Friends War Problems Committee, Paul Comly French, who was soon to become secretary of the National Service Board for Religious Objectors, and myself.

We outlined as best we could the problems likely to arise in the Army when conscription would become effective. The Colonel stressed the fact that if the local boards, the Department of Justice, and other agencies dealing with the conscientious objector before assignment to the Army did their work carefully and adequately, the problems of the Army would be small.

The following points, among others, were raised for consideration by the Army:

The conscientious objector who finds himself in military service should not be considered as a criminal, even if he is technically guilty of an infraction of military regulations because of his opposition to military service, or to combatant service, or to military control, as the case may be. A man should not be compelled to do something which he strongly feels is morally wrong.

A man should not be given cruel or brutal treatment nor the third degree, nor be confined with hardened criminals, the mentally deranged or men suffering from venereal disease. No sentence should be imposed for a period longer than the period for which, under the draft, one is liable for military service.

Every reasonable effort should be made to work out these cases first by consultation between the man involved and his superior officers; then, if necessary, and only if other methods fail of satisfactory solution, should a man be subject to formal court-martial.

Cases should be considered within twenty-one days so that the men would not be subject to long periods of imprisonment or other restrictions or punishment before their cases were reviewed. Men awaiting hearings should be free to receive and send mail.

The phrase in the conscription act "religious training and belief" should be construed liberally. Some will be church members and some will be motivated by deep ethical or humanitarian considerations which are sincerely held.

We made it clear that there was no desire to protect from military service the mere draft evader or the insincere or those guilty of infractions of military discipline for reasons other than conscientious objection to war or service under military control.

Each man assigned to the Army for noncombatant service should be furnished a card which he may keep in his possession indicating the types of service to which he may be subject and from which he may not be transferred without his consent.

If a man finds himself in the Army because of a decision by a local board or appeal board against his deep conviction, or by default, and yet the Army establishes his sincerity and depth of convictions against any kind of military service, we suggested that the Army furlough him to civilian work of national importance for the period of his military service. For the small number of "absolutists," whose major objection is to conscription itself, the Army might send these men back to the appeal board for a rehearing. The British law provided that the Minister in charge of the conscientious objectors might place such men on the C.O. register, and many of them were given complete exemption from any required service.

Colonel Partridge observed that most cases might be heard by an officers court, which was an established procedure in the Army and was more informal than a court-martial. This court would consist of four or five men — probably including the chaplain, welfare officer, public health officer, and the commanding officer or someone designated by him. The colonel hoped workable policies could be evolved by experience. The usual procedure in officers courts was to allow the man involved in the hearing to submit written or documentary evidence as well as oral, to allow him counsel or other witnesses, and to provide him with a transcript of the proceedings.

The time limit of ten days' notice before a hearing and not more than twenty-one days' delay from the first notice of the hearing seemed to the Colonel reasonable as a general rule.

I suggested that a more informal consultative procedure should be tried which I believed would benefit both the Army and the C.O. This recommendation was that in each major military installation, two or three persons from that geographical area particularly interested and informed regarding C.O. problems should sit down informally with the commanding officer and the officers court and talk over the kind of questions discussed in this interview. If the way could be left open for either the Army or civilians to raise questions as new situations arise, probably many cases could be satisfactorily solved without the formality of an officers court or the difficulty of a military court-martial.

In actual practice over the years it has been extraordinarily difficult for men already in the Army, Navy or Coast Guard to get released on grounds of conscience. Many gross miscarriages of justice have occurred within the Selective Service System because of the refusal of the draft boards to grant conscientious objector status to men who were qualified for it. Had our suggestions in 1940 been carried out by the Army, a large proportion of the estimated 60,000 to 100,000 draft evaders, war resisters and deserters now in Canada because of their opposition to the Vietnam War, would not be there in 1973 but in the United States making a useful contribution to our country. I think it is fair to say that we anticipated most of the problems which would arise, both from the standpoint of the military and from the standpoint of the conscientious objectors, except for the number of men who, seeing first- or secondhand the stark brutality of the Vietnam War, decided to desert and be done with their complicity in what they considered a moral outrage.

ELEANOR ROOSEVELT

After the conscription act was passed by Congress in September 1940, four of us drove up in an old jalopy to see Mrs. Roosevelt at her Hyde Park home. Our party included Paul Comly French, John Swomley, John Magee and myself. No closed iron gate sealed off the entrance. We drove down along the field to the house. One man was out in the yard, probably a member of the Secret Service. He pointed to the door where we should enter and where Miss Malvina Thompson, Eleanor Roosevelt's secretary, greeted us cordially. We chatted about the first lady's varied interests and vast correspondence, until Mrs. Roosevelt came into the room a few minutes later.

She welcomed us warmly and served us cider and doughnuts as we visited in front of a crackling fire. Paul Comly French, later director of the National Service Board for Religious Objectors, had requested the interview in order for us to discuss with her the speech which the President would make in a few days explaining the Selective Service legislation and setting it in motion. We asked her if she would request the President to refer in his radio address to the fact that the legislation provided for the rights of conscience by making it possible for war objectors to take civilian alternative service or, if they chose, noncombatant service in the army.

While Mrs. Roosevelt did not give us a categorical promise that she would be able to fulfill our request, she listened attentively, and seemed quite sympathetic to our plea. We certainly left the interview in a hopeful mood, but when we listened to the President's speech a few nights later there was no mention of the provisions for conscientious objectors in the law. Within a few months the President did support the right of conscientious objectors to serve abroad, as related in Chapter IV on the Starnes rider.

As we drove away, Paul French said, "I doubt if there is another country in the world where you can drive up to see the first lady of the land without being confronted by guards and a high iron fence, sit down with her and tell her you disagree with nearly everything her husband stands for. Maybe there is something to democracy after all. This is a great country when you can do what we did today!"

Representatives of about sixty national organizations arranged a dinner in Washington, May 24, 1950, to honor Eleanor Roosevelt for her activities in behalf of the United Nations and to discuss ways of strengthening the UN. At that time she was Chairman of the Human Rights Committee of the United Nations Economic and Social Council. She emphasized that the way to make real progress toward peace and democracy is to create a just economic and social order in this country.

In introducing Mrs. Roosevelt whose life had been characterized by myriad interests and boundless energy, I referred to our younger son Lee, who had just started school. When I asked him what he liked best about school, he said with evident enthusiasm, "Everything but rest!"

Colonel Lewis B. Hershey

Harold Evans, one of the founders of the War Problems Committee, Clarence E. Pickett, executive secretary of the American Friends Service Committee, Paul Comly French, and I called on Colonel (later Brigadier General) Lewis B. Hershey on September 17, 1940.[11] This was before the Selective Service Act became law and before Hershey became Director of the Selective Service System, which he headed for almost thirty years. As I recall he had been working on conscription studies and plans since 1926.

At that time Colonel Hershey was responsible for drawing up the administrative provisions of the Selective Service Act, including the regulations for the conscientious objectors. Mr. Hershey expressed his willingness to appoint an advisory board and leave most of the decisions on conscientious objectors up to the board.

The Colonel suggested that we draw up a memorandum covering the points which we felt should be included in the regulations concerning the conscientious objectors. Evans, French and myself prepared this memorandum, which was given him along with a proposed redraft of the Selective Service questionnaire for C.O.'s.

The conversation was lively and frank. With a smile the Colonel said that his grandmother was a Mennonite and his grandfather was a stonemason; he "had followed his grandfather!"

CHAPTER 17

Lobbying on the State Front [1]

Efforts to influence national legislation were greatly augmented by intensive activities undertaken by three area offices, not only on issues in Congress, but in the state legislatures of California, Illinois and Wisconsin, and more recently in Indiana.

The Northern California Friends Committee on Legislation (FCL) was formally launched at a meeting in Berkeley on May 24, 1952, after months of discussion and planning. Irving Morrissett was chosen as chairman and Catherine Corbett (later Cory) began as executive secretary. Later, when she moved to Southern California where she directed that office for several years, Trevor Thomas became head of the office in San Francisco, in April 1953.

The area offices were in the main a spontaneous development that arose out of a strong concern of local Friends. A Southern California Regional Office had begun in 1950 to work against universal military training with J. Stuart Innerst and Jean Johnson directing this campaign. This office functioned part-time and intermittently until 1954 when it was reopened on a full-time basis. Roscoe L. Warren, whose untimely death occurred on September 13, 1954, was one of the prime movers in these early developments and served as area chairman as well as regional vice chairman of the FCNL. Egbert Hayes took charge of the Pasadena office until Catherine Cory assumed those duties.

Representing both the Northern and Southern FCL's, Georges and Marjorie Weber were the first Sacramento advocates in the 1953 legislature, during which session there was a total of 372 registered lobbyists.

California has a population of approximately twenty million people — more than the population of Denmark, Sweden, Norway and half the population of Finland. The two offices grew up because, in geography, California is almost two states with the northern centers of influence in San Francisco and in the state capital at Sacramento, while the sprawling Los Angeles area is the hub of Southern California.

The Illinois-Wisconsin FCL began in April 1957, in Chicago. Carol Urner and then Mary Cadbury helped organize the office and get the program started. This office, with only a tiny staff, attempted the almost impossible task of following developments in the two legislatures in Springfield and in Madison. It expanded some when Chester A. Graham was appointed full-time executive secretary. He was followed by Vern Fina. Richard Weston directed the program in 1971-1972.

It would be hard to overemphasize the vast amount of volunteer time and dedicated leadership given these three offices by many people serving on committees and hammering out the difficult decisions on program, personnel and finances. George McCoy and George Watson were among those in the Illinois-Wisconsin committee whose prolonged participation and leadership gave a continuity and direction to its work. Thousands of people have contributed time and thought and money which have made the efforts of the FCL's and the FCNL possible and significant.

The original aim of these offices was to spend about half time on national issues in Washington and about half time on state legislation. The urgency and complexity of state questions in California seemed to demand major emphasis. The two California groups published a state newsletter combined with the *FCNL Washington Newsletter*. The Chicago office also circulated a legislative memo on Illinois and Wisconsin along with the national newsletter. Each office was free to circulate action bulletins or other FCNL publications as they chose.

SOME ISSUES IN THE CALIFORNIA LEGISLATURE

Only the barest overview of their achievements and difficulties can be recorded in the space here. Lobbying in a state legislature, particularly for an FCL advocate like Joe Gunterman who has been in Sacramento since 1961, is more direct and intimate than is possible in Congress. His office is a block away from the capitol. Not burdened by organizational and administrative details, Joe could concentrate on getting to know well many of the legislators and on following the details of legislative procedure. The California legislature is about one-fifth the size of Congress. One year not too long after the FCL had started, the committee was following 170 bills in the legislative hopper.

In the early days, one of the major national issues in Congress, supported by the regional offices, was the nuclear test ban treaty. The circulation of Trevor Thomas' *Questions and Answers About Nuclear Tests*[2] reached more than 50,000 copies. Much of their effort was directed toward challenging the various violations of civil liberties, working in behalf of disadvantaged groups like migrant and farm workers, American Indians and racial minorities, and striving for the abolition of capital punishment and for prison reform. Would it surprise the reader that, after twenty years of strenuous efforts and many advances, these same general areas are very much the priorities today? The Bureau of Census has revealed that the 1970 census shows that American Indians on the whole are behind the rest of the nation in just about every socio-economic barometer. Nearly 40 per cent of the Indian population lived below the Federal poverty level in 1969, against 13.7 per cent of the total population.

A great variety of other questions have had the attention of the FCL, including mental health, liquor control, academic freedom, and the economics of disarmament. Also, attention has been given to humane rehabilitative treatment of narcotic addicts, to extension of workmen's compensation, rights of collective bargaining, educational opportunities, health and sanitation facilities and minimum wages for the least protected groups in our society — seasonal and migrant agricultural laborers. In the civil rights field efforts have been made to remove discrimination against racial and cultural minorities and to assure equal opportunities in housing, education and employment. Another aim was to remove discrimination against aliens owning property.

Some of the legislative goals in meeting the needs of American Indians included a state Indian commission to concentrate on Indian problems; also on water rights, more relevant education, retention of Indian culture, employment, protection against exploitation and redress for violation of treaty rights.

In 1962, Henry Lohmann, secretary of the Northern California FCL, Cecil Thomas, peace education secretary of the San Francisco American Friends Service Committee, a political scientist from the Stanford Research Institute, and a representative of the Lockheed Corporation organized a monthly seminar of defense industry officials who flew into the San Francisco airport to discuss the problems of converting from military to civilian production if and when serious defense cutbacks might result from disarmament agreements.

As examples of regional programs in California, let us very briefly trace two of these issues — civil liberties and capital punishment — for a period of about a decade.

CIVIL LIBERTIES IN CALIFORNIA

California in 1952 — during the hysterical days of Senator Joseph McCarthy's largely unfounded diatribes against alleged subversives, Communists and traitors — was a hotbed of repressive laws and loyalty oaths. The atmosphere in 1953 in Sacramento for the biennial legislative session was fearful. Legislators were afraid to stand on principle. The FCL stood almost alone in opposing repressive laws and special loyalty oaths. Georges Weber volunteered as the first FCL advocate. Almost no progress was made on FCL-supported legislation. But the committee doggedly believed that an improvement could come from a concerned and informed citizenry if they kept working at it.

By 1955 the tide began to turn. A bill was defeated that would have required all tax-exempt groups, including churches, to screen those using their facilities. One of the main functions of the FCL was to serve as a catalyst in cooperation with other nongovernmental groups. The *FCL Story of the 1955 Legislature* reported that more letters were written and more legislators visited than at any time in recent history. Public-spirited organizations took positions, alerted their members, and sent their most capable representatives to Sacramento. FCL was coordinator of efforts to defeat a bill which would have denied tax exemption to nonprofit organizations who knowingly allowed their property to be used by "subversives" as identified by the U.S. Attorney General's list. Another related bill would have provided that refusal to answer any questions before a legislative, judicial or executive body should be grounds for the loss of state license for registration in businesses or other activities requiring licenses.

In 1953, seven anticivil liberties bills had been introduced and all became law. In 1955, eleven bills restricting civil liberties were introduced, of which nine were defeated.

In 1957, there were sixteen bills restricting freedom to speak and to assemble, and freedom from unreasonable search and seizure. No *major* restrictive legislation passed both Houses.

By 1959, Coleman Blease, as full-time advocate for the California

FCLs, helped initiate a greater number of bills and supported or opposed more legislation than the Committee had been able to undertake in any previous year. The thirteen new members in the Assembly and the ten new members in the Senate often cast the deciding votes on liberal legislation. The American Civil Liberties Union cooperated closely with the FCL. The two FCL offices and other civil liberties forces were better organized than they had been previously.

Bills to repeal special oaths of nondisloyalty cleared committees and were debated, but there was not yet enough sentiment in the legislature to pass these repealers. Two years previously the FCL had sponsored a constitutional amendment to restore the traditional oath generally used in the United States for swearing in officials. Most Friends have not objected to the usual oath taken by officials to uphold the Constitution, if it did not contain a phrase accepting military service. Some Friends affirm rather than swear the oath in line with early Quaker practices.

Progress was made in securing more protection against excesses by the police. However, attempts to outlaw electronic eavesdropping were defeated.

In 1961, as in the previous four sessions, the unremitting battle continued to the last day of the session to remove the statutory effects of the McCarthy era, which had whipped up panic over Communism and had led Americans to turn to fear and suspicion of each other. Thirty proposed restrictive measures were turned aside, but the FCL and the ACLU were unable to secure the passage of positive measures in the area of loyalty and special oaths. The most persistent and difficult to kill were those bills directed against teachers.

Madge Seaver, who served some time as chairman of the Northern California FCL executive committee, in testimony before an assembly committee, presented the case against the Levering Act and similar bills requiring a special nondisloyalty oath. She said in part:

> . . .Our first objection to affirming that we are not disloyal is that the presumption of disloyalty in the required oath is an affront. Those among us who have conscientiously refused to take such oaths do so because we believe our loyalty is plainly evident in all our acts. When loyalty to God has been in conflict with our loyalty to the law of the country, Friends go directly to the authorities, announce this fact, and willingly suffer the penalty of the law.
>
> Our second objection is based on our experience in the 17th century

and since then that those whose meetings are secret and actions not open to public scrutiny appear to be willing to take an oath of nondisloyalty. Therefore, such test oaths do not catch the disloyal; they merely screen out those of scrupulous conscience. Since there has not been an indictment for falsely swearing to this present oath since its enactment, we must conclude that it has not been useful in the present case in identifying any who may have been planning to overthrow the government. [3]

We have traced only a few of the many facets of civil liberties on which legislative effort was focused during the early years in California and which has helped change the climate of public opinion for the better.

Criminal Justice, Penal Reform and Capital Punishment

Justice Curtis Bok once said: "Some day we will look back on our present system of dealing with criminals with the same horror as we now do the Spanish Inquisition." Fair treatment for the offender and penal reform has been another sustained concern in the California legislature.

Capital Punishment

Another perennial issue, in both the Midwest and California, has been the abolition of capital punishment. Trevor Thomas prepared a very strong case against capital punishment in a widely circulated 24-page pamphlet entitled *This Life We Take* which was first published in 1955 and revised in 1959. After years of agitation, dating back to the early 1950's, Governor Edmund Brown called a special session of the California legislature in 1960 to consider abolition of the death penalty. Among the leaders in the struggle were Assemblyman Lester McMillan and Senator Fred Farr. McMillan had said earlier:

"The death penalty is an evil scar on the face of justice. Capital punishment masquerades as protector for the public, sympathy for the victim, and justice for the murderer. In truth it is none of these. It is simple vengeance." [4]

It was Senator Farr's view that:

In my visits to death row at San Quentin and to other prisons, I have been impressed with a singular fact. There is nothing to distinguish the crimes of the men on death row from those of hundreds of others receiving lesser penalties except for one fact — in almost all cases those on death row are poor and friendless. [5]

A series of appalling murders dissolved or quieted much of the potential support for abolition. Even after television hearings and watering down an abolition bill to a three-year moratorium, the measure was lost in the Senate Judiciary Committee 7-8. As a result, no bill reached the Governor's desk in 1960.

Nation-wide attention was later focused on the Caryl Chessman case. Some of us in Washington tried until the minute of the execution without avail to get a Supreme Court Justice to stay the execution. I believe this was the last execution in California.

The *Illinois-Wisconsin Newsletter* reviewed the book by Milton Machlin and William Reed Woodfield entitled *The Ninth Life* (New York: G. Putnam Sons, 1961). The authors became interested in the case, questioning whether Chessman was guilty of the crime for which he was convicted in spite of his plea that he was innocent. Among other miscarriages of justice, they pointed out that there had been suppression of evidence, failure to investigate other clues, and refusal of the Court to provide the defense with a daily transcript.

Some years afterward FCL led an effort in California to try to get an injunction against any further executions there. Where will the cycle of violence end if we reinstate murder by the state as penalty for murder by an individual?

The U.S. Supreme Court on June 29, 1972, ruled that discretionary death sentencing — when the judge or jury has an option to condemn the defendent or merely imprison him — violates the U.S. Constitutional protection against cruel and unusual punishment. But mandatory death statutes, under which anyone convicted of the crime is executed with no special concessions by judge or jury, are constitutional, according to the Court decision.

So the scene shifted in the California legislature for a drive either to reinstate the death penalty within the Supreme Court restrictions or provide for mandatory life imprisonment or for at least 25 years for certain crimes. Both were opposed by the FCL, the American Civil Liberties Union, the National Association for the Advancement of Colored People and like-minded groups. None of the measures passed in 1972.

THE CALIFORNIA LEGISLATURE: 1972

The January 1973 *FCL Newsletter* reports that the record of the 1972 session of the California legislature, which now meets annually for the general legislation instead of biennially as it did when the Friends Committee began lobbying there, was in many ways a disappointing session. The legislature, on two of the most critical issues before it, fumbled and bumbled on adequate financing for the schools and did nothing on reapportionment.

More than ever before the FCL played a major role in bringing together lobbyists from groups with similar concerns for weekly strategy meetings. The FCL again took leadership in the California Housing Coalition, which sponsored legislation for stronger tenant rights and for an expanded supply of housing for low-income groups. The aim of the FCL is to support the rights of individuals to grow and create, each according to his own insights and abilities. It seeks to represent those who are unable to represent themselves, such as prison inmates. And it works toward solutions to problems on which no one else is yet working — as FCL did in the first efforts to better nutrition for infants and pregnant women.

One important victory for citizens' groups and for a first-term courageous Senator, Peter Behr from San Rafael, was the passage of a measure requiring committee votes to be made public and printed in the daily *Journal*. One loophole remains because recorded votes are not required on actions by subcommittees.

California's prison system is one of the largest in the world, and it does have various advanced provisions for food, clothing and medical care. One of the basic faults is the fact that the prisoner has virtually no rights. He is stripped of the opportunity to make decisions and choices. Deprived of this opportunity, he cannot develop a sense of responsibility nor grow in self-respect.

He also does not have the right to an objective and fair hearing when others make major decisions affecting him — decisions regarding his length of sentence, his time on parole or his return to prison. He suffers from what has been called the "psychological torture" of uncertainty.

Over recent years the legislature, partly through FCL efforts, has made small moves toward checking the virtually absolute power of the Department of Corrections over the day-by-day lives of the men and women in its institutions.

An FCL-supported bill which would have established the office of prison ombudsman, an independent officer to investigate prison and corrections staff complaints, and which passed both Houses was vetoed by Governor Reagan.

The ombudsman's work could be expected to lessen the chance for riots in California prisons. Prison riots often grow out of the prisoners' feeling that they have no other way of calling their grievances to the attention of someone outside the system. A special FCL field worker spent weeks in the districts of key legislators on committees that would be considering the bill.

Many other bills designed to protect the rights of prisoners failed of passage. Two FCL-sponsored measures were among the casualties. One would have built wage credits for prisoners working on prison jobs, on the basis of what they could draw in unemployment insurance benefits if, after release from prison, they were jobless and willing and able to work. The other would have provided workmen's compensation benefits, payable upon release, for prisoners who suffer major permanent disabilities on prison jobs. Two minor measures with FCL support were enacted. The first permitted prison inmates to attend on-campus classes at community colleges. The second allowed colleges to count inmate students in the average daily attendance for the purpose of collecting state reimbursement.

Some progress was made in considering drug addiction as a health problem rather than something for criminal sanctions but only very small appropriations were voted for such programs. Also successful moves toward better alcoholism prevention and treatment were minor.

Legislation to help low income persons with their housing problems had an uphill fight in the 1972 legislature. As happened to several other progressive measures, a bill to establish a housing and development agency to pump additional financing into housing for low and moderate income persons was vetoed by Governor Reagan.

Two school lunch programs were vetoed by the Governor. One would have appropriated $100,000 for a 25 per cent grant to school districts to assist the poorer school districts to get the cafeteria equipment needed to start or expand a school lunch program. Only 113 of California's 341 school districts have school lunch programs. The other bill would have required school districts without lunch programs to establish child nutrition programs unless they could show that their pupils' nutritional needs were being met otherwise.

FARM LABOR LOSES

A bill to bring agricultural workers into the unemployment insurance program was vetoed by the Governor. Farm workers were, as usual, at a disadvantage in legislative battles because they did not have even one full-time lobbyist in the Capitol halls to match the day-by-day work of nine lobbyists employed by four major grower groups. A pesticide safety bill supported by farm workers died; one backed by agribusiness became law.

The passage by Congress of the Civil Rights Act of 1964 was briefly reviewed in the chapter on civil rights. But it was not until 1972 that the California legislature passed relevant enforcement measures to conform with federal law. Another step forward was the inclusion of domestic workers in FEPC (fair employment practices) coverage.

This partial summary of measures with which the California FCL concerned itself in the 1972 legislature portrays the complexity and the frustration involved in making minor progress toward basic human rights and points up the necessity of sustained and persistent efforts year after year to advance the frontier of human rights and justice to the less advantaged individuals and groups.

Illinois-Wisconsin FCL

Among the numerous measures that the Illinois-Wisconsin FCL supported in one or both legislatures or featured in their *Newsletter* were abolishing residency requirements for recipients of public assistance, state supervision of radioactive material, mental health legislation including diagnostic centers and schools for mentally handicapped children, improvement in the Illinois parole system and equal job opportunities for minorities. The Committee took an active part in the successful effort to get ROTC made optional at the University of Wisconsin.

As has been done continuously in California, voting records of legislators have been compiled and circulated when possible. Chester Graham helped organize the Illinois Committee for Abolition of Capital Punishment and provided active leadership for it for a time.

The committee worked for a Fair Employment Practice Commission, for a Governors Commission on Alcoholism, for education for families and children of migrant workers, for ending discrimination in housing, and for state unemployment compensation for agricultural workers. Another goal was to lower the voting age and to encourage peace candidates to speak out on peace issues.

The Illinois-Wisconsin FCL exerted a great deal of effort on national issues including food for the hungry, opposition to conscription and the ending of bomb tests. In trying to combat the hysteria over bomb shelters the December 1961 *Illinois-Wisconsin Newsletter* asked, "How big should a fall out shelter be? It should be big enough to hold 3 billion people," or all the inhabitants of the earth. At another time in calling for general disarmament and a reorientation of foreign policy, it was asserted that there would be no peace as long as nations continue the risk of a world conflict by error, miscalculation, irrational action or design.

Menominee Indian Reservation Termination

One of Chester Graham's deep concerns was for the welfare of the Indians in Wisconsin and especially the Menominee tribe whose reservation status was finally terminated in 1962 without adequate preparation for the transition.

Norman Thomas once said on trusting the Russians, "No government under the religion of the sovereign state is wholly trustworthy, including our own. Ask the American Indians!"

Chester Graham testified before the Menominee Study Committee of the Wisconsin Legislative Council on the need to expand that Study Committee to include representatives from all American Indian tribes in Wisconsin. He urged that it be made a permanent legislative study committee concerned for the welfare of all American Indians in the state. For example the Bad River reservation was subject to flooding, and this problem could be studied by the committee.

Chester followed closely the legislative developments about the Menominees as the terms and timetable for termination of their federal wardship were under consideration and tried to support the legitimate demands of the Menominees. They were opposed to opening up their forest lands to the public for fishing and hunting because these rights were crucial to their livelihood. FCL supported the proposals for operating the forests on a sustained yield basis so there would be continuous income. The Menominees wanted a separate county set up for them.

Another FCL goal was to hold the federal government to certain economic responsibilities for easing the burden of the transition from federal control. Menominee Enterprises was set up to carry on the major lumber industry and other tribal economic activities. Legislative efforts were made to increase scholarship aid, in part because there were no doctors or lawyers among the Indians.

One basic conflict was between the Indian tradition of owning land in common by the tribe, and the white man's desire to get water-front locations for residences and recreation or to gain title to areas in the forest, and to secure individual land holdings.

In short, the Menominee termination story, while seemingly

desirable in principle to put people on their own rather than to remain federal wards, was disastrous in practice, as portrayed some time ago in a TV documentary. Adequate training and preparation was not made for assuming the burden of taxation for schools and roads and for managing their own economic life. Not enough protection was given the Indians against the exploitative inroads of the white man.

Indiana Friends Committee on Legislation

One of the promising recent developments has been the organization in October 1971 of the Indiana Friends Committee on Legislation. At the end of 1973, the general chairman was Les Paulsen with Becky Mullin serving as general secretary. Becky served a year as intern in the national FCNL office. A state newsletter goes to each Friends meeting in the state.

Illustrative of lobby efforts in 1973, the IFCL has supported legislation in the state legislature for rehabilitation of alcoholics, for more humane treatment of offenders, including provisions for public defenders for those unable to pay for counsel and permission for 14-day leaves from prison, has backed ratification of the Equal Rights Amendment to the Federal Constitution, and has opposed allowing Sunday sales of liquor, and has lobbied against the reinstatement of capital punishment.

More members of the Society of Friends reside in Indiana than in any other state in the Union. Let us hope that sufficient moral and financial support will be forthcoming to assure a vigorous program directed toward the Indiana State legislature. In the United States some of our worst government is at the local and state level. All legislatures need the encouragement and needling of religiously oriented citizens if government is to meet its responsibility to the poor, the mentally and physically ill, and the unemployed. Better housing and better schools are widespread needs.

Some Lessons from The Area Offices

It would be very desirable if there could be strong citizens' groups following legislation in every state, adequately financed and ably staffed, which were seeking on a nonpartisan basis to defend and expand the principles of justice and human well being as over against selfish or prejudiced or exploitative measures. In addition to area offices in California, Indiana and Illinois-Wisconsin, volunteer groups have been organized at one time or another in New York City, in New Jersey and in Virginia. The League of Women Voters works in many states on a limited number of issues. In a few states councils of churches or other religious groups focus on the legislature. There is a growing number of public interest organizations like Common Cause and Ralph Nader's Public Citizens, but special-interest lobbies still tend to dominate state legislatures.

FINANCES

In these affluent days with two or three cars in the family, often a swimming pool and a boat in the back yard, it is still difficult to finance a vigorous program of peace and social justice particularly for a nontax-exempt organization. The FCNL has never been in a strong enough financial position to subsidize the area offices except in a very limited way while getting started. In fact the FCNL has had its difficulties most of the time in raising the funds for its own budget.

The Northern California office has been able to develop more support than the other three and is currently running a budget of approximately $70,000 or almost one-third of the national FCNL budget. At one time Lucy Hancock in San Francisco and Delmore Huserick in Pasadena concentrated on financial cultivation and were able to broaden the base of participation and support considerably. The Illinois-Wisconsin and the Southern California offices have much of the time limped along financially, with staff sometimes underpaid and with few resources for the programs which they wanted to undertake in their regions.

One variation from the national pattern has been the practice of having individual and group membership at ten and twenty-five dollars, plus appeals for contributions above that amount.

Staff turnover has been relatively frequent for various reasons, including the willingness to live on the modest salary which the area offices have been able to pay. I do praise the dedication of the FCL staffs over the years for their earnest efforts to carry out their programs under great difficulties.

RELATIONS WITH THE FCNL

When establishment of area committees was under consideration in the FCNL executive committee, Edward Evans argued strongly for virtual autonomy for the area offices in the selection of staff and decisions on policy and program. But the executive committee opted for joint approval of key staff and general policies. This led to mutual strain between the California Committees and the offices and staff of the national Committee partly over questions of legislative policy and procedure, but particularly over selection and appointment of area staff.

After prolonged negotiations it was finally agreed in 1964 that for all practical purposes the area committees and offices would be autonomous. There would continue to be close cooperation and coordination of activity on national issues when possible. The *FCNL Washington Newsletter* would be circulated with the monthly state newsletter, and representatives of the area committees would serve on the FCNL General Committee, and hopefully would be able to attend the annual policy making General Committee Meeting in Washington. The areas would also use *Action Bulletins* and other FCNL publications as desired. This arrangement has worked out reasonably well on the whole, but some problems of coordination and mutuality still remain.

RELATIONS WITH CONSTITUENCY

In the early days of legislative activity in California, the two executive secretaries, Trevor Thomas in San Francisco and Catherine Cory in Pasadena, were an imaginative, driving, activist team. Their concentration on programs and the many activities inherent in running and financing an organization beamed toward Sacramento and Washington left them little time for the careful cultivation of their constituency and the amount of circulating around among the Friends and other potential supporters, the thoughtful discussion of controversial issues and the attempt to reach the wide consensus that would have been desirable. Many churches in California Yearly Meeting were deeply concerned about evangelism, winning of new members and the building of new churches, rather than much activity in the field of social action. Several churches were in reality community churches with little emphasis on traditional Friends testimonies on peace and opposition to war and militarism, concern for the rights of the individual citizen and disadvantaged groups, and willingness to take unpopular stands. In one Friends church which I visited, most of the members were employed in one of the three nearby military installations.

There were disagreements, sometimes perhaps with too much self-righteousness on both sides, and California Yearly Meeting withdrew its official support and the naming of representatives on the FCNL General Committee and also its official relationship with the American Friends Service Committee. Many members of the yearly meeting have continued their loyal support, but there is still not the amount of mutual trust and cooperation that is desirable in corporately tackling the great unsolved problems of our time. Nor has the coordination between the north and south area offices always been easy and smooth.

CHAPTER 18

The FCNL and Its Critics

In 1970, a student applied for a Quaker leadership grant to visit Quaker organizations and to work for two months in the summer in the FCNL office. He finally recalled his application because of pressure from his family and his pastor, partly on the grounds that his pastor told him that "J. Edgar Hoover in a speech in the fall of 1969 classified the FCNL as 'communistic' or 'subversive.' " George I. Bliss wrote to J. Edgar Hoover, asking if he could confirm or refute this allegation. Hoover wrote back on August 13, 1970, "In reply to your letter of August 10th, I can assure you I did not make the statement about the Friends Committee on National Legislation attributed to me."

Since most of the issues on which the FCNL takes a position are controversial in the sense that people of good will may differ on them, it was expected from the start that criticisms would be voiced about its policies and operations. The Committee claims no infallibility. It deals with many complex questions for which there may be no simple or completely satisfactory answers.

There have been some letters over the years expressing objections to some Committee policies, but relatively few when the number and diversity of our constituency are considered.

One Friend in Illinois Yearly Meeting wrote an open letter to his fellow members criticizing the FCNL as in effect setting up a political creed for Friends to follow and objecting especially, that of the 90 points covered in the Statement of Legislative Policy, about 40 per cent seemed to him to advocate increased governmental bureaucratic control. He stressed the value and necessity of individual leading and individual action which in his view had been the strength historically of the Society of Friends. The writer of the letter asserted:

...Historically we have believed that we should not act as a Society as long as a small minority expressed opposition to that action. . . .

It would appear that the logical historical method would be for the leaders of FCNL to follow their concerns as concerned individuals. How can they represent themselves as official spokesmen for a group when many of the group sincerely believe that many of the ideas so advocated are contrary to God's plans and opposed to the best interests of those who presumably are being benefitted by the proposal?

. . .As long as the Friends Committee on National Legislation continues to use that name, it is speaking for all Friends in the eyes of those outside the Society. . . .

The world is beset by many extremely difficult problems. There are some of us who believe that we are more likely to come to the right answer, to find a solution to some of these problems, if the entire membership is faced with the responsibility of seeking these answers with God's leadership rather than turning over these decisions to a small group, no matter how well qualified and sincere this group may be.... [1]

Criticism reached its peak when in April 1959 an eleven-page letter was mailed from Glen Ridge, New Jersey, to members of the FCNL General Committee. It had been signed by 62 individuals from 46 households. Omitting those few from the areas served by the California and Illinois-Wisconsin offices, the staff could identify only two or three who had attended a general or area FCNL meeting, or who had come into the FCNL office with their doubts and suggestions. Only one had contributed substantially (he told a friend that he was in sympathy with most of the FCNL positions), and only five were currently receiving the *Washington Newsletter*.

Their four main objections were:

1. That its methods and procedures cannot help conveying to the public that it speaks for the Religious Society of Friends.

2. That the Committee takes positions in direct variance to those which many individual Friends feel they must follow.

3. That "pressure techniques" not of a religious nature are used to influence legislation. Some of the issues dealt with were political rather than religious.

4. That the FCNL does not give both sides of a question.

This criticism led to a great deal of correspondence and a conference in New York and in Philadelphia with some members of this group in an effort to reach a meeting of minds. This attempt was not completely successful. The staff and officers have tried very hard to retain good personal relations and dialogue with our critics and not let differences of opinion become a matter of personal antagonism. If a criticism was justified, and many of them were, we have sought to remedy the situation. If it was an honest difference of opinion, we have sought to recognize and respect it, even if contrary to the policy established at our annual meeting. Where an agreement could not be reached, it was a matter of regret to the staff and meant considerable emotional strain to them. We tried to recognize that no policy of the FCNL should be above review, debate or criticism, and that there was vast room for improvement of its work.

A careful answer to this communication was mailed to each signer by Charles Darlington, chairman of the General Committee.[2] His reply ran along the following lines:

In response to the first criticism, efforts were intensified to make clear that the FCNL did not presume to speak officially for the Society of Friends by inserting explicit disclaimers in the *Newsletter*, in the Statement of Legislative Policy, and in testimonies before the Committees of Congress.

Darlington pointed out that when Edward F. Snyder, then legislative secretary, testified on bills relating to national security before the Internal Security Sub-Committee of the Senate Judiciary Committee on May 1, 1959, the following colloquy took place:

Sen. Keating: I commend you for the statement that you don't speak for all Friends. We so frequently hear people come in and say, "I speak for 10 million people," or "I speak for 100,000 people."

Of course, anyone in a legislative hearing knows it is inaccurate because any organization worth its salt permits democratic procedures and we all know that there is no unanimity amongst all of them.

I wanted to get that into the record because it is so refreshing to hear a statement like that. . . .

Edward Snyder: I must say that the Friends cherish their right to hold their own opinions and so we very specifically make this statement. . . .

As for the second criticism, prolonged effort has always been made in revising the Statement of Legislative Policy to take comments and criticisms into account and to seek consensus, if not unanimity. One year the statement was held up three months over the item of civil liberties, seeking a revision upon which two members from Indiana and the rest of the policy committee could agree. However, if an organization is to be prophetic and actively seek a better world, it has to take positions ahead of those who are satisfied with the status quo.

There was merit to the criticism that the Statement of Legislative Policy covered too wide a range of issues and in places was more dogmatic than it might have been. The Statement of Legislative Policy was considered as a guide for the *Newsletter,* testimonies and legislative activities. It was thought of as something more than a working paper, but was not a political creed as the Glen Ridge letter charged. It did not rest on the presumption of infallibility, and it was subject to frequent revision. It was viewed as an educational document for study and improvement.

It was assumed that each individual Friend had a right to his own religious philosophy or his political views. Most of them were pretty strong in exercising that right. However, the General Committee was widely representative. It was made up of appointments from nineteen yearly meetings and ten Quaker organizations plus about forty Friends nominated to make the General Committee even more representative among its then membership of approximately two hundred Friends from coast to coast.

In regard to the third charge of pressure tactics, the Committee's guiding philosophy was expressed in the earliest Statement of Policy, dated March 7, 1944, as follows:

> The Committee does not intend to press its concern in the legislative field by the political pressure methods of lobbies maintained in their own narrow interests. It expects to work in the manner and spirit of Friends, presenting our point of view to individual members of the House and Senate and, when occasion arises, to administrative officials, exploring with them the problems to be solved, endeavoring to win the assent of reasonable minds and enlist sympathy with the objectives sought. [3]

The Committee has worked very hard in opposition to conscription and universal military training, in behalf of the peaceful processes of the United Nations, in support of disarmament and for a generous program of sharing with a disadvantaged world. The staff, however, could not remember ever having received a complaint from a member of Congress that he felt that we were using unfair pressure upon him.

As for the accusation that the FCNL was too political, the General Committee, which revised and approved the policy statements when up for consideration, believed that the problems of peace, justice and freedom were numerous, interrelated and complex. This accounted, in part, for the variety of issues dealt with in the policy statements from year to year. A true religious concern ought to be directed toward all of life and not compartmentalized. Each year priorities were recommended and a few selected for intensive work.

What was religious about federal aid to education or the Bricker amendment, our critics asked? Some of us hoped that federal aid to education might help in equalizing the opportunities of disadvantaged groups such as Indians and Blacks. Children in any section of the United States should not be discriminated against because of their place of birth. The FCNL looked upon the proposed Bricker amendment regarding treaty-making powers as a serious block to the development of the United Nations and to the process of securing far-reaching disarmament.

The fourth criticism leveled at the FCNL was that it did not give both sides of a question. This problem troubled me because I have always wanted eight pages rather than the usual four in our *Newsletter*, with four pages of legislative news and forecasts and four pages devoted to one or more issues in depth. Two notable *Newsletters* presented the pros and cons of recognition of the People's Republic of China and its seating in the UN. The Library of Congress ordered 150 copies of one of these newsletters for use in its correspondence. The August-September 1972 *Newsletter* summarizing the basic positions of Presidential candidates Nixon and McGovern is another case in point. Orders flooded in for more than 100,000 copies, the largest printing in FCNL history. But lack of money and editorial time, and the fact that many of our constituents preferred a brief newsletter which could be quickly read, have precluded the regular publication of an eight-page newsletter.

The editors have striven for accuracy so far as facts were concerned and very seldom have the facts presented been called into question. Editorial views are, or course, always open to difference of opinion. It was not expected that our readers should depend alone on material assembled and circulated by the staff. The flier entitled "Religion, Politics and You" urged our readers to "inform themselves through careful reading of periodicals, pamphlets and books, selected for *diversity of viewpoint*" (emphasis supplied).

Over the years the Committee has circulated many in-depth studies on a great variety of legislative or administrative policies.

In September 1960 a meeting was held with Friends from New York, Philadelphia, Vermont, Wilmington and St. Louis, who were questioning whether the FCNL should do anything in the field of domestic, economic, social, educational or welfare issues. They wanted to cut back the operations of the Committee to work mainly on disarmament and UN affairs. This inhibited the Committee some from doing more in the domestic field until the urban crisis of the late 1960's.

In 1963 some members of California Yearly Meeting were unhappy about the strong stand which the California Legislative Committee had taken on one or more of the issues of civil liberties, civil rights, abolition of the death penalty and other such measures. They sought to have the legislature withhold credentials from the FCL representative as not being representative of all Friends. An assembly committee hearing in Sacramento was convened as a result. The credentials in question were granted prior to the hearings, so the hearings became a forum for the viewpoints of both groups. FCL legislative work in Sacramento continued, after members of the legislature read the statement in the *FCNL Newsletter* that the Committee does not claim to speak for all Friends.

This posed again the historic Quaker dilemma. Should a Quaker group go ahead unless there is consensus — which has been the usual Quaker procedure in local and yearly meetings — or should a minority prevent any public presentation or action at all on Quaker concerns and insist that its view prevail?

As explained earlier in this history, the FCNL has earnestly sought consensus where possible, has tried to operate on the sense of the meeting, has listened to dissenting points of view with openness and respect, but has felt some responsibility to move ahead if there was general support to do so, without waiting for concurrence on a given question by the last reluctant Friend. This has meant considerable soul-searching on the part of the officers and staff. No policy or action is above criticism or judgment, and we know there is room for improvement in both policy and action. Time and God will have to be the final judges on the relevance, the timeliness, the methods and the efforts to influence legislative decisions in Congress and in State Legislatures.

CHAPTER 19

Some Reflections on Thirty Years in Washington

We feel very strongly that the public has a right to know about the public's business and that one of the most important parts of the public's business is the decision making of Congress.
Senator William V. Roth of Delaware

The world certainly is in a pretty depressing condition at the present time. About the only consolation is a somewhat humorous one which President Lowell wrote me a few days ago, in reply to congratulations which I sent him on his birthday. He said, "We all like to think we are doing some good in a bad world; and although one is only too conscious of how little good one can do, one's real consolation is how much more useless still one would be if the world was so good that no effort was required to improve it."
Dr. George H. Blakeslee, Professor
of History and International Relations, Clarke University, in
sending me his best wishes for a
Happy New Year, December 30, 1938

Kenneth Boulding, noted economist, author and Quaker philosopher, used to warn us that one of the most dangerous things in the world is to try to do good. So it behooves a legislative organization and a lobbyist to weigh the past and peer into the future with a measure of humility and a search for perspective.

Let us look for a moment at the dark side of the picture.

When I first came to Washington to begin work with the FCNL in 1943, I had a violent revulsion from which I have never completely recovered. I said impetuously to a friend of mine: "It seems to me the chief industry in Washington is sending other men to their deaths." "Yes," was the reply, "that is exactly what we are doing." And, I might add, not many Congressmen or Congressmen's sons were in the front lines.

Over against our aspirations for peace in 1943, one must list the Second World War which left the world divided into two major rival camps, the Korean War, which, in my judgment, set back American foreign policy in some ways for a quarter of a century, and the devisiveness and futility of twenty years' involvement in Indochina. To this list should be added the military interventions in Lebanon, Cuba and the Dominican Republic. Although I think it is fair to say that the desire for peace among the American people is stronger now than ever before, the obstacles to peace are enormous. The task still remains to take away from governments the power to make wars and to build instead effective institutions for peace.

In a world where half of God's children are still undernourished or malnourished, and in a country where some thirty million people are below or near the poverty line, our government has almost the largest military budget in history.

In a democracy where faith in the good intentions and integrity of government is the cement that holds us together, we have witnessed the erosion of that faith, due in part to the deceptions perpetrated in the name of national security during the Vietnam War and in part to the conniving and skulduggery of the Watergate operations and campaign practices in 1972 now being revealed.

The Watergate investigations have revealed the sordid length to which efforts to reelect the President have gone: electronic buggings, burglary, and the break-in of Democratic Party headquarters, millions of dollars in unaccounted-for funds, huge cash payments for cover-ups and pay-offs, and character assassination of leading contenders for the presidency, including Muskie, Humphrey, Jackson and McGovern, not to mention the distortions and innuendoes of the campaign, which were not entirely restricted to the Republicans.

These are but a few of the dark elements in the picture. The temptation for many people is to despair of efforts to influence national policy and to reform government practices. But to acquiesce in evil and injustice is to perpetuate it. Edmund Burke said that the only thing necessary for the triumph of evil is for good men to do nothing.

For a moment let us look at the brighter side. In the thirty years which have been sketched in this history, there have been many advances. In many of these the FCNL played an active part. The United Nations has replaced the defunct League of Nations and now has a membership of 134 nations as of September 1973. Probably soon it will have universal membership. Around it are clustered a host of international agencies working on economic development and technical assistance, food and population, health, communications and a wide range of international problems.

Discriminatory immigration legislation has been modified. Social Security and Medicare now benefit our older citizens. After thirty-two years of military conscription, the nation has switched to a volunteer army. A considerable thaw in the cold war has taken place and relations with the Soviet Union and the People's Republic of China are much improved.

These are a few in a much longer list of positive changes for the better. But we must not confuse a moment's resting place with the journey's end.

During the last twenty years, spokesmen for our government have set forth goals that are far from accomplished but which we must work toward with determination. There is a strong temptation to outrun history and assume that, because something is desirable, it is also possible without the long and excruciating efforts which may be necessary to bring it about. On the other hand, there is the temptation to believe that because things are as bad as they are or because advance seems agonizingly slow and difficult, change is impossible.

One goal toward which little relative progress has been made is to insure the world's population — still exploding at an ominous rate — an adequate diet. Much of the technology of food production and family limitation is known. But the political, social and personal will to use those techniques has been weak.

A second goal in the United States has been for all individuals to have access to as much education as they can benefit from and will need for using their God-given abilities. Is the wisdom exercised by the American people equivalent to the sum of their knowledge and their power in the world?

A third goal is to eliminate discrimination because of race, creed, sex or color. The Supreme Court decision of May 17, 1954, outlawing segregation in education, (five cases, including Topeka, Kansas, *Brown vs. Board of Education*), and the Civil Rights Act of 1964 have given us some of the legal framework within which to work for equality of opportunity in housing, education, employment — an equality that recognizes the worth and dignity of every individual.

The fourth goal is the elimination of dire involuntary poverty which could be erased by a series of measures including an assured minimum income. President Nixon proposed steps in this direction in 1971. An inadequate bill passed the House of Representatives but was bottled up in the Senate Finance Committee under the chairmanship of Senator Long of Louisiana and abandoned by the Nixon Administration. In our affluent society in the United States, the elimination of such poverty is now economically possible; therefore changing that situation is a task for which we are morally responsible. Cushing N. Dolbeare told the House Ways and Means Committee in March 1973, that the "wealthiest 10 per cent of our families receive 29 per cent of all income and own over 55 per cent of the wealth, while the poorest 10 per cent receive only one per cent of the income, and owe more than they own." [1]

In 1959, the governments of Great Britain, the Soviet Union and the United States gave lip service to the goal of general disarmament. So far, nations have been willing to disarm other nations but are very reluctant to reduce their own huge expenditures. Citizens must insist that governments do more on disarmament than talk out of both sides of their mouths. In June 1973, the President and Party Secretary Brezhnev signed agreements promising efforts to prevent nuclear war and to continue active negotiations for limiting offensive nuclear weapons. There is still no total freeze on nuclear weapons and no agreement for a nuclear weapons roll-back, but at least talks are to continue in a considerably more friendly atmosphere. We now have an Arms Control and Disarmament Agency to work persistently on world disarmament.

One of our constituents wrote us that if John Woolman in forty years was unable to get all his fellow Quakers to give up their slaves, the Friends Committee on National Legislation should not be discouraged if in twenty years it had not succeeded in getting the nations of the world to give up war.

The story is told of the man and his little son who came to visit Congress and were sitting in the gallery when the chaplain rose to pray at the opening of the session. The boy leaned over to his father and asked what that man did. The father replied: "He gets up and looks at Congress and then prays for the country." There are some times when one is tempted to feel that way, but most of the time, I think, Congress is an exciting, challenging place. It has been a rare privilege to have had close association with Congress over the years.

Someone characterized democracy as the worst form of government except for all the rest. In our democracy Congress is a major place where conflicts of interest are resolved. Oftentimes these conflicts are not solved in the best possible way nor as promptly as they should be. Few, if any, decisions of Congress please everybody. It is easy to criticize Congress without recognizing that it is a more accurate mirror of the characteristics of the American people than we would like to admit.

An important opportunity in our democracy is that there are so many places where the concerned citizen can share in the democratic process — citizen discussion and action at the precinct and county level, participation in political party activities, and voting at election time after studying the records of the candidate. The individual citizen or organized group can send letters and wires to members of Congress, or to the President or to those in administrative positions. He can visit members of Congress in their districts or in Washington. He can testify before Congressional Committees and can participate actively in public interest lobbies like the Friends Committee on National Legislation. But if democracy is to work satisfactorily, citizens must pay the price to make it function.

When it comes to actual lobbying, if there is something for which a visitor can praise the member of Congress, he should commend him for it. If the visitor differs with him, he should try to understand the Congressman's point of view, respect it, but present his own convictions forthrightly. If the Congressman is not available, the visitor can talk to his legislative assistant, who often does much of the research and thinking for his superior, and who frequently knows more about a certain subject than he does. It is helpful if a memo or pertinent material can be left or a follow-up letter sent.

When I went to see a tall, energetic Colorado Congressman to thank him for voting a certain way, he shook my hand and nearly twisted my arm off at the elbow. "You would be surprised," he said, "how many people ask me to do things and how few ever thank me for it."

I can remember very, very few examples of outright discourtesy by a Congressman, and then I always blamed myself for an inadequate approach. Many times one does not get to see a Congressman because he is out of his office or closeted with a visitor, or perhaps working on a speech. I tell constituents to telephone their Representative if the question is urgent, remarking that most of them are no further away than the price of a bushel of corn. It is amazing how much is done on the telephone these days, though no doubt also much time is wasted.

A Maine Congressman said to me during the height of the UMT

controversy that he did not believe his constituents were interested in the question because he had received virtually no mail about it. The absense of mail on an issue may have a profound effect on the lack of interest in a given subject. Gripe mail and mail against a measure often exceed correspondence in favor of legislation. Petitions have limited value and masses of identical letters, telegrams or cards are discounted. "The American Legion has had a meeting in my district," said a Philadelphia Representative to me, pointing to a stack of 75 identical post cards on his desk.

CONGRESSIONAL REFORM AND CONGRESSIONAL ETHICS

One of the dominant impressions of my years in Washington has been the almost total inability of Congress to reform its antiquated procedures, to organize itself to deal with the budget as a whole, or to establish needed priorities.

The various appropriations bills are, for the most part, handled separately. They are discussed in relation to administration requests, but not much consideration is given to weighing one appropriation against another or in a pinch what appropriation is more important than another in serving the total national well-being. As just one example of the need to change national priorities, in 1973, it still seems more important to the Congress to build new weapons systems than it does to enlarge the program of the Arms Control and Disarmament Agency with the aim of shifting expenditures to vitally needed domestic programs of health, education and scientific research. There seems to me to be no effective legislative process of weighing one priority in legislation against another.

Congress belatedly has passed a measure, aimed at improving the overall budgeting process, which will require Congress to examine the totals, setting itself target figures through a budget resolution, before acting on the several authorization and appropriation bills. Once the customary appropriations process is completed, Congress would then have to review both the target totals and the various bills, reconciling any discrepancies. But this procedure will only work if Congress acts much differently than they do now.

Fair Rules of Procedure. Wilmer Cooper, FCNL associate secretary, urged the Senate Rules Subcommittee on July 6, 1954, to adopt a five-point program of fair rules of procedure for Senate Committees. Cooper commented in his plea for such rules of procedure that:

. . .our great nation is in a sorry state of affairs if its chief lawmakers are unable to govern themselves in the process of governing the rest of us. . . . [2]

This was at the height of the hysteria over the unsupported charges of subversion by Senator Joseph McCarthy and the abuse of witnesses before committees such as the House Un-American Activities Committee. Wilmer Cooper questioned the appropriateness of Congressional committees inquiring about the opinions and beliefs of witnesses except in cases involving Senatorial confirmation of appointments. He urged a series of safeguards for witnesses appearing before committees based on a Statement of Policy on Civil Liberties adopted by the FCNL Executive Committee on April 8, 1954. The last twenty years have seen a great improvement in the treatment of witnesses before committees of Congress.

Recorded Votes. Some significant and encouraging steps toward voting reform have been made in the last two years. Formerly a House member could shield himself in anonymity in the teller votes which were not recorded. Under that procedure members walked down the center aisle for yea and nay votes and were counted but not identified in the *Congressional Record*. Now those votes are recorded by name. Voice votes, of course, are not recorded by name. The FCNL worked actively with other organizations in the Coalition on Military Policy and National Priorities for these and other changes in Congressional procedures.

Secrecy in Committees. In 1972, 40 per cent of all Senate and House Committee meetings were closed, according to a tabulation by *Congressional Quarterly*. Senator William V. Roth, a first-term Senator from Delaware, introduced an amendment to require all Senate Committees to hold meetings in public unless a majority voted at each meeting to close its doors. This amendment was beaten by a roll call vote 38-47. Those voting against the amendment included 12 out of the 13 chairmen of the standing committees. The Senate then adopted on March 6, 1973, a milder proposal, endorsed by the Rules and Administration Committee, which granted each standing committee the right to set up its own rules on secrecy. This action had the effect of overturning Rule 25 under which open mark-up sessions were prohibited. Mark-up sessions are those in which a committee decides on the substance and details of legislation to be reported out of committee which then goes on the calendar for eventual consideration on the floor.

The House, on March 7, 1973, voted a somewhat similar proposal encouraging open committee meetings but allowing any committee to make the decision in advance of the meeting. The House also adopted a provision that officials of the federal government, but not lobbyists, could be present at closed meetings to assist in drafting legislation.

These measures stirred up lively debate. Opponents argued that state secrets would be revealed and that open meetings of certain committees like the Senate Finance Committee would give organized lobbies the opportunity to try to stampede the committee. Further, it was claimed that it would be embarrassing to the Senate Appropriations Committee because they often set artifically high appropriation levels to build a strong bargaining position with the more tightfisted House Committee, so that a more adequate appropriations bill would emerge from the conference. It would seem to me that committee meetings, including mark-up sessions, should be open to the public, even at the expense of some candor at times, unless they entail some very delicate and sensitive matter of foreign policy involving other governments or where the character of a person might be unfairly maligned. Confirmation hearings, where the appointees' own views are under scrutiny, are usually held in open session.

While the FCNL has long advocated many Congressional reforms, an intensive drive was made in 1973, among others by Common Cause, the National Committee for an Effective Congress, the League of Women Voters and the United Auto Workers.

Seniority. The seniority system — I call it the senility system — allowed the ranking majority member of a committee to remain in power as long as he was in Congress and as long as his party was in control of that house of Congress. In the House, the Democratic Study Group secured a modification of the seniority system which required that every standing committee chairman be subject to the approval of the Democratic caucus in a recorded vote at the start of each Congress. No chairman was dethroned, but all 21 do have the threat of possible dismissal over them. Another reform in the House was to limit each member to the chairmanship of one subcommittee.

To facilitate more party discipline and more legislative planning, a steering and policy committee was created, chaired by the speaker and made up of 23 members to make recommendations on legislative priorities and party policy. Some more use is made of party caucuses to discuss legislation before it comes to the floor.

Committee chairmen should be freely elected by secret ballot for their innate ability for that particular job and not be elevated to that position because of surviving the political rat race, often from a one-party area. As was indicated in the chapter on civil rights, many committee chairmen have come from Southern states where, because of poll taxes, intimidation and other restrictions on voting, they were able to stay in Congress by the votes of a small minority of their constituents.

Filibuster. The FCNL has long advocated a more effective limitation of filibuster in the Senate, but being concerned with safeguards for minority rights on questions of peace and justice, we have not gone as far as some of our civil rights colleagues in seeking the abolition of extended Senate debate. The 1963-64 Statement of Legislative Policy maintained that:

> An important element in a democratic society is the right of a minority to express its views and obtain wide discussion of all sides of a major question. Neither railroading tactics by a majority nor filibuster tactics by a minority are in the public interest. We think it desirable for the Senate to be deliberate in its procedures, thus permitting public attention to focus on issues which may not earlier have received adequate consideration. But after reasonable time for presenting all germane points of view, we believe it should be possible for the Senate to end debate and express its will directly on pending legislation. [3]

Present regulations require a two-thirds vote of those present and voting to shut off a filibuster by cloture. The filibuster has been used most often against civil rights legislation. While the filibuster issue is not as acute as it was before the Civil Rights Act of 1964, legislative procedures should be modified to provide for closing debate after full discussion by a simple majority vote.

Disclosure. For many years, Senators Paul Douglas of Illinois and Clifford Case of New Jersey advocated full disclosure of financial assets and liabilities and income of members of Congress and federal officials in higher positions. A few members of Congress have given this information voluntarily, but no adequate disclosure legislation has been passed. Adequate disclosure would include travel expenditures, campaign contributions and miscellaneous gifts received. Present regulations do provide for reporting fees received for speeches made by members of Congress and for reporting campaign contributions of $100 or more. The reporting of campaign contributions is often circumvented by the use of shadow committees or other subterfuges, and the law is not being enforced against members of Congress who may have violated it. The Clerk of the House is supposed to police the members of the House but he is merely an employee of the Congress and must obtain approval from a special House Committee before forwarding reports of suspected serious violations of the Act to the Department of Justice.

As one method of avoiding even the tacit implication of political obligations or favoritism, Senator Paul Douglas directed his staff to return any gifts in kind which came to his office which it was estimated were worth more than a very few dollars.

Election Reforms and Campaign Spending. The revelations in the Watergate scandal have revealed starkly the need for sweeping election reforms. Vast rivers of money were spent in the last presidential campaign, millions of it unaccounted for, which had been received before the April 7, 1972, deadline after which campaign contributions were supposed to be publicly reported. The *New York Times*, June 23, 1973, reports that the total raised to re-elect the President was $54.6 million, but attorneys for Common Cause, which brought suit to compel disclosure of pre-April 7 fund-raising and expenditures, estimate the total raised at $58 million.

In October 1974, as an aftermath of the Watergate election scandals, Congress passed a landmark campaign reform bill which unfortunately exempted the House of Representatives from public financing. In essence this exemption boiled down to the unwillingness of House members to finance their opponents and to yield any of the advantages which incumbents have. The House turned down public financing of House campaigns by a 187-228 vote.

This measure sets spending limits on presidential primaries of $10 million per candidate for all primaries and in presidential general elections to $20 million per candidate. Senate primaries are restricted to $100,000 or eight cents per eligible voter, whichever is greater. Senate general elections are limited to $150,000 or twelve cents per eligible voter, whichever is greater. House primaries and general elections are limited to $70,000 each.

For presidential nominating conventions there would be optional public funding and for presidential general elections voluntary public funding. In presidential primaries there could be matching public funds up to $4.5 million per candidate. All federal money for public funding of campaigns would come from the federal income tax dollar check off.

There are strict limits on the amount each individual or organization can contribute and provisions for full disclosure of campaign contributions.

Enforcement would be in the hands of an eight-member, full-time bipartisan Federal Elections Commission to be responsible for administering election laws and the public financing program. Candidates would be barred from running for federal office for an entire term plus one year if they failed to file reports with the commission.

This measure, except for the House public financing exemption, is very much in line with the FCNL statement on Legislative Policy approved in February 1972, and with the article by Samuel Levering in the August-September 1973, *Washington Newsletter.*

New Faces and New Leadership Needed in Congress. In an elective system not based on proportional representation, any point of view has to get more than 50 per cent of the vote or at least more than the other leading candidate in order to win. Since the liberal or prophetic point of view is usually a minority point of view, this weights Congress on the conservative side and often puts a handicap on needed new legislation and leadership against the vested interests of the status quo.

While the 1974 elections brought in about ninety new members of Congress, many of them younger than the incumbents, yet both Houses are still too much in the grip of elderly conservative committee chairmen.

There is still the need to get more good people to run for Congress — men who have the character and ability to serve their district and their country well, but who may not be heavily endowed with this world's goods. And while they have an obligation to seek the best interests of their constituents and their nation, their staying in Congress ought not to depend on the amount of gravy they can get for their area in military installations, dams, post office buildings and other inroads into the federal purse.

Overall Budget and Priorities. One desperately needed reform is to develop some procedure for considering appropriations as a whole, both as to total cost and in relation to well-considered national priorities. For the most part each major appropriations bill is taken up quite independently of other appropriations and often with a minimum of debate.

For years, I used to be horrified at the procedure in the House of Representatives on military appropriations. It was not uncommon for the printed hearings ranging anywhere from 1200 to 2000 pages — with heavy deletions for national security reasons — to be released one or two days before the bill went to the House floor. This gave members who were not on the Appropriations Committee almost no time for examining the proposed expenditures. Debate on the bill was controlled by the ranking majority and minority members of the committee and few members not on the committee got a chance to enter the debate in any meaningful way. Debate time for noncommittee members and for total consideration of the bill was sharply limited.

Appropriation measures often get to the floor very late in the legislative timetable. Supposedly, all appropriations for the ensuing fiscal year are to be acted upon before the close of the current fiscal year on June 30. More and more frequently now, appropriations are extended by a continuing resolution and the actual final action on a given appropriation may be months after the beginning of the fiscal year, July 1.

Presidential Power Versus Congressional Power

In our system of checks and balances among the three branches of government — the judicial, the executive and the legislative — the balance is constantly shifting, especially between the Congress and the Administration. It is not too much to say that, over the last few years, the military and the Administration under Presidents Johnson and Nixon have largely been out of control, especially in regard to the Vietnam War.

Congress is now struggling to regain what many members of Congress believe is their rightful balance of power vis-a-vis the executive. This conflict has been acute over war powers and over the impoundment of funds.

There is not space here to speculate why Congress has allowed its relative power to decline. While it is desirable that Congress regain its rightful authority, the brutal fact is that both the Congress and the Executive have been guilty of grave misuse of power. On the side of Congress, to name only two, are the passage of the Formosa Resolution and the Gulf of Tonkin Resolution, giving the President a virtual blank check on the use of military power, already briefly described in this history. Both the Executive and the Congress need the constant scrutiny of citizens. This is only one of the reasons why lobbies in the public interest are so necessary.

James M. Banner, Jr., professor of history at Princeton University, in an article in the *New York Times*, July 14, 1973, observed that:

> Regulations governing Congressional lobbying are worthless, and as a result, the special-interest lobbyists swarm over Capitol Hill without any accountability to the public. Lobbyists for the aircraft industry, the fuel industry and the milk industry, which walk away with billions of

dollars of favors each year, do not have to indicate the sources of their funds, the nature and amount of their lobbying, nor their links to voluntary associations which urge their members to lobby. . . . Before we turn leadership of government over to Congress, we need a new and tough lobby-disclosure law.

Congress is governed by no ethics regulation, no law forbids a member of either house from holding a position with a law firm which may be doing business with the government. . . . Before we yield to the alluring arguments in favor of a better balanced Government, Congress ought first to prove its own fitness to govern by passing a tight conflict-of-interest law.

A part of the answer to the proper Congressional exercise of authority would be more adequate committee staffs so that Congress could have more of the facts behind departmental requests and could reach independent judgment based on the evidence they need. Congress has failed to correct abuses in the classification of documents. It has little research capacity of its own. "No man's thinking is better than his information" was a slogan hammered into us in graduate school. Abe Martin, a newspaper columnist, whose wisecracks used to enliven the 1920's, used to say, "Better not to know so much, than to know so many things that ain't so."

IN RETROSPECT

It is easy for a religious legislative committee to get so absorbed in legislative maneuvers, trying to get measures in Congress passed or defeated, that it may lose its concern for the moral and spiritual climate in which government ought to operate as decisions are made affecting the lives and welfare of people. Senator Mark Hatfield of Oregon has complained that nobody has come into his office to pray with him over the grave questions which he has to decide.

Much more time ought to be spent in quiet wrestling with the deeper issues of right and wrong, with the temptation to be expedient at the price of principle, or with the agonizing question at what point compromise should be made in order to further a desired goal. Very few political issues are a clear-cut choice between being totally right and being totally wrong.

More encouragement and support should be given to members of Congress to speak out and to take unpopular stands as a matter of principle. Barbara Grant and I had tea in the Senate dining room in the Capitol with Senator Wayne Morse of Oregon soon after he switched parties. He had lost all his seniority so that he was at the bottom of the totem pole in both parties. We were deeply impressed by the high price in loneliness that the Senator was paying at that time for his convictions.

There were many, many letters I should have written and telephone calls I should have made to members of Congress to commend or challenge them for their actions.

Looking back on three decades of legislative activity, the conviction deepens that what is needed is not just a patch here and there on often outmoded institutions, but a whole new radical, revolutionary approach toward the world about us.

The epistle of June 6, 1972, of the London Yearly Meeting of Friends said in part:

> A political awareness has been growing among us in recent years. This yearly meeting has seen it taking form as a fresh testimony. We have once again been bidden to seek first the kingdom, but now a social, economic and political, as well as a spiritual kingdom. We have been reminded of the revolutionary nature of the mission of Jesus, and of the radical social action of early Friends. Without such action now our Religious Society will become a religious irrelevance.
>
> We have heard the urgent summons to join in the building of a new city, and to live by its values, even while we inhabit the old, with its too frequent denial of human dignity. To that end we must inform ourselves, master our material and train our faculties for a lifelong commitment to service. Our endeavor must be to bring compassion and justice from the periphery to the center of power. . . . ⁴

Many of our young people are striving to simplify their lives, to cut drastically their own living expenses, to experiment with cooperative living, and to seek to build a society that does not rest on exploitation and war. They are rightly insisting that the process of far-reaching peaceful, nonviolent change has to be telescoped in time. There is no such thing as immediate peace or immediate justice, but the future has to be envisioned and striven for now.

Such a vision calls the religiously motivated citizen to live in creative tension with the world around him and to seek to build a society of love and brotherhood for the children of God on earth. Striving for justice becomes a life-long passion.

This fragmentary history of Quaker efforts, a few of them successful, to influence the decisions of government in the direction of peace, justice and freedom has, I hope, given some evidence of the value and necessity of citizen action motivated by a commitment to humanity as a whole.

If the better world of tomorrow is to come, more and more people must, in their minds and actions, live today in that world of tomorrow, hoping and believing that that world of tomorrow will come. That better world of tomorrow will not come just by wishing for it. To realize that vision will take an inordinate amount of persistent and intelligent effort. It is incumbent upon the individual not only to try to be good, but also, individually and in concert with others to try to be effective.

APPENDIX I

FRIENDS ATTENDING THE CONFERENCE TO CONSIDER ORGANIZING A COMMITTEE ON NATIONAL LEGISLATION
at Richmond, Indiana
June 11-12, 1943

David K. Bruner ....Earlham, Indiana
Harold Chance ....Lansdowne, Pennsylvania
Pauline Clampitt...........................New Providence, Iowa
Roy Clampitt...............................New Providence, Iowa
Alvin T. Coate ....Indianapolis, Indiana
Eva D. Edgerton...............................Dayton, Ohio
Edward W. Evans ....Philadelphia, Pennsylvania
Thomas A. Foulke...........................Ambler, Pennsylvania
James Furbay.....................................Marion, Indiana
Harold Guthrie ....New Providence, Iowa
Milton Hadley ....Richmond, Indiana
George W. Hallett, Jr. ....New York, New York
Lois Halloway...............................Barnesville, Ohio
Stanley Hamilton ....Richmond, Indiana
Kelsey Hinshaw ....North Loup, Nebraska
Seth B. Hinshaw.......................Asheboro, North Carolina
Ralph Howell...............................Yellow Springs, Ohio
Mrs. Ralph Howell ....Yellow Springs, Ohio
Herbert Huffman...............................Indianapolis, Indiana
Agnes King Inglis...............................Washington, D.C.
Emily Cooper Johnson...................Philadelphia, Pennsylvania
Murray S. Kenworthy...........................Fairmount, Indiana
Samuel R. Levering ....Ararat, Virginia
M. Albert Linton ....Philadelphia, Pennsylvania
Albert J. Livezey................................Barnesville, Ohio
Millard Markle...............................Richmond, Indiana
Nellie Markle...............................Richmond, Indiana
Arthur B. Maxwell ....Union City, Indiana
Mary B. Maxwell ....Union City, Indiana
Sumner Mills ....Indianapolis, Indiana
Erma Mott ....Indianola, Iowa
Lewis G. Mott ....Indianola, Iowa
J. Curtis Newlin...........................Poughkeepsie, New York
Roy L. Newlin...............................Earlham, Iowa
Ray Newton...........................Philadelphia, Pennsylvania

Lillian White Shepard .... Richmond, Indiana
Fred Smith .... Richmond, Indiana
Edith Reeves Solenberger .... Upper Darby, Pennsylvania
Allison Stinetorf .... Richmond, Indiana
Floretta Stinetorf .... Richmond, Indiana
Clayton Terrell .... New Vienna, Ohio
Gilbert E. Thomas .... Barnesville, Ohio
Percy M. Thomas .... Richmond, Indiana
Bert Thornberg .... Union City, Indiana
Olive Thornberg .... Union City, Indiana
Ellen L. Tjossem .... Paullina, Iowa
Merle O. Tjossem .... Paullina, Iowa
J. Barnard Walton .... Philadelphia, Pennsylvania
Norval Webb .... Richmond, Indiana
Allen J. White .... Washington, D.C.
Caroline Wills .... Oak Park, Illinois
Charles M. Woodman .... Richmond, Indiana

APPENDIX II

FRIENDS COMMITTEE ON NATIONAL LEGISLATION

OFFICERS

General Committee Chairpersons

Murray S. Kenworthy	1943-1946
Sumner A. Mills	1947-1948
David E. Henley	1949-1953
Samuel R. Levering	1954
Delbert E. Replogle	1955-1958
Charles J. Darlington	1959-1965
Stephen L. Angell, Jr.	1966-1974 —*

Executive Committee Chairpersons

Thomas A. Foulke	1943-1947
Willis H. Satterthwaite	1948-1950
Richard H. Rhoads	1951-1954
Samuel R. Levering	1955-1972
Marian D. Fuson	1973-1974 —

EXECUTIVE SECRETARIES

E. Raymond Wilson	Executive Secretary	1943-1961
	Executive Secretary Emeritus	1962-1974 —
Edward F. Snyder	Legislative Secretary	1955-1961
	Executive Secretary	1962-1974 —

Employees: November 1, 1943 - December 31, 1974

Our heartfelt thanks go to many, many volunteers who have given a great deal of time interviewing members of Congress, assisting in mailing and distributing documents, clipping newspapers, assembling and indexing archives and performing various other services which have been invaluable in forwarding the work of the FCNL, but who are not listed here by name. Especially noteworthy were the eighteen winters which retired teacher Floyd Voris spent in the mailing room. He celebrated his ninetieth birthday by climbing the 555-foot high

---

*— indicates continuing service as of 12/31/74.

Washington Monument.

Following is the list of those who have been on the FCNL payroll at least a few days. The designation for each one does not adequately portray the variety of activities which many of the staff have performed.

Elizabeth R. Abell, typist; 10/9/51 - 10/30/51
Ayse Neylan Akra, student, summer work; clerk; 5/5/61 - 7/14/61
Helen G. Alexander, office secretary; 1/3/72 - 12/31/72
John C. Alexander, mail clerk and printer; 1/7/69 - 12/31/72
William Alexander, research; 3/1/55 - 5/31/55
Edward T. Anderson, human rights secretary; 7/1/68-12/31/70
Dale Andrew, intern; 9/4/73 - 8/30/74
Frances Andrews, typist; 11/15/46 - 12/19/46
Peter B. Ashelman, student, summer work, clerk; 7/17/61 - 8/18/61
Mary Ellen W. Atkinson, mailing clerk, addressograph; 2/5/65 - 3/19/65
Marquita Attaffer, clerk; 3/13/53 - 5/8/53
Thomas B. Atwater, intern; 9/3/74 - 12/31/74 —

Karl Bach, office secretary; 1/9/74 - 12/31/74 —
C. Lloyd Bailey, associate secretary; 7/1/47 - 9/30/51
Tom Ballman, student, clerk; 38 hours, between 2/2/62 - 3/23/62
Edward W. Beals, clerk; 6/28/51 - 9/30/51
Robert H. Berman, Antioch student, clerk; 3/31/58 - 7/18/58
Susan H. Berry, office secretary; 7/2/73 - 12/31/74 —
Diana Washbon Bird, legislative secretary; 9/7/71 - 8/25/72
George I. Bliss, associate secretary; 8/7/67 - 12/31/74 —
Helen L. Bliss, office secretary; 9/11/67 - 8/31/71
Paul Nick Block, administrative secretary; 7/3/72 - 12/31/74 —
Ray Constance Blumenfeld, Antioch student, clerk; 2/21/66 - 3/24/66
Elizabeth J. Boardman, office secretary; 9/1/65 - 8/26/66
Eugene P. Boardman, Friend-in-Washington; 9/1/65 - 8/26/66
David M. Bolling, alternative service, office secretary; 3/4/68 - 6/6/69
Margaret E. Borgers, office secretary; 1/2/68 - 8/2/68
Gunthilt B. Bowen, office secretary; 7/30/62 - 12/18/62
Gloria K. Bradford, UMT, typist; 12/1/50 - 5/31/51
Evelyn W. Bradshaw, administrative assistant (office); 6/1/73 - 12/31/74 —
Jeremy Brecker, alternative service, research; 3/1/67 - 12/25/67
Paul E. Brink, editor; 9/8/69 - 12/31/74
David Burk Brown, printer, clerk; 8/25/52 - 12/31/52
Doris E. Brown, office secretary; 1/1/63 - 12/31/74 —
Dorothy A. Brown, office secretary; 7/12/65 - 8/27/65 & 6/15/66 - 8/18/66
Holmes Brown, intern, research; 2/24/71 - 8/31/71
Walter Brown, clerk; 6/17/68 - 8/30/68
Katharine Brownlee, clerk; 11/30/53 - 12/9/53 & 1/21/56 - 2/17/56,
Beth Burbank, intern, research; 7/7/71 - 7/28/72

Frank Cadwell, intern; 9/5/72 - 8/24/73
Judith Caro, clerk; 11/16/53 - 12/9/53
Philip R. Carter, intern, research; 6/15/70 - 6/10/71
Evelyn B. Clarke, office secretary; 9/20/71 - 12/31/71
Janis Cohen, office secretary; 6/2/69 - 2/12/70
Mario Collaci, UMT, research; 11/12/47 - 12/31/47
Harold B. Confer, human rights secretary; 5/21/73 - 12/31/74 —
Samuel Cooper, carpenter; 10/25/52 - 11/28/52
Wilmer A. Cooper, associate and administrative secretary; 10/1/52 -
  4/10/59
Catherine C. Cory, 10th Anniversary, Philadelphia; 9/1/53 - 12/15/53
Robert H. Cory, Jr., associate secretary for UN Affairs; 2/1/67 - to
  present, part-time
Naomi Cotter, Antioch student, switchboard; 1/2/56 - 3/24/56 &
  9/30/57 - 10/25/57
Linda Cudi, typist; 5/6/62 - 6/1/62

Linda A. Darrow, office secretary; 11/10/70 - 6/30/71
Norma Davis, typist; 7/15/54 - 12/30/54 & 1/16/56 - 2/17/56
Mary Kay Dewees, student, clerk; 6/4/62 - 8/22/62
Marianna Brown Diggs, office secretary; summer - 1963, 1964, part-time
  1967-68-70.
Eleanor Douglas Doak, research; 9/1/44 - 3/30/45
Geraldine Doleman, clerk-typist; 5/10/53 - 6/12/53
James Driver, clerk; 9/1/53 - 9/15/53
Billy Lou Dubois, Antioch student, switchboard; 10/17/56 - 12/28/56 &
  5/2/57 - 8/2/57

Ruth Early, FIW office secretary; 9/16/60 - 6/2/61
Margaret Ebeling, research; 4/14/47 - 7/15/48
William B. and Judith Edgerton, Friends-in-Washington; 3/1/68 -
  6/28/68
Diane E. Edwards, intern; 6/17/70 - 6/25/71
Mary Evans, Antioch student, switchboard; 1/2/55 - 3/31/55
William S. Evans, Wilmington College student, clerk; 1/6/69 - 3/21/69

Robert A. Fangmeier, UMT, research; 12/1/50 - 3/15/51
Rosemary Fassnidge, clerk; 4/11/66 - 6/10/66
Leah B. Felton, office secretary and librarian; 9/15/69 - 9/30/73
Geneva Fledderjohn, clerk-typist; 1/15/68 - 1/26/68
Martha Fleischer, office secretary, 1/2/73 - 6/29/73, intern, 9/4/73 -
  8/30/74
Anne Forsythe, research; 10/1/46 - 11/30/46
Catherine Foreman, office secretary; 6/3/74 - 12/31/74 —
M. Elaine Fuller, office secretary; 10/21/66 - 11/17/67

Carol Lee Gallagher, clerk-typist; 9/15/51 - 9/12/52
Joan L. Gibbons, research; 10/1/55 - 8/17/56

Carmen Gnegy, clerk; 4/4/52 - 6/6/53
Robert C. Gnegy, bookkeeping, mailing and printing; 4/23/51 - 7/27/53
Annette P. Gottfried, research; 8/7/67 - 2/9/68
Chester A. Graham, UMT, lobbyist; 12/10/47 - 3/31/48
Barbara S. Grant, research assistant; 10/8/47 - 6/30/51 & 7/23/53 - 9/15/53
Eugenia Victoria Grant, office secretary; 4/2/73 - 4/13/73
Thomas Dan Griffiths, clerk; 8/11/67 - 8/31/67
Warren Griffiths, associate secretary, 9/8/54 - 7/29/55, 9/1/56 - 8/31/57 & 7/2/67 - 8/25/67
Priscilla Grissett, research; 10/1/58 - 12/18/59

Jeanette Hadley, administrative assistant; 11/3/43 - 6/2/72
Milton H. Hadley, UMT lobbyist; 1/1/52 - 3/15/52
Ruthanna Hadley, UMT typist; 10/20/47 - 3/31/48
Helen R. Hagen, typist; 3/7/67 - 3/24/67
Elenor Hall, office secretary and bookkeeper; 8/12/47 - 9/30/49
Sarah Smith Halloran, clerk; 10/17/61 - 12/27/68
T. Spencer Hand, clerk; 11/5/51 - 11/30/51
Joan M. Haner, FIW office secretary; 2/7/62 - 4/27/62
Annanelle Hardt, switchboard, office secretary; 2/21/56 - 7/31/56
Charles H. Harker, Jr., administrative secretary; 5/4/59 - 12/31/69
Gordon L. Harris, mail department; 2/24/65 - 9/10/65
David Hartsough, program secretary; 10/1/62 - 9/30/64 & 2/9/66 - 9/11/70
Sally Hawes, office secretary; 7/5/54 - 12/20/55
Stephen A. Hawk, mail clerk; 9/6/66 - 11/28/66 & 1/25/68 - 9/8/68
Neil D. Haworth, printing and mailing department; 7/6/53 - 6/22/55
Kathryn J. Hiltner, receptionist, typist; 1/29/63 - 6/23/64
Waldo F. Hinshaw, alternative service, printing and mailing department, 8/29/60 - 8/31/62
Richard C. Hiscock, alternative service, mailing department; 1/24/67 - 4/3/67
Robert Hollister, student, clerk; 6/4/62 - 8/29/62
Harvey Holmes, janitor; 10/1/48 - 9/15/52
William T. Holmes, janitor; 1/1/60 - 4/29/60
Anne M. Holzinger, intern; 9/3/74 - 12/31/74 —
Edward Honnold, intern; 9/3/74 - 12/31/74 —
Charles F. Hough, alternative service, mailing department; 7/26/65 - 3/24/67
Roland S. Hufford, mailing department; 7/1/58 - 9/1/61

Michael L. Ingermann, office secretary, alternative service; 10/1/58 - 9/30/60
J. Stuart Innerst, Friend-in-Washington; UMT 12/1/50 - 4/30/52 & 2/8/60 - 8/31/60 & 1/1/61 - 12/31/61

David T. Johnson, intern; 3/24/70 - 3/12/71
Sandra Johnson, research; 10/19/64 - 3/19/65
John Albert Jones, alternative service, clerk; 4/6/67 - 7/28/67
John B. Jones, summer intern; 1949
Margaret E. Jones, switchboard, typist; 9/1/53 - 12/15/53
Marilyn Joslin, office secretary; 10/1/49 - 6/30/53

Peter Jay Kapenga, intern; 7/1/71 - 7/28/72
John R. Kellam, research; 11/3/43 - 8/31/44
Dorothy M. Kelley, office secretary; 2/11/57 - 6/3/60
Mary Jean Kennedy, clerk; 6/1/47 - 6/25/47
Marie S. Klooz, UMT and office secretary; 1/8/55 - 9/29/55
Gretchen L. Koenig, Wilmington College student; 1/10/69 - 3/21/69
Maaret Korkula, typist; 12/26/53 - 12/31/53
Eve Anne Kulberg, office secretary; 9/18/73 - 5/31/74
Todd Luken Kummer, student, summer work; 6/21/65 - 9/3/65
Lola Kyle, office secretary; 9/24/70 - 10/26/70

Lawrence Alan LaMotte, intern; 7/1/71 - 4/7/72
Dawn G. Lander, office secretary; 2/28/62 - 7/13/62
David Wayne LaVoy, mailing department; 4/24/67 - 9/11/70
Charles D. Lee, clerk; 12/12/51 - 12/31/51
Maud W. Lee, clerk; 11/30/51 & 12/4/51
Helen M. Levering, student, summer work; 6/4/61 - 8/31/61
Miriam L. Levering, Friend-in-Washington; 3/10/72 - 1/26/73
Samuel R. Levering, Friend-in-Washington; 2/22/72 - 12/28/73
Judith A. Lhamon, office secretary; 4/18/66 - 9/16/66
T. Proctor Lippincott, alternative service, office secretary; 10/13/64 -
   10/14/66
George Loft, UMT & doctor's draft; 1/1/48 - 6/30/48, 11/20/50 -
   12/14/50 & 5/1-28/53
Constance Longshore, office secretary; 6/13/60 - 5/19/61
Rose R. Lowe, office secretary; 6/5/61 - 3/23/62
William George Lunsford, human rights secretary; 3/15/71 - 3/30/73

Nancy L. Machler, Bennington College student, research; 1/5/58 -
   3/13/58
Antoinette Mailliard, office secretary; 8/5/51 - 12/21/51
Jeannette E. Marley, clerk; 11/14/51 - 11/23/51
Rollin P. Marquis, assistant secretary, finance; 10/1/56 - 8/30/57
Dorothy E. McCombs, UMT janitor; 1/1/55 - 7/15/55
William G. McDevitt III, intern; 4/12/72 - 7/28/72 & 9/6/73 - 8/31/73
Thelma McMillan, office secretary; 3/16/60 - 6/16/61
Marilyn D. McNabb, office secretary; 9/14/66 - 1/12/67
Clifford Mesner, intern; 9/4/73 - 8/30/74
Mary H. Mikesell, typist; 4/8/70 - 5/8/71

Zorita W. Mikva, UMT research; 9/16/51 - 6/30/52
Paul I. Miller, associate secretary; 2/1/54 - 10/29/54
Morris R. Mitchell, UMT research; 11/1/47 - 11/30/47
Patricia A. Moles, research program secretary; 3/2/70 - 5/31/72
Rebecca S. Mullin, intern; 9/5/72 - 8/24/73
William Rhoads Murphey III, associate secretary; 2/4/52 - 7/31/52

Sally Nash, student, typist; 2/11/60 - 5/20/60
Frances E. Neely, legislative associate secretary; 1/1/57 - 12/31/74 —
Jonathan Newkirk, program secretary for Vietnam; 9/8/70 - 7/16/71
Florence Noffsinger, typist; 3/10/54 - 4/15/54 & 6/25/54 - 7/30/54
Augusta Noss, Antioch student, switchboard; 10/23/56 - 6/21/57

Denise O'Connor, office secretary; 9/5/61 - 7/3/64
Arnold Olena, research; 12/10/45 - 1/15/46

Bonnie Packer, research; 3/4/68 - 5/30/69
Patricia Parkman, research & typist; 3/23/56 - 9/27/57
Guy M. Patterson, clerk; 2/2/62 - 2/6/62
Diana Ruth Payne, office secretary; 3/2/72 - 8/17/73
Barrie A. Peterson, research, Princeton student; 2/3/69 - 2/27/70
Dutton S. Peterson, UMT lobbyist; 12/1/47 - 5/28/48
William S. Petty, high school student, clerk; 7/13/67 - 9/1/67
Frances C. Pheils, clerk-typist; 3/30/54 - 7/2/54
J. Franklin Pineo, Twentieth Anniversary; 1/28/63 - 11/15/63
Richard Post, Friend-in-Washington; 2/20/73 - 5/31/74
Ora Pottenger, bookkeeper; 9/15/44 - 3/30/45

Ralpha Randall, clerk-typist; 3/31/49 - 6/15/49
James M. Read, legislative secretary; 3/11/46 - 7/1/47
Rutha Mae Rigby, office secretary; 7/10/64 - 10/2/64
Mary Elizabeth Riggs, Antioch student, switchboard; 3/31/58 - 8/1/58
Marjorie J. Risley, telephone operator and archives; 6/22/70 - 7/31/70
Marcella Rothman, secretary, clerk; 9/15/51 - 10/15/51

Henry Schilling, clerk and office finance secretary; 11/20/52 - 3/31/53
Jean Scott, Antioch student, switchboard; 1/16/56 - 3/30/56
Ben Seaver, Friend-in-Washington; 4/6/63- 5/16/63
Carolynn Seitter, UMT typist; 1/12/48 - 6/26/48
Anne E. Shipley, office secretary; 1/7/46 - 1/15/47
Karen Shirley, Antioch student - switchboard; 3/30/59 - 7/10/59
Antoinette L. Simmons, office secretary; 3/6/56 - 10/26/56
Mary Jane Simpson, research; 1/11/54 - 9/28/56
Nora Singer, Antioch student, switchboard; 7/30/58 - 12/29/58
Clifford Smith, clerk-typist; 4/23/48 - 6/5/48
Mary Emlen Smith, office secretary; 1/30/47 - 4/11/47

John E. Smothers, secretary; 9/22/68 - 12/20/68

Edward F. Snyder, legislative secretary; 4/1/55 - 1/31/62; executive
secretary; 2/1/62 - 12/31/74 —

Kenneth C. Southard, clerk; 10/10/47 - 10/24/47

Sarah Anna Southern, Bennington student - office secretary; 1/8/58 -
3/10/58

Clara R. Stahl, bookkeeper; 3/19/51 - 7/29/51

Herbert C. Standing, business manager, bookkeeper; 6/1/53 - 11/15/55

Clifford E. Stanley, mail room manager; 7/1/62 - 6/25/65

Judith R. Starbuck, research secretary; 9/7/64 - 8/25/67

Alice Stout, bookkeeper to administrative assistant; 4/1/45 - 2/28/46,
10/4/48 - 3/20/51, 10/1/52 - 9/10/53 & 10/15/55 - 12/31/74 —

Harry Stults, summer intern; 1949

James H. Taylor, office secretary; 8/30/71 - 8/8/72

Kathleen (Betty) R. Taylor, office secretary; 11/1/67 - 9/26/69

Richard W. Taylor, Friend-in-Washington; 6/17/63 - 6/30/64

Thomas T. Taylor, Jr., manager of printing and mailing; 6/1/54 -
9/30/55

Cecil A. Thomas, Friend-in-Washington; 1/15/62 - 5/29/62

Richard W. Thompson, intern; 7/7/71 - 6/30/72

Allen F. Treadway, manager of printing and mailing; 9/6/55 - 6/20/58

Carolyn Smith Treadway, office secretary; 9/27/55 - 10/15/56

Marcia L. Trimmers, office secretary; 6/29/71 - 9/24/71

Etsuko (Eppie) Umeki, office secretary; 2/1/50 - 10/12/51

Floyd Voris, volunteer; 11/51 - 4/68

George A. Walton, UMT, legislative secretary; 1/8/51 - 4/18/51

Ada F. Wardlaw, writing; 3/10/58 - 2/27/59 & 1/11/60 - 3/11/60

Gordon M. Weatherford, multilith operator; 5/11/53 - 6/4/53

Barbara Werner, office secretary; 8/22/73 - 12/21/73

Beverly LaRue Stanley Wetherald, office secretary; 2/1/53 - 7/30/54

Lawrence M. White, administrative assistant; 12/1/60 - 7/13/62

Ann A. Wilkerson, office secretary; 1/9/67 - 9/8/67

Ila Jane Williamson, bookkeeper; 2/1/47 - 8/22/47

E. Raymond Wilson, executive secretary; 11/3/43 - 1/31/62
executive secretary emeritus; 2/1/62 - 12/31/74 —

Clarence N. Wise, custodian; 5/6/60 - 12/31/74 —

Elizabeth J. Terrell Wolff, office secretary; 6/8/53 - 8/15/55

Carol Woodworth, Antioch student, switchboard; 1/1/57 - 3/28/57

Grace S. Yaukey, financial secretary; 4/7/54 - 4/30/54 & 9/11/56 - 6/7/57

Grace E. Yoder, typist; 10/20/47 - 6/19/48

Jane L. York, Antioch student, switchboard; 4/19/68 - 6/21/68

Betty Ann Hershberger Zisk, office secretary and research; 6/9/52 - 9/30/55

Ellen Lee Ziskind, Antioch student, switchboard; 12/28/58 - 5/27/59

APPENDIX III

NORTHERN CALIFORNIA FCL 1952-1973

Chairpersons, Executive Committee

Irving Morrissett	1952
S.J. Patterson	1953-1955
Madge Seaver	1956-1959
	1962-1963
Robert R. Grinstead	1960-1961
	1963-1967
Richard Jay	1968
Margaret Brooks	1969- October, 1972
Isaiah Meyer	October, 1972-1973-

Executive Secretaries

Catherine Corbett Cory	1952
Trevor Thomas	1953-1959
Lucy Hancock	January-April, 1960
Henry Lohmann	May, 1960- June, 1963
Robert Mang	July, 1963-June, 1966
Michael L. Ingermann	July, 1966-1968
Doris Sloan	1969-1973-

Legislative Advocates in Sacramento

Georges and Marjorie Weber	1953-1957
Coleman Blease	1958-1959
Robert McLane	1960
Joseph Gunterman	1961-1973
Laura Magnani, Assistant	1971-1973

Other Sacramento Staff

Betty Cornelius	Pat Medeiros
Douglas Douglas	Romi Meier
Neil Gebhart	Helen Perkins
David Groton	Nancy Strawbridge
Jimmy Martinez	Suzanne Velasco
Fielding McGehee III	

Other Northern California Staff

Sheila Andres	Robert Jenks
Martha Bennett	Constance Jordan
Betty Black	Stephen Lohmann
Rebecca Carter	Julia Marble
Irene Clurman	Carolyn Matthews
Ellis Colton	Mac McGehee
Janice Comer	Ann McGiffen
Virginia Davis	Sue O'Hara
Donald Davisson	Vivian Parks
Kevin Feigen	Lydia Piehl
Laurel Givens	Rosalie Pizzo
Lucy Hancock	Virginia Pope
Sara Howard	Myfanwy Thornton

SOUTHERN CALIFORNIA FCL 1952-1973

Executive Committee Chairpersons

Nov. 17, 1952-Sept. 1954	Roscoe L. Warren
Oct. 1954-Jun. 1956	J. Stuart Innerst
Jul. 1956-Dec. 1961	Ernest Von Seggern
1962	Myrtle Marshall
1963	Carl Hedeen
1964-Oct. 1965	J. Stuart Innerst
Nov. 1965-Jan. 1966	Myrtle Marshall, Randolph Pyle
Feb. 1966-Nov. 1966	Lewis Unnewehr
Dec. 1966-to date	Kenneth Morgan

Executive Secretaries

Nov. 1952-Nov. 1954	Egbert M. Hayes
Nov. 1954-Dec. 1958	Catherine Cory
Dec. 1958-Aug. 1960	Ralph Schloming
Sept. 1960-Dec. 1961	J. Stuart Innerst
Jan. 1962-Nov. 1962	Miles Hollister
Dec. 1962-Dec. 1963	J. Stuart Innerst
Jan. 1964-Jul. 1966	Henry Schroerluke
Jul. 1966-Jul. 1968	Margaret McCarroll
Sept. 1968-to date	James Pino

Other Southern California Staff

Ann Austin	Kathy Hall
Kitty Barragato	Delmore Huserik
Marion Beardsley	Jean Johnson
Phyllis Brewster	Stephen Johnson
Audry Brown	Patricia Pendleton
Elizabeth Campuzano	Pearl Raymond
Julie Crist	Margaret Simkin

ILLINOIS-WISCONSIN FCL

Chairpersons

George Watson	1957-1960
Walter Frank	1961-1964
George R. McCoy	1965
Tom Findley	1966-1967
George McCoy	1968-1973

Co-chairpersons:
Tom Findley   1968
Charles Lombard   1971

Executive Secretaries

Carol Urner	1957-1958
Chester Graham	1959-1962*
Wilfred Reynolds	1962
Marian Peters	1963-1964
Vera Fina	1965-1968
Richard C. Weston	1969-1971
Barbara Hausman Elkins	1972-1973

*Chester Graham, Wisconsin Secretary — 1963-1964

OTHER STAFF

Sally Barclay
Mary Cadbury
Kenneth Calkins
Neil Haworth
Marian Peters
Jean Watson

INDIANA FCL 1971-1974

Chairperson: Les Paulsen
Secretary: Rebecca Mullin

REFERENCES

Chapter 1
The Quakers Started Something

1. "Some REASONS Humbly proposed to the *Lords Spiritual and Temporal* assembled in Parliament, why the *Quaker's Principles and Practices* should be Examined, and Censured or Suppressed." Photocopy on file, FCNL Archives, Document Group 47, Series L, Box 1, Folder, Why the Quakers Should be Censured, 1699. Swarthmore College Peace Collection (hereafter identified as SCPC).

2. Barry R. Nager, "The Jury That Tried William Penn," *American Bar Association Journal,* Vol. 50 (February 1964), pp. 168-170.

3. Don C. Seitz, ed., *The Tryal of William Penn and William Mead [for causing a tumult at the sessions held at Old Bailey in London the 1st, 3rd, 4th and 5th of September, 1670]* first published in 1719 (Boston: Marshall Jones Co., 1919).

4. Thomas E. Drake, *Quakers and Slavery in America* (New Haven: Yale University Press, 1950), p. 86.

5. Ibid., p. 87.

6. Ibid., p. 102.

7. Ibid., pp. 163, 169.

8. Ibid., p. 126.

9. Ibid., p. 108.

10. Ibid., p. 175.

11. Ibid., p. 129.

12. Ibid., pp. 103-05.

13. Ibid., p. 192.

14. Margaret E. Hirst, *The Quakers in Peace and War,* (New York: Doran, 1923), p. 448. Charles A. and Mary R. Beard, *Basic History of the United States,* New York: Doubleday, 1944), p. 280, estimate total cost of Civil War above $10 billion.

15. Rayner Wickersham Kelsey, *Friends and the Indians: 1655-1917* (Philadelphia: Associated Executive Committee of Friends on Indian Affairs, 1917), pp. 62, 63.

16. Ibid., p. 90.

17. Ibid., Chapter VIII, "Grant's Policy," pp. 162-199.

18. *The American Friend,* New Series 28, No. 14, July 18, 1940, p. 299.

19. The material for this section on the three years of activities by the Friends War Problems Committee preceding the launching of the Friends Committee on National Legislation (hereafter designated FCNL) was largely drawn from the four boxes of archives of the Friends War Problems

Committee, DG47, A, B, C, D; and the Diary of Paul Comly French, all on deposit in the Swarthmore College Peace Collection. Also the minutes of the Representative Committee of the two Philadelphia Yearly Meetings in the Swarthmore and Haverford Friends Historical libraries.

Chapter 2
The First Protestant Lobby

1. This chapter is based on material in the SCPC depository for FCNL Archives, including Friends War Problems Committee DG 47, Series A, Boxes A, B, C, and D; and FCNL DG 47, Series A, Boxes 1-5. Also Vol. 1, *FCNL Washington Newsletter* and Vol. 1, *FCNL Minutes*, which are on file at the FCNL office in Washington, D.C.

Other sources include the Diary of Paul Comly French, and the records of the National Service Board for Religious Objectors, Boxes A-1 and A-6, in SCPC.

2. DG 47, War Problems Committee, Box C, Folder, Thomas A. Foulke File, 1943-44, SCPC.

3. DG 47, Series A, Box 1, Folder, Organizational Meeting, Richmond, Indiana, June 11-12, 1943, SCPC.

4. DG 47, Series A, Box 1, Folder, Statements of Purpose and Policy, SCPC.

5. *Dept. of State, Treaties and Other International Agreements of the United States of America, 1776-1949*, Vol. 3, p. 822, Pubn. 8464.

Chapter 3
What A Church Lobby Is Up Against

1. Jeremiah 22:1, 3. King James Version.

2. Matthew 25:35-40. *Good News for Modern Man* translation, American Bible Society, 1959.

3. Quoted in article "Should the Church Lobby?" *Engage* 3, No. 4, (Board of Christian Social Concerns of the Methodist Church, October 15, 1970).

4. Charles J. Zinn, *How Our Laws Are Made*, 92nd Congress 2d Session, House of Representatives, 1972, Document No. 92-323; *Enactment of a Law — Procedural Steps in the Legislative Process*, 90th Congress, 1st Session, 1967, Senate Document No. 35.

5. See Kirby Page, *Individualism and Socialism* (Farrar and Rinehart, New York, 1933), Chapter 3, a review of fourteen measures (including women's suffrage and free universal education) which are now considered an accepted part of our society but which took a long time to achieve.

6. John C. Bennett, ed., *Christian Ethics in a Changing World* (Association Press, New York, 1966), p. 163.

7. E. Raymond Wilson, "Are We Serious About Social Action?" *The Christian Century* 82, No. 6, February 10, 1965.

8. Luke Ebersole, *Church Lobbying in the Nation's Capital*, New York, Macmillan, 1951.

9. James A. Nash, "Church Lobbying in the Federal Government: A Comparative Study of Four Church Agencies in Washington." (Ph.D. Dissertation, Boston U., 1967).

10. James L. Adams, *The Growing Church Lobby in Washington* (Grand Rapids, Michigan: Eerdmans, 1970). He describes the agencies currently working in Washington in pages 209-285.

11. Ibid., p. 219.

12. Ibid., p. 287.

13. Ibid., p. viii.

Chapter 4

The Starnes Rider — A Case History in Lobbying

1. The documentary material on which this chapter is based is mainly in the FCNL archives, DG 47, Series E, Box 1, and *FCNL Washington Newsletter* Nos. 2, 8, 9, 21, 31, SCPC; and in *FCNL Minutes*, Vol. 1, and in *Testimonies and Statements*, Vol. 1, in the Washington FCNL office.

2. *House Subcommittee on Military Appropriations for 1945, May 17, 1944.* Pickett Testimony, pp. 626-637. Testimony by John Rich, pp. 638-640. On file in DG 47, Series E, Box 1, Folder, A Brief History of the Efforts to Repeal the Starnes Rider.

3. Ibid. June 17, 1944, Stimson letter, p. 87.

4. Letter from Frank Aydelotte, March 24, 1944, to E. Raymond Wilson, DG 47, Series E, Box 1, Folder, Starnes Rider Correspondence, April-June 1944, SCPC.

5. DG 47, Series E, Box 1, Folder, Conscientious Objectors, 1943-45, A Brief History of the Efforts To Repeal the Starnes Rider, SCPC.

6. DG 47, Series E, Box 1, Folder, Starnes Rider Correspondence, 1945-46, SCPC.

7. Mulford Q. Sibley and Philip E. Jacob, *Conscription and Conscience: The American State and the Conscientious Objector, 1940-1947.* (Reprint: New York, Johnson Reprint Corporation, 1965). For a description of the origin of the Frozen Fund, see pp. 132-133 and 219-220; legislative history of the Frozen Fund, pp. 297-300.

Paul Comley French's Diary contains many references to his efforts on this problem over three-year period from 1943 to 1946. SCPC.

The material on the Frozen Fund is largely drawn from FCNL files in DG 47, Series E, Box 5, which includes a review memorandum by Jeanette

Hadley, May 12, 1959, and from *FCNL Washington Newsletter* Nos. 37, 41, 42, 65, 67, 73, 79, and 81.

8. *FCNL Memorandum* No. 22, September 17, 1943.

9. *The Reporter*, Vol. 2, No. 7, October 1, 1943, SCPC.

10. H.R. 200, January 3, 1945.

11. H.R 1938, February 13, 1947.

12. S. 2496 by Sparkman and Saltonstall passed the Senate on June 8, 1950, on the unanimous consent calendar.

Chapter 5
The Battle To Feed the Hungry

1. The information in this chapter is drawn from the seven boxes on food and relief in the FCNL Archives in the SCPC. DG 47, Series J, Boxes 1-7; the bound volumes of FCNL minutes, newsletters, and testimonies; *Seminars and Conferences*, Vol. 1, and *Miscellaneous*, Vol. 1, all on file in the FCNL office in Washington, D.C.

2. *Hearings before the Senate Judiciary Subcommittee To Permit the Supplement of Relief Supplies*, April 25, 1946, pp. 28-31.

3. *Hearings before the Senate Civil Service Committee To Amend the Trading with the Enemy Act so as To Permit Certain Aid to Civilian Recovery*, April 9, 1947, pp. 14-19.

4. See bound volume *FCNL Testimonies and Statements*, Vol. 1, FCNL, Washington, D.C.

5. *Hearings before the House Committee on Agriculture on A Joint Resolution To Prevent the Use of Grain for Nonessential Purposes during the Period of Shortage*, James Vail, August 2, 1946, pp. 25-30.

6. See bound volume, *FCNL Testimonies and Statements*, Vol. 1, on file at the FCNL office, Washington, D.C.

7. *Hearings before the House Banking and Currency Committee on Allocation of Grain for Production of Distilled or Neutral Spirits for Beverage Purposes*, E. Raymond Wilson, Jan. 27, 1948, pp. 122-124.

8. See *FCNL Testimonies and Statements*, Vol. 1, FCNL, Washington, D.C.

9. See FCNL bound volume on *Seminars and Conferences*, FCNL, Washington, D.C.

10. *FCNL Memo*, No. 30, March 28, 1956.

11. E. Raymond Wilson, "Japan Journey," Chapter 26, "CAC Representatives Visit Hokkaido Relief Area," DG 70, SCPC.

12. DG 47, Series J, Box 4, Folder, International Commodity Clearing House Proposal, 1949, SCPC.

13. DG 47, Series J, Boxes 3 and 4, Folders, Food for India, 1951, and Folder, Interviews by E. Stanley Jones, SCPC.

14. DG 47, Series J, Box 7, Three Folders, Grain for India, 1956-57, SCPC.

15. DG 47, Series J. Boxes 6 and 7, Eleven Folders on Food for China, 1961-63, SCPC.

16. DG 47, Series A, Box 59, Folder, Government Officials, Interview with President Kennedy by Six Quakers, May 1, 1962. The letter from Edward F. Snyder to President Kennedy on August 1, 1962 is filed in DG 47, Series J, Box 7. There is also a record on tape of the Kennedy interview by each of the participants on file in SCPC.

17. *Hearings before the House Committee on Agriculture on Agricultural Act of 1961*, May 24, 1961, pp. 841-846.

18. *Hearings before the Senate Banking and Currency Committee on Government Guarantees of Credit to Communist Countries*, November 22, 1963, pp. 243-246.

19. *Hearings before the Senate Committee on Agriculture on the Food for Freedom Program and Commodity Reserves*, March 8, 1966, pp. 398-407.

Chapter 6
I Was A Stranger

1. Material for this chapter was drawn from the *FCNL Washington Newsletters*, bound volumes, I-III; *FCNL Testimonies*, bound volumes I-IV; and the Immigration and Refugee Boxes, all at the FCNL Library in the Washington, D.C. office archives; and the *FCNL Action Bulletins and Memos*, bound volume I; and DG 47 Boxes 3, 4, and 5; and the FCNL Statements of Legislative Policy and Annual Reports 1944-1970 in loose leaf volume, all at SCPC.

2. DG 47, Series G, Box 3, Folder, Palestine Refugees, 1949-50, SCPC.

3. *FCNL Newsletter*, No. 64, June 13, 1949, and *Congressional Record*, June 2, 1949, Vol. 95, Part 6, pp. 7137-7140 and 7147.

4. *FCNL Washington Newsletter*, No. 42, June 17, 1947.

5. FCNL Statement on Immigration and Citizenship approved by the General Committee, Dec. 3-4, 1955, and filed in loose-leaf volume of "FCNL Legislative Policies," SCPC.

6. FCNL 1961 "Legislative Report," p. 11, loose-leaf volume, Annual Reports, SCPC.

7. DG 47, Series G, Box 3, Folder, Dolliver Bill concerning Bearing of Arms, H.R. 2286, 1947-48. This folder contains copy of letter to Rep. Brooks Hays.

Chapter 7
What Liberties Should A Person Have?

1. Information for this chapter was drawn from the bound volumes of

FCNL Washington Newsletters, the bound volumes of testimonies at the Washington office of the Committee, and also DG 47, Series G, Boxes 1 and 2 in the SCPC.

2. Loose-leaf volume, FCNL Statements of Legislative Policy, SCPC.

3. Ibid.

4. Ibid.

5. Ibid.

6. Ibid.

7. See FCNL bound volume of *Testimonies and Statements* FCNL office, Washington, D.C.

8. *Congressional Quarterly Almanac* (Congressional Quarterly, Washington, D.C., 1972), p. 87.

9. *Hearings before the House Judiciary Subcommittee*, No. 5, May 3, 1955, pp. 245-258. *Hearings before the Senate Judiciary Subcommittee on Wiretapping*, May 12, 1954, pp. 209-225.

10. See footnote 2.

11. DG 47, Series A, Box 30, Folder, National Civil Liberties Clearing House, SCPC.

12. DG 47, Series G, Box 1, Folder, Statement against the Mundt-Nixon Bill, May 13, 1948, SCPC.

13. *Hearings of the House Un-American Activities Committee*, March 21-23, 28-30; April 4; May 2-4, 1950, pp. 2226-2229. Hearings on H.R. 3903 and H.R. 7595 (legislation to outlaw certain Un-American and subversive activities).

14. DG 70, E. Raymond Wilson, *Occasional Papers, Testimonies and Statements before Congress*, March 31, 1950, SCPC.

15. See *FCNL Memo*, No. 12, December 23, 1954, "The Case of Dr. Edward U. Condon." Also DG 47, Series G, Box 2, Folder, Civil Liberties Cases — Dr. Edward U. Condon, SCPC.

16. *Congressional Record*, Vol. 194, Part 2, March 9, 1948, pp. 2476-79. The remarks by Congressman Sabath on the House Un-American Activities Committee release on Dr. Condon were stricken from the printed record by motion of Congressman Rankin.

17. *FCNL Memo*, No. 12.

18. Ibid.

19. Ibid.

Chapter 8
A Matter of Justice

1. Findings of the Second Friends Seminar on American Indian Affairs held in Albuquerque, New Mexico, Feb. 4-7, 1960. DG 47, Series G, Box 6, Folder, American Indians, 1956-64, SCPC.

2. Quoted by Walter Taylor, Indian Committee Representative to the Seneca Nation of Indians, in hearings of the Subcommittee on Indian Affairs, Senate Committee on Interior and Insular Affairs, March 2, 1964.

3. The story of the visit of William Savery and his committee to the Seneca Indians is told in the "Journal of William Savery," *The Friends Library*, I (Philadelphia: Joseph Rakestraw, 1837), pp. 349-368.

4. Arthur E. Morgan, *Dams and Other Disasters* (Boston: Porter Sargent, 1971), Chap. 10 — "The Upper Allegheny" and Chap. 11 — "The Kinzua Dam."

5. The quotations from Cannon, Ickes, Heron, George Washington, the War Department in 1962, John F. Kennedy and the *Christian Century* are from the pamphlet "The Kinzua Dam Controversy — A Practical Solution without Shame," published in 1961 by the Kinzua Project of the Indian Committee of the Philadelphia Yearly Meeting of Friends. This pamphlet was circulated by the FCNL to its action list on human rights. DG 47, Series G, Box 6, Folder, American Indians, 1956-1964, SCPC.

6. "The 1964 Crisis for Seneca Indians," a report from the Indian Committee, Philadelphia Yearly Meeting, Feb. 1, 1964. DG 47, Series G, Box 6, Folder, American Indians, 1956-1964, SCPC.

7. *Congressional Record*, 110 Part 16, August 20, 1964, p. 20560.

8. Theodore Hetzel has testified at least five times regarding American Indians, often on behalf of FCNL: 1955, 1956, twice in 1964, and 1966.

9. See Findings of Second Friends Seminar referred to in footnote 1.

10. *Congressional Record*, 117, Part 2, Feb. 9, 1971, p. 2240.

11. *FCNL Washington Newsletter*, No. 49, Feb. 26, 1948.

12. *Hearings before the Senate Subcommittee on Interior and Insular Affairs on the Alaska Native Land Claims, S. 835*, March 16, 1971, pp. 378-379.

13. *Congressional Record*, 117, Part 36, Dec. 14, 1971, pp. 46784-88.

14. Jacobus ten Broek, Edward N. Barnhart, and Floyd W. Watson, *Prejudice, War, and the Constitution* (U. of California Press, 1954), p. 325.

15. Ibid., p. 332.

16. Allan R. Bosworth, *America's Concentration Camps* (New York: Norton and Company, 1967), pp. 236-240. See also Bill Hosokawa, *Nisei: The Quiet Americans* (New York: Morrow, 1969), pp. 445-449; and Dillon Meyer, *Uprooted Americans* (U. of Arizona Press, 1971), pp. 252-256.

17. Mike Masaoka, *Pacific American*. (The Pacific American is the official publication of the Japanese-American Citizens League, pub. in Los Angeles.)

18. Bosworth, p. 236.

19. Ibid., p. 246.

20. "Protest to Politics: The Future of the Civil Rights Movement," *Information Service* 44 (No. 7, National Council of Churches, March 7, 1955). Reprinted from *Commentary*, p. 25, pub. American Jewish Committee, Feb., 1955.

21. Harry A. Ploski and Ernest Kaiser, ed., *The Negro Almanac*, 2nd ed. (New York: The Bellweather Co., 1971), p. 28.

22. *Congressional Quarterly Almanac*, 20, 1964, p. 368.

23. From a release of the Commission on Religion and Race, National Council of Churches, Washington, D.C., June 12, 1964.

24. *Hearings before the Subcommittee on the War on Poverty Program of the House Committee on Education and Labor*, Part 2, April 20, 1964, p. 1043.

25. DG 47, Series A, Box 71, Folder, Richard Taylor, Appreciation Letters, 1964, SCPC.

26. *FCNL Washington Newsletter* No. 2, Dec. 10, 1943. A major source of this newsletter was the handbook issued by the National Committee to Abolish the Poll Tax, "Why the Poll Tax Is A National Issue" (Washington, D.C. n.d.).

27. Ibid.

28. "Voting in Mississippi," A report of the United States Commission on Civil Rights, 1955, pp. 70-71. The figure of one Black registered in Chichsaw County was for January 1, 1964.

29. *Congressional Quarterly Almanac*, 1964, pp. 381-382.

30. FCNL bound volume, *Testimonies and Statements*, vol. 1, FCNL office, Washington, D.C.

31. Ploski and Kaiser, pp. 267-270.

32. DG 47, Series G, Box 6, Folder, Amici Curiae: David Scull and Thompson Restaurant Case, 1949, SCPC.

33. Bound volume II *FCNL Testimonies and Statements*, 1951-55, FCNL office, Washington, D.C.

Chapter 9
Involving the U.S. in the UN

1. Material on the San Francisco Conference which established the United Nations in 1945, the Dumbarton Oaks proposals for the UN Charter, and the Delegations to the Middle Powers, both of which preceded the San Francisco Conference, are in DG 47, Series I, Box 4, SCPC. See also *FCNL Newsletters* Nos. 12, 13, 14, 16 (with the January 14, 1945 FCNL Statement appended), 17, and 18. No. 18 contains 14 amendments to the Dumbarton Oaks Charter proposed by FCNL.

2. DG 47, Series I, Box 4, Folder, Friends Recommendations for the UN Charter, April 30, 1945, SCPC.

3. 1965 bound volume of FCNL Publications, SCPC.

4. DG 47, Series I, Box 5, Folder, United Nations Tenth Anniversary — Resolutions by Mrs. Bolton — Initiative by FCNL.

5. *Hearings on UN Bonds before the Senate Foreign Relations Committee*, Feb. 19, 1962, pp. 187-189.

6. DG 47, Series A, Box 59, Folder, Government Officials, State, 1962, SCPC.

7. 1970 bound volume of FCNL Publications, SCPC.

8. FCNL activities 1963-70, drawn largely from yearly legislative reports in yearly publication volumes, and in cumulative loose-leaf volume of FCNL annual reports on file in SCPC.

Chapter 10

The Birth of Two New Organizations: 1960-1961

1. George Sullivan, *The Story of the Peace Corps*, 2nd ed. (New York: Fleet Publishing Corporation, 1965), Chapter 1, p. 19.

2. *Hearings on Foreign Assistance and Related Agencies for 1972, Part 1, House Subcommittee on Appropriations*, June 30, 1971, pp. 721-832.

3. *FCNL Washington Newsletter*, No. 244, Jan., 1964.

4. The story of the Peace Corps is drawn from *FCNL Washington Newsletters*, Annual Reports, Bound Volume IV of *Testimonies and Statements*, and Edward F. Snyder, "Capital Weighs Peace Corps," *Quaker Life*, February, 1961, pp. 36-37.

5. *Congressional Record*, 106, part 4, March 7, 1960, pp. 4707-4709.

6. DG 47, Series L, Box 1, Folder, Proposed Party Planks, 1932-64, SCPC.

7. *Hearings on the Disarmament Agency, Senate Foreign Relations Committee*, August 16, 1961, p. 263.

8. U.S. Arms Control and Disarmament Agency, *Twelfth Annual Report to the Congress*, Dec. 31, 1972, p. 20.

9. *Hearings before the House Foreign Affairs Committee on* "To Amend the Arms Control and Disarmament Act," Sept. 11, 1963, pp. 77-86.

10. *FCNL Washington Newsletter*, No. 244, Jan. 1964.

11. *Arms Control Achievements*, 1959-1971, ACDA Publication, No. 59, October 1, 1971.

12. *Hearings before the Senate Foreign Relations Committee* on the "Strategic Arms Limitations Agreements," June 30, 1972, pp. 429-431.

Chapter 11

Fighting Militarism for Thirty Years

1. David Hunter Miller, *The Drafting of the Covenant* (New York: G.P. Putnam's Sons, 1928), II, p. 48.

2. The fuller statement of the conference appears in *The American Friend* (new series), 32, No. 23, (Nov. 16, 1944), p. 460.

3. DG 47, Series D, Box 9A, SCPC.

4. *Hearings on Universal Military Training, House Select Committee on*

Post War Military Policy, 1945. D. Robert Yarnell, pp. 179-182. Norman Thomas, pp. 227-232.

5. H. Res. 325 was introduced by Rep. Martin, June 17, 1945, S.J. Res. 126 by Sen. Hoey, Dec. 6, 1945. Similar or identical bills were introduced by Sen. Styles Bridges of N.H. and by Reps. Louis Ludlow of Ind., Jerry Voorhis of Cal., James Geelan of Conn. and Gerald Landis of Ind.

6. Harrop A. Freeman, "The Constitutionality of Peacetime Conscription," *Virginia Law Review*, 31, No. 1, (Dec. 1944).

7. Miller, II, pp. 72, 99.

8. *Ibid.*, II, p. 146. For a discussion of the objectives of France and Italy, see Miller, I, pp. 65-67 and 170-171; and II, p. 264.

9. *Documents of the Conference for the Reduction and Limitation of Armaments,* (Geneva, 1932), I, pp. 119-120.

10. "An Attack on Draft Armies," *The Literary Digest*, 90, Sept. 18, 1926, p. 14.

11. E. Raymond Wilson, *Occasional Papers*, III, Jan. 24, 1947. See also DG 47, Series D, Box 7, Folder — President's Commission on UMT, 1947, SCPC. Printed copies of the hearings before the President's commission were never released.

12. John M. Swomley, *An Analysis of the Report of the President's Advisory Commission on Military Training* (Washington, D.C.: National Council against Conscription, July 7, 1947). Filed in same folder as above.

13. National Security Training Commission, *Universal Military Training, Foundation of Enduring National Strength* (U.S. Government Printing Office, October, 1951(. DG 47. Series E, Box 13, Folder, UMT, Foundation of Enduring National Strength, SCPC.

14. John M. Swomley, *The Facts Behind the Report* (National Council Against Conscription, January, 1952). Filed in same folder as above.

15. Rainer Schickele and Glenn Everett, "The Economic Implications of Universal Military Training, *"Annals of the American Academy of Political and Military Science,"* (Sept. 1945), pp. 102-112.

16. *U.S. v. Seeger*, (380, U.S. 163, 1965)

17. *Hearings on Amending and Extending the Draft Law and Related Authorities by the Senate Committee on Armed Services*, April 17, 1967, pp. 359, 370.

18. *FCNL Memo*, No. 166, May 17, 1967.

19. *Congressional Record*, 117, Part 14, pp. 18777-78.

Chapter 12
Dare the World Disarm?

1. *U.S. Arms Control and Disarmament Agency, Twelfth Annual Report*, January 1 to December 31, 1972, p. 20.

2. *FCNL Memo*, No. 57, March 19, 1958.

3. *FCNL Memo*, No. 58, April 15, 1958.

4. *FCNL Memo*, No. 62, August 15, 1958.

5. *FCNL Memo*, No. 89, November 15, 1960.

6. *FCNL Memo*, No. 107, May 16, 1962.

7. DG 47, Series D, Box 35, Folder, International and Civilian Control of Atomic Energy, SCPC.

8. *Congressional Record*, 91, Part 6, p. 8337, H. Res. 336.

9. Public Law No. 79-585, *Congressional Record*, Vol. 92, Part 13 (Index), Senate Bills & Resolutions, p. 567.

10. U.S. Senate, *Special Committee on Atomic Energy, Atomic Energy Act of 1946. 79th Congress, 2nd session, Senate Report 1211, April 19, 1946.*

11. *Information Service*, 25, no. 16 (New York: Federal Council of Churches, April 20, 1946), p. 4.

12. *Congressional Record*, 92, Part 1, p. 426, S. Res. 219.

13. DG 47, Series D, Box 36, Folder, History of International Negotiations on the Atom Bomb and Atomic Energy — Summary of articles in *The New Republic*, April 3, 10, 17, 1950, SCPC.

14. Information on the seven National Conferences on Disarmament can be found in DG 47, Series D, Box 28, SCPC.

15. DG 47, Series D, Box 28, Folder, Seventh National Conference on World Disarmament and World Development, Working Paper, 1961, SCPC.

16. Ibid.

17. FCNL *Washington Newsletter*, No. 115, June 4, 1953. *Congressional Record*, 99, pp. 5945-5951.

18. See the chapter on Memorable Interviews for the appeal made to Presidential candidate Eisenhower before his election, for leadership toward disarmament.

19. *U.S. News and World Report*, 34, April 24, 1952.

20. FCNL *Washington Newsletter*, No. 117, August 1, 1953. *Congressional Record*, 99, pp. 10261-10270.

21. DG 47, Series D, Box 37, Folder, Appeal to President Eisenhower and Premier Khrushchev To End Nuclear Tests. Also, Wilson, *Occasional Papers*, Vol. 5, 1958-1961, DG 70, SCPC.

22. Ibid.

23. Wilson, *Occasional Papers*, Vol. 5.

24. DG 47, Series A, Box 57, Folder, AFSC — Peace Education — Memorandum from Raymond Wilson to Stewart Meacham, Feb. 20, 1962, SCPC.

25. *Congressional Quarterly Almanac*, 19 (1963): p. 1018. A short chronology of test ban talks is printed on p. 250.

26. *Hearings before the Senate Appropriations Subcommittee on State and Judiciary*, Nov. 12, 1963, pp. 2418-2423.

27. *Hearings before the Subcommittee on State and Judiciary of the House Appropriations Committee on the Nuclear Test Ban Treaty*, August 27, 1963, pp. 917-923.

28. FCNL *Washington Newsletter*, No. 241, October, 1963.

29. Loose-leaf binder, FCNL, Policy Statements, SCPC.

30. DG 47, Series D, Box 40, Folder, Civil Defense Correspondence, Frances Neely File, 1963, SCPC.

31. Ibid.

32. *Hearings before House Appropriations Subcommittee on Independent Offices*, April 19, 1962, pp. 918-925.

33. *Hearings before the Senate Appropriations Subcommittee on Independent Offices, 1963*. August 14, 1962, pp. 1073-1084.

34. *Hearings before the House Armed Services Committee*, June 18, 1963.

35. Ibid.

36. *Hearings before the House Appropriations Subcommittee on Independent Offices*, April 21, 1964, pp. 836-37.

37. DG 47, Series D, Box 30, Folder, Disarmament Information Service, SCPC.

38. DG 47, Series D, Box 44, SCPC.

39. DG 47, Series A, Box 50, Folder, Letter to President Kennedy, SCPC.

40. E. Raymond Wilson, *Occasional Papers*, Vol. 6, 1962-65, SCPC. Also, DG 47, Series A, Box 59, Folder, Interview with Pres. Kennedy by Six Quakers, May 1, 1962, SCPC. See letter to Defense Secretary McNamara, Series A., Box 59, Folder, proposal to name Polaris submarine "William Penn," SCPC.

41. FCNL *Memo*, No. 107, May 16, 1962. See also Kennedy interview in Chap. 5, "The Battle To Feed the Hungry."

42. See Folder, interview with Pres. Kennedy, cited in footnote 40.

43. *Congressional Quarterly Almanac*, 14 (1958), pp. 253-55.
Congressional Quarterly Almanac, 15 (1959), p. 304.
Congressional Record, 105, Part 10, July 9, 1959, pp. 13119-13131.

44. *Hearings before the House Appropriations Subcommittee on the Department of Defense*, January 20, 1959.

45. FCNL *Memo*, No. 35, June 12, 1956.

46. *Hearings before the Senate Foreign Relations Subcommittee on Control and Reduction of Armaments, on S. Res. 93 and S. Res. 185*, Part 8, June 8, 1956, pp. 418-437.

47. *Congressional Record* 115, Part 6, March 24, 1969, pp. 7206-7215.

48. *New York Times*, April 4, 1969.

49. FCNL, *The Big Hand in Your Pocket* (Washington: FCNL, 1960), p. 27.

50. *New York Times*, June 22, 1969.

51. Richard A. Fineberger, "Setting the Record Straight — America's Chemical and Biological Warfare Program," *Lithopinion*, 7 (Fall, 1972), no. 3, issue 27. See also his article "No More Chemical Biological War?" in the *New Republic*, Dec. 2, 1972.

52. Daniel S. Greenberg, "Test Tube Warfare: The Fake Renunciation," *World Magazine* (August 15, 1972). Reprinted in the *Congressional Record*, 118, part 163, October 11, 1972, pp. 17481-2.

53. Col. Stanley D. Fair, "The Chemical Corps: Alive, Well, and Visible,"

Army, April, 1972, pp. 29-31.

54. Memo to the Scientists' Committee on Chemical and Biological Warfare, by Richard Novick of the Public Health Research Institute of the City of New York, "United States Chemical and Biological Weapons Program at Fort Dietrick and Edgewood Arsenal: Current Status, Dec. 1, 1972." (typed)

Chapter 13
Wars, Revolutions, and Interventions

1. *Hearings before the Senate Committee on Foreign Relations, S. 938, A Bill To Provide for Assistance to Greece and Turkey*, March 31, 1947, pp. 118-119.

2. Ibid., Charles G. Bolte, pp. 93-95.

3. Henry G. Cadbury, *Hearings before the House Committee on Foreign Affairs on H.R. 2616, A Bill To Provide for Assistance to Greece and Turkey*, April 3, 1947, pp. 234-245.

4. Barbara S. Grant and E. Raymond Wilson, "Some Questions and Comments about the North Atlantic Treaty and the Accompanying Rearmament Program," April 25, 1949, DG 47, Series H, Box 20, SCPC.

5. *Senate Foreign Relations Committee Hearings on the North Atlantic Treaty*, May 11, 1949, pp. 758-784.

6. *NATO: Facts and Figures* (Brussels: NATO Information Service, 1969), p. 74.

7. Phone conversations with FCNL, May 31, 1973, from Clement Lapp, Assistant Director, Cuba Refugee Program, Social and Rehabilitation Service, Department of Health, Education and Welfare.

8. Robert Lyon memo to Nancy Duryee, April 20, 1961, DG 47, Series H, Box 3, Folder, April 1961 (1), SCPC.

9. Ed Duckles letter to Nancy Duryee, April 26, 1961, DG 47, Series H, Box 3, Folder, April 1961 (1), SCPC.

10. *Congressional Quarterly Almanac*, Vol. XVIII, 1962, p. 340.

11. Dept. of State Press Release, No. 76, TV Report by Sec. of State Dean Rusk, Feb. 2, 1962. DG 47, Series H, Box 4, Folder, Cuba, Feb., 1962, SCPC.

12. DG 47, Series H, Box 6 contains documents and newspaper clippings on the missile crisis. Robert F. Kennedy, *Thirteen Days: A Memoir of the Cuban Missile Crisis* (New York: Norton, 1969) gives a very readable and detailed account of the day by day discussions and decisions of the Executive Branch, Oct. 16-28, 1962. McNamara statement on p. 16.

13. Ibid.

14. "FCNL Legislative Report," Loose-leaf Volume, 1962, SCPC.

15. AFSC, *Search for Peace in the Middle East*, rev. ed. (New York: Fawcett, 1970).

16. *Congressional Record*, Vol. 104, Part 11, July 16, 1958, p. 13978.

17. *The Nation*, 200, No. 20 (May 17, 1965), p. 517.

18. *FCNL Washington Newsletter*, No. 261, June 1965.

19. A fairly comprehensive collection of documents dealing with the Korean War is to be found in DG 47, Series H, Boxes 15 and 16, SCPC.

20. The full text of the memorandum of E. Stanley Jones regarding his interview with President Truman is in DG 47, Series H, Box 15, Folder, E. Stanley Jones interviews, August 7-8, and September 1, 1950.

Chapter 14
Vietnam: 1954-1968

In these two chapters on Vietnam, our principal sources for FCNL activities were the Yearly Reports and the material in the FCNL annual bound volumes 1965-1971. We are also indebted to the *Congressional Quarterly* and the *News Dictionary* published by Facts on File for some of the information on military and political developments during the years 1967-1971. The FCNL file on Vietnam on Jan. 1, 1974, in the SCPC is in DG 47, Series M, Boxes 1-17.

1. For more information on the background of Vietnam, see *The New Yorker*, 48, Nos. 19-23 (July 1-29, 1972), and Bernard Fall, *Last Reflections on A War* (Garden City, N.Y.: Doubleday and Co., 1967).

2. *New York Times*, April 17, 1954.

3. Marvin E. Gettleman, *Vietnam: History, Documents, and Opinions* (Greenwich, Conn.: Fawcett Books, 1965), p. 157.

4. James Avery Joyce, "SEATO: False Alibi," *The Christian Century*, 84, (Nov. 8, 1967), p. 1426.

5. Clergy and Laymen Concerned about Vietnam, "Fact Sheet on the Vietnam War," April 15, 1970, SCPC.

6. Joyce, p. 1428. The full legal case against U.S. military involvement, answering the State Department's arguments point by point, is presented in "Vietnam and International Law," a study prepared by a panel of well-known American lawyers and political scientists and published by O'Hare Books (New York: 1967).

7. *FCNL Washington Newsletter*, No. 129, May 25, 1954.

8. *FCNL Washington Newsletter*, No. 138, March, 1955.

9. *FCNL Washington Newsletter*, No. 226, July, 1962.

10. H.J. Res. 1145, S.J. 189, PL-88-408.

11. Clergy and Laymen Concerned, "Fact Sheet on the Vietnam War," April 15, 1970.

12. Letter of Frances Neely to Hugh Gallagher, Office of Senator E.L. Bartlett, June 2, 1967, in DG 47, Series M, Box 1, Folder, Frances Neely File, Jan.-July, 1967, SCPC.

13. E. Raymond Wilson, *Occasional Papers*, Vol. 6, March 19, 1965.

14. *FCNL Washington Newsletter*, No. 278, Jan., 1967.

15. "Vietnam: Challenge to the Conscience of America" was a cooperative effort of the following groups:

American Baptist Convention, Division of Christian Social Concerns
Church of the Brethren Service Commission

Department of Christian Action and Community Service, United Christian Missionary Society (Disciples of Christ)

Division of Christian Citizenship, Executive Council, Episcopal Church

Division of Peace and World Order, Methodist Board of Christian Social Concerns

Friends Committee on National Legislation

National Newman Student Federation

Unitarian Universalist Association, Department of Social Responsibility

United Church of Christ, Council for Christian Social Action

United Church Women

United Presbyterian Church in the USA, Office of Church and Society

University Christian Movement

The Commission on Social Action of Reform Judaism commended this program to its constituent organizations and congregations.

The International Affairs Commission of the National Council of Churches commended this program to its member churches as an important means of exchange and expression of issues concerning Vietnam.

16. *FCNL Memo*, No. 157, August 16, 1966.

17. FCNL, Annual Bound Volume, Vietnam Section, 1966, SCPC.

18. *FCNL, Statements on Legislative Policies*, loose-leaf volume, SCPC.

19. *FCNL Legislative Report, 1967*, bound volume, pp. A-C, and "Vietnam" section.

Chapter 15
The Later Years of Vietnam: 1969-1973

1. *Congressional Quarterly Almanac*, vol. 25 (1969), Congressional Quarterly, Washington, D.C. 1970, pp. 857-9, 1000.

2. *Congressional Record*, vol. 115, Part 6, March 25, 1969, pp. 7403-7526.

3. *FCNL Memo*, No. 192, October 16, 1969.

4. *News Dictionary*, 1970, Facts on File, New York, 1971, pp. 303-4. *Congressional Quarterly Almanac*, 1970, p. 89A.

5. *U.S. President's Commission on Campus Unrest, Report*, United States Government, September 1970, p. 18.

6. *Congressional Record*, vol. 116, Part 13, June 2, 1970, p. 17868.

7. FCNL *1970 Legislative Report*, January 1971, p. 16.

8. *FCNL 1970 Publications, Testimonies and Statements*, May 1970.

9. *FCNL 1971 Publications, Letters to Congress and the President*, July 16, 1971.

10. *Keesing's Contemporary Archives*, Keesing's Publications Ltd. (of London), Bristol, England, vol. 18, 1971-72, p. 24725.

11. *Congressional Quarterly Report*, vol. 29, (1971, no. 2), (Statement by

House Conferees), Congressional Quarterly, Washington, D.C., 1971, p. 71.

12. Gallop Poll Report, "In view of the developments since we entered the fighting in Vietnam, do you think the U.S. made a mistake sending troops to fight in Vietnam?" July 1971, p. 3.

13. FCNL *1970 Legislative Report*, January 1971, p. 22.

14. These figures were given in a talk by David Perry at a Haverford Friends Forum on January 6, 1974. He had recently returned from the AFSC Da Nang Rehabilitation Unit in South Vietnam.

15. Reprinted by AFSC, 1969 along with a letter from Biafra, under the title "Looking Through A Hole into Hell: Two Wars, Two Letters," on file in DG 47, Series M, Folder, Publications Regarding Vietnam, Jan.-June, 1969.

16. *New York Times*, June 20, 1973.

Chapter 16
Some Memorable Interviews

1. This interview is reported more fully in DG 47, Series A, Box 24, SCPC.

2. The full text of Eisenhower's inaugural address is reprinted in *U.S. News and World Report*, 34, Jan. 30, 1953, pp. 98-99.

3. *U.S. News and World Report*, 50, January 30, 1961.

4. *U.S. News and World Report*, 34, April 24, 1953.

5. An open letter from Japanese Christians dated June 27, 1960, reviews the protests against the treaty, the arbitrary action of the government party in ratifying the treaty in the absence of the opposition party, the demand for the resignation of the Prime Minister, the reasons for hoping Eisenhower would not come to Japan, and regret for the violence against Mr. Hagerty, Eisenhower's advance emissary, DG 47, Series H, Box 24, Folder, Open Letter from Japanese Christians Opposing Eisenhower Visit, SCPC.

6. This interview is reported on more fully in DG 47, Series A, Box 25, Folder, Adlai Stevenson Interview, Oct. 20, 1952, SCPC.

7. Letter to E. Raymond Wilson, Nov. 4, 1952, filed in DG 47, Series A, Box 25, same folder as above, SCPC.

8. FCNL *Memo*, No. 32, April 25, 1956.

9. These interviews are reported on more fully in DG 47, Series A, Box 52, Folder, Washington Staff Conference, SCPC.

10. Paul Comley French Diary, Sept. 13, 1940, SCPC.

11. A fuller report on this interview can be found in Friends War Problems Committee minutes, Sept. 23, 1940, DG 47, Series A, Box A, and Paul Comley French Diary, Sept. 23, 1940, SCPC.

Chapter 17
Lobbying on the State Front

1. The Newsletters, Minutes and other publications of the Northern and Southern California FCLs through 1964 are contained in five bound volumes on file at the FCNL office in Washington, and also one bound volume of publications of the Illinois-Wisconsin FCL. Later publications of the area offices are contained in the annual bound volumes on file both in the FCNL offices and in Swarthmore College Peace Collection.

2. First published in August 1957.

3. *The Story of the 1961 California Legislature*, p. 14.

4. *The Story of the 1959 California Legislature*, p. 29.

5. Ibid.

Chapter 18
The FCNL and Its Critics

1. Open letter by Clifford Haworth to the members of Illinois Yearly Meeting, February 12, 1959. Illinois-Wisconsin Friends Committee on Legislation, bound volume of *Minutes and Legislative Letters*, Vol. 1, 1957-1964 FCNL Office, Washington, D.C. Also letter and correspondence in DG 47, Series A, Box 47, Folder Ha, SCPC.

2. DG 47, Series A, Box 46, Folder, Charles Darlington, FCNL Chairman. Also bound volume of FCNL Minutes for 1959, FCNL Office, Washington, D.C.

3. 1944 FCNL Statement on Policy, loose-leaf volume, SCPC.

Chapter 19
Some Reflections on Thirty Years in Washington

1. *Hearings by the House Ways and Means Committee on General Tax Reform*, March 5, 1973, pp. 165-174.

2. *Hearings by Senate Rules Committee*, July 6, 1954.

3. *FCNL, Statement on Legislative Policy* 1963-64, DG 47, Loose-leaf volume, SCPC.

4. London Yearly Meeting of Society of Friends, proceedings 1972, pp. 256-7.

INDEX OF PERSONS

INDEX OF SUBJECTS

Nestled behind the new Senate Office Building, the headquarters of FCNL [see arrow] are convenient to all parts of "the Hill." Shown are the Capitol, the two Senate Office Buildings, the Supreme Court, and corners of the Library of Congress, and one of the House Office Buildings.

Quaker Delegation to President Kennedy, May 1, 1960.
Left to right: David Hartsough, Dorothy Hutchinson, Henry J. Cadbury,
Edward F. Snyder, Samuel R. Levering, George Willoughby.

Seminar of Quaker Farmers from nineteen states visits the Department of Agriculture Experiment Station at Beltsville, Maryland, 1956. An earlier seminar was held in 1950. [Photo by Merton Scott]

FCNL Staff 1973

First row: Marian D. Fuson, Chairman, Executive Committee; Edward F. Snyder, Executive Secretary; Paul E. Brink. Second row: Martha Fleischer, Rebecca Mullin, Nick Block. Third row: Doris Brown, Leah Felton, Robert Cory. Fourth row: Diane Payne, William McDevitt, Samuel R. Levering, Friend-in-Washington; Stephen Angell, Jr., Chairman, General Committee. Fifth row: Richard Post, Friend-in-Washington; Frank Cadwell, Evelyn Bradshaw, Alice Stout, Miriam Levering, Friend-in-Washington. Not present when picture was taken: Frances Neely, George Bliss, E. Raymond Wilson, William Lunsford.

The Annual Meeting of the General Committee establishes basic policy and sets yearly priorities. 4-H Center, Washington, D.C., 1964.

Charles F. Harker, Associate Secretary, and Stephen P. Angell, Jr., FCNL General Chairman, rejoice over Jeanette Hadley's devoted service as dedicated staff member for 29 years.

Delegation calls on Soviet Ambassador Mikhail A. Menshikov during the Quaker Peace Witness, 1960.

E. Raymond Wilson confers with Senator Hubert Humphrey regarding disarmament and food for peace.

A friendly visit with Senator Arthur V. Watkins of Utah. Left to right: Francis Bacon, Lansdowne, Pa.; Otto Hofmann, Austin, Tex.; Virginia Apsey, Hastings-on-Hudson, N.Y.; Senator Watkins; Evelyn Young, Wilmington, Del.; Sam Legg, Poughkeepsie, N.Y.

FCNL Tenth Anniversary, Philadelphia, Pa., November 24, 1963. Left to right: M. Albert Linton, active in launching the committee; Robert James, dinner chairman; Supreme Court Justice William O. Douglas, speaker; Lydia Stokes; E. Raymond Wislon. More than 600 attended the dinner, one of 22 Anniversary Celebrations.

Charles Darlington, FCNL General Chairman, greets Paul Hoffman, Director of the UN Development Program, at the Twentieth Anniversary Dinner, Philadelphia, Pa., 1963.

Some members of the FCNL Organizing Conference in 1943 return for the Twentieth Anniversary Observance, Earlham College, Richmond, Indiana, 1963. E. Raymond Wilson [extreme left], Executive Secretary Emeritus, and Edward F. Snyder [extreme right], Executive Secretary, were not present in 1943. Those who were, L to R: Clayton Terrell, James Furbay, Ethel Furbay, Norval Webb, Amie Webb, Albert Livesey, Eva D. Edgerton, Mary Edith Hinshaw, Samuel R. Levering, Seth Hinshaw.

Mrs. Dorothy Guadalupe was the 10,000th person to sign the Petition asking President Eisenhower to Cease Nuclear Testing, July 24, 1957. Ben Seaver, Peace Education Secretary, AFSC, San Francisco; Trevor Thomas, Executive Secretary, FCL of Northern California; Mrs. Dorothy Guadalupe.

Edward F. Snyder and J. Stuart Innerst, Friend-in-Washington, talk with Congressman William G. Bray of Indiana [center] about U.S. military policy, 1960. [Del Ankers Photo]

FCNL cooperates with many religious and other nongovernmental organizations. Four colleagues exhibit pens used by President Lyndon Johnson, May 27, 1965, in signing amendments to the Arms Control and Disarmament Act. Left to right: Methodist Bishop John Wesley Lord of the Washington area; Edward F. Snyder, FCNL; Rodney M. Shaw, Methodist Board of Christian Social Concerns; Robert Van Deusen, Director, Office of Public Affairs and Government Relations, Lutheran Council in U.S.A.

Edward Anderson   *William Lunsford*   *Harold Confer*

Human Relations Secretaries

George Bliss
Finance/Promotion Secretary

Frances Neely
Legislative Secretary

E. Raymond Wilson and Charles Harker, Administrative Secretary, confer with FCNL General Committee Chairman Charles Darlington [center] after his testimony against Draft Extension, in the Senate Armed Services Hearing Room, March 12, 1963.

Volunteers play a big role in FCNL operations. Floyd Voris, on left, 93 years young, was a volunteer for 18 winters; Polly Renee, center, part-time volunteer; Charles Hough, on right, on alternative service, manager of mail room, 1966.